Fashion Business Cases

Fashion Business Cases

A Student Guide to Learning with Case Studies

Leslie Davis Burns
Bloomsbury Fashion Business Cases, Editor-in-Chief

Haekyung Yu
Bloomsbury Fashion Business Cases, Regional Editor, Asia

Lorynn Divita
Bloomsbury Fashion Business Cases, Regional Editor,
USA and Canada

Michael Beverland
Bloomsbury Fashion Business Cases, Regional Editor, Australia

Natascha Radclyffe-Thomas
Bloomsbury Fashion Business Cases, Regional Editor,
UK and Europe

FAIRCHILD BOOKS
NEW YORK · LONDON · OXFORD · NEW DELHI · SYDNEY

FAIRCHILD BOOKS
Bloomsbury Publishing Inc
1385 Broadway, New York, NY 10018, USA
50 Bedford Square, London, WC1B 3DP, UK

BLOOMSBURY, FAIRCHILD BOOKS and the Fairchild Books logo
are trademarks of Bloomsbury Publishing Plc

First published in the United States of America 2021

For legal purposes the Acknowledgments on pp. x–xi constitute
an extension of this copyright page.

Cover design: Eleanor Rose
Cover image: © Yagi Studio / Getty Images

Library of Congress Cataloging-in-Publication Data
Names: Burns, Leslie Davis, author.
Title: Fashion business cases : a student guide to learning with case studies / Leslie Davis
Burns, Bloomsbury Fashion Business Cases, Editor-in-Chief [and four others].
Description: New York, NY : Fairchild Books, Bloomsbury Publishing Inc, [2021] |
Includes bibliographical references and index.
Identifiers: LCCN 2020018971 | ISBN 9781501362996 (paperback) | ISBN 9781501363016 (pdf)
Subjects: LCSH: Clothing trade–Case studies. | Fashion–Economic aspects–Case studies.
Classification: LCC HD9940.A2 B86 2021 | DDC 746.9/2068–dc23
LC record available at https://lccn.loc.gov/2020018971

ISBN: PB: 978-1-5013-6299-6
          ePDF: 978-1-5013-6301-6

Typeset by Integra Software Services Pvt. Ltd.
Printed and bound in the United States of America

To find out more about our authors and books visit www.fairchildbooks.com
and sign up for our newsletter.

CONTENTS

Part 5   Merchandising Management and Retailing

Part 6 Entrepreneurship and Fashion Law

Introduction 268

Introductory Cases

Intermediate Cases

PREFACE AND ACKNOWLEDGMENTS

Professionals in the global fashion industry constantly make decisions that affect the organization and operations of their fashion businesses—including decisions around strategic plans, marketing and branding strategies, merchandising management, retailing, fashion law, product design and development, and supply chain management. They apply a broad range of skills to this decision-making—abilities to analyze situations, evaluate alternative courses of action, recommend optimal strategies for moving forward, and assess the effectiveness of strategies. Students in fashion programs, the industry professionals of the future, practice and acquire these skills through a variety of experiential learning activities that are built into their courses and programs. One such experiential activity is the fashion business case study. A fashion business case study is a written description of a "real life" business problem, issue, or opportunity in the fashion industry. The case study method (or case method) of teaching and learning is a powerful tool for students to apply concepts introduced in courses to real-life situations, dilemmas, or opportunities faced by professionals and companies in the fashion industry. As an outcome of analyzing fashion business case studies, students learn concepts and at the same time practice problem-solving and communication skills necessary for their future success. *Fashion Business Cases: A Student Guide to Learning with Case Studies* consists of forty introductory, intermediate, and advanced case studies on topics related to situations, dilemmas, and opportunities faced by professionals and companies in today's global fashion industry. The cases studies included are organized around five general topic areas:

1) Textiles, Design, Product Development, and Sustainability
2) Marketing and Branding
3) Manufacturing, Supply Chain, and Technology
4) Merchandising Management and Retailing
5) Entrepreneurship and Fashion Law

Fashion Business Cases: A Student Guide to Learning with Case Studies provides step-by-step guidelines for students to successfully complete case study analyses. The assignments and activities presented with each case study provide students with an opportunity to express, support, defend, and present conclusions and recommendations. In addition to the step-by-step guidelines for students that are incorporated in this book, ancillary materials include an *Instructor's Guide* with teaching notes for each of the cases.

This book is a wonderful collaboration between *Bloomsbury Fashion Business Cases (BFBC)* and Fairchild Books, an imprint of Bloomsbury Publishing. *BFBC* is part of Bloomsbury Fashion Central, a digital hub for interdisciplinary research in fashion and dress. Case studies included in this book were written by scholars from around the world and reprinted, by permission, from the *BFBC* resource. Prior to publication in *BFBC*, cases were reviewed and edited by content and editorial specialists. *BFBC* was made possible because of the vision and leadership of those currently and previously with the Digital Resources Division at Bloomsbury Publishing including Kathryn Earle, Hannah Crump, Tomas René, Selina Mahar, Abigail Le Marquand-Brown, and Holly Shore. The regional editors of *BFBC*, Lorynn Divita, Haekyung Yu, Michael Beverland, and Natascha Radclyffe-Thomas, played a crucial role in the creation of this book. Their superb reviewing and editing of case studies included in *BFBC* assures that the collection includes relevant, timely, and high-quality cases.

The editorial team at Fairchild Books, specifically Emily Samulski, Jenna Lefkowitz, and Edie Weinberg, understood the need for a learning guide for students around case studies, identified the opportunity for collaborating with *BFBC*, and adapted the cases for inclusion in the book. Without their leadership, this book would not have been possible. It has been my great pleasure to serve as editor-in-chief of *BFBC* since its inception and to work with Fairchild Books in adding this important contribution to the library of resources they offer to fashion students.

Leslie Davis Burns
Editor-in-Chief, *Bloomsbury Fashion Business Cases*, 2017–2020

The publisher wishes to gratefully acknowledge and thank the editorial team involved in the publication of this book:

Acquisitions Editor: Emily Samulski

Development Editor/Editorial Assistant: Jenna Lefkowitz

Art Development Editor: Edie Weinberg

In-House Designer: Eleanor Rose

Production Manager: Ken Bruce

Project Manager: Rebecca Willford

Bloomsbury Digital Resources Commissioning Team: Tomas René, Abigail Le Marquand-Brown, Selina Mahar, Holly Shore

DISCLAIMER

LIST OF CONTRIBUTORS

Bethan Alexander
Course Leader—MA Fashion Retail
London College of Fashion
London
UK

Maher Anjum
Director
Anjum-James Associates Limited
London
UK

Helen Beney
Lecturer—Fashion Business
London College of Fashion
London
UK

Michael Beverland
Professor of Fashion Enterprise
RMIT
Melbourne
Australia

Margaret L. Bishop
Adjunct Professor—Graduate Studies:
  Supply Chain management
Parsons School of Design
NY
USA

Flora Brunetti
Adjunct Professor—Marketing and
  Management
LIM College
NY
USA

Nina Bürklin
Research Associate and Doctoral Candidate
LMU Munich
Munich
Germany

Leslie Davis Burns
President
Responsible Global Fashion LLC
OR
USA

Yoori Chae
PhD candidate in Apparel Studies
University of Minnesota–Twin Cities
MN
USA

Justine Davidson Ruby
Senior Lecturer—Fashion Management
Nottingham Trent University
Nottingham
UK

Lorynn Divita
Associate Professor of Apparel
  Merchandising
Baylor University
TX
USA

Lynne Hammond
Director—Business & Management
  Program
London College of Fashion
London
UK

Rosanne P. Hart
Adjunct Professor—Fashion Media &
  Public Relations
Southern Methodist University
TX
USA

Lisa Hodgkins
Faculty Librarian
Pima Community College
AZ
USA

Matalie Howard
Assistant Professor of Family & Consumer
  Science
Liberty University
VA
USA

Joanne Hurley
Lecturer—BA Hons Fashion Branding and
  Communication
Birmingham City University
Birmingham
UK

Iva Jestratijevic
Assistant Professor
University of North Texas
TX
USA

Kim K.P. Johnson
Professor Emerita—Retail Merchandising
  Program
University of Minnesota
MN
US

Chanjean Jung
Practitioner
South Korea

Hakan Karaosman
Postdoctoral Researcher in Sustainability
  Integration in Luxury Fashion Supply
  Networks
Politecnico di Milan
Milan
Italy

Anthony Kent
Professor—School of Art & Design
Nottingham Trent University
Nottingham
UK

Anjum Khan
Director of Asian Business Chambers of
  Commerce
Greater Birmingham Chambers of Commerce
Birmingham
UK

GiHyung Kim
Department of Clothing and Textiles
Sookmyung Women's University
Seoul
South Korea

Su Yeon Kim
Department of Human Environment and
  Design
Yonsei University
Seoul
South Korea

Ae-Ran Koh
Yonsei University
Seoul
South Korea

Camille Kraeplin
Associate Professor—Journalism
Southern Methodist University
TX
USA

Jennifer Kyungeun Lee
Assistant Professor—Fashion Business
  Management
FIT
NY
USA

Myles Ethan Lascity
Assistant Professor—Journalism
Southern Methodist University
TX
USA

Yoon-Jung Lee
Department of Home Economics Education
Korea University
Seoul
South Korea

Sheng Lu
Associate Professor—Fashion and Apparel
  Studies
University of Delaware
DE
USA

Priscilla Martinez
Baylor University
TX
USA

Rachel Matthews
Head of Fashion
Collarts
Melbourne
Australia

Clare McTurk
Principal Lecturer and Educational
    Lead—Fashion Buying
Manchester Metropolitan University
Manchester
UK

Anne Peirson-Smith
Assistant Professor—English
City University of Hong Kong
Kowloon
Hong Kong

Patsy Perry
Senior Lecturer—Fashion Marketing
University of Manchester
Manchester
UK

Roxanne Peters
Intellectual Property Lecturer
University of the Arts London
London
UK

Luis Quijano
Liberty University
VA
USA

Natascha Radclyffe-Thomas
Course Leader—BA (Hons) Fashion
    Marketing
London College of Fashion
London
UK

Jongeun Rhee
Professor—Operations and Management
University of Wisconsin–Stout
WI
USA

Nancy A. Rudd
Faculty Emeritus—Consumer Sciences
The Ohio State University
OH
USA

Eda Sanchez-Persampieri
Director of the Center of
    Entrepreneurship
St. Francis College
NY
USA

Marie Segares
Assistant Professor—Management &
    Information Technology
St. Francis College
NY
USA

Amanda Grace Sikarskie
Assistant Professor of Art,
    Art History, and Design
Michigan State University
MI
USA

Celia Stall-Meadows
Associate Professor—Fashion Marketing
Northeastern State University
OK
USA

YoungJee Suh
Lecturer
Seoul Occupational Training College
Seoul
South Korea

Caroline Swee Lin Tan
Lecturer—Entrepreneurship
RMIT
Melbourne
Australia

Rosemary Varley
Subject Director for Marketing and Retail
London College of Fashion
London
UK

David S. Waller
Senior Lecturer—Marketing Discipline
    Group
University of Technology Sydney
Sydney
Australia

Helen J. Waller
Verge Gallery
University of Technology Sydney
Sydney
Australia

William Webb
Senior Lecturer—Retail Management
London College of Fashion
London
UK

Valerie Wilson Trower
Associate Lecturer—Fashion Business
London College of Fashion
London
UK

Agnieszka Witońska-Pakulska
Legal counsel
Pakulskikancelaria
Kielce
Poland

Haekyung Yu
Professor
Incheon National University
Incheon
South Korea

PART ONE

Learning through the Case Study Method

Chapter 1

The Case Study Method of Learning

Leslie Davis Burns

In This Chapter You Will Learn

- What to expect when you are assigned a fashion business case study to analyze.
- The objectives of using a fashion business case as a learning tool.
- Approaches to analyzing fashion business cases.

You've Been Assigned a Fashion Business Case Study—Where to Begin?

As a student in a fashion-related major or enrolled in a fashion-related course, you have been given an assignment to analyze a fashion business case. The general expectations of this assignment are for you to evaluate the business case and then justify and present your conclusions and recommendations. You may be asking many questions about this assignment: Where do I begin? What process would be most effective in carrying out this type of analysis? How much time will I need to devote to this assignment? What is the best way to present my results and conclusions? How will this assignment be graded? This chapter introduces you to the case study method of learning—why you were assigned a fashion business case study, what you can expect to learn from the assignment, and the process for completing your analysis.

What is a fashion business case study?

Why do you believe you were assigned a fashion business case to analyze for this course? The answer is that the assignment will facilitate your thinking and making decisions like a professional in the fashion industry. Professionals in the fashion industry are constantly addressing challenges and opportunities and making strategic decisions that affect the future success of their companies. Whether it's an individual in a junior-level product development position making a decision about an optimal material choice for a particular product or a senior level marketing analyst making a decision about an optimal strategic course of action for the entire company, professionals at all levels in a fashion business constantly make decisions that affect the organization and operations of their companies. These decisions may not have a single "correct" answer. Instead, fashion professionals must weigh the advantages and disadvantages of options and then decide on the best plan of action according to the criteria they have established. These same issues, opportunities, challenges, and strategic decisions form the basis of fashion business case studies. The case studies included in this book will ask you to take the role of fashion professionals and make decisions according to their perspectives. This exercise allows you to not only practice thinking like a professional in the fashion industry but also analyze the strategic approaches of fashion companies.

The case studies included in this book are written by international faculty, instructors/ tutors, and professionals with expertise in fashion business topics. The case studies are written and organized around the following areas:

1 Learning objectives of the case.
2 Introduction, overview, and background information associated with an issue, challenge, opportunity, or dilemma that a professional in the fashion industry or a fashion brand company is currently facing or has faced in the past.
3 A specific business problem addressed in the case.
4 Business questions to guide your analysis.
5 References and further readings to assist you in your analysis.

Fashion brand companies include all businesses that are involved with the design, development, production, marketing, and retailing of fashion products. As students, you are asked to take the role of a fashion industry professional to address the issue, challenge, dilemma, and/ or opportunity identified in the case study; develop and evaluate options; and justify your decision for the best plan of action.

Background information for the case studies is based on public information about an actual company or situation (possibly including interviews) and/or faculty expertise in an area for hypothetical (but realistic) situations or companies. Background information may also include additional outside readings or media. In the case study method, you are asked to review and analyze this background material; evaluate multiple alternative solutions; recommend and justify an optimal solution for the professional or company; and predict the outcomes of the chosen solution. Fashion business cases provide you with opportunities to apply and practice critical thinking; analytic, evaluative, problem solving; and communication skills. These are essential skills for your success in today's fashion industry—and the primary reason case studies are assigned in fashion-related courses.

Integration of case studies into courses

You will find that case studies are integrated into a range of courses at all levels from first-year/introductory courses through to graduate-level courses. Case studies for introductory courses are generally short and focus on a single concept, topic, or issue. As a way of introducing you to concepts, introductory case studies may, in fact, have a "correct" answer or single most optimal solution. For example, a case study in an introductory textiles or product development course may introduce you to properties of textiles/materials and ask you to evaluate and compare the textile/material options for a particular product category and then recommend and justify the optimal textile/material to use. For this type of case study there may, in fact, be an actual optimal textile/material for the product category. As another example, a case study in an introductory fashion merchandising course may introduce you to markdown calculations for a particular retail situation and ask you to evaluate different markdown percentages and recommend and justify the optimal percentage for the situation. Again, for this type of case study, you would be expected to accurately calculate the markdown percentages.

Case studies for intermediate courses are generally longer and focus on the inter-relationships among concepts where you would be expected to integrate knowledge and applications. Intermediate case studies may have multiple "correct" or optimal solutions. You will be expected to evaluate the options and justify the solution you recommend. For example, a case study in an intermediate product development or sourcing course may ask you to evaluate the advantages and disadvantages of sourcing the production of a particular product category in several countries. You would be expected to consider multiple factors in comparing the sourcing options and recommending and justifying the optimal country for sourcing production of that particular product category using established criteria for the recommendation. As another example, a case study in an intermediate merchandising management course may ask you to weigh the advantages and disadvantages of adding a product category to the mix of merchandise offered by a particular retailer. You would be expected to evaluate the situation from multiple perspectives and then recommend and justify whether the retailer should add this product category to their mix of merchandise offered.

Case studies for advanced courses include multi-faceted issues and topics that require you to assess internal and external factors associated with the issue or topic. Advanced cases are typically longer and may be used for term/semester-long assignments. As with intermediate cases, advanced cases would also have multiple "correct" or optimal solutions and you would be expected to evaluate the options and justify the solution you recommend. For example, a case study in an advanced retail management course may ask you to evaluate and justify strategic initiatives for a large retailer around corporate social responsibility. You would be expected to evaluate initiatives with respect to the retailer's mission, size, and strategies for product design and development, sourcing, marketing, and distribution. Based on this evaluation you would then be expected to recommend a series of initiatives for the retailer.

Case studies are also integrated into courses across subject matter topics: textiles, product development, design, branding, marketing, manufacturing, supply chain management, merchandising, retailing, sustainability, entrepreneurship, and fashion law. Some case studies will be assigned as in-class activities where short written responses and/or small group or larger class discussions would be expected. Other case studies will be assigned as out-of-class assignments with the expectation that you will conduct research and present your results as a written paper, oral presentation, and/or design solution. With all types of assignments, you will be expected to analyze the case study, evaluate alternative solutions or courses of action, and recommend and justify an optimal solution or course of action.

Learning through Fashion Business Cases

As you can see, the case study method of learning is a powerful tool for you to learn and apply concepts introduced in courses to real-life situations, strategies, opportunities, and dilemmas faced by professionals and companies in the fashion industry. In the process of analyzing fashion business cases you will practice problem-solving and communication skills necessary for your future success. In addition, you will be exposed to a variety of issues and situations within the fashion industry, understanding that such opportunities and dilemmas are not unique to a particular company but are part of working within the fashion industry. As a result of the case study method, you will demonstrate your ability to:

- Diagnose and articulate a problem, issue, or opportunity faced by a professional and/or company in the global fashion industry.
- Analyze and critically evaluate alternative solutions to the particular problem, issue, or opportunity.
- Present and justify ideas, decisions, or solutions.
- Actively listen to others and express and defend your thoughts to others.
- Think like a professional in the global fashion industry.

The power of learning from case studies comes not only from your analysis of the case study but also from written assignments, group/class discussions, and other formats for communicating/presenting the results of your analysis. For example, you may be required to complete written analyses and/or oral presentations around the case study. Case studies integrated into design courses may include assignments whereby you are asked to justify and present a design recommendation. Because the case study method of learning is inductive and experiential, sometimes with no single "correct" answer, you may disagree with conclusions or recommendations made by others in your class. However, these assignments and activities will provide you with an opportunity to express, support, and defend your conclusions and recommendations as well as learn from others in your class.

Approaches to Successfully Completing Fashion Business Case Studies

Although students vary in their approaches to fashion business case analyses, this section discusses general guidelines to inform the approach that will work best for you to successfully complete your case study assignment and tips for successfully completing your analyses.

Steps for completing your case study assignment

1. Read through the entire case study including the assignments.
The first step is to carefully read the case study and all assignments associated with the case study. This careful reading will give you a sense of the scope and complexity of the case study as well as what is being expected of you. Depending on the length and complexity of the case study, estimate the amount of time you believe will be necessary to complete the assignments, including time for researching the topic, completing the case study analyses, communicating your conclusions and recommendations, and practicing a presentation (if assigned). In general, you will need a minimum of two hours to prepare a short 1,000-word case study and a minimum of four hours for longer cases. If the case study assignments span over the course of a term or semester, note time allocations for completing the assignments over the time span indicated.

As you read the case study, think broadly about and note concepts and issues introduced in the case study. Also note the professional in the fashion industry from whose perspective the case study analysis will be written/communicated. As you complete the analysis, evaluation, and recommendations, you will take the role of and present your analysis from the perspective of this individual. Think about what their general approach to these concepts and issues would be.

2. Conduct preliminary research related to the fashion business case.
The next step is to conduct preliminary research into background information related to the fashion business case, including topics and issues introduced in the case study and information about the company. If the case study includes a list of readings and references, that is a good place to start. Textbooks and other resources assigned for the course may also provide essential background information related to topics and issues introduced in the case. Become familiar with the historical context for the problems or issues introduced in the case study. Also become familiar with the company; this will include referring to the company's website and trade publications that have reported on the company or the issues and topics in the case. In some cases, interviews with industry professionals and/or field observations (e.g., visiting a retail store) may be useful. You will also want to become familiar with terminology introduced in the fashion business case. If you are not familiar with industry terminology, look up the definitions and how the terms apply to this case study. Lastly, as part of your research, identify theoretical frameworks or models that may be relevant to the topics introduced in the case study.

3. Read the entire case study again; this time, as you go along, identify key facts relevant to the issue.
Now that you have conducted preliminary research on the topics and the company introduced in the case, the next step is to read the entire case study again. This time take notes about areas of analysis; list all possible problems and concerns, being sure to look at causes of the problem area, not just the symptoms of the issue or problem. Also note the key facts that will guide your analysis, evaluation of options, and recommendations regarding optimal solutions, decisions, or courses of action. Refer to the business questions and other assignments as guidance for the analysis you will be expected to complete. Create an outline of the questions that you will address and determine that you have the necessary research and background information to address these questions. Review the results of the preliminary research and identify topics that you will need to conduct further research.

4. Develop your conclusions and recommendations.
Reflect on the areas of analysis, study relevant information, and begin noting your responses to each of the areas. Outline the possible solutions or courses of action you are considering. At this stage, be creative in developing these alternative courses of action. Next, establish the criteria to be used in assessing the optimal solution or course of action—think about what priorities the professional and/or company would have. Outline the advantages and disadvantages for alternative solutions or courses of action you are considering, assessing each alternative based on the information in the case, the criteria established from the perspective of the professional and/or company, and the research you have conducted, including relevant theoretical frameworks and/or models associated with the topics introduced in the case study. This research will be used to inform your analysis, final justifications, and conclusions. Be sure you are approaching the conclusions and recommendations from the same perspective (of a particular professional and/or company) that the case analysis is written/communicated.

5. Review your conclusions and formulate a set of recommendations along with justifications for the conclusions.
Review the list of possible solutions or conclusions you are considering. As you review this list, answer the following questions:

1   What do you believe is the optimal solution? Why?
2   Do the advantages of your recommendations outweigh the disadvantages? If not, do you need to rethink your conclusions?

3 What do you believe are the strongest justifications for your conclusions? Why?

4 Are your conclusions and recommendations consistent with the perspective of the industry professional and/or company presented in the case? If not, do they need to be re-evaluated in order to be consistent?

6. Prepare your analysis.
Review the assignments and expected presentation format for communicating the conclusions and recommendations associated with the case study. You are now ready to start outlining how you will communicate or present the case study analysis. Chapter 2 focuses on strategies for effectively presenting your analysis, conclusions, and recommendations.

Tips for success

As you prepare your analysis cases for presentation, you should consider the following:

1 Carefully evaluate all information presented in the case.

2 List all possible problems and concerns, being sure to look at causes of the problem area, not symptoms.

3 Use textbook material, current articles, and other resources (e.g., library materials, websites, interviews, field observations) to research the situation, problem, and alternatives.

4 Use your own personal experiences around the topics that may inform your conclusions and recommendations.

5 Be creative in developing alternative courses of action.

6 Assess each alternative based on the information in the case and the criteria established.

7 Be ready to defend the selected course of action.

Summary

Fashion business case studies are excellent learning tools for applying and evaluating concepts, topics, and issues in today's fashion industry. The typical fashion business case study provides an overview and background information associated with an issue, challenge, opportunity, or dilemma a professional in the fashion industry or a fashion brand company is currently facing or has faced in the past. You are asked to take the role of a fashion industry professional to address the issue, challenge, opportunity, or dilemma; develop and evaluate options; and justify your decision for the best plan of action. As such, fashion business cases provide you with opportunities to apply and practice critical thinking, analytic, evaluative, problem solving, and communication skills. You will find case studies integrated into a range of courses at all levels and across subject matter topics. You will need to follow a systematic approach when completing a case study assignment, paying attention to key facts presented in the case study, evaluating alternative solutions, taking the perspective of the fashion professional, and justifying your recommended course of action.

Further Reading

Ellet, William (2018). *The Case Study Handbook, Revised Edition: A Student's Guide*. Boston, MA: Harvard Business Review Press.

Chapter 2

Presenting Fashion Business Case Studies

Leslie Davis Burns

In This Chapter You Will Learn

- A general approach for presenting your case study analysis, conclusions, and recommendations.
- Best practices for a variety of case study presentation formats including written, oral, and design presentations.
- Criteria for evaluating case study assignments and presentations.
- Methods for integrating your case study analysis into portfolios, internship or job interviews, and theses and dissertations.

Presenting Your Case Study Analysis

Having followed the steps outlined in Chapter 1, you are now ready to present your case study analysis. This chapter discusses creating effective presentations to communicate your evaluation, conclusions, and recommendations. It also discusses how to integrate your case study analysis into portfolios, theses and dissertations, and interviews for internships and jobs.

To achieve the greatest learning from fashion business cases you should follow a systematic approach that is based on the business questions associated with the case study and the analysis you completed along with your conclusions, recommendations, and justifications. These will be presented in one or more formats including written analyses, oral presentations, debates, role-playing, poster presentations, design presentations, videos, and class discussions. A general outline for communicating/presenting your analysis, conclusions, and recommendations associated with the case study is provided below. This outline can be used for any presentation format. Remember that the assignment or business questions associated with the case study may ask you to address additional or specific aspects included in the case study. These aspects should also be included in your presentation.

1. Introduction and background: presentation of facts surrounding the case.
Your presentation should begin with an overview of the background of the business situation introduced in the case study, including the name and general organizational structure of the company, relevant information about the industry sector, historical context of the issue or problem, and the perspective from which the case study is being analyzed. This section will include the research that was conducted as part of your case study analysis: from textbooks, journal articles, trade publication articles, and/or appropriate website information as well as from any interviews you have conducted and/or observations you have made. The introduction should not simply repeat the background information included in the case study but provide an integrated summary that demonstrates a comprehensive understanding of the background of the industry sector, topic, and opportunity, issue, or problem that forms the basis of the case study.

2. Identification of the concerns, issues, problems, and/or opportunities.
After introducing background information about the industry sector, company, and topic, the next section of the analysis is to clearly identify the concerns, issues, problems, or opportunities evident in the situation introduced in the case. This section should answer the questions: What is the issue or opportunity for this individual and/or company? Why is it an issue or opportunity? What key facts should be considered in addressing the issue or opportunity? Research that was conducted as part of your case study analysis, including relevant theoretical frameworks and/or models, will also be included in this section.

3. Listing and evaluation of alternative solutions and/or courses of action.
The case study will most likely ask you to make a recommendation as to an optimal solution or course of action to an issue, problem, opportunity, or dilemma being faced by a fashion brand company and/or professional. In most cases, the company and/or professional will evaluate alternative solutions or courses of action, weighing the advantages and disadvantages of each before making a recommendation. Therefore, the next section of the presentation should present this evaluation and decision-making process. In this section a list of the alternative solutions and/or courses of action, along with the advantages and disadvantages of each, should be presented. Remember, these alternative solutions and/or courses of action should be presented from the perspective of the company and/or industry professional upon whom the analysis is based. The merits of alternative solutions and/or courses of action should be compared and weighed according to criteria identified by this same company and/or industry professional.

4. Recommendation and justification of the optimal solution and/or course of action.
After the advantages and disadvantages of the alternative solutions and/or courses of action have been evaluated according to the criteria identified, a recommendation is made regarding the optimal solution and/or course of action. Therefore, the next section of the presentation is your recommendation of an optimal solution and/or course of action along with a justification for this recommendation. The main questions you will address in this section are: What is the best solution or course of action for the business problem? and Why is this the best solution or course of action? Remember, the justification for this recommendation must be supported with evidence collected through the research process and should be from the perspective of the company and/or industry professional identified in the case study. This supporting evidence will be based on the research you conducted as part of your case study analysis (from textbooks, journal articles, trade publication articles, and/or appropriate website information). Supporting evidence may also include personal experiences, interviews, or observations.

5. Plans for implementing the recommended course of action.
For some cases, you will be expected to also present plans for implementing the recommended solution or course of action. This requirement results in your thinking through all aspects of implementation, including logistical strategies for these plans. Depending on the case study, your plan may be from the perspective of the industry professional identified in the case study or from other industry professionals.

6. Identification of possible follow-up issues.
The presentation of some case study analyses will include a section on possible follow-up issues. The most common of these is being asked to identify metrics and strategies for determining the effectiveness of the recommended solution or course of action. Questions addressed in this section include:

1 How would the fashion professional and/or company know if the recommended optimal solution or course of action was successful?
2 What metrics will be needed to make this assessment?
3 How will the metrics be measured and analyzed?
4 Are there any unintended consequences of the decision?
5 What are the next steps for the fashion professional and/or company in moving forward?

7. Bibliography or references.
The presentation should include your list of references and other resources used in conducting the research for your analysis, using a standard format for citations and references (e.g., APA, Chicago Manual of Style, Harvard).

8. Guidelines for outline allocations
As a general framework, allocate the following percentages of your presentation to its various sections included in the outline. Please note the importance of listing alternative solutions and/or courses of action, and the recommendation of and justification for an optimal solution or course of action.

1 Introduction and background information: 15%
2 Identification of the concerns, opportunities, issues, and/or problems: 15%
3 Listing and evaluation of alternative solutions and/or courses of action: 25%
4 Recommendation and justification of the optimal solution and/or course of action: 25%
5 Plans for implementing the recommended course of action, if applicable: 10%
6 Identification of possible follow-up issues: 5%
7 Bibliography or references: 5%

Written Case Study Analyses

Written assignments are a commonly assigned format for presenting your case study analysis, recommendations, and justifications. Through these assignments, written communication skills are enhanced, specifically organization, sentence structure, appropriate grammar and spelling, appropriate citation of references, and appropriate use of industry terminology. If written assignments are expected, follow the section guidelines previously outlined and the specific assignment questions provided by your instructor.

Written case study papers should be typed (single or double-spaced) and include headings if they assist the reader with the organization of the case analysis. Supporting evidence for your recommendation and justification needs to be included. Cite all work using the preferred formatting for citations within the written document and in the bibliography/references section of the written analysis.

Oral Presentations

Oral presentations are also a commonly assigned format for presenting case study analyses, recommendations, and justifications. There are several oral presentation formats. You may be asked to:

- Present your analysis to the entire class or to a smaller group or subset of the class.
- Record your oral presentation and upload it onto a digital platform.
- Present your analysis through oral debates or role-playing activities.

Presenting case study analyses through oral presentations enhances oral communication and organizational skills. Oral presentations may be assigned independently of or in conjunction with written assignments associated with the case studies.

Oral presentation guidelines

As with written assignments, the guidelines outlined previously and the specific assignment questions provided by your instructor can be used for oral presentations. However, oral presentations are more than simply reading your written assignments out loud. A presentation should be delivered in an organized and thoughtful manner that effectively communicates your analysis, evaluation of alternatives, recommendation, and justification. When developing your presentation, you will want to consider the length of time allotted for the presentation and divide the presentation sections to fit the allotted time.

Practicing your presentation is a necessary step, allowing you to build confidence in your delivery, ensuring that the timing of the presentation meets the requirements, and creating an opportunity for you to assess and revise the content as necessary. Practice the presentation as you would deliver it in person: maintain eye contact, use your notes sparingly, be confident and relaxed, and dress in a manner that does not distract from the presentation. You may want to audio or video record your presentation and review it, taking the role of a member of the audience. Pay attention to the speed of delivery, phrasing and emphasis, voice volume, logical flow of thought, any fillers that should be avoided (e.g., "um," "like," "and, uh"), and any gesturing that the audience may find distracting. You may also practice your presentation in front of friends or peers, asking them to comment and make suggestions around the content and delivery of the presentation.

One question you might have is whether visual tools (e.g., Microsoft PowerPoint slides) should be used to accompany the oral presentation. Some assignments (e.g., a voice-over of a PowerPoint slide show, a product design, or a poster design) necessarily require such visuals to be an integral part of the presentation. For other oral presentation formats, however, visual tools may be optional. With these oral presentation formats, visuals can add interest to your presentation, but they should only be used if they reinforce or add relevant information to the presentation. Slides with text should be simple (e.g., bullet points only) and readable (at least 24-point font with a sans serif typeface), focusing on key points. In addition, during your presentation you should not read from the screen but use the slides as a way of adding interest to the presentation. Any images used should be large enough and appropriately cited. Animations and special effects should be avoided unless they add to the information or a point being made in the presentation.

Debates

Fashion business cases lend themselves to the debate format of oral presentations when recommended solutions and/or courses of action for the case can be argued from more than one perspective. In the debate format some students will present and provide evidence for one of the perspectives; others will present and provide evidence for another of the perspectives. Through this oral presentation format, you will learn to defend your perspective while at the same time learning from the arguments made regarding the defense of other perspectives. In most cases, with the debate format of presentation you will be working with teams of students who share your perspective. However, you may be asked to prepare justifications and defenses for both perspectives. In these situations, you may be randomly assigned to present and defend one of the perspectives. Debates are typically organized in "rounds," with each round allowing the teams to present their arguments for and against the particular solution or course of action each is defending. Once they have heard the others' arguments, each team will have an opportunity to respond to that argument in the form of a rebuttal. Debates are evaluated based on how well each team prepared for and presented their arguments.

Role-playing

Some fashion business cases lend themselves to role-playing oral presentations. If you are assigned a role-playing presentation of the case, you will take the role of a fashion business professional and present the information from the perspective of the individual. Taking the perspective of a fashion professional is inherent in your analysis of many fashion business cases. That said, role-playing exercises are most common in classroom oral presentations where the presenter takes the role of a fashion professional and the audience (others in the class) takes the role of others in the fashion industry to whom the fashion professional is making a recommendation. For example, you may be asked to take the role of:

- A marketing research professional who is providing recommendations to senior marketing leadership of a fashion brand company around brand position or brand identity strategies.
- A product developer for a fashion brand company who is providing recommendations to the company's senior leadership around strategies for addressing problems with the quality of a particular product.
- A fashion retail buyer who is negotiating terms of sale with a sales representative for a fashion brand.
- A sourcing analyst who is explaining the implementation of the fashion brand company's code of conduct to a group of managers of contract factories.

As you can see, role-playing activities provide opportunities for you to practice effective oral communication as a professional in the fashion industry.

Design Presentations

In addition to written and oral presentations, case studies may ask you to present your analysis and recommendation in the form of a visual design. Design presentations follow the same approach as described earlier; the only difference is that the recommendation is made visually. Examples of design presentations include:

- The design of a fashion product that solves an issue or problem as identified in a design brief. For example, a design brief may ask a designer to use a zero-waste design strategy for a particular product category. The presentation will be the design and justification that represents this strategy.
- A poster that visually summarizes your analysis, recommendation, and justification. Posters may require images, charts, tables, or other visual tools to effectively communicate content.
- A marketing tool that visually presents an optimal solution for a marketing issue, opportunity, or dilemma. For example, you may be asked to create a visual display or website, to effectively communicate to consumers the impact of a fashion brand company's sustainability initiative.
- A flow-chart or model that presents an optimal solution for a process for a fashion brand company. For example, you may be asked to analyze and recommend an optimal management process for assuring supply chain transparency including a flow-chart for this process.
- The design of a textile/material that represents an optimal solution for an issue or dilemma a fashion brand company is facing. For example, you may be asked to evaluate options and design the specifications for a material that best meets performance standards for a particular fashion product category.

Design presentations are typically accompanied by written and/or oral presentations; but remember, the design should "stand on its own" as a means of communicating your analysis of the issue, problem, opportunity, or dilemma included in the case study. Design presentations are graded according to the quality of the presentation and effectiveness of the design in meeting the criteria outlined in the assignment.

Class Participation and Discussions

Case studies make excellent prompts for class discussions of the specific topics or issues introduced in the case and of more general topics related to the case study. Therefore, you may be expected to participate in class discussions as part of the case study assignment. With courses that meet in person, class discussions are generally oral; with courses that meet online, class discussions can be written or video-based in nature. Class discussions enhance your learning from classmates' comments and also enhance your communication skills, particularly your ability to organize your thoughts and speak confidently with little or no time for preparation.

Class discussions may take on many formats. The discussion leader (typically your instructor) may pose specific questions related to the case study. You may also be asked to present one or more sections of the case study. For example, you may be asked to take on the role of one of the following:

- Case Opener—you will summarize the key issues of the case.
- Action Plan Presenter—you will describe an optimal solution and justification or present a response to one of the discussion questions.
- Participant—you will ask questions, provide alternative perspectives, and defend those perspectives.

Presentations may be made in small groups or to the entire class. If small groups are used, conclusions drawn by the group will be expected for several cases and presented to the entire class.

Because there is generally more than one "correct" answer to the case study opportunities, issues, problems, and questions, you may find that you disagree with the conclusions or recommendations made by others in your class. This can and should result in lively discussion. However, to get the most out of these discussions, the following ground rules will facilitate a constructive discussion:

1 No one should be humiliated for anything they say—personal attacks should not be tolerated. However, if you are not prepared, your comments are careless, or your thoughts are not clear, you may feel embarrassed. Embarrassment and humiliation are not the same thing.

2 Rude or offensive comments or class behavior, including bigotry of any kind, should not be tolerated. Your discussions are to be civil, with every student showing proper respect for the beliefs and the dignity of every other student.

Your instructor or class may develop additional ground rules for discussions as appropriate for the context and goals of the class discussion.

Evaluation of Case Study Presentations

Evaluation of case study presentations will vary according to the format of presentation required. However, across formats, case study analyses will be evaluated based on the following criteria:

1 Care with which facts and background knowledge are researched.
2 Accuracy of the background information presented.
3 Demonstration of the ability to clearly identify and state problems and issues.
4 Use of appropriate analytic techniques in identifying feasible solutions/plans of action.
5 Evidence of sound logic/argument.
6 Consistency between analysis and recommendations.
7 Ability to formulate reasonable and feasible recommendations for action.

Next Steps: Including Case Study Analyses in Portfolios, Capstone Projects, and Interviews

Now that you have completed your case study analysis, think about how you might use this assignment as you communicate your experiences in design or learning portfolios, as the basis for capstone projects such as theses and dissertations, or during interviews for internships and positions within the fashion industry. Case study analyses that result in written and design presentations can be included in portfolios to show evidence of your abilities to analyze a problem or opportunity, evaluate alternatives, and recommend and justify an optimal solution. These analyses also show evidence of your writing and/or design skills.

Case study analyses can also be used as a basis for capstone projects. Some college or university degrees require that students complete a capstone project, such as a thesis or dissertation, that demonstrates a student's ability to conduct research, integrate information from a variety of reliable sources, evaluate and justify strategies, and draw conclusions. Case study analyses may serve as a basis for these types of capstone projects, often requiring that the student identify an issue or opportunity in the fashion industry, write their own case study, evaluate and justify alternative strategies, and present their recommendation and conclusions.

Case study analyses can also be effectively integrated into interviews for internships and jobs within the fashion industry. Behavioral interviewing is a common technique used by interviewers. In this technique, the interviewer will ask about past behaviors and experiences in order to predict your behavior in the future and determine if you have the skills necessary for the internship or job. For example, the interviewer might ask:

- "Give me an example of when you were faced with a dilemma and had to solve it."
- "Describe a decision you made that might have affected others in a company."
- "Provide an example of a difficult situation that you had to resolve. What steps did you take?"

Early in your career, you may not have a great deal of professional experience in order to answer these questions. This is where your case study analyses come into play. For these types of questions, you can begin by saying "As part of my coursework, I successfully completed a case study analysis that addressed this type of situation," and then continue with your description of the case and the resulting analysis.

The S.T.A.R. method is the most common approach for answering behavioral questions. Using this method, you briefly describe each of the following:

- Situation: describe the situation outlined in the case study including the dilemma, opportunity, problem, or issue and business questions.
- Task: explain the task or assignment you were asked to complete, including the presentation format (e.g., written, oral, design).
- Action: describe the process or approach that you took to address the dilemma, opportunity, problem, or issue, including the criteria you used to evaluate the possible solutions.
- Results: describe the results of your analysis, including the recommended optimal solution and/or action plan and the justification for this recommendation.

As you can see, your case study analysis and presentation are ideal assignments to demonstrate that you can think like a successful professional in today's global fashion industry.

Summary

Your case study analysis will be presented in one or more formats including written analyses, oral presentations (including debates and role-playing), design presentations, and class discussions. Your presentation should begin with an overview of the background of the business situation introduced in the case study. After introducing background information, the next section of the analysis is to clearly identify the concerns, issues, problems, or opportunities evident in the situation introduced in the case. Next, the presentation should present the evaluation and decision-making process. In this section a list of the alternative solutions and/or courses of action, along with the advantages and disadvantages of each, should be presented. The next section of the presentation is your recommendation of an optimal solution and/or course of action along with a justification for this recommendation. You may also be expected to present plans for implementing the recommended course of action and/or include a section on possible follow-up issues. Case study presentations are evaluated according to the degree to which you have effectively outlined, justified, and presented an optimal solution or action plan. Your case study presentation can effectively be incorporated into learning or design portfolios and used as a basis for capstone projects such as theses and dissertations or as an example of your decision-making abilities in interviews for internships and jobs.

PART TWO

Textiles, Design, Product Development, and Sustainability

Introduction

This section includes case studies that focus on the decisions that professionals in the fashion industry make related to textiles, design techniques, and product development, all with a focus on environmental sustainability. Designers and product developers within the fashion industry use design briefs as guidelines for making these decisions. A design brief "outlines the design and development of lines offered by a fashion company and assures that all areas of the fashion company have a common design strategy for their lines" (Burns and Mullet 2020, p. 142). Components of a design brief include:

- Objectives of the line.
- Description of the target customer for the line.
- Design inspirations and theme of the line.
- Design requirements.
- Supply chain calendar and schedule for the line completion.

(Burns and Mullet 2020, p. 144)

Based on the objectives of the line, target customer, and design criteria outlined in a design brief, designers and product developers weigh the advantages and disadvantages of textiles, materials, and design strategies.

The case studies included in this section incorporate environmental sustainability as a criterion for which the advantages and disadvantages of alternative decisions are weighed. According to the U.S. Environmental Protection Agency (2019), "to pursue sustainability is to create and maintain the conditions under which humans and nature can exist in productive harmony to support present and future generations." Fashion brand companies use a number of strategies to pursue and enhance environmental sustainability including:

- Use of environmentally responsible materials.
- Reduction of water consumption over the life cycle of the product.
- Decreased use of energy from fossil fuels and increased use of renewable energy sources.
- Reduced textile waste.

(Burns 2019, p. 58)

The case studies included in this section represent challenges and opportunities for fashion brand companies in meeting objectives, design requirements, and supply chain calendars while creating environmentally sustainable lines. You will be required to analyze alternative solutions and courses of action that result in the global fashion industry's effective pursual of environmental sustainability.

See also the following chapters/cases on sustainability and corporate social responsibility:

- Chapter 13, H&M Under Attack: How Greenpeace Threatened a Brand's Reputation in Sustainability by Rosanne P. Hart and Camille Kraeplin (Public Case).
- Chapter 20, H&M Post-Rana Plaza: Can Fast Fashion Ever Be Truly Ethical? by David S. Waller and Helen J. Waller (Public Case).
- Chapter 22, Youngone Corporation: Global Sourcing and Corporate Social Responsibility by Yoon-Jung Lee and Yoori Chae (Public Case).
- Chapter 23, Making Fashion Transparent: What Consumers Know About the Brands they Admire by Iva Jestratijevic and Nancy A. Rudd (Public Case).
- Chapter 25, Growth of Green Apparel Manufacturing Strategies in Bangladesh—The Sustainable Road Ahead by Maher Anjum and Lynne Hammond (Scenario Case).
- Chapter 39, Approaching CSR with a New Kind of Transparency: How eCommerce Retailer Everlane Set New Industry Standards in Brand Communication by Nina Bürklin (Public Case).
- Chapter 40, Patagonia: Creative Sustainability Strategy for a Reluctant Fashion Brand by Rosemary Varley, Natascha Radclyffe-Thomas and William Webb (Public Case).

References and Further Reading

Burns, Leslie Davis (2019). *Sustainability and Social Change in Fashion*. New York: Fairchild Books/ Bloomsbury.

Burns, Leslie Davis and Kathy K. Mullet (2020). *The Business of Fashion: Designing, Manufacturing, and Marketing*. New York: Fairchild Books/Bloomsbury.

United States Environmental Protection Agency (2019). "What is Sustainability?" Accessed December 10, 2019. http://www.epa.gov/sustainability/learn-about-sustainability#what

Chapter 3

FABSCRAP: Building Stakeholder Awareness for Reducing Fashion Industry Waste

Margaret L. Bishop

The fashion industry relies on a constant flow of new styles to fuel its revenue growth and shareholder profit. Young consumers demand an ever-changing offering of new clothing to update their wardrobes. Older consumers seek new arrays of interior textiles to freshen their homes. Meanwhile, brand shareholders demand profit growth. To satisfy both their consumers and their shareholders, fashion and interior textile brands develop tens of thousands of new cut-and-sew products every year. The efforts to fill consumer demand and shareholder expectations result in unprecedented textile waste. In the United States, much of that waste is generated in the heart of New York City.

Entrepreneurial firm FABSCRAP collects pre-consumer textile waste from leading fashion brands and design rooms. Volunteers sort the scraps, so they can be diverted from landfill to be recycled, reused, or upcycled. Founded as a charitable organization with the goal of improving sustainability in the fashion industry, FABSCRAP also conducts outreach to build awareness of textile waste and engagement across its community of stakeholders. As a small lean organization, the firm is challenged to grow sustainably and to maintain awareness and engagement across its vast and diverse stakeholder groups.

Learning Objectives

Upon completion of this case, students should be able to:

- Identify and prioritize the organization's different stakeholder groups.
- Evaluate the effectiveness of FABSCRAP's current awareness and engagement efforts.
- Identify and evaluate contemporary, cost-effective tools for growing awareness and engagement among FABSCRAP's stakeholders.

- Formulate messaging appropriate to FABSCRAP's mission, the targeted stakeholder group(s), and available communication tool(s).
- List key metrics for evaluating the success of a communications plan to build awareness and engagement.

Introduction

Fashion is built on change, requiring a constant flow of new styles. The continuous demand for new products creates a behemoth design, product development, manufacturing, and sourcing ecosystem, using fabrics and trims to sample and manufacture new styles. As younger consumers grow more concerned about reducing environmental harm, the conflict between environmental concern, fashion's need for constant change, shareholder profit demands, and the textile waste fashion generates is growing. Fashion brand companies use a number of strategies to address this issue. One strategy that has been promoted by several fast fashion retailers is returning used garments to retailers for recycling or charity. However, because of the growth in consumption, the inability of most used clothing to be resold, and challenges with recycling, returning garments to retailers for recycling or charity does not solve the problem alone. Focusing on both pre-consumer textile waste and post-consumer textile waste is necessary.

The fashion industry in New York City accounts for 180,000 jobs, nearly \$11 billion in wages, and \$2 billion in tax revenue annually.[1] It also contributes to the city's overall vibrancy. Fashion is vitally important to New York City. In 2016, former New York City Department of Sanitation employee, Jessica Schreiber, established FABSCRAP as a 501C3 charitable nonprofit organization in the city of New York. The company contracts with fashion and interior textiles firms to collect pre-consumer textile waste. Volunteers separate paper and metal, and sort the scraps according to fiber content. Large scraps and fancy trims that can be upcycled go to FABSCRAP's store. Single-fiber (e.g., 100 percent cotton, 100 percent polyester, or 100 percent wool) scraps are consolidated for recycling; mixed-content scraps without elastane are sent for shredding to make shoddy or stuffing material; scraps containing elastane (including spandex and Lycra®) go to landfill.

To sustain its nonprofit business model, FABSCRAP must continually build awareness of pre-consumer textile waste among its stakeholders and must maintain a pipeline of volunteers to sort a growing inventory of scraps. FABSCRAP leadership conducts guest lectures at New York City's fashion universities and industry events to build awareness and stakeholder engagement across designers, brands, consumers, and the community at large. The firm maintains Twitter, Instagram, and Facebook feeds; it also enjoys word-of-mouth advertising. The firm employs a client engagement manager. In August 2017, the company also hired an individual to manage outreach.

Business Problem

FABSCRAP is a small, lean organization with diverse stakeholders across public and private sectors and the community at large. As a condition of its business status, FABSCRAP must undertake activities to grow stakeholder awareness of the textile waste problem. To sustain its current business model, the firm relies on a continuous flow of unpaid volunteers to sort the textile scraps it collects.

Company goals

New York City residents discard over 200,000 tons of post-consumer textile waste annually.[2] During her work at the New York City Department of Sanitation, FABSCRAP founder Jessica Schreiber identified a need to reduce pre-consumer textile waste being sent to landfill by the city's fashion producers. Schreiber identified three destinations for such waste: landfill, recycling, and upcycling. Passionate about upcycling, cognizant of the city's laws requiring businesses to recycle their pre-consumer textile waste, and knowledgeable about the technical limitations of textile recycling, Schreiber founded her company to address New York's pre-consumer textile waste problem. FABSCRAP seeks to reduce pre-consumer textile waste by increasing awareness of this waste problem, changing industry behavior, generating greater consumer awareness of sustainability, and maximizing upcycling and recycling of pre-consumer textile scraps.

Stakeholders

The group of individuals with an interest in FABSCRAP and/or reducing textile waste in New York City is varied. Businesses operating within the city are required to recycle their textile waste if it comprises more than 10 percent of their commercial waste. Socially concerned consumers want to reduce environmental harm from landfill sites. Commercial textile recyclers need a reliable source of usable scraps. Fashion and interior textile brands want to win favor with shareholders and consumers by demonstrating good sustainability practices. Eco-friendly designers, artists, and craft groups need affordable sources of interesting raw materials.

FIGURE 3.1 FABSCRAP collects fabric scraps from commercial businesses for recycling and reuse. © DON EMMERT/AFP via Getty Images

Process

Because of chemical differences between fiber types, and technical constraints of textile recycling equipment, many fabric scraps made from fiber blends cannot be recycled. Common examples include cotton/polyester, wool/nylon, and wool/polyester. Furthermore, due to its chemistry, popularly used fabrics containing elastane cannot be shredded for secondary use. However, design and product development teams working under tight deadlines with lean staff are generally unwilling or unable to sort their textile waste by fiber content.

FABSCRAP offers an important service. It contracts with clients to collect textile and apparel waste, removes labels and metal, sorts the textiles by fiber content, and directs the sorted scraps to the most appropriate end-of-life destination: upcycle, recycle, or landfill. FABSCRAP provides each client with data on its individual contributions. To comply with the feedback terms of its client contracts, demonstrate the importance of its service, and maintain its own company integrity, FABSCRAP must collect reliable data against key metrics. By September 2017, the company had collected more than 48,000 pounds of scraps. Appendix 1 shows data on the number of clients, and waste collected and sorted through September 2017.

The company uses school presentations, its website, and the social site Eventbrite to recruit and schedule volunteers to sort the scraps. Following a thirty-minute educational orientation, volunteers sort for two hours. Afterward, they may shop the take-home scraps for thirty minutes. Volunteers may select and take home five pounds of scraps, for free, for their own upcycling use; they may purchase additional scraps at a modest price. The firm uses factory workspace in the Queens borough of New York City, accessible by a combination of subway and a ten-minute walk. Appendix 2 shows volunteer data.

Outreach

FABSCRAP's client engagement manager attracts and involves community members through educational presentations and volunteer-based operations. In addition to its presentations at New York City's fashion universities, trade shows, and other industry events, FABSCRAP builds awareness through social media and word of mouth. Schreiber and FABSCRAP's client engagement manager conduct university presentations and industry events. The firm maintains an informative website (FABSCRAP.org) and social media feeds (Facebook, Instagram, Twitter); it sends periodic e-mail blasts to a subscriber list. FABSCRAP management has compiled limited data on the growth and effectiveness of its social outreach. The company's new outreach manager administers digital communications. Appendix 3 shows available outreach data.

Through August 2017, the company's website messaging has emphasized the textile waste problem; the simplicity and convenience of FABSCRAP's service; and the benefits to brands and volunteers of recycling/upcycling textile waste. E-mail blasts have emphasized volunteer opportunities and benefits.

Resources

FABSCRAP rents space within a factory. Utilities and security are provided by the building. In August 2017, FABSCRAP contracted an independent delivery service to collect waste from the clients and deliver it to the sorting site. Collections are made once a week.

Using the volunteer model, the collection and sorting process requires few resources other than people and time. With its current sorting stations, FABSCRAP can accommodate six volunteers per shift. The company can conduct ten shifts per week, excluding holidays. Restrictions on factory access preclude evening, weekend, or holiday shifts.

Twofold Business Problem

To remain relevant within its community and adhere to the terms of its 501C3 status, FABSCRAP must continually grow awareness of the problem of pre-consumer textile waste among its stakeholders. For financial viability, operational function, and growth, the company must also build and maintain ongoing stakeholder engagement to ensure a steady and growing clientele and a reliable pool of volunteer sorters. To remain viable and to grow, FABSCRAP must address these two problems without substantially increasing expenses.

Business Questions

Cost-effective outreach to build awareness and engagement is critical for FABSCRAP to achieve the success it desires. Several key questions must be answered in addressing FABSCRAP's challenges. They are as follows:

1   What are FABSCRAP's business goals?
2   Who are the company's different stakeholder groups? What does each group want from FABSCRAP? How does what they want differ across groups?
3   How do the different stakeholder groups rank in importance, in relation to FABSCRAP achieving its goals?
4   How should FABSCRAP measure its performance against what its key stakeholders want?
5   What challenges does FABSCRAP currently face in growing and maintaining (a) stakeholder awareness and (b) stakeholder engagement?
6   What vehicles and/or activities would be most effective for FABSCRAP to economically and efficiently build and maintain stakeholder awareness and stakeholder engagement?
7   What messaging would best help the company build awareness?
8   What messaging would best help FABSCRAP build and maintain stakeholder engagement?
9   What metrics would enable the company to best measure change in awareness and change in engagement?

Appendices

APPENDIX 1 *Clients and Waste*

Total Clients and Pre-Consumer Waste Collected (Pounds)

Year	2016								2017									TOTAL
Month	May	Jun	Jul	Aug	Sep	Oct	Nov	Dec	Jan	Feb	Mar	Apr	May	Jun	Jul	Aug	Sep	
New Clients	1	0		1	4	5	1	6	3	5	10	4	7	10	6	13	10	86
Total Clients	1	1	1	2	6	11	12	18	21	26	36	40	47	57	63	76	86	86
Total Waste Collected	386	136	193	778	603	507	260	1,068	4,166	3,919	3,508	1,877	5,425	4,914	6,716	7,582	6,101	48,139
Total Waste Sorted*	0	0	0	0	0	0	0	1,037	207	741	1,895	765	1,165	2,268	3,076	2,488	2,519	16,161
Metal Paper Plastic**	0	0	0	0	0	0	0	0	24	325	439	330	266	351	804	657	533	3,729
Total for Reuse	0	0	0	0	0	0	0	277	25	71	431	90	418	447	919	1,045	1,070	4,793
Total Mixed Fiber	0	0	0	0	0	0	0	594	140	213	545	160	232	715	672	512	665	4,448
Total Single Fiber	0	0	0	0	0	0	0	0	2	57	250	38	107	229	269	90	97	1,139
Total with Spandex	0	0	0	0	0	0	0	167	16	74	229	147	142	528	412	183	154	2,052

*   Waste sorted prior to December 2016 was rolled into the December figures.

** Includes paper labels, hangers, staples, tape, zippers, etc.

APPENDIX 2 *Volunteers*

	Volunteers													
Year	**2016**				**2017**									**TOTAL**
Month	**Sep**	**Oct**	**Nov**	**Dec**	**Jan**	**Feb**	**Mar**	**Apr**	**May**	**Jun**	**Jul**	**Aug**	**Sep**	
Total Number of Shifts	0	0	0	0	2	9	10	8	10	13	13	23	18	106
Total Volunteer Signups*	0	0	0	0	11	45	64	60	64	86	75	85	72	562
AM	0	0	0	0	6	25	34	30	29	39	55	55	36	309
PM	0	0	0	0	5	20	30	30	35	47	20	30	36	253
No-shows	0	0	0	0	1	4	16	20	27	23	27	17	10	145
Max Volunteers/ Shift	0	0	0	0	6	5	6	6	6	6	6	6	6	
AM	0	0	0	0	6	5	6	6	6	6	6	6	6	
PM	0	0	0	0	5	5	6	5	6	6	6	6	6	
Repeat Volunteers**	0	0	0	0	3	5	27	21	18	20	18	32	28	172

*   Includes individuals who signed up but did not attend.

** Volunteers who have worked one or more prior shifts within the 12-month period; only counted if volunteer worked the session (i.e., excludes no-shows).

APPENDIX 3 *Outreach*

Outreach: Presentations, Website, E-Mail Blasts, and Social Media Followers																
Year	**2016**						**2017**									**TOTAL**
Month	**Jul**	**Aug**	**Sep**	**Oct**	**Nov**	**Dec**	**Jan**	**Feb**	**Mar**	**Apr**	**May**	**Jun**	**Jul**	**Aug**	**Sep**	
Presentations																
Number	1	1	1	7	7	1	2	1	6	2	2	4	2	2	5	44
Hours	1	2	0.5	7	7	0.5	2.5	2	12	2	2	6.5	1.5	5	5.5	57
Facebook	N/A	N/A	N/A	N/A	N/A	N/A	N/A	N/A	N/A	N/A	N/A	N/A	N/A	N/A	N/A	N/A
Instagram	N/A	N/A	N/A	N/A	N/A	N/A	N/A	N/A	N/A	N/A	N/A	N/A	N/A	N/A	N/A	N/A
Twitter	N/A	N/A	N/A	N/A	N/A	N/A	N/A	N/A	N/A	N/A	N/A	N/A	N/A	N/A	N/A	N/A
Total SM Followers	N/A	N/A	N/A	N/A	N/A	N/A	N/A	N/A	N/A	N/A	N/A	N/A	N/A	N/A	N/A	N/A
Website	N/A	N/A	1,141	811	2,985	1,239	1,523	1,341	1,270	2,684	1,144	1,245	1,273	1,981	1,660	20,297
Initial Source of Leads																
Direct	N/A	N/A	N/A	N/A	N/A	N/A	N/A	N/A	N/A	N/A	N/A	N/A	N/A	N/A	N/A	8,262
Google	N/A	N/A	N/A	N/A	N/A	N/A	N/A	N/A	N/A	N/A	N/A	N/A	N/A	N/A	N/A	7,879
Huffington Post	N/A	N/A	N/A	N/A	N/A	N/A	N/A	N/A	N/A	N/A	N/A	N/A	N/A	N/A	N/A	527
Facebook	N/A	N/A	N/A	N/A	N/A	N/A	N/A	N/A	N/A	N/A	N/A	N/A	N/A	N/A	N/A	456
Other	N/A	N/A	N/A	N/A	N/A	N/A	N/A	N/A	N/A	N/A	N/A	N/A	N/A	N/A	N/A	1,511

Notes

1   City of New York, "Fact Sheet: Celebrating and Supporting New York City's Fashion Industry," September 3, 2014. http://www1.nyc.gov/office-of-the-mayor/news/858-14/fact-sheet-celebrating-supporting-new-york-city-s-fashion-industry

2   RefashionNYC. http://www.1.nyc/gov/assets/dsny/zerowaste/residents/re-fashionyc.shtml

References and Further Reading

Allwood, Julian M. Well Dressed? The Present and Future Sustainability of Clothing and Textiles in the United Kingdom." Accessed September 2017. https://www.ifm.eng.cam.ac.uk/uploads/Resources/Other_Reports/UK_textiles.pdf

Bishop, Margaret. "Is Fast Fashion Selling Under the Guise of Green?" Accessed August 2017. https://apparelmag.com/fast-fashion-selling-under-guise-green

Cline, Elizabeth L. 2013. *Overdressed. The Shockingly High Cost of Cheap Fashion*. New York: Portfolio/Penguin.

FABSCRAP. https://www.FABSCRAP.org

Waste Not, Want Not: FABSCRAP Founder Jessica Schreiber on Reusing and Recycling." Accessed August 2016. http://nyctextileweek.com/waste-not-want-not-fabscrap-founder-jessica-schreiber-on-reusing-and-recycling/

Wicker, Alden. "This Entrepreneur Has a Surprising Way to Make Fashion More Ethical." Accessed August 2017. https://www.mindbodygreen.com/0-26027/this-entrepreneur-has-a-surprising-way-to-make-fashion-more-ethical.html

Definitions

Cut-and-sew: The process of cutting fabric and sewing the components into finished products such as garments.

Interior textiles: Fabrics and other textile products designed for use in residential and/or commercial spaces; interior textiles include upholstery, carpeting, curtains, bed and bath linens, and kitchen linens.

Metric: A measurement useful for benchmarking progress against a target or goal.

Pre-consumer: Raw materials or product that has not reached the consumer.

Recycling: Processing pre- or post-consumer waste into raw materials for use in other products.

Stakeholder: Someone who has an interest in the activities and/or success of a business or organization; may have an ownership stake.

Sustainability: Meeting the needs of the present without compromising the ability of future generations to meet their own needs. (Definition from *1987 World Commission on Environment and Development*).

Upcycling: Creating a higher value opportunity for reusing a product or its components.

Chapter 4

Lenzing Group and Eileen Fisher

Leslie Davis Burns

Eileen Fisher Inc. launched an ambitious Vision 2020 with goals and commitments to expand their environmental and social sustainability practices. As part of fulfilling these commitments, they are exploring current practices and procedures. Currently, Eileen Fisher is using viscose rayon for several product categories and is exploring alternatives to this fiber such as TENCEL® produced by Lenzing Group. They are also exploring closed-loop textiles such as Lenzing's Refibra® fibers. Students are asked to take the role of a decision maker for the Eileen Fisher fashion brand to evaluate environmentally sustainable alternatives to viscose rayon and a possible partnership with Lenzing for a closed-loop fiber for an upcoming collection.

Learning Objectives

Upon completion of this case, students should be able to:

- Describe a company's target customer/market.
- Evaluate environmentally sustainable alternatives to rayon produced using the viscose method for specific product categories.
- Define closed-loop processes for textiles and evaluate textiles that incorporate closed-loop processes.
- Evaluate advantages and disadvantages of partnerships between fiber companies and fashion brands to achieve environmental sustainability goals.

Introduction

Lenzing Group

Headquartered in Austria, Lenzing Group is "the world's leading producer of wood-based cellulose fibers" producing brand names including TENCEL®, Lenzing Viscose®, Lenzing Modal®, Lenzing FR®, and Refibra® (Lenzing 2018a). Lenzing Group is also "committed to the principles of sustainability and sets the highest environmental standards in the industry" and has received the European Award for the Environment by the European Union for the TENCEL® manufacturing process and the Ökotex Sustainability Award for Product Innovation given by OEKO-TEX®.

With wood being the natural raw material for Lenzing fibers, Lenzing strives "to source wood and pulp exclusively from non-controversial sources, preferring suppliers participating in credible forest certification programs." Moving beyond wood pulp as its base material, Lenzing introduced Refibra™ fibers of the TENCEL® brand made from post-industrial/pre-consumer cotton textile waste. In this process Lenzing takes fabric scraps, removes dyes and resins, and produces a cotton cellulose pulp. This pulp is blended with wood pulp adding only solvent and water; the solvents are then recycled. According to Lenzing (2018b), "based on the technology of TENCEL® fibers, Refibra® fibers are an extraordinary innovation and most likely the most sustainable fibers from natural raw materials." In 2016 Lenzing announced that Patagonia, a US apparel brand well known for its sustainability standards and initiatives, would be their first apparel brand and retail partner for this new TENCEL® fiber.

Eileen Fisher

Headquartered in New York, USA, Eileen Fisher Inc. is a certified B Corporation in the fashion industry and is well known for its sustainability initiatives. Several years ago, Eileen Fisher Inc. outlined an ambitious strategic plan, Vision 2020 (Eileen Fisher 2018b) which served as a blueprint for their corporate social responsibility (CSR) standards. Vision 2020 includes corporate commitments around environmental and social sustainability "where human rights and sustainability are not the effect of a particular initiative, but the cause of a business well run. Where social and environmental injustices are not unfortunate outcomes, but reasons to do things differently" (Eileen Fisher 2018b). In addition, Eileen Fisher is committed to becoming a more "closed-loop company" through their sourcing and manufacturing processes.

Environmental sustainability is an important aspect of the company's commitments and the company's initiatives include several components including sustainable fibers such as organic cotton and linen and sustainable and responsible wool. However, Eileen Fisher knows that becoming a truly "closed-loop company" will require more than just adopting sustainable materials. The company's take-back and upcycling program, RENEW, is testament to their willingness to explore new strategies and opportunities to create closed-loop and upcycling processes (Eileen Fisher 2018a). "Here's how it [RENEW] works: you bring back your old EILEEN FISHER clothes we find them another home. When your clothes can no longer be worn, we remake them into one-of-a-kind designs—and we save the scraps, because they're tomorrow's raw materials."

Business Problem

As part of their Vision 2020 process, Eileen Fisher is examining current processes and exploring opportunities to meet their sustainability initiatives. This includes examining materials, processes, and partnerships. For example, Eileen Fisher currently uses rayon produced using the viscose method for several product categories. To further their commitment of using environmentally sustainable materials, the company realizes that an alternative to rayon is needed. As such, TENCEL® is one of the fibers they are exploring as a replacement for rayon.

In addition, a variety of closed-loop strategies are being evaluated. One possible strategy is partnering with Lenzing to use closed-loop processes for fibers/fabrics for their apparel merchandise. As part of the team of designers and merchandisers creating a plan of action for Eileen Fisher for sustainable fibers, you are to investigate sustainable alternatives to viscose rayon and a possible partnership with Lenzing for a closed-loop fiber for use in an upcoming collection for Eileen Fisher.

Business Questions

1   Give a description of Eileen Fisher and their target customer.
   a. Who is the target customer for Eileen Fisher?
   b. What are the primary merchandise offerings of this brand and where is the brand sold?
2   Describe Eileen Fisher's approach to sustainability.
   a. What are Eileen Fisher's values and initiatives around sustainability?
   b. What environmentally responsible fibers are currently being used by Eileen Fisher? Why are these fibers considered environmentally responsible?
   c. Why is rayon made using the viscose method not considered environmentally sustainable?
   d. List and evaluate three fibers that are suitable environmentally responsible alternatives to viscose rayon.
   e. In your opinion, what action should Eileen Fisher take to move forward with finding an alternative to viscose rayon?
3   Eileen Fisher is exploring a possible partnership with Lenzing around a closed-loop fiber for an upcoming collection.
   a. What are Lenzing's strengths and weaknesses as a corporate partner for Eileen Fisher?
   b. In your opinion, should Eileen Fisher become a fashion brand/retailer partner with Lenzing? Why or why not? Provide a justification for your recommendation and cite relevant references.

References and Further Reading

Braham, Emily. 2017, May 8. Closing the Loop on Sustainable Fashion. *Forbes*. Accessed January 10, 2018. https://www.forbes.com/sites/ashoka/2017/05/08/closing-the-loop-on-sustainable-fashion/#6410c5a12f3f

Eileen Fisher. 2018. Sustainable Fibers: Choosing TENCEL over Viscose. Accessed January 10, 2018. https://www.eileenfisher.com/sustainable-fibers/choosing-tencel-over-viscose/

Eileen Fisher. 2018a. Renew. Accessed January 10, 2018. http://www.eileenfisher.com/renew/

Eileen Fisher. 2018b. Vision 2020. Accessed January 10, 2018. http://www.eileenfisher.com/vision-2020/

Lenzing. 2016. October 6. Patagonia Picks Up TENCEL® Made from Cotton Fabric Waste. Accessed January 10, 2018. http://www.carvedinblue.lenzing-fibers.com/patagonia-picks-tencel-made-cotton-waste/

Lenzing Group. 2018a. Botanic Fibers. Accessed January 10, 2018. http://www.lenzing-fibers.com/tencel/refibra/

Lenzing Group. 2018b. Investor's Fact Sheet. Accessed January 10, 2018. http://www.lenzing.com/en/investors/factsheet.html

The background for this case study is based on publicly available information. The business problem of Eileen Fisher and Lenzing Group creating a partnership around closed-loop fiber is speculative only and not based on publicly available and/or documented information from Eileen Fisher Inc or Lenzing Group.

This case study was adapted by permission from Burns, Leslie Davis (2017) in: *Instructor's Guide for Fashion Fibers: Designing for Sustainability* by Annie Gullingsrud. New York: Fairchild Books.

Definitions

Closed-loop textiles: Textiles made from recycled, reused, or waste materials that have the potential of being used again and again.

Corporate social responsibility: A company's business approach and strategies around sustainable development including economic, environmental, social, and cultural sustainability. Strategies typically go beyond regulatory mandates.

Product development: "The creation of products with new or different characteristics that offer new or additional benefits to the customer. Product development may involve modification of an existing product or its presentation, or formulation of an entirely new product that satisfies a newly defined customer want or market niche." (http://www.businessdictionary.com/definition/product-development.html).

Rayon: A regenerated cellulosic fiber manufactured using a viscose or high wet modulus process. Lyocell is a sub-category of rayon in which the cellulose fiber is obtained by an organic solvent spinning process.

Target market: The specific group of consumers at which a product or service is aimed.

Upcycling: A process by which recycled, reused, or waste objects and/or materials are used to create a product of a higher quality or value than the original object and/or material.

Chapter 5

Natural or Synthetic Dyes?

The Preservation of Indigenous Textile Dyeing Techniques

Luis Quijano and Matalie Howard

As environmental regulations in developed countries become more strictly defined, there is an increasing need for sustainable measures for textile dyeing. In Teotitlan del Valle, Mexico, the textile dyeing techniques of indigenous cultures, using natural dyes, stretch back more than 1,000 years. However, due to a rise in urbanization prompting young adults to move from small rural towns to big cities, these techniques are facing extinction. Thus, the knowledge passed down from generation to generation of weavers and artisans is subsequently lost. To meet the needs of fast fashion, Teotitlan del Valle became increasingly receptive to using synthetic dyes. However, realizing the environmental hazards that emerge with synthetic dyes, some of its artisans have returned to the usage of natural dyes, to restore historical traditions and in response to concerns regarding the environmental and health risks of synthetic dyes. In this case study, students will distinguish the differences between natural and synthetic dyes, recognize the advantages and disadvantages of each method, and determine the best choices to meet the community's needs. Finally, this case study will promote dialogue and problem-solving methods that can encourage the preservation of the textile dyeing techniques of indigenous cultures.

Learning Objectives

Upon completion of this case, students should be able to:

- Compare and contrast the advantages and disadvantages of natural and synthetic dyes.
- Think critically from the perspective of a fashion designer whether natural or synthetic dyes would be best for their company and provide reasons to justify your decisions.

- Analyze the challenges associated with the preservation of textile dyeing techniques of indigenous cultures.
- Propose methods that could be implemented to preserve indigenous textile dyeing knowledge.
- Identify ways in which modern technology and online platforms can promote knowledge of indigenous textile dyeing techniques to a wider, digital audience.

Introduction

The textile and apparel industry has significantly contributed to the economies of various developing countries. *Textile dyeing*, the process of imparting color onto textiles and clothing, is an important stage in the fashion design and manufacturing process. The textile dyeing industry in Southeast Asia alone aimed to reach approximately $6 billion by the beginning of 2017 ("Booming textile dyeing industry in emerging countries" 2014). Most textile dyeing facilities are located in economically developing nations in the Asian Pacific region. Textile dying can create enormous amounts of textile *effluents* and textile waste that is discharged and dumped into the oceans, rivers, and lakes near manufacturing sites. Thus, the way a designer or company chooses to dye their apparel and textiles, whether using natural or synthetic dyes, has consequences and impacts on the local environment.

Natural dyes have been used since the origins of civilization and are derived from sources such as plants, food, animals, fruits, insects, and minerals. Because of their organic sources, natural dyes are perceived to be harmless. However, natural dyes can be as dangerous, if not more so, than synthetic dyes due to the fact that natural dyes require *mordants* (a compound used to hold down the molecules of the dye onto the fabric, preventing the dye from washing off the fabric). Synthetic dyes have been used in apparel since William Henry Perkin discovered *mauveine*, the first synthetic dye, in 1856. Since the creation of mauveine, the use of synthetic dyes has accelerated due to their lower cost and *colorfastness* (the ability of a textile to resist color loss or fading due to a variety of environmental conditions such as laundry, sunlight, perspiration, etc.). Furthermore, synthetic dyes on average can achieve a better color consistency.

When evaluating which dyes are preferable to use for a business, the following factors should be taken into consideration:

1 Cost: Depending on the garments being created, natural dyes may be increasingly more expensive. According to Live Science (Yoquinto 2012), up to 70,000 cochineal bugs are needed to produce a pound of a vibrant, red dye. Natural dyes are valued for their pure aesthetic; however, arable land is required to produce materials such as cotton, the easiest textile for natural dyes to adhere to. Synthetic dyes stick to fabrics easily, do not lose pigmentation, and are available in a wide array of colors. However, synthetic dye factories create an enormous amount of pollution in neighboring water sources.

2 Product specification and needs: To make sure the most appropriate type of dye is used on a fabric, one must know the fabric content and the desired color the fabric will be dyed. In today's industry, there are a variety of dyes with various specializations and functions. For instance, dyes that work best with cotton might not work with the same efficiency with polyester. Another important aspect to consider in the dyeing process is the quantity of textiles to be dyed.

FIGURE 5.1 Textile effluents in the water, 2014 © Pixabay C00 Creative Commons. Textile dyeing effluent that has washed into a body of water. Depending on the dyes used, environmental effects can be costly for the communities surrounding the production site.

3 Environmental impact: It is part of a company's social responsibility not to harm or, at the very least, to minimize the ecological effects of its dyes upon the environment. Thus, choosing the wrong type of dye on a fabric within a business can have adverse effects on the environment. The World Bank in 2011 (Scott 2015) estimated that textile dyeing processes accounted for more than 17–20 percent of all global industrial water pollution. With these considerations in mind, the decision between using natural and synthetic dyes and between specific types of dyes within these categories becomes important, and most fashion designers do not realize that this carries such an environmental impact. Figure 5.1 shows the potential impact of synthetic dyes on a body of water.

Business Problem

Introduction

Teotitlan Del Valle is a small, rural artisan village near Oaxaca, Mexico, known for their hand-stitched rugs. Containing a population of 5,600, around 75 percent of Teotitlan's population is involved in an aspect of weaving according to the *New York Times* (Goode 2017). One estimate states that there are 2,000 or more looms in the village, a ratio of 1:3 looms per person. In order to meet the needs of fast fashion, Teotitlan gradually shifted to using mainly synthetic dyes. However, recently there has been a shift in Teotitlan back to embracing natural dyes to revive indigenous textile dyeing techniques that stems from concerns about the environmental and health risks of synthetic dyes. In an era where knowledge of natural textile dyeing techniques is dangerously close to being lost, innovative methods of retaining the knowledge are being sought.

Historical overview of Teotitlan Del Valle

Teotitlan Del Valle is a weaving village in which the locals pride themselves on sustaining Zapotec culture through its weaving (called *laadi* in local Zapotec). Furthermore, most villagers still retain Zapotecan culture and customs; a majority still speak Zapotec. For most of the people, their livelihood relies on textiles in some aspect, and textile making is the major economic activity in the village. The craft of weaving can be traced back to 500 BC in Teotitlan Del Valle. Previously known as the Zapotecan capital in the eleventh and twelfth centuries, they are internationally known for their colorful weavings and tapestries. For instance, while under the subjugation of the Aztecs, their financial tribute was paid in the form of weavings.

Women were the first Teotitlan weavers, making cotton clothes and blankets, but men began to learn weaving as the Spaniards began to colonize. For centuries, the families of the Zapotec weavers of Teotitlan have handed their knowledge of weaving traditions down through their children with the art of weaving in many families going back six or seven generations. During the beginnings of the Spanish conquest, weavers shifted their focus to producing ponchos and blankets made from wool. The Spaniards introduced the Zapotec people to more advanced technology consisting of the spinning wheel, larger looms, steel needles, and other textile-production equipment that allowed the weavers to create products from heavier materials. As the centuries passed, the weaving of these items shifted from the needs of the local community to garnering revenue from the tourism and trade industries.

Rise of the wool rugs

As weaving became a method of survival and trade between indigenous cultural groups and Spanish conquistadores, the market for Teotitlan's distinct weaving techniques increased. Creating items for trade and tourism caused the functionality of their items to change and subsequently, their styles to change as well. During the second half of the twentieth century, when the development of air travel resulted in an increase in tourism, demand for their handwoven Zapotec weavings rose to an all-time high. US importers, seeing a potential and opportunity to market Teotitlan weavers' quality hand-made rugs, asked for the people of Teotitlan Del Valle to increase their production and brought them Navajo-inspired rug designs. These new rugs were sold at lower prices in comparison to the indigenous designs to people seeking to decorate their homes with Southwestern flair. To meet the high demand, some of the weavers from Teotitlan Del Valle went to neighboring regions with higher elevation so that they could herd more sheep and produce greater quantities of wool. It was a win-win situation for both sides. Businesses delivered cheaper items while at the same time the people of Teotitlan Del Valle rose in prosperity in the midst of an impoverished region.

Zapotec rugs, commonly known also as Oaxacan rugs, vary in shape and size and commonly range from $25 to $500. Naturally dyed pieces from the more prominent weavers in Teotitlan

Del Valle can range upward of several thousand dollars. According to the Smithsonian (Selcraig 2003), "What was a mom and pop cottage industry 30 years ago—based on a centuries-old, pre-Spanish weaving tradition—has turned into a multimillion-dollar phenomenon involving a couple of hundred families and multinational importers ... Farming families who once produced a few 5-by-7-foot rugs each month on the side now employ 10 to 15 weavers to meet the demands of American importers who order several thousand rugs each year."

Natural or synthetic dyes?

With the rise in production, the majority of Zapotecan weavers producing rugs use synthetic dyes. By the time American businesses discovered Zapotecan rugs, synthetic dyes had become widely used. As a result, accommodating the requests of these businesses was easy due to synthetic dyes simplifying the dyeing process. Synthetic dyes also reduced the costs and provided greater overall convenience in the design process, although there were several downsides associated with their use. In the midst of rising concerns about synthetic dyes perpetuating health and environmental hazards, a select few of Teotitlan Del Valle's weavers have shifted to using natural dyes.

In an interview for the *New York Times* regarding the use of natural dyes in Teotitlan Del Valle, Mexico, Schafer (Goode 2017) stated, "Every family has their own recipe, and every family does their dye process differently." For instance, one such family in Teotitlan Del Valle is able to combine seven or eight natural elements, creating more than forty vivid colors. Figure 5.2 showcases the beautiful hues achieved with the use of natural dyes. The majority of elements used to make the natural dyes are available within the community. The only element requiring importation is *cochineal*—a gorgeous, valued red dye—and indigo. These dyes give the rugs a more vivid, illustrious display in comparison to synthetic dyes. Furthermore, the

FIGURE 5.2 Himalayan weavers use native textile dyeing techniques and produce vibrant colors from their dyes. © Wikimedia Commons. Himalayan weavers use native textile dyeing techniques and the vibrant colors produced from their dyes. Although natural dyes typically cost more than their synthetic counterparts, the hues that can be achieved from natural dyes may attract the consumer.

natural dyes that are created for the use of the Zapotec rugs can be considered environmentally friendly because the mordants they use are hazardless and free of toxins.

Preserving indigenous textile dyeing techniques

With the average weaver in Teotitlan Del Valle earning more than the average white-collar worker, their town has taken huge steps, transformed from a village where a majority live in poverty to one where a majority are financially secure. Although the transformation of this weaving town is beneficial to the lives of the villagers, it also has its drawbacks. Children growing up in the current state of Teotitlan Del Valle now seek to move to bigger cities, breaking away from learning the native dyeing techniques that were passed down from generation to generation. As a result, the wealth of knowledge this town possesses has been placed on the brink of extinction. One of the families that decided only to use natural dyes is currently in the process of making a book with various recipes. Uncertain of how the artisans will pass their knowledge down to future generations, the community of Teotitlan Del Valle needs to develop methods that will promote the preservation of their indigenous textile dyeing techniques. The questions before them now are whether they should use natural or synthetic dyes, and how they should go about preserving their methods for natural textile dyeing and innovative weaving techniques.

Business Questions

Major question

After weighing up advantages and disadvantages of natural and synthetic dyes, in the role of a Teotitlan del Valle artisan, which stance would you advocate and why?

Study questions

1 List some differences between natural and synthetic dyes. What are the advantages and disadvantages of using natural and synthetic dyes for the community of Teotitlan del Valle?
2 What are the hardships Teotitlan del Valle faces in preserving their indigenous cultural weaving techniques, and what has brought about their current hardships?
3 What methods are used to preserve indigenous cultural sewing techniques?
4 In what ways can digital technology and online platforms sustain indigenous cultural weaving technique knowledge to a wider, digital audience?
5 Should the Teotitlan cater to large businesses, or limit their production to more high-end, but labor-intensive artisanal production methods?

YouTube links

Links to YouTube videos that further explain dyeing in intriguing ways:

1 The Chemistry of Natural Dyes—Bytesize Science. https://www.youtube.com/watch?v=Gwk1B66dvAM

2 How Does Fabric Get Its Color?—Buzzfeed Blue. https://www.youtube.com/watch?v=JIz4DZ84kko

3 Made in Peru | Natural Dyes—Alternative (Spoken in Spanish, but subtitles in English; beautiful graphics). https://www.youtube.com/watch?v=fuC6EofKmnI

4 How to Dye Fabric: Rit DyeMore Synthetic Dye—OnlineFabricStore.net. https://www.youtube.com/watch?v=hoR6w_j281I

References and Further Reading

Booming Textile Dyes Industry in Emerging Countries. 2014, September 8. Fibre2Fashion. Accessed December 20, 2017. http://www.fibre2fashion.com/industry-article/7422/booming-textile-dyes-industry-in-emerging-economies

Cohen, A. C. and I. Johnson. 2012. *J. J. Pizzuto's Fabric Science*. New York: Fairchild Books, 163–180.

Goode, E. 2017, September 17. In Mexico, weavers embrace natural alternatives to toxic dyes. *New York Times*, p. D1. Accessed November 14, 2017. https://www.nytimes.com/2017/09/18/science/mexico-textiles-natural-dyes.html

Schafer, N. n.d. Weaving & Dyeing in Teotitlan del Valle. Accessed December 20, 2017. http://oaxacaculture.com/textilesweavingdyeing/weaving-dyeing-in-teotitlan-del-valle

Scott, A. 2015, October 19. Cutting out Textile Pollution. *Chemical & Engineering News*. http://cen.acs.org/articles/93/i41/Cutting-TextilePollution.html

Selcraig, B. 2003, November 1. Dream Weavers. Accessed December 19, 2017. https://www.smithsonianmag.com/arts-culture/dream-weavers-92832342/

Yoquinto, L. 2012, April 27. The Truth about Red Food Dyes Made from Bugs. Live Science. Accessed December 20, 2017. https://www.livescience.com/36292-red-food-dye-bugs-cochineal-carmine.html

Chapter 6

Sewing for the Soil

A Social Enterprise

Yoon-Jung Lee and Yoori Chae

Sewing for the Soil is a social enterprise in Korea, established in 2008. The company initially focused on the production of wedding gowns with eco-friendly corn fibers but has since expanded its business to include eco-friendly wedding services. In 2014, Sewing for the Soil gained widespread attention in Korea when it planned and directed the eco-friendly wedding of the iconic celebrity couple, Hyori and Sangsoon Lee. This event kindled an interest in small and eco-friendly weddings among many young Koreans. The main strands of the company's business now include an eco-friendly wedding service (consulting, execution, and rentals) and eco-friendly uniform production. This case study provides an introduction to the concept of social enterprise, and then presents the business activities of Sewing for the Soil. It allows students to examine how the purpose and operation of the business of social enterprises differ from those of regular companies. The case also offers students an opportunity to reassess the social and environmental issues that the fashion industry may need to address in order to grow toward sustainable development. Students will suggest strategies for social enterprises in the fashion business to be profitable while pursuing social values.

Learning Objectives

Upon completion of this case, students should be able to:

- Define the concept of social enterprise.
- Explain differences in the purpose and operation of social enterprises and regular companies.
- Explain challenges social enterprises face in meeting both social and business objectives.

- Assess social and environmental issues that the fashion industry may need to address in order to grow toward sustainable development.
- Recommend strategies for social enterprises in the fashion industry to be profitable while pursuing social values.

Introduction

Environmental and social issues in the fashion industry

The fashion industry has been often criticized for its lack of attention to environmental problems associated with the supply chain, from the production of raw materials to final products for consumers. For example, pesticides and fertilizers used at cotton plantations are known to be a major factor causing soil deterioration. Chemicals used in the dying process need to be strictly controlled to avoid water pollution. Moreover, the fashion industry deliberately shortens product life cycles in order to generate demands for new products. In other words, by generating new fashion trends and accelerating the disposal of existing styles, the fashion industry pushes consumers to buy new apparel products, resulting in a tremendous amount of waste.

In addition to the environmental issues, critics have pointed to the fashion industry's humanitarian problems. The chemicals used in the production of apparel products not only harm the environment, but also the human body. Serious social problems include wages that are too low for workers to lead decent lives, poor working conditions, overtime labor, and child labor.

In addition to the issues listed above, many other problems in the fashion industry have been publicized, and the level of criticism has intensified. As more practitioners in the fashion industry realize the seriousness of the problems, companies have started engaging in corporate social responsibility (CSR) practices by inspecting their companies themselves and contributing to the public welfare through donations, the promotion of environmentally friendly production and marketing practices, the sponsorship of diverse events, and partnerships with academic institutions to solve problems being faced by fashion brand companies.

Social enterprises

In general, companies aim to create and maximize financial profits. Therefore, the resources that companies own are centered on activities that generate financial value. Social enterprises also seek to generate profits and financial value, however, they are distinguished from regular companies in that they prioritize creating social value over financial value. They should also be distinguished from nonprofit organizations, which do not aim to generate financial profits. In the case of social enterprises, a portion of the profits they generate are reinvested for social purposes.

Green designer Kyoung-jae Lee and Sewing for the Soil

After majoring in fashion design at college, Kyoung-jae Lee worked as a costume designer for a Korean broadcasting station. Her job was to create costumes for TV actors. She was satisfied with her salary and the job was quite stable. However, she found little meaning in the job.

Within a year, she decided to quit and live in the countryside of Gangwon province to help a local community run a guesthouse business. While living in the countryside following the cycle of nature, she became deeply appreciative of nature and aware of many environmental issues. The combination of her talent as a designer and interest in environmental issues led her to hold a solo fashion exhibition with the theme of environmentally friendly design. The title of the exhibition was *Sewing for the Soil*. After the exhibition, some brides-to-be contacted Kyoung-jae asking if they could wear the eco-friendly wedding gowns that had been exhibited. As the number of customers increased, Kyoung-jae officially started the eco-friendly wedding dress business in 2008 under the same name, Sewing for the Soil. Her business further expanded to provide wedding planning services. In addition to making wedding gowns and directing weddings, Sewing for the Soil currently produces eco-friendly uniforms and lifestyle products. It has been registered as a social enterprise in Korea since 2010. It is a small-sized enterprise with only three employees but it has grown rapidly. The sales volume had doubled five years after Kyoung-jae started the business and reached 1 billion won in 2014.

Products and service

Sewing for the Soil's business activities are largely divided into two strands—wedding and uniform—with the wedding strand representing the bigger portion. Their wedding business not only includes wedding gown production, but also the planning of wedding ceremonies. In addition to uniform manufacturing, the company also produces household products such bags and towels made of eco-friendly materials. These are frequently used as promotional items. The uniform and lifestyle products are sold through business-to-business (B2B) or business-to-government (B2G) commerce.

Eco-friendly wedding gowns. Most brides in Korea rent wedding gowns from wedding rental shops, as the wedding gown is considered a ceremonial garment only. With the exception of high-end wedding gowns made of silk, gowns are normally made of synthetic fibers, which are not biodegradable in a landfill. A problem with these gowns is that they are abandoned after several rentals when are no longer wearable due to frequent modification for brides with different body sizes. As a result, rental gowns made of synthetic fibers generate a great deal of landfill waste, resulting in an environmental problem.

Sewing for the Soil makes eco-friendly wedding gowns using natural and renewable fibers such as corn fiber, pulp fiber made from traditional Korean paper, and nettle, all of which are biodegradable. Moreover, unlike most wedding gowns, Sewing for the Soil's dresses are not made from fabrics that have undergone optical whitening processes. Accordingly, the wedding gowns made by the Sewing for the Soil have a slight ivory tone instead of bluish white.

The use of eco-friendly materials is not the only means by which the company pursues its motto to help conserve the environments. The firm has developed designs that extend products' lifespans. Their wedding gowns, for example, can be worn in different situations after simple modifications and alterations. Their basic bridal dress is a simple knee-length dress, suitable for a reception party. To give the bride an elegant look for the wedding ceremony, the company lends the brides a maxi-length bell-shaped skirt to wear over the basic dress. The brides return the bell-shaped skirt after the wedding, and the company provides alterations so that the dress may be worn in daily life, resulting in a longer product lifespan.

Eco-friendly weddings. The environmentally friendly ethos of Sewing for the Soil is reflected not only in its wedding gowns, but also in the overall wedding services it provides. An example is the firm's wedding invitations. The main purpose of a wedding invitation

FIGURE 6.1 A bridal dress (with and without the maxi over-skirt). (Source: picture taken by Kyoung-jae Lee).

FIGURE 6.2 Invitation cards and the bridal bouquet. (Source: picture taken by Kyoung-jae Lee).

is to convey information. The card is therefore usually thrown away when its purpose of information delivery is over. In addition to using soybean oil ink on recycled or non-wood pulp paper instead of a less eco-friendly solvent ink on ordinary paper, Sewing for the Soil's invitations are designed to have a second life as a desktop picture frame. For bouquets and boutonnières, flower roots are left uncut so that the flowers may be re-potted after the wedding event. Also, flowerpots, rather than cut flowers, are used for the flower decorations in the wedding hall. When the wedding ceremony is over, the groom and the bride give the flowerpots to their guests as a thank-you gift.

Small weddings. In Korea, marriage is not just about the relationship between a couple, but about the whole family. Many people are invited to the wedding ceremony to congratulate the wider family as well as the bride and groom. The number of people at a wedding signifies the social power of the family. Sometimes an extravagant wedding ceremony and reception party are held for the sole purpose of showing off the family's wealth and power. Bucking the trend of extravagant, conspicuous wedding expenditure, Sewing for the Soil promotes small weddings that focus more on the couples and the meaning of the wedding itself. The main office building of Sewing for the Soil is a house with a small garden, and the garden is used as a venue for couples who want a small wedding of fewer than 100 guests. The company has also worked with public agencies such as the Ministry of Gender Equity and Family and the City of Seoul to use the City Hall and other public buildings as venues for small weddings.

Ma-eul weddings. In Korea, a handful of luxurious wedding gown rental shops and bridal hair/makeup salons dominate the wedding industry. Wedding planners connect gown rental shops and bridal hair/makeup salons in neighborhoods known as "wedding towns." Moreover, most popular wedding venues have established links with food caterers. In this system, couples have limited choices and only a small number of business owners benefit.

Sewing for the Soil strives to boost the local economy. The company is located in Seongbuk District, which is an old region of Seoul with a rundown neighborhood. The industries of the region are predominantly small businesses. Instead of contracting hair/makeup salons in a wedding town, the company looks for talented hair/make-up artists employed in small local salons based in the neighborhood of the wedding venue. Sewing for Soil actively seeks potential partner salons through diverse channels, including articles in magazines. One important criterion for selection is the opinion of the potential partners' employees. This reflects Kyoung-jae's philosophy of respect for human welfare. She believes employees' opinion of a salon mirrors the salon owners' respect for people, and that only people with respect for human welfare would take seriously the environmental and social impacts of their businesses.

In terms of the wedding meal, rather than contracting catering companies, Sewing for the Soil buys food from local small restaurants and brings it to the wedding site. The company also hires underprivileged people such as women whose careers have been interrupted or elderly people for the jobs of preparing additional foods or decorations for the wedding ceremony.

Eco-friendly uniforms. Most work uniforms are made of synthetic fibers. However, Sewing for the Soil makes uniforms (e.g., company uniforms, doctors' coats, and patient gowns) with eco-friendly materials such as organic cotton, nettles, recycled PET fibers, and corn fibers, which are less harmful to the environment. The fabric is also colored using natural dyes rather than chemical dyestuffs. In addition, as with the wedding gowns, Sewing for the Soil designs products with a longer lifespan. One example of this was the campaign uniforms made for the election camp of a mayoral candidate. The company found that the uniforms

FIGURE 6.3　Ma-eul wedding. (Source: picture taken by Kyoung-jae Lee).

FIGURE 6.4　Neighborhood ladies preparing the feast. (Source: picture taken by Kyoung-jae Lee)

used during an election campaign are usually discarded after the election—especially if the candidate loses. Therefore, Sewing for the Soil made uniforms that could be used as an apron, with easily removable slogans.

Wedding gowns and uniforms are mostly manufactured in-house, except for large orders which are outsourced to regional manufacturing facilities. Sometimes, packaging jobs are outsourced to the Seongbuk Center for Independent Living People with Disabilities.

Promotion

Kyoung-jae interacts with potential customers through her blog. Although Sewing for the Soil have not put time or money into promoting the business, Kyoung-jae and her designs have received a great deal of publicity from the start and have been covered in many news articles and magazines. Sewing for the Soil became widely known to the South Korean public in 2014 after they organized an eco-friendly wedding for an iconic Korean celebrity couple, Hyori and Sangsoon Lee. Since then, Kyoung-jae has been a guest speaker at eco-friendly events, and she has received numerous awards concerning environmental issues. These activities have provided wide exposure in the press. Kyoung-jae and her company are covered by the press about twenty times a year.

Business Problem

Limited variety and supply of eco-friendly materials

After having decided to make eco-friendly wedding gowns, Kyoung-jae worked on obtaining different kinds of eco-friendly materials that could be used for clothes at home and abroad. She acquired corn fibers (PLA) by contacting a Japanese company that she saw at an exposition in Japan. However, other than corn fiber, Kyoung-jae discovered a very limited number of materials she could use. In the past, the Korean government has supported research and development of eco-friendly materials, thereby increasing the possible options available. Due to low demand many of these materials were not distributed for long and currently the materials available for eco-friendly wedding gowns lack diversity and are even decreasing in quantity.

Performance standard of eco-friendly materials

In the early days of her business, Kyoung-jae made eco-friendly patient gowns for a hospital. After delivering the products, she received a phone call from the hospital saying that all the patient gowns had shrunk. It turned out that the temperature at which the clothes were sterilized was higher than she had imagined. Hospitals usually sterilize patient gowns at 130 degrees Celsius, but the fabric Kyoung-jae had used could only withstand 110 degrees Celsius. Therefore, Kyoung-jae had to remake the products with a fabric that could be boiled at 130 degrees Celsius. This resulted in a major financial loss.

Unlike fabrics that are widely used for clothes, the detailed specifications of many eco-friendly fabrics are generally not known well. One reason for this is that eco-friendly fibers and fabrics were developed for purposes other than for clothing. On one occasion, Kyoung-jae was asked to make a dress with eco-friendly materials for the host of an environmental film festival. She made the dress with a fabric made of corn fiber. However, on the night before the festival, she burned the dress while ironing it, not realizing that fabrics made of corn fiber are not resistant to heat and can melt easily. Kyoung-jae had to stay up all night remaking the dress in order to deliver it before the festival.

Communicating the value of an eco-friendly business to the clients and customers

As a social enterprise, the major goal of Sewing for the Soil is promoting the value of eco-friendly business. Communicating with the clients and end consumers and to the wider society is a major challenge for the company. It is also related to the demand for their products.

Uniforms produced in an eco-friendly way with wider eco-friendly materials typically carry a higher unit price than other products. Most companies prefer vendors with the lowest price, above all other factors. It is therefore difficult to persuade customers to spend additional money on eco-friendly products, even when the designs are better. Unless the company shares the same values as Sewing for the Soil and is willing to spend additional money on eco-friendly uniforms, a lot more effort is required to persuade potential customers than would be required for ordinary uniforms.

Cannibalization and stagnant market growth

Kyoung-jae tries to share her values with her employees and teach her business know-how to them through rigorous training. On one occasion, however, an employee informed her with no advanced notice that she was quitting. Unable to find an immediate replacement, Kyoung-jae suffered a great deal. When she later received the news that the ex-employee had started a similar business, she felt betrayed. This was not the first time it had happened; several other previous employees of Kyung-jae have also started similar businesses. In addition to these problems, the market growth for eco-friendly weddings and uniforms is stagnant, due to the generally sluggish economy.

Business Questions

Major questions

1 One of the challenges Kyoung-jae faces is the supply and performance of materials that fit with her environmentally responsible philosophy. What materials would you recommend to Kyoung-jae to meet this challenge? Why?

2 Another challenge that Kyoung-jae faces is communicating the social values of her company to potential consumers. Describe three strategies that Kyoung-jae may use to more effectively communicate the values and benefits of Sewing for the Soil? What metrics should she use to assess the effectiveness of these communication strategies?

3 At first, Kyoung-jae was upset by her former employee starting the same business after quitting her company. However, she decided to look at the situation from a different perspective and has now begun to work with those previous employees on a project of promoting the values of eco-fashion.

   a. How would you perceive this situation? Is this increased competition a threat or an opportunity to Kyoung-jae's business?

b. Why do you think the market for eco-friendly fashion products is slow to grow?

c. The prices of eco-friendly products—including wedding gowns, uniforms, and even small weddings—are usually higher than that for ordinary products. What would be the best strategy for Sewing for the Soil to compete in the market when it is hard for them to compete in terms of price?

Study questions

1 What are the differences between social enterprises and regular companies?

2 What social and environmental issues do you think the fashion industry may need to address, in addition to the ones Kyoung-jae focused on?

3 What kind of efforts should be made, and by whom, in order to expand the market for eco-friendly materials and fashion products?

4 Do you think Sewing for the Soil is a sustainable business? Why or why not?

Chapter 7

Re;Code

Upcycling Deadstock Fabrics into a Fashion Brand

Ae-Ran Koh and Su Yeon Kim

Creating upcycling fashions from post-consumer waste is an important and timely topic for today's global fashion industry. This study discusses challenges addressed by fashion brands creating upcycled fashion products using the case of Re;Code.

Re;Code was launched in 2012 as a subsidiary label of Kolon Industries, a US$9.7 billion textile company founded in South Korea during the 1950s. The driving force behind Re;Code is a consideration for the environment; by adapting traditional methods of apparel design and creation in projects such as "Re;Nano" and "Re;Table," Re;Code aims to reuse leftover materials and ex-stock clothing that would otherwise have been disposed of by Kolon Industries. Re;Code thus acknowledges the problem of textile waste and concurrently reduces the environmental damage caused by its parent company, Kolon Industries. Evidence of the company's impact on the wider social landscape will be demonstrated via interviews with individuals directly impacted by the work of Re;Code, such as those involved in the "Sharing Space" "Re;Table" initiative. The upcycling fashion ideas of "Re;Code," such as the zero-waste design project of "Re;Nano," global projects, exhibitions, and campaigns, are also introduced. Students will analyze the challenges of launching a new upcycling fashion line for this giant textiles firm and will offer brand reinvention ideas that promote a sustainable fashion-consumption culture.

Learning Objectives

Upon completion of this case, students should be able to:

- Understand the business structure of a textiles company in South Korea.

- Discuss the opportunities and threats of launching a new brand which is focused on sustainability and innovation.

- Understand upcycling as a method not only of redesigning old products but also as a sustainable method of creating a new item of clothing which has a longer shelf-life.

- Illustrate the necessity of the adoption of an upcycled manufacturing system for sustainable fashion brands.

- Describe Asian fashion brands' approaches to globalization by explaining how fashion brands in developing countries strategically stress or disguise their ethnic background for global brand expansion.

- Explore the varied creative ideas which can be utilized by sustainable fashion brands, by expanding the scope of everyday living items including industrial materials, such as tents, military supplies, car interior supplies, etc., which have functional, symbolic as well as environmental values.

Introduction

Re;Code is an upcycling fashion brand known for creatively reusing left-over materials and old-stock clothing. Launched in 2012, as a label of a leading textile giant of South Korea, the Kolon Group, Re;Code has transformed series of clothing using better designs and with added environmental value. Kolon Group, founded in 1957, is the largest Korean textiles manufacturing company; the company is well known for being the thirtieth largest Korean Chaebol (a large industrial conglomerate run by an owner). As an early manufacturer in the Korean nylon industry, Kolon Group has made a significant contribution to national economic growth over the last sixty years. The company first adopted a mass-production manufacturing system in 1960s and has become an iconic corporation in Korea's fashion market. Kolon Group has since expanded to produce chemicals, other industrial materials, and fashion materials as well as fashion products under Kolon Industries.

The Kolon Group was originally founded in 1957 as Korea Nylon Inc. In 1969 Korea Polyester Inc. was established, and from 1981, Korea Nylon Inc. and Korea Polyester Inc. merged to create a single materials company, the Kolon Corporation. Following the business adopting a holding company structure, Kolon Industries was established in 2010 as an independent subsidiary company of the Kolon Corporation. Kolon Industries focuses solely on the production of chemicals, materials, and fashion. As of the end of 2017, Kolon Industries hold around 40 percent of the total sales volume of the Kolon Corporation.

TABLE 7.1 *Company Profiles of Kolon Group, Corp.*

Type of Industry	Textiles Manufacturing
Founded	1957
President	Lee, Won Man
Number of Employees	11,289
Sales Volume of 2016	US$9.767 billion
Operating Profit	US$136 million
Subsidiary Companies	Kolon Industries, Inc., Kolon Global, Inc., etc.

Source: Financial Statement of Kolon Group, Corp. (2017).

TABLE 7.2 *Sales Volume of Five Divisions of Kolon Industries, Inc.*

	Specialty Product Category	**Sales in 2016 (US$)**
Industrial Material	Functional fibers, high-performance fibers	1.74 billion
Chemical	Hydrocarbon resin, phenolic resin	817 million
Film/Electronic Material	Polyester film, electronic materials	474 million
Fashion	Outdoor, sport, golf, men's and women's wear	1.137 million
Fashion Material	Polyester chip, yarn, and fabric	395 million
Total		4.56 billion

Source: Financial Statement of Kolon Industires, Inc. (2017)

Kolon Industries, Inc. currently has five major business divisions, namely, industrial materials, chemical, films/electronic materials, fashion, and fashion materials. The company is planning to globalize its automotive materials, advanced materials, optical films, chemical, and fashion businesses.

The fashion division of Kolon Industries, Inc. recorded sales figures amounting to US$1.137 million in 2016. The division currently manufactures diverse categories of fashion products including outdoor, sports, and golf wear under the brand names of Kolon Sport, Head, Jack Nicklaus, Elord, WAAC, Elord Club, and Honma; and silhouettes, suits, and casuals under the brand names of Customellow, Cambridge Members, Club Cambridge, GGIO II, Brentwood, and Spasso for men. Additionally, it offers casualwear under the Lucky Chouette brand, as well as pant suits, long dresses, pants, rider jackets, and marine looks under the Jardin de Chouette for women label; casualwear under the Henry Cottons, Series, Epigram, Shirtsxseries, and Re;Code brands; leather goods under the Couronne name; shoes under the Suecomma Bonnie label; sneakers under the Supercomma B brand; and premium fashion wear under the Marc Jacobs, Berluti, Neil Barrett, Loewe, etc. names.

Over its sixty years of manufacturing history, Kolon Industries has continuously been concerned about sustainability issues in the fashion industry. Kolon Industries recognized that all left-over materials and unsold products from their company were being burnt—this was not only an enormous waste of resources but also incredibly damaging to the environment. The company decided that a solution would be to create a new fashion brand within its corporation which was responsible for sustainable zero-waste fashion production. Re;Code was thus launched in 2012 to help tackle the problem of material waste created by their parent company. This has been achieved through modifying traditional methods of garment design to create zero-waste products, investing in alternative handcrafting methods of production over mass-based machine creation, and beginning initiatives which aim to educate end-users on a more sustainable way of consuming fashion, such as "Re;Table."

Re;Code has been clever in securing powerful PR support from its mother company, Kolon Industries, Inc. They stage museum exhibitions, eco forums, produce high-fashion collections, and collaborate with famous foreign designers, traditional costume designers, as well as independent young designers, such as Sung-Do Kang and Jae-Woong Jung who were both winners of the international televised fashion design competition "Project Runway Korea." Re;Code has a series of collections which are creatively designed and crafted, and achieves favor with many sustainability-conscious customers. Re;Code delivers the brand values of being sustainable, ethical, and green, as they recreate with the disposed materials generated from Kolon Industries, Inc's diverse business sectors.

This case study aims to introduce Re;Code's unique approach to reducing textile waste, not just in upcycling new clothes but also in creating innovative projects which encourage an awareness of the environmental harm of material waste and ways to reduce this going forward. The brand's zero-waste initiative "Re;Nano," which involves clothing being made into detachable parts so as to allow individuals to restyle their own items, and "Re;Table," which educates individuals about upcycling and provides them with the sewing skills to do so, are two such projects which are examined in closer detail here. As well as pioneering the world of upcycling education and projects, Re;Code also makes contributions to the wider community in helping vulnerable individuals get back into work via their disassembling schemes.

Re;Code's ethical approach to production is drawing extensive attention from fashion brands who consider sustainability an important brand identity.

Business Problem

Brand stories of Re;Code

Code is defined as "a concept used to represent something" or "a series of letters, numbers, or symbols assigned to something for the purpose of identification." Phrases such as "culture code" are used to describe unique features that are encoded in some form of information which help to identify a specific culture. The brand name "Re;Code" came from the company's idea to give a new code to the old stock fabrics and clothing. This "Re-Code" is not a complete reset of the existing code in that the brand does not attempt to conceal the previous identities of garments in their upcycling. Instead, Re;Code figuratively melts and merges the code associated with multiple old garments to create one which is newly amalgamated. Therefore, Re;Code could be defined as a brand which creates new life from old clothing through its combining of multiple old codes—the new code of every garment is made up entirely and singularly of only those codes which could be found in the individual garments prior to their upcycling.

Some of the materials that Re;Code give a new life to come from third-hand old stock clothing which were unsold in the brand shop, unsold in the brand's private discount stores, and consequently were due to be incinerated. Re;Code also uses pre-consumer stocks, as well as other unreleased military materials and industrial materials created by Kolon Industries, that have small scratches or flaws but that are too good to be burned away. Kolon Industries, which manufactures and sells US$4.56 billion worth of fashion materials and clothing, spend more than US$3 million annually to burn their own old stock. The incineration system requires a substantial amount of budget, but a more important issue is that it also pollutes the surrounding environment.

Re;Code has three main collections: the military collection, the industrial collection, and the inventory collection. The collections are each defined by the materials from which the garments within the collection have been made: the military collection utilizes military equipment which suffers defects or has passed its expiration date; the industrial collection utilizes industrial materials, such as car airbags or seats, which suffer defects; and the inventory collection utilizes clothing and other materials (such as tents) created by Kolon Industries which have remained unsold for three years or more. Re;Code sources its raw-fabric from tents, military supplies, car interior supplies, mass-produced and unsold inventory garments, and the materials used in upcycled fashion have unique brand stories. Kyung-Ae Han, a creative director and vice president of Kolon's Fashion Division II, has stated that the ability of upcycled fashion to have this unique brand story is highly desirable. Re;Code features women's jackets made from sports jackets and car seat fabric, and curtains made from air bags and dog wear. Every material used by Re;Code in upcycling shows the history of the material.

In the military collection, military equipment became the materials, such as military supplies passed the expiration date, and some defective products or goods which would be incinerated without even being used on the ground. Because the quality of the fabric used in military clothes, tents, and parachutes is verified, these not only have the best durability but also their own unique color, graphic, and vintage mood, as shown in Figure 7.1.

Industrial materials discarded from defective products are also important materials. Re;Code use fabrics that once functioned as the material for an air bag or car seat. Since parts like a car seat's head lining directly come in contact with the human body and are made with soft high-quality materials, these materials can be used directly as clothes, accessories, and other goods (Figure 7.2).

In the inventory collection (manufactured from products which have remained unsold for three years or more), garments interestingly show the background of each material piece by retaining the former fashion brand's logo uncut and even emphasized. Old fashioned clothing which was no longer attractive to consumers, was redesigned and reborn with trendy designs. Since upcycling fashion and sustainable production has become one of the most recent and important fashion trends, Re;Code emphasizes the necessity of recycling and upcycling of

FIGURE 7.1 Military collection of Re;Code upcycling Kolon Industries' military supplies. © Kolon Industries. Used with permission.

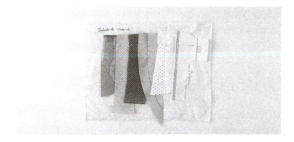

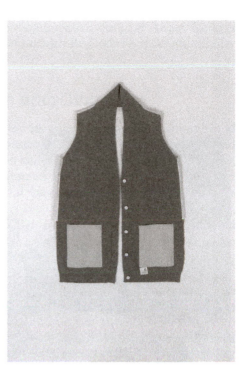

FIGURE 7.2 Industrial collection of Re;Code upcycling Kolon Industries' automobile interior supplies. © Kolon Industries. Used with permission.

their own inventory products. For example, Figure 7.3 demonstrates how Kolon Industries' other fashion brands' inventories are made clear in Re;Code's garments. The tree shape logo of Kolon Industry F&C's sportswear brand, and the logo of Brentwood, Kolon Sports, and the menswear brand, have been kept and emphasized on the items' cuffs and hems.

Working with independent designers hoping to enter the market, the collection gives them a platform for exposure to gain a foothold in the market place through collaborative design and inclusion in Re;Code's collection. Designer collaborations have included renowned UK upcycling brand Junky Styling, and famous Korean fashion designers Andee Kang, Jaewoong Jeong, and Byung Mun Seo. Working together with independent designers, Re;Code recycles and redesigns clothing that has been left in the inventory for a long time. By decreasing waste it is eco-friendly, giving added value to the products for its customers. Working with a broad range of materials, Re;Code creates jackets, bags, and tops for men and women from military fabrics, tents, uniforms, and parachutes, as well as fashioning used car air bags into purses, totes, and shirts. Each item in the collection has a story and creates a new culture of value in place of waste.

Re;Code also work with individuals who are intellectually disabled at the "Goodwill Store"; they are trained to deconstruct the salvaged materials collected from Kolon Industries in order to prepare them for reinterpretation and redesign. This helps these individuals get into work and thus give back to the community. Designs are produced in highly limited numbers with six being the maximum in any style, and each one labelled with the total number of designs produced. Each piece is then created by a master craftsman in their atelier store, where Re;Code invite independent fashion designers, so the craftsman can be deeply involved in the design process and share their ideas of upcycled fashion. Re;Code believes that worth grows through collaboration and creates new value through sharing. The brand also supports hearing impaired youth through the purchasing of hearing aids and

since 2015, and has received "Good Business Model Awards" for generating a responsible economy and helping others benefit from economic growth. Re;Code has demonstrated a business model where value is created for everyone involved in the process. Ms. Kyung-Ae Han, creative director and vice president of Kolon's Fashion Division II, found three sewing artisans in Anyang, versed in every part of making clothes, to work with designers to create new designs from the inventory clothing (Figure 7.4). She also sought out independent designers for collaborations, and worked with inventories from companies such as Bluefit and the company who manufacture Korean Air Force cargo parachutes. The brand run a communal art shop in Myeong-dong Cathedral, where a library, audiovisual room, and open workshops deliver Re;Code's messages about sustainable fashion.

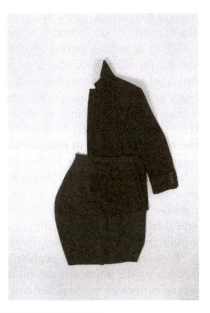

FIGURE 7.4 Examples of the creative and versatile designs of Re;Code. © Kolon Industries. Used with permission.

"Sharing Space" and "Re;Table" to involve consumers in upcycling

Re;Code invests much on their brand marketing to better deliver their brand identity toward their potential customers. "Sharing Space" (Figure 7.5) is an initiative ran by Re;Code in Myeongdong Catholic Cathedral Archdiocese of Seoul, Korea. The church has collections of more than 1,500 books regarding environmental issues and sustainability issues as well as more than 200 videos related to the environment for users to pick and view for free. Upcycled clothing, accessories, and lifestyle items are also exhibited. On weekends, Re;Code open upcycling handicraft workshop classes within the church and all the proceeds from the event are donated to charity.

On December 17, 2017, fifty people who had loved to participate in the project of "Sharing Space" that year, were invited to the church, and they enjoyed the Christmas atmosphere through listening to Christmas carols and sharing grapes, cheese, and chocolate cookies which were offered to promote the idea of zero-waste lifestyles. At this event "Re;Table" (Figure 7.5), Re;Code's consumer involvement campaign helping their customers to make their clothing repair kit by themselves, was also run. Here, all visitors participated to make their own sewing kit. The raw materials, yarns, buttons, and making tools were provided. Members of the college-student community, who are known as "Thinkers," were also invited. These "Thinkers" appreciated Re;Code's approach to communicate better with their consumers.

> It's a great idea to let their potential customers to embrace the necessity of sustainable living. This sewing kit that I made looks awkward, but it's what I made by myself, and I like it. With this, I can repair or give a new breath to my old clothes. This big and sharp pair of scissors could be a great help to recreate many of my old jeans. They also give numbers of upcycling ideas on their website. (A member of college student community, Thinkers)

Additional consumer interviews were conducted with whomever visited the brand's "Sharing Space " to investigate how successfully the brand is coming up with better targeted "Creating Shared Value" ideas that suggest more sustainable consumption values to their end-users. They were also asked what they thought about sustainable fashion in general. They elaborated on the creative philosophy of Re;Code and identified green fashion as a trend of the future.

> If you look closely at Re;Code's fashion creations, you can see what kind of textiles they were in their former life. The young designer from the Re;Code design competition makes stylish dresses and skirts from old trousers and shirts. Green fashion denotes fashion that is sustainable and that follows ethical principles. It is a growth sector, and upcycling which involves recycling waste materials into valuable new products. That is the latest trend. (Participant of "Sharing Space")

Lots of young independent fashion designers are participating in Re;Code product design. Mr. Sung-Do Kang, who participated in the design competition *On-Style Project Runway Korea* season 4, recently joined the design team of Re;Code and mentioned that,

> Upcycling takes used textiles from their old context and rearranges them to create something new and unique. Memories associated with old items of clothing are woven into new garments. This enables our customers to keep these memories alive as they wear and display them in a new form.

Upcycling is not just giving new life to existing clothing but it should also provoke consumers to wear this clothing more and for longer. Mr. Kang also mentioned that all of his designs were created with extensive trend forecasting, so they can be worn in more than three ways and maintain a longer wardrobe life.

FIGURE 7.5 "Sharing Space" and "Re;Table." © Kolon Industries. Used with permission.

Upcycling design inspirations and ethics

Zero-waste design projects of "Re;Nano"

Re;Code directly promotes sustainability within their products through their fashion line "Re;Nano." "Re;Nano" is one of Re;Code's product lines that reuse all left-over pieces of materials as well as subsidiary materials left from the making process of the brand's other collections. They promote zero-waste design projects emphasizing the necessity of effective dismantling and recreation process in detail. Zero-waste fashion refers to items of clothing that generate little or no textile waste in their production, and it can be considered a part of the broader sustainable fashion movement. Re;Code has their own design approach in conscious pattern-making for zero-waste design, and they keep in mind that fabric is a notable resource and should not be wasted for any style options. However, zero-waste design is far more than effective pattern-making.

"Re;Code's garments come with instructions on how to up-cycle, recycle or donate the pieces so no product goes to waste," the creative director of Re;Code, Ms. Han said, adding that the outfits showcased in the brand's zero-waste collection can each be styled into seven or more different looks by playing with detachable parts. It is a clever approach to encourage their end-users to wear their clothing to promote zero-waste. Not only does Re;Code eliminate waste during the design and manufacturing processes, they also consider post-consumer zero-waste fashion by providing clothing that can be worn frequently for longer periods of time.

Collaborations with foreign designers

Re;Code attempts to globalize the brand and continues to perform collaborations with a number of European fashion designers from the UK, France, Denmark, and Italy. For example, the first collaboration with Danish designer Henric Viscov in 2016, titled "Inside Out," presented the value of upcycling, and the second collaboration with the French creative group, Andrew Crews showed a collection titled "environmentalism" in Fall/17 Paris Fashion Week. Re;Code's upcycling design ideas were well delivered in the collection, mixing futurism, craftsmanship, and the love of nature. However, the everlasting identity of Re;Code became even more cemented by telling the stories of working with Korean independent designers. The "Arumjigi project" kept the Korean tradition by reinterpreting traditional costume design with a contemporary edge (Figure 7.6).

Re;Code are trying to globalize their brand by collaborating with European fashion designers, at the same time they cannot neglect their Korean brand DNA. This study illustrates how they try to embody their ethnic background into their global brand expansions. Lastly, Re;Code invests much in their brand marketing to better deliver their brand identity toward their potential customers. This case study investigates how they are coming up with better-targeted "Creating Shared Value" ideas that might generate more sustainable consumption values.

Handcraft production to involve local communities in production

Contemporary Korean culture values the aid given by the fashion industry to others who could be considered less fortunate within society. Re;Code comprises a production team titled "Good Will" (Figure 7.7), which is made up of individuals with intellectual disabilities who have been trained to dismantle the old materials from Kolon Industries so that they may be upcycled. Re;Code have started to expand this production team outside of its main

FIGURE 7.6 Re;Code collections with independent designers. © Kolon Industries. Used with permission.

warehouses, so that smaller teams also operate in minority groups within local communities in Korea. In doing so, Re;Code has begun to help rehabilitate and train individuals (particularly women) who have been exposed to violence. In this way, Re;Code is not only more able to cope with the time consuming demands of upcycling materials (such as those contributed to by the complexity of having to dismantle old garments, and construct new ones from these old materials) by employing a much larger staff force, but is also able to help minority communities in Korea, both by providing financial support and by reintegrating them into society. Moreover, through promoting the fact that real individuals and not machines have made the clothes of the label (such as in the promotional images of Figure 7.6), Re;Code may discourage consumers from throwing away the items they have bought upon wearing them a nominal number of times, as consumers may recognize the increased value in the product caused by it being handmade. Re;Code thus also promotes both a more sustainable and inclusive way of living. By helping other fashion companies recognize the value in training staff who may require assistance getting into work, by creating clothes sourced from products which are more environmentally friendly, and by promoting handcrafted fashion which is potentially less likely to be thrown away by consumers, Re;Code could lead to a more sustainable culture of consumption being adopted both in Korea and globally.

Business Questions

Since Re;Code is a relatively new and experimental brand within the Korean market, it has not been regarded as a representative brand of Kolon Industries. However, their strong mission to elaborate the ideas of sustainable manufacturing ethics in the market is achieving conscious attentions from the global market. Recently, Re;Code has attempted to globalize the brand by adopting different culture codes and collaborating with famous European designers.

FIGURE 7.7 Re;Code's handcraft production team, "Good Will." © Kolon Industries. Used with permission.

Should Re;Code be aiming to globalize their business in order to expand their brand and promote sustainable fashion consumption, or should they instead focus on supporting regional communities?

Study questions

1   What opportunities and threats are involved for a textiles manufacturing company launching a new brand which upcycles their left-over and old stock fabrics?

2   Investigate a couple of examples of globalization strategies taken by other foreign fashion brands; discuss what they do to communicate with global consumers.

3   Discuss the meaning of zero-waste design and sustainable fashion and investigate what other upcycled brands deal with those missions. How would you increase consumer consciousness on sustainable fashion?

References and Further Reading

Financial Statement of Kolon Industries, Inc. 2017. "Condensed Financial Statement: Consolidated Version." *Kolon Industries*. Accessed April 24, 2018. https://www.kolonindustries.com/Eng//Service/service02.asp

Jang, Seung-Ho 2017. Personal communication with Seung-Ho Jang, marketing manager of Re;Code.

Re;Code 2018. "KOLONmall: Re;Code." *KOLONmail*. Accessed April 25, 2018. https://www.kolonmall.com/Content/445

Chapter 8

Turning Ocean Plastics into Sustainable Product Innovations

The Strategic Collaboration of Adidas and Parley for the Oceans

Nina Bürklin

The leading sportswear company Adidas and the environmental initiative Parley for the Oceans joined forces in 2014 to tackle the problem of increasing marine pollution caused by plastic waste. The goal of their strategic collaboration was to foster environmental sustainability by raising awareness for the cause and initiating specific activities within their stakeholder network. As part of its corporate social responsibility strategy, Adidas partnered with the New York-based not-for-profit organization, Parley for the Oceans, to collaborate on innovative product development and education. By transforming plastic waste into newly spun fibers through 3D-printing, they aim to create a revolutionary product design and a new type of supply chain management that can set standards for the industry. Focusing on limited editions, Adidas has released newly developed sports shirts as well as a variation of shoes from the Ultra Boost series that are each made of approximately eleven recycled plastic bottles. Through exclusive distribution, limited editions, and marketing communications the sportswear company has managed to raise awareness among a variety of stakeholders, such as customers, suppliers, and employees. Nevertheless, the question arises of how far limited editions are scalable in order to serve customer needs worldwide. Building on the successful collaboration with Parley for the Oceans, possible next steps for the sustainability efforts of the sportswear company must be defined and planned. While this partnership marks the beginning of a far-reaching stakeholder integrating initiative, more actions need to follow. Hence, advantages and disadvantages of current and future collaborations should be considered and evaluated.

Learning Objectives

Upon completion of this case, students should be able to:

- Develop a thorough understanding of a company's stakeholder network by identifying and describing relevant stakeholder groups of the strategic collaboration between Adidas and Parley for the Oceans.

- Identify potential benefits and harms of a strategic partnership regarding the topic of environmental sustainability on the one hand, and the effect on (potential) customers on the other hand.

- Critically revise the idea of product innovations and the related concept of limited editions with regard to potential investments, access to tangible and intangible resources, and acceptance rates by customers.

- Identify, evaluate, and develop current and future stakeholder initiatives around the strategic partnership to foster environmental sustainability according to Adidas's corporate social responsibility strategy.

Introduction

Every year, massive amounts of plastic waste enter the oceans leading to environmental pollution and deterioration of the sea and the animate beings in it. The sportswear supplier Adidas and the New York-based not-for-profit organization Parley for the Oceans joined forces in 2014 to tackle the worldwide problem of environmental pollution caused by the dumping of plastic waste in the sea. Parley for the Oceans comprises a community of creators, thinkers, and leaders who "come together to raise awareness for the beauty and fragility of our oceans and collaborate on projects that can end their destruction" (Parley for the Oceans 2017), while Adidas is engaged in various corporate social responsibility (CSR) activities to foster sustainability for which they have received worldwide recognition. Their joint stakeholder network includes creative thinkers, employees, and customers in the fashion industry, local communities affected by marine pollution, and environmental scientists. Together, they strive to increase awareness for the cause and aim to develop new product solutions as well as innovative communication strategies on the topic of recycled synthetics retrieved from the oceans.

Founded in 1949, Adidas Group is one of the leading suppliers worldwide in the sportswear industry and has a very broad portfolio of shoes, clothes, and equipment for sports and lifestyle. For the sportswear giant, turning pollution into high-performance products is just part of a wider scheme to raise awareness of environmental problems. Within the ambit of their CSR strategy, the global sportswear supplier is engaged in initiatives that foster sustainability in the context of oceans worldwide. For example, Adidas employees are educated about the cause of ocean waste, environmental protection, and the risk of further marine pollution. Further, in 2016, Adidas banned plastic bags from all their stores worldwide in order to decrease the waste created by this material. In a similar vein, Parley for the Oceans comprises personalities from creative industries around the globe who are sympathetic to the marine deterioration and who want to highlight the cause. Combining expertise on materials and technology such as 3D-printing with a global initiative to raise awareness, Adidas and Parley for the Oceans aim to instigate an industry-wide change. Among their new product developments are shoe soles with fibers spun from ocean waste, such as Adidas Ultra Boost, which are made from gillnets,[1] and soccer jerseys made from recycled materials. In their joint effort, they've managed to produce various collections of shoes that are each made of eleven plastic bottles. Through these activities, they position themselves as industry leaders in terms of innovation and environmental sustainability.

Business Problem

Environmental sustainability and the problem of ocean waste

Every year, several million tons of plastic waste reach the oceans worldwide, which leads to massive contamination of one of the most important ecosystems of our planet. Plastic waste can be found in all oceans across the globe as it builds up huge islands of waste, reaches greater depths of the sea, and remains there for a very long time. Through incident solar radiation and salt water, plastics are broken down into smaller and smaller pieces that animals often mistake for plankton and die after ingestion of the plastic. Plants are damaged and humans absorb resulting micro plastics through food consumption. One of the biggest problems is that more and more plastics enter the oceans in direct or indirect ways every year. A report released by the Ellen MacArthur Foundation in 2016 forecasted that by 2050, there will be more waste in the oceans than marine animals. With plastics estimated to make up almost 80 percent of the total marine debris in the world's oceans, the collaboration of Adidas and Parley for the Oceans is making waves in sustainability. The two partners have come together to contribute to the cleanup of oceans worldwide. Through the collaboration they continue their mission to transform plastic waste from the sea into fashionable trainers and clothing.

A strategic partnership

With their "Ocean Plastic" strategy of "Avoid, Intercept, and Redesign," New York-based Parley for the Oceans wants to save the oceans and put an end to marine deterioration. While the not-for-profit organization has initiated various corporations to recycle ocean plastics, their ultimate goal is to get rid of plastics all together and instead use environmentally friendly alternatives.

The international group Adidas, with headquarters in Herzogenaurach (Germany), employs more than 60,000 people worldwide and generated sales of €19.3 billion in 2016. Their core brands are Reebok, Adidas, TaylorMade, and CCM Hockey. For several years, they have integrated aspects of sustainability into their corporate strategy as the following quote by Kasper Rorsted, CEO of Adidas shows: "We are one of the very few companies that integrate sustainability into their business model, which becomes most visible in the fact that we take sustainability to the product level" (Rorsted 2017). CSR initiatives of Adidas regularly receive worldwide recognition from leading sustainability indices, for example the Dow Jones Sustainability Index (DJSI) or the FTSE4GOOD Index to measure a company's performance based on environmental, social, and governance practices. In 2015, Adidas was integrated into the DJSI for the sixteenth time. Furthermore, Adidas was ranked third in the list of "The World's Most Sustainable Companies" by the Toronto-based media company Corporate Knights in 2015.

The partnership with Parley for the Oceans started in 2014 and has since continued and expanded to a range of activities. Among others, it has included the product development

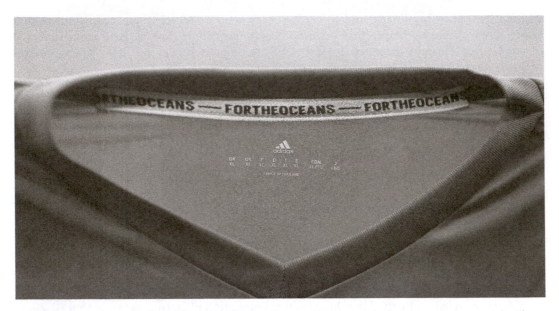

FIGURE 8.1 A special edition FC Bayern Munich soccer jersey made from recycled materials. Photo by Matthias Hangst/Bongarts/Getty Images.

and marketing of the Ultra Boost Shoe as well as the education of Adidas employees and a special edition of soccer shirts for the renowned soccer club FC Bayern Munich. Cyrill Gutsch, founder of Parley for the Oceans, says of the partnership: "We are really excited to have Adidas supporting us in this journey and showing how you can take concrete steps in the right direction" (Adidas 2016).

Further company engagement on the topic of environmental sustainability has become visible in different areas of Adidas's operations. The latest sustainability report by the sportswear supplier explained several initiatives that had been implemented. By the end of the first quarter in 2016, plastic shopping bags were no longer given to customers in Adidas stores which led to the elimination of roughly 70 million plastic bags. Furthermore, the report stated that over 700 employees engaged in roughly 33,000 volunteer hours in 2016. Together with partner COTY, the company also discontinued the inclusion of microbeads in body hygiene products by the end of 2015. By 2020, Adidas plans to substitute all toxics used for dying processes or as plasticizer with non-hazardous substances. Additionally, drinks will no longer be provided in plastic bottles during meetings at the headquarters in Herzogenaurach, Germany.

Innovation in product development and design

Since trainers like the Adidas Ultra Boost have traditionally been made from PET, the question arose, why not use recycled ocean plastics for the production of sports shoes?" Adidas and Parley for the Oceans announced their strategic partnership to fight the problem of plastic waste in the oceans at the climate change conference COP21 in 2015. Through their collaboration they want to show it is possible to generate a profit while decreasing the amount of marine pollution. The not-for-profit organization assisted by turning waste into thread which was used to create the running shoes first presented in December 2015. It was the first shoe ever to be created with a sole made by 3D-printing with fibers that integrated recycled polyamide and fishing nets salvaged from the sea. Though only a prototype, the shoe was a good example of how sustainability and design could be developed through innovation. It was the starting point for further product developments and new types of supply chains. Eric Liedtke, Head of Global Brands and Member of Executive Board at Adidas, commented upon the cooperation by stating: "The ambition is to continue to innovate to help athletes while looking at every way possible to do less harm. […] While we will not compromise on the integrity of our innovations for the sake of sustainability efforts, we will look to build sustainability into every innovation" (Peters 2015).

FIGURE 8.2 Eric Liedtke, Head of Global Brands and Member of Executive Board at Adidas, speaks on stage at the United Nations x Parley For The Oceans Launch Event on June 29, 2015, in New York City. Photo by Jamie McCarthy/Getty Images for Parley for the Oceans.

In November 2016, the first limited edition of the shoe Ultra Boost Uncaged was released. At the same time, the soccer players of FC Bayern Munich played their match in tricots made from recycled ocean plastics collected in the Maldives. In a further bid to end pollution, the sportswear brand joined forces with the environmental initiative for the second time in the summer of 2017, when another wave of product innovations entered the market. Three variations of shoes were presented to the public in May 2017: Ultra Boost 3.0, Ultra Boost X, and Ultra Boost Uncaged.[2] Each pair is constructed using an average of eleven plastic bottles and features laces, heel linings, and sock liner covers from recycled PET material. The blue colorway that adorns all three pairs, according to Adidas, was inspired by the shades of the ocean. For their new collection of swimwear, the ocean plastic is converted into a technical yarn fibre named Econyl, which offers the same properties as the regular nylon used in making swimwear. The designs are inspired by the origins of the recycled yarn, with graphic prints in shades of blue intended to reflect a seascape.

Selective distribution and exclusivity

The distribution of the Parley-branded products is very selective. So far, all products are strongly limited and resemble exclusivity. For example, only 7,000 pairs of the first shoe Ultra Boost were offered. Generally, the products made from recycled ocean waste are only available in selected Adidas stores and in the Adidas online shop. The price for a pair of trainers is set comparably high at €200 for each pair. Nevertheless, Adidas aimed to produce 1 million pairs of shoes from ocean plastic in 2017. The company's long-term goal is to completely eliminate pure synthetics from the value chains. With the support of beach cleaners and environmental activists, at least 11 million plastic bottles will be collected in coastal regions to be used in the production of sports products.

Stakeholder initiatives to increase awareness for the cause

In order to reach not only customers, but also other relevant stakeholder groups, Adidas and Parley for the Oceans set up different initiatives to tackle the problem of marine pollution through plastic waste. In the years 2015 and 2016, two groups of twenty Adidas employees each participated in the Parley Ocean School. The concept combined creating awareness for the protection of the oceans with experience-based learning on the open sea. The employees were engaged in beach cleanups along the coast and learned more about the current state of the oceans during Parley Talks with marine experts. Furthermore, they explored the opportunities and necessity of cross-cultural collaborations through youth education initiatives and experiences with the local community. The goal was to educate and motivate a new group of ambassadors for the cause in order to spread knowledge in the private and work-related environments of Adidas employees.[3]

During the week of World Oceans Day in 2017, Adidas and Parley for the Oceans partnered with the mobile application Runtastic to raise awareness of the deterioration of oceans. In order to make a global statement, all three parties asked the sports community to participate in a global movement called "Run for the Oceans." The goal was to engage as many people as possible to actively start thinking and acting to tackle the problem of ocean waste. Over 35,000 runners participated by tracking their running data through Runtastic and sharing it on social media. Besides the digital engagement, an offline running event was executed in New York City with renowned runners, environmentalists, and influencers to raise awareness for the cause of marine deterioration. Throughout the year 2017, the collection made from recycled ocean waste was extended to include further garments. Moreover, different product ranges such as the Adidas by Stella McCartney product line, will potentially integrate shoes and sports clothing made from recycled plastic fibers in the future. Demonstrating their will to further enhance environmental sustainability, the collaboration had ambitious goals and wanted to succeed in producing 1 million sneakers from Parley plastics by the end of 2017.

Business Questions

1   Who are the stakeholders of this strategic collaboration? In class, identify all relevant stakeholders and their roles. Next, form groups of three to four people who each represent one stakeholder group and discuss its stake as well as its goals.

2   What are the potential benefits and risks of the bespoke product innovations? Explain and discuss the concept of limited editions. How closely is the concept of exclusivity linked to the strategic collaboration and to environmental sustainability?

3   Who is the target customer of the products made from ocean waste? What is their need and what is important to this customer regarding environmental sustainability? Develop a customer persona that reflects the personality, goals, behavior, and lifestyle that Adidas is targeting.

4   Identify and develop two new initiatives within the strategic partnership of Adidas and Parley to further engage relevant stakeholders in the context of environmental sustainability, including specific measurements for their success. For each initiative, discuss potential risks and benefits.

Notes

1   For an example of the Adidas Ultra Boost sneaker see: https://circuitsandcableknit.com/shoes/adidas-x-parley-gillnet-sneaker-getting-limited-edition-launch/

2   An example of the Ultra Boost Uncaged sneaker can be viewed at: http://www.businessinsider.de/adidas-releases-new-parley-ocean-waste-plastic-shoes-2017-4?r=US&IR=T

3   To see images and find additional information on the initiative, please visit: http://www.parley.tv/updates/2017/1/12/parley-ocean-school-maldives-2016

References and Further Reading

Adidas. 2016. "Adidas Group Sustainability Progress Report 2015." Accessed August 2017. https://www.adidas-group.com/media/filer_public/9c/f3/9cf3db44-b703-4cd0-98c5-28413f272aac/2015_sustainability_progress_report.pdf

Ellen MacArthur Foundation. "The New Plastics Economy—Rethinking the Future of Plastics." Accessed November 2017. https://www.ellenmacarthurfoundation.org/publications/the-new-plastics-economy-rethinking-the-future-of-plastics

Parley for the Oceans. 2017. Accessed June 2017. http://www.parley.tv/#fortheoceans

Peters, Adele. 2015. "This Sneaker Was 3-D Printed From Ocean Waste." Accessed August 2017. https://www.fastcompany.com/3054494/this-sneaker-was-3d-printed-from-ocean-waste

Post, James E., Lee E. Preston, and Sybille Sachs. 2002. *Redefining the Corporation*. 1st edn. Stanford: Stanford University Press.

Rorsted, Kasper. 2017. "Adidas Reiterates Commitment to the Oceans and Publishes 2016 Sustainability Progress Report." Accessed August 2017. https://www.adidas-group.com/en/media/news-archive/press-releases/2017/adidas-reiterates-commitment-oceans-and-publishes-2016-sustainab/

Sachs, Sybille and Edwin Rühli. 2011. *Stakeholders Matter: A New Paradigm for Strategy in Society*. Cambridge: Cambridge University Press.

Chapter 9

Applying Circular Economy Principles in Luxury Fashion: Petit h

Patsy Perry and Hakan Karaosman

As one of the world's most iconic luxury brands, Hermès is known for its heritage and excellence in craftsmanship and materials. However, the pursuit of product excellence in order to maintain the high status of luxury brands often results in significant waste of raw materials. As one of the world's most polluting industry sectors, fashion has come under increasing scrutiny in terms of its environmental responsibility, and many companies are engaging with a variety of initiatives to reduce the environmental impact of business operations. The circular approach is an alternative to the linear system of "make, use, dispose," and advocates that resources should be kept in use for as long as possible before being recycled or regenerated, for example, by reusing waste materials, designing for longevity, and recycling. Some of these approaches have been successfully adopted in the fast-fashion and outdoor sectors but may conflict with traditional luxury brand values of exclusivity, excellent quality, and uniqueness, especially in the highest level of absolute luxury. This case considers the challenges and opportunities for a luxury fashion house in pursuing circularity, including how to harness design, creativity, and innovation; how to develop and disseminate technical and motivational capabilities toward circularity; and whether luxury fashion can be aligned with circular economy principles. The case takes the perspective of Pascale Mussard, who set up the Petit h division of Hermès in 2010 with the aim of repurposing waste raw materials into new objects of desire, and explores the challenges she faced.

Learning Objectives

Upon completion of this case, students should be able to:

- Explore the definition of a luxury brand in the context of fashion.
- Compare linear and circular approaches in the fashion industry.

- Analyze the barriers to and facilitating factors of adopting a circular approach in luxury fashion.
- Evaluate the opportunities for value creation from using waste raw materials in luxury fashion.
- Describe ways in which circularity could be communicated to luxury consumers through various types of marketing messages.

Introduction

Originally founded as a saddlery shop in 1837, Hermès International SCA is a French family-owned company which specializes in design, manufacturing, and marketing of luxury leather goods, apparel, and homeware. Its main focus is on leather saddlery, footwear, and bags, but it also sells clothing and accessories, perfume, tableware, and watches. It is present in Europe, Asia, the Pacific region, and the Americas, via a network of over 300 exclusive stores, its website, and airport duty free outlets (Hermès 2018b). It is one of the world's most iconic luxury brands and sits in the Absolute segment, which makes up 25 percent of the luxury market (D'Arpizio 2016). Absolute luxury brands are characterized by elitism, heritage, and exclusivity. Hermès price points are considerably higher than other luxury brands such as Louis Vuitton, Dior, and Prada and its iconic Birkin and Kelly handbags are made to order with notoriously long waiting lists. Most Hermès products are manufactured in its own production units in France, which include tanneries and leather goods workshops, as well as textile, porcelain, and crystal manufacture (Hermès 2018b). In 2016, it employed 12,834 people worldwide (Statista 2018). Its key strengths include its strong brand identity and the creativity and skills of its artisans (Chaboud 2017). In terms of size, it is smaller than the luxury industry leaders LVMH and Richemont, however, it is significantly more profitable, with net profit outperforming the industry average as well as both industry leaders (Deloitte 2017). Hermès aims to conduct its business in a way that respects its ecological, social, economic, and cultural environment and focuses on maintaining authenticity in each product, which entails respecting natural raw materials and developing artisanal skills, primarily in France (Hermès 2018c). It provides considerable information in its annual reports, including appendices which detail water and energy consumption and CO_2 emissions of operations, as well as information about employees, local community support, and responsible trading partnerships. It is one of the few luxury companies to disclose information about its first- and second-tier production sites (product manufacturing and material processing), most of which are located in France, and the environmental and social impact of its factories on local communities.

Luxury is a profitable and growing fashion market, with some of the world's most valuable and recognizable brands, providing symbolic benefits to consumers and supporting artisanal skills in many regions. However, it is not immune from the environmental problems that ensue from mass-market fashion production operations. The environmental impact of luxury fashion is significant as change happens each season, with new colors and materials required as more frequent collections are launched. The pursuit of product excellence generates significant amounts of waste materials in order to ensure the highest levels of quality. These issues present a challenge to adopting a circular approach in terms of designing for longevity and reusing waste materials. So far, luxury fashion houses have not engaged with circular approaches as well as the fast fashion and outdoor apparel sectors (for example H&M's and Patagonia's use of pre- and post-consumer recycled textiles, or Adidas' and Gant's use of ocean plastic waste as a raw material), but as a high profile industry sector, luxury brands are at increasing risk of reputation loss if they do not engage with the sustainability agenda.

Business Problem

Sustainable fashion may be considered an oxymoron; while sustainability is about durability, fashion is about change. The current system for producing, distributing, and utilizing clothing operates in an almost completely linear way of take-make-dispose (Ellen MacArthur Foundation 2017). In fashion, clothing is produced from virgin raw materials, purchased and used by consumers, then disposed of. However, this linear system generates a significant environmental and social footprint, and leaves economic opportunities unexploited. The circular economy proposes an alternative flow model by emphasizing product, component, and material reuse, remanufacturing, refurbishment, and repair, which is cascaded throughout the product value chain and cradle-to-cradle life cycle (Korhonen et al. 2018). It refers to an industrial economy that is restorative by intention; aims to rely on renewable energy; minimizes, tracks, and eliminates the use of toxic chemicals; and eradicates waste through careful design (Ellen MacArthur Foundation 2017). A circular fashion economy implies that materials and products are used and circulated among users for as long as possible, in an environmentally safe, effective, and just manner. Waste is regarded as a resource for other processes to take place in society, so the use of virgin materials is minimized. Natural resources, including energy, are used effectively during both production and consumption. Renewable energy sources are prioritized, and all materials are free from hazardous substances and chemicals, in order to enable safe and pure material flows in society and prevent or minimize undesirable environmental impacts (circularfashion.com 2018). A circular approach should be used throughout the business, including design, sourcing, production, and reuse/recycling, as advocated by Circularfashion.com (2018):

- Fashion products should be *designed* with high longevity, resource efficiency, non-toxicity, biodegradability, recyclability and good ethics in mind.
- Similarly, they should be *sourced and produced* with priority given to local, non-toxic, renewable, biodegradable and recyclable resources, as well as efficient, safe and ethical practices.
- Moreover, the products should be *used* for as long as possible, through good care, repair, refurbishment and sharing among multiple users over time (through rent/lease, second-hand sales, swapping etc.).
- Thereafter, the products should be *redesigned* to give the material and components new life.
- Lastly, the material and components should be *recycled and reused* for the manufacturing of new products. If unfit for recycling, the biological material should instead be composted to become nutrients for plants and other living organisms in the ecosystem. (emphasis in original)

Changing the current linear system and moving toward circularity could deliver significant environmental, social, and economic benefits. The European Commission estimated that circular economy type economic transitions could create 600 billion euros annual economic gains for the EU manufacturing sector alone (Korhonen et al. 2018). However, some circular approaches may conflict with traditional luxury brand values of exclusivity, premium quality, and uniqueness, especially in the highest level of absolute luxury, where nothing less than perfection is tolerated. Luxury's focus on product excellence and the highest quality results in significant amounts of waste materials. For example, a belt should be made up of a single piece of animal hide, rather than lots of small pieces sewn together, so each hide may only yield one or two belts. This results in wastage of materials as only the very best parts of animal furs, hides, or reptile skins are utilized. To protect the high status of the luxury brand, unsold products may be destroyed rather than offered for sale at a discount. Imperfect products may also be destroyed to protect the brand name, rather than being sold as seconds. Commercial pressures, demanding fashion calendars, and organizational complexities also impede the pursuit of reducing material waste in production. Materials purchased last season may not be used for the next season due to trend changes. Craftsmanship is pivotal and expert production techniques are necessary to achieve excellence in luxury products—however, expertise only comes with experience and sometimes things can go wrong, which may result in imperfections in the final product and consequently lead to material wastage and product destruction. Luxury houses have tended not to address sustainability in terms of waste, choosing to destroy defective or surplus goods (Stylebubble 2013).

Petit h

Pascale Mussard set up the Petit h division of Hermès in 2010, where she was creative director until 2018. She is the great-great-great-granddaughter of the saddle-maker Thierry Hermès, who originally founded Hermès as a saddlery shop in 1837, and the niece of Jean-Louis Dumas, who transformed the fashion house into a highly successful global luxury brand during the late 1970s. Pascale worked in a number of departments of the company, including fabric purchasing and communications, before moving into Petit h. Driven by sustainability-focused creativity, she developed a creative vision for Petit h that was underpinned by environmental consciousness. She collected unused, discarded or undesirable materials from Hermès' many ateliers and workshops, such as discarded leather or silk, broken crystal or porcelain, as well as unused samples or remnants of discontinued lines, ever since she joined the Hermès group in 1978, and stored them in an "Ali Baba's cave of treasures" (Hermès 2013). An initially small box of discarded items grew over the years to become an impressive storage room that is now used as a source for inspiration to create beautiful and exquisite new products.

> Where do Hermès leftovers come back to life? At petit h, the daring design office where remnants form the art of finds to come. (Hermes 2018a)

Petit h is part-laboratory, part-atelier. Designers play with ideas, toy with possibilities (Stylebubble 2013), and have the freedom to experiment with creativity and new techniques as long as objects created are functional and in keeping with Hermès' understated style (Israel 2013). Nevertheless, Petit h follows the heritage of Hermès in product development and respects the core values embodied in its history. The story of Petit h is thus combined with Hermes' own story: the story of being in France, of having an atelier in France, of using the most exquisite materials, of having the best quality, and of being the very best of the best. Petit h's philosophy is not about using defective or damaged materials, but if those parts are cut away, the remainder can be repurposed so that all Petit h products are still perfect (Stylebubble 2013), in keeping with Hermès' brand values. For example, a Birkin

FIGURE 9.1 Hermes is well-known for their luxury handbags. Discarded materials from Hermes products are reused and repurposed to create products under the brand, Petit h. © Victor VIRGILE/ Gamma-Rapho via Getty Images

bag's scratched sides would be removed and replaced with the bulge of a felt hat to create a completely new Birkin-hat hybrid (Stylebubble 2013). Similarly, a discarded piece of crystal that might not be beautiful for a glass is still crystal and can be reused for another purpose, or parts from a broken porcelain mug could be recut and transformed into a necklace. Thus, discarded materials are reused to create something original, new, and beautiful. Petit h does not see imperfections as incommensurable with the concept of luxury. For example, wrinkles in leather are not necessarily defects, but represent authenticity because each animal has its own life and its own skin full of memories and signs of life, which becomes a captivating story of the material. In this way, no material is unworthy (Hermès 2013). Petit h items are marketed as "one of a kind" items and the lack of consistency is promoted as a positive characteristic:

> Each petit h piece is unique. The color or the pattern of your product will be a surprise within the color scheme selected. (Hermes 2018d)

Petit h products have been described as whimsical (Bagaholicboy 2013; Architectural Digest 2014) and playful (Stylebubble 2013). The line includes leather accessories such as charms, patches, passport holders, and pouches; silk items such as tote bags, shoelaces, bracelets, and necklaces. Other creations include desktop dumbbells in crystal and crocodile, light fittings made from refashioned porcelain teapots, and a crystal umbrella tray (Israel 2013). By purposefully focusing on such small goods, Petit h does not overstep the line into the ready-to-wear or footwear territory of the main brand Hermès (Stylebubble 2013). Initially, Petit h creations were offered for sale in pop-up events in Hermès boutiques around the globe. Now, the creations are also sold on Hermes' website (https://www. hermes.com/us/en/petit-h/#||Category), although currently available to US customers only. Initially, Hermes set up a dedicated Pinterest board for Petit h (Bagaholicboy 2013) but this no longer exists.

Although the creative director always had a dream of reusing materials and creating beautiful designs by using what was left behind, she nevertheless encountered a number of challenges in setting up Petit h. "Why?" was what everyone in the company said at the time (Stylebubble 2013). First, she had to convince the Hermès family members that she was respecting the brand, its core values, and its long heritage by fashioning new products from waste materials. Then, she needed to show the artisan craftspeople that it was still possible to design beautiful products from materials with imperfections, such as broken porcelain or crystal and wrinkled leather. At first the craftspeople were skeptical of Pascale's idea, as the culture was to strive to achieve the best possible quality, so convincing them to produce things out of waste or imperfect materials required a significant change of mindset. She also had to convince the designers to allow her to recreate new objects from their pieces (Israel 2013). Pursuit of excellence in the Petih h line was also important, as time makes things expensive, and even if waste materials are used, human resources needed to be diverted from the main line. As objects were created in very limited quantities, there was little room for error in the Petit h atelier—as it would be ironic to waste the "waste materials" that were being repurposed in the first place (Stylebubble 2013). Pascale explained in 2013: "the idea is to create exceptional objects that are unique in their spirit of invention and in the quality of their execution" (Israel 2013). Last but not least, she needed to learn how to create technical and management resources to disseminate knowledge on circular economy throughout the relevant parts of the business, including design, production, and marketing.

Business Questions

1   What were the barriers to adopting a circular approach for Hermès?

2   Why should Hermès create products from waste materials under their name?

3   What were the barriers for Hermès, as an established luxury fashion house and iconic brand, to create products from waste materials under their name? Can such a line coexist alongside its main line?

4   How should know-how be developed, disseminated, and maintained within the company?

5   How could Hermès educate internal and external stakeholders, including consumers, employees, and designers, about the circular economy?

6   How could Petih h promote products made from waste?

7   How could Petit h be scaled up for a greater impact?

8   How should designers, material experts, and marketers in Hermès collaborate in pursuit of a circular approach?

9   Can imperfection be aligned with luxury? Provide reasoning for your opinion.

10 Should sustainability and circularity be communicated to luxury consumers? If not, why not? If so, how?

11 What might be the challenges for incorporating circular principles into luxury brand management at the highest level of absolute luxury?

12 Are the principles of sustainability compatible or incompatible with those of luxury, given luxury's focus on unique, valuable, and rare materials?

References and Further Reading

Achabou, Mohamed Akli and Sihem Dekhill. 2013. "Luxury and Sustainable Development: Is there a Match?" *Journal of Business Research* 66 (10): 1896–903.

Architectural Digest. 2014. "Hermès Launches Petit h Line of Quirky Accessories." Accessed April 1, 2018. https://www.architecturaldigest.com/story/petit-h-hermes-article

Bagaholicboy. 2013. "Hermès Petit h." Accessed April 1, 2018. http://bagaholicboy.com/2013/06/hermes-petit-h/m

Bendell, Jem and Anthony Kleanthous. 2007. *Deeper Luxury: Quality and Style When the World Matters*. Woking: WWF–UK.

Brun, Alessandro and Cecilia Maria Castelli. 2013. "The Nature of Luxury: A Consumer Perspective." *International Journal of Retail & Distribution Management* 41 (11/12): 823–47.

Chaboud, Isabelle. 2017. "Hermès: Behind the Scenes of the French Luxury Gem." *The Conversation*, July 11. Accessed April 1, 2018. https://theconversation.com/hermes-behind-the-scenes-of-the-french-luxury-gem-80551

Circularfashion.com 2018. "Origin of the Concept 'Circular Fashion.'" Accessed April 1, 2018. https://circularfashion.com/circular-fashion-definition/

D'Arpizio, Claudia. 2016. "Altagamma 2016 Worldwide Luxury Market Monitor." *Bain & Co*. and *Fondazione Altagamma*, October 20. Accessed April 1, 2018. https://altagamma.it/media/source/ALTAGAMMA%20WW%20MARKETS%20MONITOR%202016.pdf

Deloitte. 2017. "Global Powers of Luxury Goods 2017." Accessed April 1, 2018. https://www2.deloitte.com/content/dam/Deloitte/global/Documents/consumer-industrial-products/gx-cip-global-powers-luxury-2017.pdf

Ellen MacArthur Foundation. 2017. "What is a Circular Economy?" Accessed April 1, 2018. https://www.ellenmacarthurfoundation.org/circular-economy

Fionda-Douglas, Antoinette and Christopher M. Moore. 2009. "The Anatomy of the Luxury Fashion Brand." *Journal of Brand Management* 16 (5/6): 347–63.

Hermès. 2013. "Inside Hermès petit h - Episode n°1." YouTube, October 7. Accessed April 1, 2018. https://www.youtube.com/watch?time_continue=17&v=NZVBC2XrAPw

Hermès. 2018a. "The Big petit h Studio." Accessed April 1, 2018. https://www.hermes.com/ca/en/story/22741-petit-h/

Hermès. 2018b. "Group Overview: Stores and Manufactures." Accessed April 1, 2018. https://finance.hermes.com/en/Group-overview/Stores

Hermès. 2018c. "La Maison Hermes." Accessed April 1, 2018. https://www.hermes.com/uk/en/faq/maison-hermes-uk/#la%20maison%20herm%c3%a8s

Hermès. 2018d. "Petit h." Accessed April 1, 2018. https://www.hermes.com/us/en/petit-h/#//Category

Israel, Katrina. 2013. "Upcycling on Bond Street? Oui, Says Hermès with its Petit h Exhibition." *Wallpaper*, November 20. Accessed April 1, 2018. https://www.wallpaper.com/fashion/upcycling-on-bond-street-oui-says-herms-with-its-petit-h-exhibition

Kapferer, Jean-Noël. 2010. "All that Glitters is not Green: The Challenge of Sustainable Luxury." *European Business Review*, November/December: 40–44.

Kapferer, Jean-Noël and Anne Michaut-Denizeau. 2017. "Is Luxury Compatiblewith Sustainability? Luxury Consumers' Viewpoint." In *Advances in Luxury Brand Management*, Journal of Brand Management: Advanced Collections, edited by Jean-Noël Kapferer, J. Kernstock, T. Brexendorf and S. Powell, 123–56. Cham: Palgrave MacMillan. https://doi.org/10.1007/978-3-319-51127-6_7

Introduction

This section includes case studies that focus on the challenges and opportunities professionals in the fashion industry face and the decisions they make in the areas of fashion marketing and branding. Marketing is the "management process that connects product offerings with the values, wants, needs, and behaviors of customers" (Burns and Mullet 2020, p. 3). Marketing research is conducted to better understand the marketplace for a fashion brand company's products and services and used to inform decisions related to the marketing and brand strategies that the fashion brand company will implement. Fashion brand professionals must weigh advantages and disadvantages of implementing marketing and brand strategies that align with the fashion brand company's mission and objectives.

Creating, developing, implementing, and maintaining an effective brand strategy is imperative for the success of a fashion brand company. A successful fashion brand is distinct, innovative, consistent, well-positioned in comparison with competing brands, and reflects an identity that creates a positive and unique image in consumers' minds (Hameide 2011). Marketing for a fashion brand's products and a distinctive brand identity are created through a mix of company-controlled communications (e.g., advertising, social media, visual merchandising) and consumer experiences with the brand.

Fashion brand professionals are constantly addressing changes and opportunities in the fashion marketplace to better position their brands and effectively promote them. The case studies in this section explore challenges and opportunities that fashion brand companies face related to maintaining a distinct and positive brand identity, the impact of changing consumer dynamics on branding and marketing, and the role of marketing in the "see now, buy now" supply chain calendar.

References and Further Reading

Burns, Leslie Davis and Kathy K. Mullet (2020). *The Business of Fashion: Designing, Manufacturing, and Marketing*. 6th ed. New York: Fairchild Books/Bloomsbury.

D'Arienzo, William (2016). *Brand Management Strategies*. New York: Fairchild Books/Bloomsbury.

Divita, Lorynn (2019). *Fashion Forecasting*. 5th ed. New York: Fairchild Books/Bloomsbury.

Hameide, Kaled K. (2011). *Fashion Branding Unraveled*. New York: Fairchild Books.

Chapter 10

Only Bright Lights for Uniqlo?

Devising Strategies for Suburban Growth

Myles Ethan Lascity

Japanese specialty-store retailer of private-label apparel, Uniqlo, has outlets around the globe, but their expansion in the U.S. market has seemingly stalled. Since 2005 the retailer has had a presence in the United States, first with several mall locations before it switched to using flagship stores as a market entry strategy. As such, flagships now dot fashion-forward areas, including in New York's SoHo district, San Francisco's Union Square, and Chicago's Michigan Avenue; the chain also opened an 89,000-square-foot global flagship along Manhattan's famed Fifth Avenue. Despite growth that saw locations increase from one U.S. store in 2011 to several dozen stores by 2017, Fast Retailing, Uniqlo's parent company, has been struggling to turn a profit in the United States, which resulted in the closure of some suburban stores.

This case study implores students to think about why Uniqlo might have a strong base of support in urban areas but has trouble moving into more suburban locations. Further, it asks students to devise promotional strategies that might allow Uniqlo to introduce itself into smaller markets.

Learning Objectives

Upon completion of this case, students should be able to:

- Analyze market segmentation and demographic differences between urban and suburban consumers.
- Examine the expansion of Uniqlo and its partial failure and postulate reasons for it.
- Identify and describe creative ways for a fashion brand to expand.

Introduction

Uniqlo, the Japanese specialty store of private-label apparel, has become a prominent fashion brand from Tokyo and Singapore to Paris and London. Recently the chain has taken on the North American market, seeking to expand its presence in the United States and Canada. In 2011 it was reported that Uniqlo and parent company Fast Retailing were seeking to challenge U.S. staples H&M, Zara, and Gap, and planned to open 200 stores by 2020. Uniqlo would be playing catch-up; at the time it had three locations, compared to more than 100 for H&M and 49 for Zara.

Despite this, Fast Retailing CEO and market analysts expected room for a growth. "Uniqlo brings in a broader customer base and is a bit more classic and tailored," NPD Group chief analyst Marshal Cohen told Reuters. "They will appeal to a slightly more affluent shopper."

Uniqlo's U.S. initiative started in 2005 when the retailer opened three mall-based stores in New Jersey. However, the growth has appeared unsteady. In 2006, a 36,000-square-foot flagship store was opened in New York City's SoHo district, but the New Jersey locations were shuttered the following year. Uniqlo was relegated to the single flagship store through 2011, when it began its aggressive expansion.

Business Problem

In 2010 Uniqlo signed a lease on what would become its Fifth Avenue, global flagship store. The store would be 89,000 square foot spread across three floors, substantially larger than the nearby flagship locations of Abercrombie & Fitch and H&M. (For comparison, an NFL football field covers 62,400 square feet.) This plan led the *New Yorker* to ask, "Just how did the Japanese discount brand become the hottest retailer in the city?"

FIGURE 10.1 The window display for the Denver Uniqlo store, the brand's first branch in Colorado. The text refers to Denver by its nickname "Mile High City." Photo by Helen H. Richardson/The Denver Post via Getty Images.

The global flagship store opened in 2011 followed by a third New York City flagship in Herald Square. In 2012 Uniqlo opened a 29,000-square-feet flagship in San Francisco and the chain has expanded from these two U.S. bases since. Largely, this strategy might be deemed a "flagship market entry strategy," where large, eye-catching stores help retailers make a statement. Flagships have been called the best articulation of a brand image and are widely understood to be a cultural flash point for brand managers and consumers alike.

By 2014 Uniqlo was expanding into three new markets: Los Angeles, Boston, and Philadelphia. The growth was assisted by several glocalization campaigns that aimed to localize the brand.

A Twitter campaign asked users to tweet slang from the locations, sponsored Buzzfeed articles extolled the virtues of Philadelphia and Boston, and advertisements featured celebrities with ties to the cities, including actor Glenn Howerton and celebrity chef Kristen Kish.

Uniqlo would eventually open five stores in and around Philadelphia. In May the first Pennsylvania store opened at the King of Prussia Mall, the second largest mall in the United States. This was followed by a flagship store in Center City, Philadelphia, and suburban mall

FIGURE 10.2 The digital display was visible behind the brown paper as workers cleared the Uniqlo location at the King of Prussia Mall on June 20, 2017. The store's final day of operation was June 18. Myles Ethan Lascity.

locations in Cherry Hill, New Jersey, and Willow Groves and North Wales, Pennsylvania. The flagship's opening was celebrated with "Love Fest" in the city's Fairmont Park which featured brand promotions and a concert by Questlove.

However, Uniqlo's expansion seemingly stalled again. Stores within the United States operated at a loss in 2015, and by 2016, the chain shuttered locations in Danbury, Connecticut, Staten Island, New York, Northridge, California, and the Willow Grove and Cherry Hill locations. In June 2017 Uniqlo also closed the King of Prussia location, leaving only two stores of the original five stores in and around Philadelphia.

The company blamed limited brand awareness and reiterated the importance of the U.S. market to the *New York Post*.

"The brand penetration in big cities such as New York, San Francisco and Chicago is good," the company's CEO Tadaski Yanai reportedly said during an earnings call, "but not in the suburbs."

Business Questions

1 What are three key differences between people who live in urban areas and suburban locales? How might this affect their purchasing decisions?

2 Why might be the Uniqlo brand be better known in cities like "New York, San Francisco and Chicago," but not in suburban locations? What could be done to increase recognition in suburban locations?

3 Imagine working with Uniqlo on its expansion into the suburbs. What promotions would you suggest the brand should undertake to increase recognition of the brand in suburban locations? Why?

4 Do you feel that promotional activities such as Buzzfeed listicles and hashtag promotions are useful as branding tools, and do they result in increased sales? Why or why not? Do you engage with retailers who ask you to use specific hashtags? Why or why not?

References and Further Reading

Brooke, Eliza. 2015. "Uniqlo Plants to Curb U.S. Store Openings, Citing 'Limited' Brand Awareness." *Fashionista*, October 8. https://fashionista.com/2015/10/uniqlo-store-openings

Fickenscher, Lisa. 2016. "Uniqlo's Struggles Cause Fashion Chain to Close Stores." *New York Post*, June 20. http://nypost.com/2016/06/20/uniqlos-struggles-cause-fashion-chain-to-close-stores/

Mattioli, Dana. 2012. "Uniqlo Expansion Takes Retail Out to West Coast." *The Wall Street Journal*, April 9. https://www.wsj.com/articles/SB10001424052702304587704577333740754213030

Moor, Liz. 2007. "Branded Spaces." In *The Rise of Brands*. New York: Berg.

Moore, Christopher M., Anne Marie Doherty and Stephen A. Doyle. 2010. "Flagship Stores as a Market Entry Method: The Perspective of Luxury Fashion Retailing." *European Journal of Marketing* 44 (1–2): 139–161. doi: 10.1108/03090561011008646

Thompson, Carig J. and Zeynep Arsel. 2004. "The Starbucks Brandscape and Consumers' (Anticorporate) Experiences of Glocalization." *Journal of Consumer Research* 31 (3): 631–642. doi: 10.1086/425098

Urstadt, Bryant. 2010. "Uniqlones." *New York*, May 9. http://nymag.com/fashion/features/65898/

Wahba, Phil. 2011. "Uniqlo Starts U.S. Expansion, Eyes 200 Stores." *Reuters*, October 13. http://www.reuters.com/article/us-fastretailing-idUSTRE79C7IG20111013

Zukin, Sharon. 2005. "How Brooks Brothers Came to Look Like Banana Republic." In *Point of Purchase: How Shopping Changed American Culture*. New York: Routledge.

Definition

Glocalization: The process of adapting a global brand to give it attributes tailored to a local market.

Chapter 11

The Future for Under Armour

Maintaining Brand Equity

Lisa Hodgkins

US athletic apparel company Under Armour, Inc. has experienced large-scale and consistent growth since it was established in 1996, but the company has a continuing need to maintain brand equity as they compete worldwide with other athletic-wear giants. This case study asks students to consider elements of successful branding, formulate ideas for targeting new customers, and recommend ways in which Under Armour can enhance the image and prestige of their brand.

Learning Objectives

Upon completion of this case, students should be able to:

- Understand aspects of brand development.
- Recommend enhancements or adjustments to the brand's image.
- Explore Under Armour's online presence and compare it with its competitors'.
- Consider potential target markets and create a persona for the brand.
- Suggest new products or designs which would appeal to their target markets.

Introduction

Under Armour, Inc., a US-based sports apparel, footwear, and accessories company, was founded in 1996 by twenty-three-year-old former University of Maryland college football player Kevin Plank when he recognized a need for an alternative to cotton sports training gear.

He created the #0037 Under Armour HeatGear® T-shirt made of lightweight fabric which could wick away sweat in hot weather; and this was soon followed by garments made with ColdGear® fabric designed to be warm but breathable in cold weather conditions (Under Armour n.d.). Plank began promoting Under Armour (UA) shirts to his former teammates, drew the attention of the National Football League (NFL), and in 1998 UA became an official supplier to the NFL Europe League. In 1998 to 1999 Plank arranged product placement in two football-themed Warner Brothers movies and by the year 2000 company revenues had reached $5 million (Funding Universe 2004; Olson 2015). Only two years later in 2002 Under Armour revenues had skyrocketed to more than $50 million (Olson 2015).

The company formed relationships with professional sports organizations both in the United States and abroad. It also expanded its links with university athletics by outfitting teams as well as supplying cobranded merchandise to sell to the public (Funding Universe 2004). Under Armour has supplied a number of US Olympic teams and established partnerships with well-known celebrities and athletes including Dwayne (the Rock) Johnson, basketball player Stephen Curry, World Champion skier Lindsey Vonn, ballet dancer Misty Copeland, Olympic swimmer Michael Phelps, tennis player Andy Murray, NFL football player Tom Brady, and supermodel Gisele Bündchen (Under Armour UK n.d.).

An in-house product development team consults with athletes and with UA's marketing team to create new products and collections (Under Armour 2018). Their merchandise is primarily manufactured outside the United States using a number of unaffiliated suppliers and manufacturers on short term contracts. The company has its own retail and outlet stores and also sells direct to the consumer through its website. It places wholesale products in a variety of channels including bricks-and-mortar venues such as sporting-goods chains, department stores, university bookstores, and professional sports team shops. Goods are also sold through independent and licensed distributors (Marketline 2017).

The company has a high-tech heritage and ethos. CEO Plank has said "I think we have a chance to play a much bigger role than just a typical apparel and footwear supplier. We want to deliver the most innovative and technical gear that delivers on our mission, which is to make all athletes better" (Harrison 2014). The company's beginnings focused on fabric technology and they continue to increase their fabric range. Under Armour is pioneering the development of body monitoring apparel which they sell to professional and college teams. Their footwear line involves innovations in design as well as digital connectivity from the shoe to the UA fitness apps. Their Connected Fitness segment develops and markets fitness tracking technology and by the end of 2017 had almost 200 million users (Hyman 2017). In 2016 the company built the UA Lighthouse in Baltimore, Maryland, a state-of-the-art center for manufacturing and design innovation which in addition to providing the facilities for developing new products, will enable UA to venture into manufacturing some of its range in-house; and in 2017 the company established a biomechanics lab and training center for footwear design in Portland, Oregon (Under Armour 2018).

Business Problem

Although Under Armour has shown consistent revenue growth throughout its existence, there was a significant drop in the value of its stock both in 2016 and 2017 (LaMonica 2017). Analysts have said this may be due in part to company overexpenditure and overinvestment, but modest revenue growth from sales did not compensate for losses (Stock Board 2017). A security breach of customer data from the UA MyFitnessPal app in March 2018 may also have had a negative impact on the company's reputation (Lamkin 2018).

FIGURE 11.1 Under Armour Store, Causeway Bay, Hong Kong. Courtesy SOPA Images/LightRocket/Getty Images.

In fiscal year 2017 there was a 5 percent decrease in sales from the North American market which brings in 76 percent of the company's total net revenue. By contrast there was a marked increase of forty six percent in international revenues, particularly in the Asia Pacific market where revenues grew by sixty one percent. (Under Armour 2018). The company is heavily reliant on sales of products though sporting goods stores, so healthy sales in that sector are vital, but brand perception is one of the most significant factors in maintaining and increasing success across markets (Marketline 2017).

As of 2018, Under Armour ranks in the top four athletic apparel companies. The company's closest rivals are Puma and Adidas, with Nike as the top-selling worldwide sportswear brand by a significant margin (Patil 2018). Continuing growth with these sportswear giants as competitors is challenging. The athletic footwear market remains strong, but the competition in this segment of the market is widespread across many clothing and sports apparel brands. Online retailers such as Amazon pose a threat to UA's retail sales, and their focus on the fitness app market means they are also competing with tech companies producing online fitness services (Marketline 2017).

Since almost all of the company's products are manufactured outside the United States, the company may not be able to adequately oversee quality control and may face an increase in counterfeit products being supplied to the market which mimic the Under Armour logo and look. Intellectual property in materials and manufacturing technologies may be held by the suppliers, so new innovations could potentially be shared with competitors. Third party distributors and licensees may mean a further lack of control over the brand (Marketline 2017).

The key to the company's success may rest in having a solid position in the masstige market, yet low-priced products and the current widespread dissemination of Under Armour goods in discount retail outlets could either provide more exposure and thus opportunities for increased sales, or have the opposite effect and impact negatively on brand image. The company did enter the upscale athleisure market by creating the "UAS" range which debuted at New York Fashion Week in 2016 but few items from this line remain available (Kell 2016).

Under Armour promotes itself as a serious brand for athletes, yet they have lost popularity among both teens and upper-income adult males—presumably two of the company's strongest target markets (Green 2018). They continue to work with celebrity partners to raise the brand profile; however, there was a setback in the company's image when CEO Kevin Plank joined President Trump's Manufacturing Council in early 2017 (Plank resigned from the Council six months after joining) (LaMonica 2017). To continue growth, the company will need to successfully identify and cater to current and future customers. Anticipating the preferences of their target markets and conveying an image of brand prestige will be crucial factors in increasing sales both in North America and worldwide.

Business Questions

Imagine you are conducting research for a brand management consulting firm employed by Under Armour:

1. Identify one element in the development of the Under Armour brand which led to the company's success and describe why this element was important in building the brand image.

2. Consult the websites of Under Armour and one of its competitors (Adidas, Puma, or Nike). Take note of visual components such as logos, photography, models, color choices, product offerings, and differentiation of product lines, etc. Explore the functionality of the websites, especially in the area of online sales.
   - Describe the strengths of the Under Armour brand image.
   - How does it compare to the brand image of the competitor?
   - Which website would be more successful in generating online sales and why?

3. Research Under Armour's use of social media to promote the brand. In your opinion does Under Armour effectively use social media (consult Facebook, Twitter, Instagram, bloggers) to build brand communities? Can you find an "influencer" on social media who independently promotes the brand and are they convincing?

4. Create a "brand persona" for the company which you believe represents a typical UA customer. Give this persona a name and include a detailed description of appearance, gender, age, place of residence, activities, beliefs, favorite items of clothing, and preferred shopping habits, etc. Next, describe a second Under Armour persona who represents a new potential target market for the brand.

5. How could the company adjust the brand image to appeal to markets outside of North America? Use a specific country as an example. Suggest a celebrity representative who could increase the profile of the brand in that country and explain why they would be a strong ambassador for Under Armour.

6 Identify one element of the design, manufacturing, or distribution chain which could be adjusted to protect the brand or increase brand value. Explain how changes to this element might impact the brand.

7 Suggest a new product or design which would appeal to one of Under Armour's target markets and explain why you believe it aligns with the Under Armour image.

References and Further Reading

D'Arienzo, William. 2016. *Brand Management Strategies: Luxury and Mass Markets*. New York: Bloomsbury.

Funding Universe. 2004. "Under Armour Performance Apparel History." Accessed March 16, 2018. https://www.fundinguniverse.com/company-histories/under-armour-performance-apparel-history/

Green, Dennis. 2018. "Teens are Abandoning Under Armour in Droves—and it's Turning into a Huge Crisis for the Brand." *Business Insider*, April 10. Accessed May 31, 2018. https://www.businessinsider.com/teens-say-under-armour-isnt-cool-2018-4

Harrison, J. D. 2014. "When We were Small: Under Armour." *Washington Post*. November 12. Accessed March 16, 2018. https://www.washingtonpost.com/business/on-small-business/when-we-were-small-under-armour/2014/11/11/f61e8876-69ce-11e4-b053-65cea7903f2e_story.html?utm_term=.ba2793d9115c

Hyman, Tori. 2017. "Under Armour Connected Fitness Surpasses 200mm Registered Users." *Under Armour Connected Fitness Blog* (blog). Accessed March 14, 2018. http://advertising.underarmour.com/blog/under-armour-connected-fitness-surpasses-200mm-registered-users

Kell, John. 2016. "Why Under Armour Debuted a Collection at Fashion Week." *Fortune.com*, September 15. Accessed March 27, 2018. http://fortune.com/2016/09/15/under-armour-fashion-week-debut/

Lamkin, Paul. 2018. "Under Armour Admits Huge MyFitnessPal Data Hack." *Forbes.com*, March 28. Accessed April 30, 2018. https://www.forbes.com/sites/paullamkin/2018/03/30/under-armour-admits-huge-myfitnesspal-data-hack/#e81efb1cc54f

LaMonica, Paul R. 2017. "Under Armour had an Awful year. Will 2018 be Better?." *CNN Money*, December 13. Accessed March 14, 2018. http://money.cnn.com/2017/12/13/investing/under-armour-stock/index.html

MarketLine. 2017. "Under Armour, Inc. SWOT Analysis." *MarketLine Company Profiles*. Accessed March 30, 2018. http://0-search.ebscohost.com.library2.pima.edu/login.aspx?direct=true&db=buh&AN=124575677&site=bsi-live

Olson, Parmy. 2015. "Silicon Valley's Latest Threat: Under Armour." *Forbes.com*, September 30. Accessed March 14, 2018. https://www.forbes.com/sites/parmyolson/2015/09/30/kevin-plank-under-armour-apps-technology/#416f4d1619a9

Patil, Siddharth. 2018. "Sportswear Brand Wars 2017." LinkedIn, March 20. Accessed April 30, 2018. https://www.linkedin.com/pulse/sportswear-brand-wars-full-year-2017-results-analysis-patil

Stock Board Asset. 2017. "Under Armour Collapses. Meanwhile CEO Builds Elitist Hotel and Whiskey Distillery." (Blog). October 31. Accessed March 14, 2018. https://stockboardasset.com/blog/under-armour-collapses-ceo-dumps-stock-builds-elitist-hotel-and-whisky-distillery-now-attempts-to-build-5-5bn-city/

Under Armour. n.d. "It started with an idea." Accessed April 30, 2018. https://www.uabiz.com/company/history.cfm

Under Armour. 2018. "Under Armour 2017 Annual Report." Accessed May 15, 2018. http://investor.underarmour.com/annuals.cfm

Under Armour UK. n.d. "*Team*." Accessed April 30, 2018. https://www.underarmour.co.uk/en-gb/Roster.

Definitions

Athleisure: Athletic-style sportswear primarily designed for casual wear.

Brand development: The process of creating or modifying a brand. Elements of brand development could include creating products which represent the brand, creating a personality and story for the brand, building a target market for the brand, differentiating the brand from others in the market, and adjusting the brand to adapt to changes in the market.

Brand image: How a brand is represented. Brand image is influenced by factors such as how products are represented in advertising, the images of the target markets and consumers of the brand, the image of the company, and the brand's role in society.

Brand equity: Perception of the value of a brand. Factors which contribute to high brand equity could include consumer awareness of the brand, prestige of the brand, and positive associations with the brand such as a perception of quality, popularity, or high ethical standards associated with the brand.

Brand value: The financial value of the brand.

Brand persona: A fictional version of the typical or ideal consumer for the brand.

Intellectual property: Intangible intellectual assets such as copyright, trademarks, design rights, and patents.

Masstige: Goods which are reasonably priced and aimed at mass markets yet are perceived to have an element of prestige.

Net revenue: The amount of income from sales after costs and expenses have been paid.

Target market: A group which has been identified as probable customers of a brand.

Chapter 12

Brand Repositioning within the Fashion Industry

Jongeun Rhee and Kim K.P. Johnson

Customers and a brand both get older. Whereas some mature fashion brands successfully reinvent their offerings, others do not. Mature brands often fail to attract future generations of customers other than their initial target market segment and consequently lose revenue. It is critical for a fashion brand to constantly create and recreate relevant meanings as well as styles to maintain their appeal across generations. Brands that continue to appeal to young consumers maintain longevity while brands that do not can quickly become obsolete. This case provides an overview of the issues that a mature menswear brand could face. These issues include the importance of establishing and revising a target market segment, revitalizing a mature brand, brand repositioning, and the use of line extensions in the fashion industry. There are several approaches that could be taken to solve the problem of declining revenues. For example, the company could diversify the brand's portfolio with the addition of new product lines or remain a single brand with a unified product offering and a clear marketing message for its targeted customers. Students are expected to identify the best approach to strategically implement a marketing mix to maintain brand equity and profitability.

Learning Objectives

Upon completion of this case, students should be able to:

- Describe the menswear sector including history and trends.
- Identify the importance of revisiting and redefining a clear target market.
- Evaluate the pros and cons of brand repositioning to gain revenues.
- Evaluate pros and cons of a line extension strategy to gain revenues.

Introduction

Company history

The company that was to become Alexander Castiglione was established in the 1930s by tailor Gregorio Castiglione. The goal of this Naples-based tailor was to create imperfect clothing for imperfect bodies. To achieve this goal, he designed, cut, and sewed a jacket that was considered to be revolutionary for the times. He removed the internal padding, shoulder pads, and linings associated with contemporary men's suit coats and replaced them with a jacket that was as soft and lightweight as a shirt. This jacket came to be considered the epitome of fine dressing and attracted fashion-conscious young men as clients. Famous customers at the time Gregorio began his business included members of the British royal family.

Following in his father's footsteps, Gregorio's son Alexander worked alongside his father learning the techniques and methods to make the unstructured jacket. Alexander worked and studied in several fashion houses, eventually returning to a town on the outskirts of Naples to set up his own business, Alexander Castiglione, with his sons, Bartolomeo and Enzo. The company enjoyed a long-established reputation for making luxury menswear but began to lose market share as dressing casual for the workplace became the norm.

The return of formal menswear

In the early 1990s, Enzo Castiglione, one of Alexander's children and now the CEO of Alexander Castiglione, opened a flagship store in New York City. The Neapolitan styles the store offered were utterly new for the times as competitors offered traditional American or British style suits. American styles were conservatively cut and baggy. British styles were cut closely to the body but made using techniques that resulted in a stiff and sometimes uncomfortable silhouette that appealed to a limited number of customers. The initial target market for the store was fashion-conscious young men between the ages of twenty-five and thirty-five.

During this period, businessmen had begun to leave casual dressing in the workplace behind and the menswear market generated significant growth (Wang 2014). However, by the time that the accepted manner of dress for professional men shifted back to formal menswear, the Castiglione brand had lost touch with its stated target market, and Enzo Castiglione was concerned about the current and future revenue of the Castiglione brand.

During this same period, earnings had remained stagnant. Castiglione menswear had continued to target fashionable young men, but Enzo Castiglione questioned whether the company was actually meeting the needs of this consumer segment. To begin to identify causes for the lack of business growth, Mr. Castiglione visited its menswear flagship store in New York City.

Enzo Castiglione started his visit by reviewing the brand's product. The store was filled with common Castiglione styles, styles that had remained relatively unchanged for the past twenty-five years. The majority of suits and sport jackets were offered in very similar fabrics and color schemes. Only a few trendy styles were being promoted in the store's windows.

Next, he took notice of customers and the pricing strategy. Mr. Castiglione found most of the store's customers were in their late forties and older. Mr. Castiglione also noted that prices were slightly higher than the store's major competitors. Prices for the high-quality fabric that Castiglione insisted on using were increasing, offering an explanation for the higher suit cost. The sales associates were providing outstanding service. There were, however, smaller competing brands offering suits in a trendier cut at a lower price point. Was price alone the explanation for stagnant sales?

Mr. Castiglione decided to consult with a brand strategy and marketing consulting firm, Cambridge Consulting Ltd. The customer profiles, revenue, and market share metrics indicated by the firm were consistent with what he observed at the store. The results of a brand equity survey with a nationally representative sample demonstrated Castiglione's market share ranked third among men aged forty-five and older whereas Castiglione ranked fifteenth among millennials, their supposed target customer.

Even though their core customer is a young man, targeting men forty-five and older may not necessarily be a bad idea as these consumers represent an increasingly large and financially powerful part of the population worldwide and are consistently more brand-loyal than their younger counterparts (Lambert-Pandraud et al. 2005). Was the company marketing to the wrong consumer group?

Business Problem

Alexander Castiglione is a well-known Italian menswear brand that needs to rebrand and reinvent its product offerings to regain market share.

Alexander Castiglione has not gained any momentum with millennials even though young men are identified as their target market. Without building stronger support from this generation of consumers, Alexander Castiglione risks declining sales over time and eroding the brand equity that the company has spent decades building.

Market segmentation and a mature brand

A fully and clearly defined target market is important in brand positioning. A target market details everything about the ideal customer of a brand from their demographic characteristics (e.g. age, income, and education) to her/his lifestyle (e.g. nutrition related habits and alcohol use). To build a target market, a company visualizes their core customer. The core customer is the ideal customer of a brand; the individual who is most likely to buy the product offerings of the brand and earn the most benefits. Targeting a specific market does not mean that a brand is excluding people who do not fit the established criteria. Rather, segmented target marketing allows a brand to focus its marketing expenses and marketing communications on the specific market of people that is most likely to purchase. This approach is an effective allocation of marketing resources and an efficient way to reach potential clients to generate business.

Although one could argue that all brands are aging, an aging brand signifies that the brand has experienced a systematic decline in popularity (correspondingly a decline in sales) over a long period of time. One approach to managing a mature brand is to discontinue it. And this could be a viable option as the marketing report indicated that Alexander Castiglione had not gained any momentum with millennials. This is an important consumer segment as the millennial generation is the largest group of potential brand consumers in history; significantly larger than even the baby-boomer generation. Failure to build a connection and customer base with this consumer group, in the long term, means Alexander Castiglione will face declining sales as well as an erosion of the brand's equity as the brand will generate revenues solely from its existing customers who are loyal but declining in numbers.

Brand repositioning and line extensions in the fashion industry

Moving forward, Mr. Castiglione and the management team envisage several options:

1 Keeping Castiglione's original target market and developing effective strategies to create connections relevant to their initial designated target customer (men twenty-five to thirty-five years old);

2 Repositioning the Castiglione brand as a strong luxury brand and offering lines to appeal to both their current loyal customers and to millennials; or

3 Repositioning the Castiglione brand to target their current customer (men forty-five years of age and older) and launching a line extension, E. Castiglione, targeting fashion-forward millennials.

A line extension would enable leveraging the Castiglione name. Mr. Enzo Castiglione needs to evaluate the size and potential growth of the menswear market and decide whether the market opportunity is momentous enough for this type of investment. The decision must come after an assessment of how Castiglione's existing resources could be effectively utilized.

Brand and line extensions in the fashion industry proliferated from the 1990s to the early 2000s. Brand managers, even managers of a luxury brand, often try to sell something to everyone to maximize their sales revenue. For example, the luxury brand Giorgio Armani extended its brand portfolio to appeal to all consumers who were fashion-conscious regardless of their age or income. Armani's extensions were mostly downward making Armani accessible to new segments of their primary target market. Similarly, many other luxury fashion brands aggressively extended their brand and line portfolios. Examples include Dolce and Gabbana, Calvin Klein, Ralph Lauren, Burberry, Hugo Boss, and Mark Jacobs. The increased revenues generated by the branded line extensions seemed to contribute to shareholder value when the economy was expanding. In contrast, as the economy went through a downturn, the brands went through significant changes. They consolidated their expanded brand portfolios. For example, all the brands noted previously simplified; Burberry and Mark Jacobs became single unified brands without any sub-brands.

In contrast to taking the line extension approach, there are luxury fashion brands that effectively target both young and old clientele: Gucci, Balenciaga, and Chanel. These companies focus on high return on investment through efficient use of existing resources rather than developing competition within their brands. What are the implications for Mr. Enzo Castiglione? Is a single unified brand approach the right direction for him to take?

Business Questions

- Given that older customers are more brand loyal than younger customers, to what extent should Alexander Castiglione continue to identify young men as the core target market for the menswear business? Who should be the core customer for the brand?

- Why is a continued review of the core customer of a brand important?

- The brand's promise is to be a menswear business that offers contemporary suits to fashion conscious men. In addition to thinking about who the core customer of the brand is, what else should Castiglione be considering to move the brand forward and gain market share? How did the brand lose its relevancy to its core customer?

- Some well-established apparel brands successfully revitalize their brands while others vanish. What do those apparel brands that successfully revitalize do that the other brands do not?
- There were three options that Mr. Castiglione was contemplating: (1) Keeping Castiglione's initial designated target customer (men twenty-five to thirty-five years old) and developing a relevant marketing mix for them; (2) Repositioning the Castiglione brand as one strong luxury brand and offering lines to appeal to both their current loyal customers and to millennials; or (3) Repositioning the Castiglione brand to target their loyal customers (men forty-five years of age and older) and launching a line extension, E. Castiglione, targeting fashion forward millennials. What are the advantages and disadvantages of each option?

References and Further Reading

Lambert-Pandraud, Raphaëlle, Gilles Laurent, and Eric Lapersonne. 2005. "Repeat Purchasing of New Automobiles By Older Consumers: Empirical Evidence and Interpretations." *Journal of Marketing* 69, no. 2 (April): 97–113.
Phan Michel, Ricarda Thomas, and Klaus Heine. 2011. "Social Media and Luxury Brand Management: The Case of Burberry." *The Journal of Global Fashion Marketing* 2, no. 4: 213–222.
Wang, Lisa. 2014. "No Signs of Slowing in the Global Menswear Market." *Business of Fashion*, July 14. Accessed July 10, 2018. https://www.businessoffashion.com/articles/fashion-show-review/signs-slowing-global-menswear-market

Definitions

Mature brand: A brand that has lost its ability to differentiate from competitors. It has no perceived competitive advantage and thus, loses equity.
Brand extension: A marketing strategy that consists of using an established brand name to launch a product line in a different product category.
Line extension: A marketing strategy that consists of using an established brand name to launch a product line in the same product category.
Return on investment (ROI): A measure of the profitability of an investment relative to the amount of money invested. It is typically reported as a percentage. A high ROI is interpreted as signaling the investment's gains compare favorably to its costs.
Segmented target market: A distinct set of consumers defined and divided into identifiable segments that have similar demographics, psychographics, geography, or other attributes.
Target market: Consumers who are most likely to buy the products and services of a brand and to earn the most benefits.

Chapter 13

H&M Under Attack

How Greenpeace Threatened a Brand's Reputation in Sustainability

Rosanne P. Hart and Camille Kraeplin

When Greenpeace launched online and on-site protests against H&M for water pollution in H&M's Chinese supply-chain factories in 2011, the fashion brand faced serious damage to its reputation as a leader in sustainability alongside plummeting sales. Despite over a dozen other apparel and footwear companies being singled out in Greenpeace's global "detox" fashion campaign, the nongovernmental organization (NGO) specifically targeted H&M, a Swedish company with more than $18 billion in sales in 2011 and 2,500 stores globally. Greenpeace pressured H&M with shock-provoking tactics such as by stationing a naked man in front of an H&M store, splashing store windows with "detox" graffiti, and creating aggressive social media posts on Twitter and Facebook.

This case critically analyzes the factors that precipitated Greenpeace's protests and activist communications tactics against H&M and considers the effectiveness of H&M's response from crisis communications and corporate social responsibility (CSR) perspectives.

Students will explore the progression of the Greenpeace detox campaign, and how and why they targeted H&M. Students will then be challenged to determine the best communications strategy for H&M to address Greenpeace's reputational threats.

Learning Objectives

Upon completion of this case, students should be able to:

- Understand how a globally executed social media campaign can threaten a powerhouse fashion brand's corporate reputation.

- Determine the importance of timing in responding to negative publicity as part of a corporate reputation management strategy.
- Define CSR and the important role it plays in brand reputation.
- Evaluate the ethics of the tactics that Greenpeace used in its environmental activism strategies and executed globally against targeted companies.

Introduction

Despite its glamorous image, the fashion industry is regarded as one the worst environmental offenders, particularly in the case of water pollution caused by wastewater discharge in textile processes. The industry has sustained numerous public relations crises, from the sweatshop revelations in Nike's supply chain in Southeast Asia in the 1990s, to the 2013 collapse of a Bangladesh factory that killed over 1,000 people, many of them contract garment workers for companies including Joe Fresh, Gap, and JCPenney. In another famous case, as part of a much-hyped "detox" campaign, Greenpeace exposed what they perceived as inconsistencies between the values H&M espoused and actual practice, weakening H&M's reputation as a leader in sustainability and a champion of the environment. Furthermore, Greenpeace's social media tactics intentionally targeted H&M's core social-media-savvy young customers, leading to a PR crisis for the international fashion brand.

In July 2011, Greenpeace launched its detox fashion campaign after identifying international apparel and footwear brands in the first of two "Dirty Laundry" reports. The first report revealed that hazardous chemicals had been found in the wastewater from two Chinese textile companies that were linked to international fashion brands. That polluted wastewater was being dumped into the Yangtze and Pearl River deltas—important drinking water sources for millions of Chinese people (Greenpeace International 2011e). At the time, the polluted wastewater discharge violated China's environmental laws (*The Huffington Post* 2012), however, these laws regarding water pollution by Chinese factories were lax and ineffective (NDRC 2010, 3) and did not regulate or mandate against specific harmful chemicals (Greenpeace International 2011b, 8).

Greenpeace's July 2011 report identified major fashion companies—including Adidas, Nike, and Puma—all of whom quickly took up the challenge to detox or eliminate hazardous chemicals from their supply chains after Greenpeace's public protests. Within a month, all three brands had responded to Greenpeace's call for "zero discharge of hazardous chemicals" (ZDHC) (Greenpeace International 2017b). The fast-fashion brand H&M, however, responded to Greenpeace's first report by denying that its products were connected to the polluting textile facilities. The company consequently came under heavy fire for water pollution caused by its Chinese contractors, especially after Greenpeace published its follow-up report *Dirty Laundry 2* on August 23, 2011.

It is important to note that H&M does not own any of its factories, but sets environmental and sustainability standards for production of H&M products by its Chinese contractors. Despite H&M's denial in its first response and statement of support for Greenpeace's efforts to eliminate harmful chemicals from wastewater discharges, H&M was again identified in the second Dirty Laundry report, which linked toxic chemicals to clothing made near the Yangtze and Pearl rivers.

Dirty Laundry 2 tested seventy-eight garments from fifteen fashion brands including Nike, Adidas, and Puma, which had already developed plans to detox their supply chains after the first Dirty Laundry report.

This second report found fifty-eight clothing items from fourteen of the fifteen fashion brands contained chemicals called NPEs or nonylphenol ethoxylates. Typically used in textile production, NPEs break down into a toxic, persistent, hormone-disrupting chemical called nonylphenol or NP when released in wastewater. NPs build up in the food chain and are hazardous even at very low levels (Greenpeace International 2011c, para 6). NPs have also been found in human tissue (Greenpeace International 2011c, 12). Four of the six H&M garments tested contained NPEs above Greenpeace research lab's limit of detection, which is "1 mg. NPE per kilogram of material" (Greenpeace International 2011c, para 6). One month after the *Dirty Laundry 2* report, H&M still had not responded to Greenpeace's challenge to commit to a ZDHC program.

Greenpeace is a powerful NGO with 2.8 million members worldwide whose activists expose damage and "threats to the environment" in a "peaceful, non-violent manner" (Greenpeace International 2017a). With offices in more than fifty countries, Greenpeace addresses environmental issues including the pollution of human water sources.

H&M became a target of Greenpeace's pressure tactics for several reasons. Firstly, the company failed to respond in a timely manner to the second Dirty Laundry report and waited almost thirty days after publication of the report to address Greenpeace's findings (Greenpeace International 2017b).

According to crisis communication expert W. Timothy Coombs, H&M's position in the industry was a second factor. "Greenpeace made H&M a priority target because it is the largest clothing company appearing in its Dirty Laundry Report" (Coombs 2014, 235).

Finally, a strong ideology for H&M is that it will provide "fashion and quality at the best price in a sustainable way" (HM.com). H&M's disposal of harmful chemicals into drinking water directly violated this principle; Greenpeace thus sought to educate H&M's socially conscious target market, millennials (Nielsen.com 2015), through the viral medium of social media. Through aggressive social media tactics, Greenpeace hoped to discredit H&M's supposed core beliefs in the eyes of their core social-media-savvy young consumers, and thus hopefully discourage them from shopping there.

H&M was an $18 billion fast-fashion powerhouse in 2011 with more than 2,000 stores across forty countries. It was also one of the earliest proponents of sustainability and had a ten-year track record for inspecting supplier factories. Greenpeace believed that if H&M would lead with a commitment to ZDHC, smaller fashion companies would follow. From a public relations perspective, the *Dirty Laundry 2* report represented a threat to H&M's leadership position in sustainability, as well as its fashion reputation with socially conscious millennials. As a result of Greenpeace's attacks, H&M's CSR reputation and its leadership in sustainability were called into question, particularly because the company waited two months after the first Dirty Laundry report to support Greenpeace's detox campaign as Nike, Adidas, and Puma had done early on.

Business Problem

Greenpeace and the dirty laundry reports

Greenpeace was founded in 1971 to protest against US nuclear testing on the Alaskan coast. Since then, Greenpeace has become a powerful international group with some three million supporters whose mission is to "save the planet" from environmental threats (Greenpeace International 2017a).

"We bear witness to environmental destruction in a peaceful and non-violent manner," reads the Greenpeace.org website. The organization advocates the use of nonviolent confrontation methods to raise awareness and generate "public debate" (Greenpeace International 2017a).

Greenpeace released its first Dirty Laundry report—*Dirty Laundry: Unraveling the Corporate Connections to Toxic Water Pollution*—on July 12, 2011. The study focused on analysis of wastewater in China, the world's largest clothing exporter (Lu 2015). It investigated wastewater discharge from two Chinese factories, Youngor Textile Complex, on the Yangtze River Delta, and Well Dyeing Factory Limited, located on a Pearl River Delta tributary. Greenpeace's research revealed hazardous chemicals from these factories' textile-manufacturing processes were flowing into these rivers that provide drinking water for millions of Chinese people (Greenpeace International 2011e).

A May 2011 Greenpeace study revealed that twenty million people living in sixteen cities (including Shanghai) across the Yangtze River Delta depend on the river for their drinking water (Greenpeace International 2011e).

During the first Dirty Laundry study in 2011, "hazardous and persistent chemicals with hormone-disrupting properties" were found in the wastewater samples (Greenpeace International 2011b). Greenpeace notified all companies included in the first Dirty Laundry report a month before its release, offering them an opportunity to respond. Most did, citing their own CSR initiatives that stressed sustainability and environmental initiatives. Greenpeace argued that the brands didn't have a comprehensive plan to manage the release of toxic chemicals into the two rivers and needed to commit to ZDHC. As a result, Greenpeace challenged big brands, such as Nike, Adidas, Puma, and H&M, to join them as "champions for a post-toxic world by eliminating all releases of hazardous chemicals from their supply chains and products" (Greenpeace International 2011b).

H&M, as well as other fashion companies listed in the report, replied to Greenpeace that they did not use the "wet processes of the Youngor Group" (Greenpeace International 2011b). H&M's letter specifically denied using the two textile facilities guilty of discharging wastewater with toxic chemicals and referenced H&M's most recent sustainability report detailing its management of water throughout its supply chain (Greenpeace International 2011b, 2011f). H&M's letter also stressed its attention since 2003 to water pollution resulting from garment manufacturing and noted that beginning in 2006 it required textile suppliers to treat all wastewater (Greenpeace International 2011b; Helmersson 2011). The letter was written by Helena Helmersson, head of H&M's CSR department. Based on Greenpeace's reaction Helmersson's letter did little to satisfy them, as H&M would soon become a target for Greenpeace's high-pressure tactics.

Greenpeace initiated a second study in August that analyzed clothing samples produced by the two Chinese factories. The findings were released in *Dirty Laundry 2*, with the impact to consumers noted in its conclusions:

major clothing brands are making their consumers unwitting contributors to increasing levels of hazardous nonylphenols in the environment and water bodies of countries where the products are purchased, as the washing of these clothing items can release residual levels of NPEs contained within the apparel, into the sewage systems. (Greenpeace International 2011c)

H&M's global reputation

H&M, founded in 1947 in Sweden, is one of the world's largest and fastest-growing clothing retailers offering "fashion and quality at the best price" (HM.com 2008, "Our Responsibility"). H&M keenly understands its target market—"the low-price, high-fashion end of the clothing sector" (Muran 2007). H&M particularly appeals to younger women who comprise its primary consumer base. The company helped pioneer "fast fashion" (comments from Ingrid Schullstrom, manager of CSR; HM.com 2008, "Our Responsibilty")—clothing styles based on runway shows that can be manufactured quickly, are popularly priced, and focus on the mainstream consumer. It enjoyed a loyal following with its wide range of on-trend clothing at "attractive prices," all delivered frequently to its stores in "prime shopping locations." As an $18 billion global fashion leader, H&M was an early adopter of CSR initiatives. In 2008, the company launched a new CSR strategy, including a sustainability vision that stated: "We … have adopted a preventative approach with the substitution of hazardous chemicals." H&M pledged that water would be one of the company's primary sustainability concerns geared toward improving suppliers' efficient use of water and their treatment of polluted water. Three years after this report, H&M would see its CSR efforts and clean-water-focused initiatives questioned as a result of Greenpeace's detox campaign. For H&M, "the campaign represented a threat to its reputation as an industry leader in sustainability, a crisis communications situation that could potentially turn its fashion-savvy customers against them" (Hart 2016).

Greenpeace's pressure tactics

Prior to targeting H&M for protests and social media attacks, Greenpeace exerted negative online communications tactics and on-site demonstrations to pressure Nike and Adidas following the initial Dirty Laundry report. Greenpeace's actions ranged from organizing flash mobs to staging a giant human "Detox" banner on a Thailand riverbank, to coordinating a naked protest with 600 people outside Nike and Adidas stores worldwide (Greenpeace International 2017b). By September 2011, H&M still had not responded to the detox campaign. Greenpeace decided it was time to take H&M to task as well. A provocative feature story, published on September 13, 2011, on Greenpeace.org, accused H&M of selling clothing made with "chemicals which cause hazardous water pollution around the world" (Greenpeace International 2011g). Greenpeace urged H&M to use its position as one of the world's largest clothing companies to "come clean" and commit to a "toxic-free future" (Greenpeace International 2011g) a gesture that would encourage other fashion brands to follow suit. The Greenpeace story emphasized that H&M's "reputation as an industry leader in sustainability is on the line" (Greenpeace International 2011g). Readers were asked to sign a petition on Twitter by retweeting Greenpeace's post: "Retweet to sign petition @HM needs to #Detox! Hazardous chemicals are so last season! #fashion #water http://act.ly/484 (Greenpeace International 2011g).

Simultaneously, Greenpeace launched social media attacks on Facebook and Twitter, posting on Facebook on September 13, 2011, that "H&M are one of the world's largest clothing companies, and they are TOX-IC! They're rushing out the latest fashions, let's see if they can be fast to catch up to commitments from Nike, Adidas, and Puma to detox their supply chains?" (Hart 2016). Greenpeace's strategic use of social media targeted H&M's Facebook audience of 8.75 million fans and more than 635,000 Twitter followers and thousands more with 1,200 petition retweets (Coombs 2014, 235). The effort sparked posts on H&M's Twitter and Facebook sites commenting on and questioning H&M's support of the detox campaign. Greenpeace added fuel to the detox fire by holding on-site protests in twelve countries, plastering large green "Detox the future" stickers across H&M store windows and even staging a sit-in protest featuring a naked man in front of an H&M store.

H&M waited a full week after the on-site protests and social media storm to address Greenpeace's demands. They chose instead to post Helmersson's blogged rebuttal on H&M's website on September 13, 2011, countering charges in Greenpeace's story. Helmersson indicated she was "surprised and disappointed" by the article, and reiterated H&M's concern for the environment and its reputation as a "conscious company" (Dubsky 2011). The following day, Greenpeace.org published a letter from Martin Hojsik, head of the detox campaign, responding to Helmersson's post by challenging the company's sixty-day delay joining the detox campaign after campaign leaders reached out early to H&M. Hojsik acknowledged how Greenpeace and H&M had collaborated in the past on European legislation regarding hazardous chemicals and efforts to seek "safer alternatives" (Dubsky 2011). However, Greenpeace's letter indicated that hazardous chemicals found in H&M garments and the lack of disclosure regarding the chemicals used in H&M factories and the toxic wastewater they discharged were key issues H&M needed to address. "What exactly does H&M have to hide?" asked Hojsik (Dubsky 2011). The letter ended by warning H&M that until they recognized "the problems your insufficient chemical management policies are causing for people and wildlife in China and elsewhere, we will keep reminding you" (Dubsky 2011). It was clear Hojsik was implying that reminders would include continued social media barrages and on-site protests outside H&M stores.

FIGURE 13.1 Greenpeace activists apply "Detox" banners across an H&M store window in H&M's headquarters' city, Stockholm. Photo courtesy Ludvig Tillman/Greenpeace.

H&M's response

Finally, following a meeting between Greenpeace and H&M at the company's Stockholm headquarters, Greenpeace published a press release on September 20, 2011, proclaiming, "Fast fashion retail giant H&M committed yesterday to eliminate the use of hazardous chemicals from all production processes associated with the manufacture of its products by 2020." Greenpeace credited its pressure tactics for solidifying H&M's support (Greenpeace International 2011d). H&M also agreed to publish a restricted substance list of all chemicals released from its supplier factories on the H&M website in October. The company promised that a more detailed list of the quantities of hazardous chemicals being discharged and the facilities responsible would be released online by the end of 2012 (Greenpeace International 2011a). Greenpeace both lauded and marginalized H&M's actions, calling them "just the first step" (Greenpeace International 2011a). Greenpeace wanted more and implied that pressure would be applied to other brands that did not act quickly to detox their supply chains. "Who's going to wait to be called out by fans for committing the latest fashion faux pas?" Greenpeace asked in a September 20 blog post. Touting its success in pressuring H&M, Greenpeace warned it would be watching closely to ensure H&M lived up to its detox commitment.

H&M's PR crisis

Throughout the detox campaign, Greenpeace's on-site and social media tactics exposed what they perceived as inconsistencies between the values H&M espoused and actual practice, weakening H&M's reputation as a leader in sustainability and a champion of the environment. Coombs posits that "social media is responsible for the growing link between crisis communication/management and the online world" primarily because social media users control content and its distribution (Coombs 2012, 21). Greenpeace and H&M were well aware H&M had more to lose than its CSR credibility; it faced losing the business of its predominantly female millennial consumers who aligned with its socially responsible values of sustainability and commitment to environmentally friendly production processes. A recent Nielsen study confirmed the importance of corporate social responsibility among millennials in purchasing decisions, with almost three-out-of-four respondents under the age of thirty-four stating they would pay extra for brands "committed to positive social and environmental impact" (Nielsen 2015, 16). Furthermore, Grace Farraj, senior vice president for public development and sustainability at Nielsen, commented: "Brands that establish a reputation for environmental stewardship among today's youngest consumers have an opportunity to not only grow market share but build loyalty among the power-spending millennials of tomorrow, too" (Nielsen.com 2015).

For H&M to continue to ignore Greenpeace's demands for H&M to do more to detox its supply chain than its current supplier Code of Conduct and factory audits, clearly posed a danger to its healthy revenue growth.

Greenpeace's social media barrage and global on-site protests disrupted traffic into H&M stores worldwide and generated negative sentiment on its Twitter and Facebook sites, resulting in a public relations crisis for the brand. Coombs points out that "negative online comments can threaten valuable reputational assets" of an organization (2012, 21). A more serious concern for H&M was the "threat to its reputation associated with the norms and values cherished by society, and socially expected obligations," according to crisis communications scholars Y. J. Sohn and Ruthann Weaver Lariscy (2014, 25). Water is an

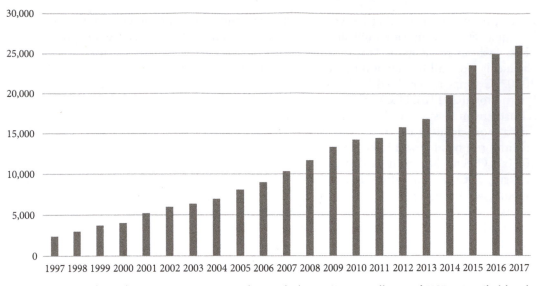

FIGURE 13.2 Chart showing H&M gross sales (including VAT) in millions of USD compiled by the authors from H&M's annual reports, 1997–2017 (Conversion from SEK to USD accurate as of August 2018).

essential life source to be managed and protected by society. Because clean water is at the crux of Greenpeace's detox campaign, Sohn and Lariscy's statement (2014) validates the severity of H&M's reputational crisis.

With its history of sustainability practices and launch of a designated CSR program in 2008, H&M aligned with many of Greenpeace's environmental goals. By waiting until Greenpeace had launched an intense global communications campaign to meet with Greenpeace representatives about the detox campaign, H&M defied prudent crisis communication and reputation management practices. Helmersson was clearly caught off-guard by Greenpeace's tactics, as she believed that H&M and Greenpeace shared similar environmental values and maintained a positive industry relationship.

How would a crisis communication strategy have helped H&M avoid the public relations crisis and reputational threat posed by Greenpeace's online and on-site attacks? Although H&M's 2011 revenues did not appear to be significantly affected by the crisis, the company's annual report stated that 2011 profits declined by 3 percent and earnings per share dropped 15 percent from the prior year (HM.com 2011b).

Business Questions

1 What impact does a company's corporate reputation have on its overall business and customers' perceptions of the company?

2 How did Greenpeace's tactics threaten H&M's corporate reputation?

3 Do you think a CSR program is more important today than ever for fashion brands? Why or why not?

4 What do you think were H&M's reasons for failing to immediately support the Greenpeace detox campaign?

5 How would you advise your CEO to respond to negative publicity around environmental violations by a key Chinese contractor that was critical to your fashion production processes?

6 Did Greenpeace ethically go too far in their communications tactics that targeted H&M because they were the world's largest clothing retailer included in the "Dirty Laundry" reports?

Epilogue

H&M's annual report for 2012 demonstrates the company going above and beyond the requests of Greenpeace's detox campaign in order to eliminate harmful chemical waste in fashion industry manufacturing supply chains by 2020. H&M joined the UN's CEO Water Mandate, committed to reporting its own and its suppliers' efficiency in water use and treatment, made public its entire supplier list of factories, and adopted strict chemical restrictions that forbid using some substances and limited others (HM.com 2013). In 2013, H&M teamed up with the World Wildlife Fund (WWF) to implement a cutting-edge water strategy, and began working closely with the Institute of Public and Environmental Affairs in China, which reports on discharge violations (Hau 2013).

H&M's efforts are particularly notable because it does not own any factories and remains dependent on its overseas contractors to comply with governmental regulations and H&M's environmental and sustainability standards. "It is impossible to be in full control," says Helmersson in a 2012 article for *The Guardian* (Siegle 2012).

In 2016, H&M was lauded by Greenpeace. Most recently a H&M news article dated July 12, 2018, on H&M's website stated, "The latest report from Greenpeace praises the progress and achievements of committed companies, like H&M group, on key areas such as water, chemicals and circularity" (HM.com 2018).

Prior classroom use of the H&M case study in the media and the business of fashion class for SMU's journalism/fashion media majors, and elements of Hart's master's research paper on H&M were incorporated into class lectures on apparel industry supply chain management, and sustainability and CSR programs implemented by fashion companies.

References and Further Reading

Burns, Leslie D., Kathy K. Mullet, and Nancy O. Bryant. 2016. *The Business of Fashion: Designing, Manufacturing & Marketing*, 5th edn. New York: Fairchild Books.

Coombs, W. Timothy. 2012. "Effects of the Online World on Crisis Communication and Crisis Management." In *Ongoing Crisis Communication*, pp. 19–29. Thousand Oaks, CA: Sage Publishing.

Coombs, W. Timothy. 2014. "Greenpeace Pressures H&M to Detox the Garment Industry." In *Applied Crisis Communications and Crisis Management*, pp. 229–238. Thousand Oaks, CA: Sage Publishing.

Dubsky Eion. 2011. "H&M can do much better," Greenpeace.org (blog), September 14. Accessed May 27, 2018. https://www.greenpeace.org/archive-international/en/news/Blogs/makingwaves/hm-can-do-much-better/blog/36793/

Greenpeace International. 2011a. "Big Brands Like H&M are Listening to You." (blog), October 26. Accessed May 23, 2018. https://www.greenpeace.org/archive-international/en/news/Blogs/makingwaves/big-brands-like-hm-are-listening-to-you/blog/37524/

Greenpeace International. 2011b. *Dirty Laundry: Unraveling the Corporate Connections to to Toxic Water Pollution*. Executive Summary. July 12. Accessed May 23, 2018. https://www.greenpeace. org/archive-international/en/publications/reports/Dirty-Laundry/

Greenpeace International. 2011c. *Dirty Laundry 2: Hung Out to Dry: Unraveling the Toxic Trail From Pipes to Products*. Executive Summary. August 23. Accessed June 1, 2018. https://www. greenpeace.org/archive-international/en/publications/reports/Dirty-Laundry-2/

Greenpeace International. 2011d. "H&M's Detox Commitment Set To Be This Season's Hottest Fashion Trend." September 20. Accessed May 27, 2018. https://www.greenpeace.org/eastasia/press/ releases/toxics/2011/hm-detox-chemicals-production/

Greenpeace International. 2011e. "Hidden Consequences: The Costs of Industrial Water Pollution on People, Planet and Profits." May 25. Accessed June 13, 2018. https://www.greenpeace.org/archive-international/en/publications/reports/Hidden-Consequences/

Greenpeace International. 2011f. "Response from Hennes & Mauritz regarding Youngor Group Co., Ltd." June 20. Accessed June 1, 2018. https://www.greenpeace.org/international/Global/international/ publications/toxics/Water%202011/detox-company-replies/20110720%20letter%20H-M.pdf

Greenpeace International. 2011g. "Will H&M Make 'Detox' The New Must-have?" September 13. Accessed June 13, 2018. https://www.greenpeace.org/seasia/ph/News/news-stories/hm-detox/

Greenpeace International. 2012. *Toxic Threads: The Big Fashion Stitch-Up*. Accessed July 21, 2018. https://www.greenpeace.org/archive-international/Global/international/publications/toxics/ Water%202012/ToxicThreads01.pdf

Greenpeace International. 2017a. "About Greenpeace." Accessed May 27, 2018. https://www. greenpeace.org/international/values/

Greenpeace International. 2017b. "Detox My Fashion." Accessed May 23, 2018. https://www. greenpeace.org/archive-international/en/campaigns/detox/timeline/

Hart, Rosanne P. 2016. "H&M Detoxes: Analyzing a Fashion Brand's CSR Reputational Crisis from a Crisis Communications Theoretical Perspective." MA diss., Kent State University.

Hau, Claire. 2013. "H&M: Water Stewardship in Fashion." *Chinawaterrisk.org*, April 9. Accessed July 21, 2018. https://www.chinawaterrisk.org/opinions/hm-water-stewardship-for-fashion/

Helmersson, Helen. 2011. "Response from Hennes & Mauritz Regarding Youngor Group Ltd." *Propertibazar*, June 20. Accessed June 13, 2018. https://propertibazar.com/article/response-from-hennes-mauritz-regarding-youngor-group-co-ltd_5ae2f1d2d64ab2361ce83043.html

HM.com. 2008. *Part I. H&M In Words & Pictures 2008*. Accessed June 13, 2018. https:// sustainability.hm.com/content/dam/hm/about/documents/en/Annual%20Report/Annual_ Report_2008_p1_en.pdf

HM.com. 2011a. *Annual Report Part 1 H&M in Words and Pictures 2011*. Accessed May 28, 2018. https://about.hm.com/content/dam/hmgroup/groupsite/documents/en/Annual%20Report/Annual_ Report_2011_P1_en.pdf

HM.com. 2011b. *Annual Report Part 2, H&M in Figures*. Accessed June 10, 2018. https://about. hm.com/content/dam/hmgroup/groupsite/documents/masterlanguage/Annual%20Report/Annual_ Report_2011_P2.pdf

HM.com. 2013. *Annual Report 2012*. March 21. Accessed June 10, 2018. https://about.hm.com/ content/dam/hmgroup/groupsite/documents/en/Annual%20Report/Annual-Report-2012_en.pdf.

H&M.com. 2016. "Quality in Focus." Accessed June 10, 2018. https://about.hm.com/en/about-us/in-focus/quality-in-focus.html

HM.com. 2018. "H&M Group praised by Greenpeace for leading the way on responsible water and chemicals management." July 12. Accessed July 22, 2018. https://about.hm.com/en/media/news/ general-news-2018/hm-group-at-greenpeace-report.html

Lu, Sheng. 2015. "Five Key Trends in World Textile and Apparel Trade." *Sheng Lu Fashion*, October 16. Accessed June 13, 2018. https://shenglufashion.files.wordpress.com/2016/07/five-key-trends-in-world-textile-and-apparel-trade.pdf

Muran, L. 2007. "Profile of H&M A Pioneer of Fast Fashion." Researchgate. Accessed September 12, 2018. https://www.researchgate.net/publication/298670045_Profile_of_HM_A_pioneer_of_fast_ fashion

Nielsen.com. 2015. "Green Generation: Millennials Say Sustainability Is A Shopping Priority." November 5. Accessed June 11, 2018. https://www.nielsen.com/us/en/insights/news/2015/green-generation-millennials-say-sustainability-is-a-shopping-priority.html

Nielsen. 2015. "The Sustainability Imperative: New Insights on Consumer Expectations." October. Accessed June 22, 2018. https://www.nielsen.com/content/dam/nielsenglobal/dk/docs/global-sustainability-report-oct-2015.pdf

NDRC. 2010. "Clean By Design: Revolutionizing The Global Textile Industry." March 23. Accessed May 23, 2018. https://www.nrdc.org/resources/clean-design-revolutionizing-global-textile-industry

Pratt, Cornelius B. 2012. "Theoretical Approaches To And Sociological Perspectives In Crisis Communications." In *Case Studies in Crisis Communications*, edited by Amiso M. George and Cornelius B. Pratt, pp. 3–27. New York: Routledge.

Siegle, Lucy. 2012. "Is H&M the New Home of Ethical Fashion?" *The Guardian*, April 7. Accessed May 31, 2018. https://www.theguardian.com/business/2012/apr/07/hennes-mauritz-h-and-m

Sohn, Y. J. and Ruthann Weaver Lariscy. 2014. "Understanding Reputational Crisis: Definitions, Properties and Consequences." *Journal of Public Relations Research* 26 (1): 23–43.

The Huffington Post. 2012. *Major Retailer's Contribute to Severe Water Pollution in China: Report.* April 23. Accessed July 20, 2018. https://www.huffingtonpost.com/2012/04/23/china-water-pollution-fashion-textile-factories_n_1445766.html

ZDHC Foundation. 2017. "About." Accessed June 12, 2018. https://www.roadmaptozero.com/about/

Definitions

Corporate social responsibility (CSR): "A philosophy whereby a company takes into consideration human rights, labor conditions, and environmental implications when making business decisions" (Burns et al. 2016, 349).

Crisis communication: A crisis is broadly defined by public relations and communication scholars as "unexpected events that engender unwholesome outcomes" for the organization (Pratt 2012, 6). Crisis communication refers to communication strategies and tactics that are designed to address the crisis and mitigate any damage to the organization's reputation.

Sustainability: A complex term that is defined from an environmental science perspective as "the quality of not being harmful to the environment or depleting natural resources, and thereby supporting long-term ecological balance" (Dictionary.com).

ZDHC: ZDHC refers to zero discharge of hazardous chemicals as well as to the nonprofit ZDHC Roadmap to Zero Programme formed in 2011 by major fashion brands to promote zero discharge of hazardous chemicals—or provide safe substitutes—within the textile, apparel, and footwear "value chain" or product life cycle. According to the ZDHC.com website, "Our mission is to advance towards zero discharge of hazardous chemicals in the textile, leather and footwear value chain to improve the environment and people's well being."

Chapter 14

"D&G Go Home Now!"

Cultural Sensitivities, Local Awareness, and Customer Relations for Luxury Brands Operating Overseas

Anne Peirson-Smith

This case investigates the controversy surrounding the luxury Italian brand Dolce & Gabbana's (D&G) response to a customer incident in Hong Kong in early January 2012, as a way of highlighting the need for forward planning to prepare organizations to deal with an unexpected incident. The case identifies a range of issues for luxury brands expanding into the Asia Pacific region, including the protection of a brand's intellectual property, awareness of, and accommodation to local cultural sensitivities and cultural alignment in strategic brand management. It also examines how a fashion brand, due to poor customer care and lack of stakeholder awareness, found itself at the center of a much wider sociocultural concern in the territory, given the new spending power and increasing presence of the emerging Chinese consumer. Initially Hong Kong shoppers, and subsequently investigative reporters, were prevented from taking photographs of the windows and interior of the Kowloon-based D&G flagship store, whereas customers from overseas and mainland China were apparently allowed to do so. The story was reported by local, regional, and global media as the crisis rapidly escalated, generating significant negative coverage for the brand. The incident snowballed involving debate on hundreds of negative Facebook posts and other social media sites and resulting in two protest marches outside the Hong Kong store. With no apparent coordinated crisis management response, the incident appeared to be spiralling out of control. The case asks students to consider the range of options open to D&G when responding to the initial incident and subsequent PR crisis to contain the situation and minimize the damage to their brand image and reputation.

Learning Objectives

Upon completion of this case, students should be able to:

- Identify the nature and profile of a brand crisis and define the conditions and characteristics that constitute a crisis.

- Describe the implications of a crisis on managing and maintaining brand image, brand identity, and brand equity.

- Differentiate between the different types of crisis in terms of whether they are functional (product output) or symbolic (core ethos espoused by the brand) in orientation, and their duration from a one-off incident to ongoing issues.

- Define the five stages that a crisis encounters throughout its life cycle covering detection; containment and communication; competence; recovery; and evaluation as a way of managing and controlling a crisis effectively.

- Understand the role of stakeholders in a crisis, including how brands need to incorporate the needs of stakeholders into their crisis response.

- Discuss the strengths, weaknesses, and risks associated with adopting provocative brand marketing communications based on an understanding of local culture for brands operating internationally, where social, political, moral, and ethical views may differ widely and determine how these localized value systems impact consumer behaviors.

- Analyze D&G's crisis case narrative, by identifying key players and events and applying crisis process theory to understand how this crisis emerged and developed.

- Provide proactive and responsive strategies and tactics in terms of preparedness planning, strategic containment, and effective communication solutions that can be implemented to minimize a crisis and its negative impact on brand image and equity.

- Propose a viable solution post-crisis to protect brand reputation and equity through the strategic implementation of preparedness planning.

Introduction

Given the complexities of conducting business in a globalized, competitive marketplace, no brand or organization is immune from having to deal with a crisis (Coombes 2007). Typically, a crisis for an organization will "start as a relatively small issue that grows out of control because insufficient attention was paid to it" (Devereux and Peirson-Smith 2009: 110). A crisis is defined as "a major occurrence with a potentially negative outcome affecting an organisation, company or industry, as well as its publics, products, services or good name. It interrupts normal business transactions and can sometimes threaten the existence of an organisation" (Fearn-Banks 1996: 1).

The study of organizational and brand crisis management has emerged from management theory and usually focuses on the ways in which organizations employ strategies and tactics to deal with an issue that has gone out of control. This issue in turn threatens a decline in public trust and results in a fractured relationship between a business and its consumers and customers, while it also elicits an openly negative public response. Organizational crises can take various forms from a one-off incident to continued problems, ranging from faulty products, employee misbehavior, or offensive brand advertising. Crises can be divided into two categories:

1   functional performance-related crises, such as a defective product incident, or
2   a more symbolic and indirect value-based type of crisis that concerns social or ethical
    issues surrounding the core beliefs espoused by the brand.

This second type of crisis does not involve specific product attributes that deliver functional benefits but instead calls into question the brand's ability to deliver the symbolic and psychological benefits that it has promised. This symbolic type of value-based crisis often involves issues such as child labor, or unethical fashion production using toxic dye, or the overuse of natural resources.

The response to an organizational crisis can range from unambiguous support through to unambiguous stonewalling at the far end of the reactive spectrum; ambiguity is another response strategy that companies might adopt, which sits within the middle of the spectrum (Dawar and Pillutla 2000). Unambiguous support constitutes the full acceptance of responsibility on behalf of the brand for the situation and unequivocal support to remedy the problem as soon as possible. This may manifest itself as an immediate voluntary product recall of a defective item, for example. At the opposite end of the spectrum, some companies may take the extreme position of denying all responsibility for the crisis or refusing to communicate or comment about it in the public domain as a form of blatant and unambiguous stonewalling. The middle ground is occupied by brands reacting to a crisis situation in a more ambiguous way, by providing inconsistent and contradictory support to stakeholders. This occurs when the brand promises in a corporate crisis statement, media interview, advertisement, or news release that they will take action by offering a free replacement of faulty goods with an apology and explanation, yet inevitably fail to provide the replacement. This form of crisis management often leaves consumers confused and resentful.

Stages of a crisis

The literature on crisis communication suggests that the crisis process typically passes through five phases:

1   *Detection of crisis*: Preparation for, and prevention of the incident. The realization that a problem has occurred and is escalating within the public domain.
2   *Containment and communication*: Respond swiftly with a controlled and coordinated response from a single organizational source, issuing an apology if needed and communicating regular updates on how the crisis is being contained and resolved.
3   *Competence*: Demonstrate a real understanding of the crisis and clear leadership to direct the crisis to a quick solution, thereby minimizing damage to the brand image.
4   *Recovery*: Implement strategies and tactics to improve the brand image, identity, and equity from a stakeholder perspective following the impact of the crisis.
5   *Evaluation and learning*: Review what was done in response to the sudden incident, how it could have been improved, and how to prevent this occurring in future.

Luxury fashion brand global influence and reach

As luxury fashion brands jostle for a position in new consumer markets, their brand strategy is not just about generating the most creatively engaging collections each season (although this is important and critical to generating positive media coverage and mediated visibility) but is also about managing their brand communications.

Luxury fashion brands represent the arbiters of taste and are signifiers of wealth and success. In order to display this, European brands, in particular, appear to rely more on emotional and abstract symbolic content within their brand communication campaigns, which may not translate well across cultures. This means that there is always the risk of what Umberto Eco called "aberrant decoding" in the misinterpretation of the sign or brand message by the receiver (Eco 1972).

This case features a range of issues that face luxury brands that are expanding into the Asia-Pacific region, including how these brands protect their intellectual property, and also how they become aware of local cultural sensitivities and cultural alignment, and incorporate this within their strategic brand management.

In recent years, Dolce & Gabbana have become well known for their controversial thoughts, which often manifest within their provocative brand communications; in 2015 the brand courted a public outcry in their openly anti-gay adoption stance and negative feelings about in vitro fertilization (IVF) in a media interview. These views resulted in an online argument with Elton John, who himself is father to two children conceived via IVF, and provoked a more widespread celebrity backlash. It also triggered a Twitter storm #BoycottDolceGabbana, which generated 30,000 responses, and an internet petition calling for the boycott of Dolce & Gabbana's goods in Macy's and Debenhams, which gained 10,000 signatures; a large protest also took place outside of the London flagship store (Gani 2015). Eventually, the duo retracted their comments and apologized for the misunderstanding, claiming that they supported freedom of choice and were only expressing their own personal views, yet decried the boycott as medieval behavior.

In Beijing, the brand also encountered a social media crisis in response to its 2017 online campaign "Dolce & Gabbana Loves China" by the Morelli brothers, which included images of models wearing luxurious D&G clothing in some older streets and locations within China, next to ordinary and often older working people. The images were criticized as intentionally displaying a backwards view of the country and avoiding displaying modern China (Liu 2017). One Weibo (a Chinese micro-blogging website) user commented, "Stop it! You intentionally show the backwards part of China. It is discrimination"; many other online commentators stated that they would not buy from the brand as it is too disrespectful (Yiling 2017). The marketing aim for the campaign was to create a media buzz ahead of the launch of its elite Alta Moda and Alta Sartorial Fashion Show; instead, the brand had to pull the campaign photographs from its Weibo and WeChat channels, though the images remained on D&G's Instagram page, which is banned in China. As a form of symbolic apologia, the brand subsequently took photos of their models in the business district where the after-show party took place, which received more positive appreciation from Instagram users. Actively taking risks and riding out the storm of criticism by hoping that it will burn itself out as the crisis ceases to be top of the news agenda is a strategy that some brands may also choose to adopt in the contemporary media saturated and socially mediated world.

Business Problem

Context

Since the 1990s, the nations in Southeast Asia have undergone rapid modernization and development, which has resulted in the rise of the nouveau riche in first and second tier Chinese cities, for example, who actively and visibly wear their wealth in the form of luxury fashion brands. As the economic world order shifts it brings with it new transglobal flows of wealth and buying power, with Asia Pacific increasingly becoming the consumption center for global luxury brands that are typified by D&G. In response to these new market opportunities, high-end, luxury brands are increasingly expanding their retail presence in urban centers, such as Hong Kong. To satisfy a growing demand for consumer goods and conspicuous consumption in rapidly developing economies, in recent years the global consumerscape has consequently shifted its focus from the West to Southeast Asia, and particularly China.

Luxury fashion brand D&G's expansion into Hong Kong and China was part of a strategic business move that intended to yield dividends by capitalizing on large-scale consumer demand. Historically Hong Kong has been considered an east–west gateway and has generally been seen as the place for brands to "try out" the market within Southeast Asia before entering the Chinese market and committing to further regional expansion.

Following the Hong Kong handover from British rule in 1997, the flow of consumers from China to Hong Kong as a Special Administrative Region (SAR) of China has been an observable trend, with increasing numbers of mainland Chinese tourists traveling to Hong Kong on shopping trips to purchase luxury brands; 60 million mainland Chinese visitors represent almost three-quarters (70 percent) of the visitor to Hong Kong annually (Hong Kong Tourism Association 2017; Ng 2018). Many retail tourists are attracted by considerations of authenticity and lower prices of up to 30 percent less for luxury goods, a wider choice, and the removal of travel restrictions under the Individual Visa Scheme (Hong Kong Business 2011). While the increasing influx of Chinese visitors has significantly contributed to the wealth of the country and an increased number of jobs, tensions have emerged among the local Hong Kong population in response to the increased visitor volume and a perceived lack of cultural empathy. The D&G crisis in this case unfolded against, and in partial response to, a tense situation and broader cultural misunderstandings arising from the volume of mainland Chinese visitors and shoppers to Hong Kong.

D&G profile and financial standing

Since starting their luxury fashion partnership in 1985 the Italian fashion design duo, Domenico Dolce and Stefano Gabbana, have crafted, owned, and controlled every part of their Milan-based business success. In 2018 D&G employ over 3,500 workers worldwide and had a global retail network and an increasing sales presence via online off-price retail platforms, such as Farfetch and YOOX Net-a-porter. The brand is no stranger to controversy and brand-crisis scenarios are notable in the use of provocative, nonconventional advertising and the infamous banning of perceived hostile journalists and editors representing *The New York Times, Vanity Fair, W magazine, WWD,* and even *Italian Vogue.* Their nonconformist and disruptive approach to business surprised the industry and their consumers when it was announced in 2011 that they would be shuttering their popular and profitable D&G diffusion line to concentrate on their signature Dolce & Gabbana collection, which they hoped would help to simplify their brand message and concentrate on critical emerging markets, such as China.

Case narrative

In the first week of January 2012 two local Hong Kong residents were prevented by a security guard from taking photos of the D&G flagship store window located in Canton Road, Tsim Sha Tsui (TST), Hong Kong, on the edge of a high-end shopping mall, Harbour City. When they protested that it was their right to take photographs of a street and pointed out that other people were also doing the same thing, the store guard allegedly replied that only "mainland Chinese" or "foreign" people were permitted to take photographs of the store due to copyright. The enraged would-be photographers contacted *Apple Daily,* a popular mass circulation tabloid newspaper in Hong Kong that is well known for its sensationalist style of journalism. The news editor dispatched a staff photographer to the store to replicate the photo-taking activity, which elicited the same response from store security guards. This time, however, the security guards threatened to smash the cameras if the photographer persisted in taking photos. Subsequently, the news reporter filed criminal charges.

Even before the story went to press the original disgruntled couple had posted their version of the "D&G bullying" incident on Facebook. In addition, a video of the security guards threatening the reporter outside of the store with his hand over the camera lens was circulated on YouTube. By the time the *Apple Daily* story was published on January 5, 2012, there was already a groundswell of negative commentary about D&G's handling of the case swirling around various forums, Facebook sites, and blogs. The *Apple Daily* article resulted in many people getting angry about the story and it erupted across all channels of communication—traditional media, virtual media, and word of mouth. Within 24–48 hours of the *Apple Daily* report, both print and broadcast media were carrying the story locally, regionally, and globally. The story consequently came to the attention of news agencies, Reuters and AP newswire. International coverage of the incident appeared in the UK-based *Daily Telegraph* with the title "D&G photo ban protest" (*Daily Telegraph* 2012).

Digital communication conduits can be effective channels to disseminate positive brand messages; however, they can also generate uncontrolled negative exposure, and things were buzzing in the "netosphere" with a firestorm of D&G criticism spreading rapidly. By January 6, there were hundreds of Facebook posts on D&G's site alleging rank racism from the Italian luxury brand and an anti-D&G protest forum had 20,000 fans supporting it. A call for a street protest under the banner of "10,000 people Photograph D&G event" emerged from the site and 1,000 protestors converged on the D&G flagship store in Canton Road, TST, on January 8, carrying cameras to photograph the store and wielding placards both denouncing D&G by telling the brand to pack up and go home to Milan and demanding an apology. The negative coverage of the crisis spread quickly and exponentially through Facebook and Twitter—alongside Milan Fashion Week's blogs and internet forums.

This mass reaction was also followed by a repeat protest a week later on January 14, when a group of protestors left a can of dog food outside the doors of the store with posters attached stating "D&G = Dog and Garbage"; "Dislike—Go"; "Discrimination and Greed"; and "Dump—Garbage" The store was so overwhelmed by the wave of photo-taking protesters that it was forced to close its doors by 3:00 p.m. on the day of the protest, along with other luxury fashion stores in the vicinity. The protests necessitated a two-week police presence, with twenty officers permanently stationed outside the D&G store.

The initial response from D&G's Hong Kong office was to issue an unsigned statement on their Facebook page reading:

> We wish to underline that our company has not taken part in any action aiming at offending the Hong Kong public.

Sensitive to their own part in the incident, the Harbour City management company (who were in charge of contracting out security personnel for the D&G stores in question) had issued an apology on their own Facebook site on January 7, the day before the first protest occurred, and blamed the incident on a lack of communication. They also implicated D&G in the event for ordering the photographic ban and causing such a crisis.

FIGURE 14.1 People protest against the banning of photographs being taken of the TST D&G store in January 2012. Photograph: Jason Lawler/Moment/Getty Images.

In the absence of any substantial explanation or apology for the incident, significant "conspiracy"-type rumors started to circulate on various Facebook sites, media reports, and on the street. These rumors suggested that a well-known, high-living senior Chinese government official from Nanjing had been shopping inside the D&G store and complained to the manager when he noticed people taking photographs, as he feared that netizens would link his luxury shopping spree to a display of corrupt spending of public money. At this time popular media myths were circulating which rumoured that Chinese consumers were buying or renting apartments in the main shopping districts of Mong Kok and Kowloon to store their luxury goods and purchases, the volume of which far exceeded what they could legally cross the border back to Mainland China with. Further rumors criticized excessive purchasing and hoarding behavior as evidence of an illegal "gray market" in luxury goods that were destined to be resold (for profit) back in mainland China, as well as a representation of the corrupt gift-giving of luxury items.

Anti-D&G sentiment in Hong Kong was at its peak across many social and traditional media channels at this point of the escalation of the crisis, as typified by the following commentary,

> In fact, this anti Dolce & Gabbana Chinese-language page sprung up on Facebook and has more than 20,000 fans, and the luxury retailer's own Facebook wall has been peppered with comments such as "One of D & G values is 'Respect for individuals'. This is be changed to 'Practice of racism is our core value [*sic*].'" (Ad Age 2012)

Brand competitors, such as Prada and Louis Vuitton, issued statements on their Facebook sites within a week of the incident occurring stating that they welcomed all possible customers and passersby to take photos of their window displays, which they deemed to be in the public domain and, as such, part of their consumer discourse. D&G, on the other hand, maintained its "No comment" stance for over fifteen days but finally broke its silence by issuing an official apology from its Milan HQ at 3:00 a.m. Hong Kong time on January 19 (SCMP 2012):

> We understand that the events which unfolded in front of the D&G boutique on Canton Road have offended the citizens of Hong Kong. For this we are truly sorry and we apologise. The Dolce&Gabbana policy is to welcome the Hong Kong people and the whole world respecting the rights of each individual and of the local laws.

By this point in the crisis, the incident had gone beyond the concerns of the protestors to involve a wider stakeholder group of opinion formers and leaders, politicians and lawyers as the situation escalated and assumed new dimensions and provoked the discussion of other related issues. The Equal Opportunities Commission sent a letter to D&G's Hong Kong head office demanding a full explanation of the incident in response to the public's complaint of racial discrimination. A tourism official also demanded that D&G apologize for discriminating against local residents and one of the contenders for the political leadership post of chief executive of Hong Kong, who had a family background in the knitwear industry, promised to raise the issue in the Legislative Council due to it threatening public freedom.

A related discussion point among wider stakeholders hinged on the issue of intellectual copyright and questioned whether an individual has the unequivocal right to take photographs in public areas. This also prompted a vigorous debate in the media; some commentators, such as the government's secretary for commerce, took the middle ground by pronouncing that the public had the right to take photographs of anything in public so long as they did not make a nuisance of themselves, and that copyright owners only had the right to protect their work from being reproduced. Legal copyright experts highlighted the woeful ambiguity of the law on this point, and some legal experts cited Section 71 of the Copyright Ordinance, which allows the filming of artistic craftsmanship displayed in public and does not recognize it as infringing an artist's copyright. Section 40, which allows the incidental inclusion of copyright material in sound or image recordings, was also cited as relevant.

Despite these discussions, many protestors pointed out that the issue of copyright within this case was invalid, especially as the reasons why these individuals were not allowed to photograph the store seemed to be tied to ethnicity. The assumption that Hong Kong photographers would take photos to steal D&G's intellectual property, while mainland Chinese and foreign people would not, led one Hong Kong lawyer publicly to label the security guard's claim that individuals were not able to photograph the store due to copyright reasons, "a lame excuse" and a whitewash.

Through strategic crisis brand management, could there have been ways of alleviating the damage, or perhaps preventing it in the first place? It is now imperative that the brand plans some form of recovery and evaluates its response to protect their current and future reputation.

Business Questions

Dolce & Gabbana's failure to contain a brand crisis in their global operations in Southeast Asia is a cautionary tale reminding global luxury fashion brands that they need to understand the cultural landscape in which they operate, and in which their various stakeholders reside, by constantly monitoring the prevailing social, economic, and political issues and being mindful of cultural values in the local marketplace as a baseline global brand management strategy.

Major questions

If you were the brand manager for D&G what would your response to this crisis be in the short, medium, and long term? How and why does your answer differ from what actually happened?

Study questions

1   What type of crisis is this, why did it start and could it have been managed differently or even prevented?

2   Who were all of the stakeholders involved in this crisis and what were their viewpoints in this case?

3   How would you evaluate the brand's response and handling of this crisis? Why?

4   Examine D&G's Hong Kong based brand crisis scenario using the response framework (detection/monitoring; containment/communication; competence; recovery; evaluation) to examine the brand's handling of the situation and identify the lessons to be learned from this.

5   Why is it important for a fashion brand to be culturally sensitive to the local market context and the needs and values of local stakeholders when operating and expanding globally? How can a brand prepare for its global operations across different geographic locations? If a brand fails to realize that it need to be more culturally aware, what do you think are the consequences?

6   What role did social media play in developing this crisis? How could this be managed and controlled by the brand?

7   Are there any circumstances under which a crisis can have a positive rather than a negative impact on a fashion brand?

8   Do fashion brands encounter and need to manage crises in a different way from other product categories and brands?

9   What did the D&G brand learn from their direct experience of this crisis case?

References and Further Reading

Ad Age. 2012. "Dolce & Gabbana's Photo Ban Angers Hong Kong Shoppers: Mainland Chinese Are Allowed to Snap Pictures but Locals Aren't; Protest Escalates on Facebook." Ad Age, January 10,2012. Accessed June 2017. https://adage.com/article/global-news/dolce-gabbana-s-photo-ban-angers-hong-kong-shoppers/232002/

Coombs, W. Timothy. 2007. "Protecting Organization Reputations During a Crisis: The Development and Application of Situational Crisis Communication Theory." *Corporate Reputation Review* 10 (3): 163–176.

Coombs, W. Timothy. 2015. *Ongoing Crisis Communication: Planning, Managing, and Responding,* fourth edition. Los Angeles: Sage.

Daily Telegraph. 2012. "One Thousand Protest Dolce & Gabbana Hong Kong Store over Photo Ban." *The Daily Telegraph*, January 9, 2012. Accessed October 10, 2013. https://www.telegraph.co.uk/news/worldnews/asia/hongkong/9001001/One-thousand-protest-Dolce-and-Gabbana-Hong-Kong-store-over-photo-ban.html

Dawar, Niraj and Madan, M. Pillutla. 2000. "Impact of Product-Harm Crises on Brand quity: The Moderating Role of Consumer Expectations." *Journal of Marketing Resources*37 (2): 215–227.

Devereux, Mary M. and Anne Peirson-Smith. 2009. *Public Relations in Asia Pacific: Communicating Effectively Across Cultures*. New York: John Wiley Publishing.

Eco, Umberto. 1972. "Towards a Semiotic Inquiry Into the Television Message." Translated by Paola Splendore. *Working Papers in Cultural Studies* 3: 103–121.

Fearn-Banks, Kathleen. 1996. *Crisis Communications: A Casebook Approach*. Mahwah, NJ: Lawrence Erlbaum & Associates.

Gani, Aisha. 2015. "Dolce & Gabbana Protesters Demand Boycott Outside London Shop." *The Guardian*, March 19, 2015. Accessed June 10, 2016.https://www.theguardian.com/fashion/2015/mar/19/dolce-gabbana-london-protests-boycott-shop

Hong Kong Business. 2011. "Three Reasons Why Mainland Tourists Shop in Hong Kong." September 2, 2011. Accessed December 21, 2018. https://hongkongbusiness.hk/retail/news/three-reasons-why-mainland-tourists-shop-in-hong-kong

Hong Kong Tourism Board. 2017. *Monthly Report-Visitor Arrivals Statistics*. December 2017. Hong Kong: HKSAR Government. Accessed February 3, 2018. http://partnernet.hktb.com/filemanager/intranet/ViS_Stat/ViS_Stat_E/ViS_E_2013/Tourism_Stat_12_2013_0.pdf

Liu, Charles. 2017. "Dolce & Gabbana Fashion Shoot on Streets of Beijing Upsets Locals." *The Beijinger*, April 23, 2017. Accessed June 20, 2017. https://www.thebeijinger.com/blog/2017/04/23/dolce-gabbana-photo-shoot-streets-beijing-upsets-locals

Ng, Kang-Chung. 2018. "Hong Kong Visitor Numbers Continue to Rise, with 5 million Tourists in March: Figures from the Hong Kong Tourism Board Show Three Quarters of the Visitors Last Month were from Mainland China." *SCMP*, April 30, 2018. Accessed September 10, 2017.https://www.scmp.com/news/hong-kong/hong-kong-economy/article/2144090/hong-kong-visitor-numbers-continue-rise-5-million

Singh, Prachi. 2017. "Dolce & Gabbana Annual Turnover Increases 9 percent." *Fashion United*, October 16, 2017. Accessed September 30, 2017. https://fashionunited.uk/news/business/dolce-gabbana-annual-turnover-increases-9-percent/2017101626313

South China Morning Post (SCMP). 2012. "Dolce & Gabbana's Apology Too Late." *SCMP*, January 19, 2012. Accessed September 20, 2017. https://www.scmp.com/article/990525/dolce-gabbanas-apology-too-late

Yiling, Pan. 2017. "Dolce and Gabbana Campaign Sparks Controversy On China's Social Media." *Jing Daily*, April 25, 2017. Accessed September 10, 2017. https://jingdaily.com/dolce-gabbana-campaign-controversy/

Definitions

Brand: A product for sale by a producer or manufacturer and distinguished from other products in the same category by its distinctive features using a unique name or symbol.

Brand equity: The potential that a brand has in terms of the power of its name and the collective goodwill that a brand accumulates.

Brand ethos: The core meaning of the brand articulating what the brand is and what is represents including characteristics of authenticity, consistency, and differentiation.

Brand identity: Aspects of a brand comprising its distinctiveness, such as its logo, colors, products, and promotional communication efforts.

Brand image: The consumer's perception of a brand and its identity based on feelings or direct experience.

Crisis: A major happening with a negative outcome potential impacting on an organization in addition to its stakeholders, outputs, and reputation.

Crisis communication: The response to a crisis situation devised to control organizational messaging about the situation to minimize any negative impact.

Netizen: A regular user of the internet.

Preparedness planning: A proactive cycle of strategic planning undertaken by an organization ensuring an effective and coordinated response during an incident before a crisis occurs.

of this journey, and consequently decided to expand her range from homeware to apparel (Lawes 2017). As a result, Bhumi began to provide its customers with a range of lifestyle apparel basics, such as T-shirts.

Although the extensions from homeware to clothing basics seemed an obvious evolution for Bhumi, their most recent extension seemed to be motivated less by fit in the "customer journey" and more by developing a lifestyle range; in 2017 Vinita decided to extend Bhumi into yoga and athleisure wear for both men and women (Baravkar 2017a). Bhumi has promoted the idea of "seed to shelf," which "refers to Bhumi's ability to follow the flow of the entire supply chain from farmers planting the organic cotton crop, to the dyes used to color the cotton fabric all the way to the finished products available on the shelf," and believes that reinforcing this requires an extension into the wider world in which consumers operate and require next-to-skin solutions (Bhumi 2018b).

The extension into athleisure was also driven by recent consumer trends, whereby people no longer see a divide between exercise and leisure more generally (Wholesale Investor 2018):

> Bhumi wants to be different from the mainstream activewear and yoga brands. With our goal to lead by example, we want to only provide socially conscious products that are high performance, functional to a variety of strength and endurance activities, that benefit the earth, that benefit humanity. We want to set off a large chain reaction, a movement for change; as we exercise and sweat in sweatshop free activewear, we are shaping the future of the world we live in. (Baravkar 2018b)

Furthermore, the brand team identified that an increased desire for "conscious consumerism" had driven the demand for spiritual activities such as yoga and meditation (Baravkar 2015b), yet few of the products available on the market reflected this same ethical ethos in terms of their material use, and treatment of workers and animals (Bhumi 2018a):

> There is a growing awareness for ethical consumerism and a growing movement of people doing yoga, meditation and other physical activities … We noticed there is a gap in the market for ethically produced and sustainable yoga and active wear, therefore, we started working on this and are now excited to launch a range that is the first of its kind in Australia. (Benton-Collins 2017)

Vinita dubbed the new extension into athleisure as the "Soul Space" range, which she positions as follows:

> We are all souls, beings of energy and light, holding space on this beautiful planet. What we choose to do with the time we have is reflected in our actions be it yoga, meditation, walking, dancing, running. As we perform these activities, wouldn't it be nice to know that what we are wearing reflects our goals of a better self, a better state of health, a better balance of body mind and soul? (Benton-Collins 2017)

Vinita states that Soul Space aims to reinforce Bhumi's ethical and spiritual associations:

> At Bhumi we want to make a positive impact on our planet and the people on it, by inspiring people to make positive choices. We are committed to finding a state of balance and beauty on this Earth which is why we at Bhumi decided to create Australia's 1st Fairtrade yoga and activewear range that adheres to our core principles of sustainability, no toxins, no child labour and an ethical supply chain. (Bhumi 2017)

The extension has also driven demand for Bhumi overseas, particularly in America, as well as a demand for other products, such as women's G-strings to be worn during yoga practice. The yoga range has also driven Bhumi to launch a range of crop tops—though difficulties with Global Organic Textile Standard (GOTS) guidelines and the associated technical challenges has, so far, prevented them from creating bras (Bhumi 2017). This line extension was made possible through Bhumi partnering with an Indian company that carried GOTS and Fairtrade certifications (Bhumi 2018a), which are able to sell Vinita offcuts of colorful fabrics (these pieces were perfect for yoga wear) (Baravkar 2018a). Using cut-offs for limited edition underwear ranges, such as Bhumi's "Pulse Cami," helps reinforce the brand's commitment to the environment and limit the amount of textile waste caused by the production process. Bhumi is also partnering with a local company, Wanderlust 2017 Sunshine Coast, to offer "Glamping by Bhumi" (Bhumi Organic Cotton 2017b). The annual four-day spiritual festival caters to over 3,000 people, many of whom practice yoga each morning, providing the brand with the perfect platform to reach new customers.

Conclusion and challenges

Bhumi have driven their growth through a range of brand extensions and relationships with like-minded partners, expanding the base of their organic fairtrade cotton products to enable consumers to achieve a conscious lifestyle. Vinita has stretched her brand from its origins in basic homeware to booming lifestyle categories such as yoga and athleisure. With each extension Vinita has focused on ensuring relevance, GOTS and Fairtrade certification, and Bhumi's brand heritage. Moreover, with each extension Bhumi has reinforced key brand associations in all its messaging. However, how far can Vinita further expand without undermining her original credentials and brand position or unique selling point? If she were to further expand the brand, which categories could she move into that would enhance the brand without fear of dilution, and how would she do so? Should she expand through line or category extensions, and what role would partners play?

As well as brand-identity concerns, there are technical challenges to further expansion. Bhumi's options are constrained by their certifications. For example, color dying and printing have to be natural, vegetable based, and GOTS certified. As a result, currently the use of color and prints requires a minimum order measured in kilometers, which represents a production level and investment that may be beyond a small label such as Bhumi. Trying to produce the athleisure range under GOTS restrictions limits the ratio of nonorganic cotton materials such as elastin; the same restrictions apply to yoga wear. Further growth areas, such as organic cotton bras, for example, require the wire to be GOTS approved.

As of mid-2018, Bhumi's scope of products is unique among Australian fashion brands. Nonetheless, other brands, focused on children's or women's wear do exist and potentially could expand into similar categories and compete with Bhumi.

Business Questions

1   Why did Vinita extend her brand? What benefits has she enjoyed?
2   List all of Bhumi's brand extensions. Which are line extensions and which are category extensions? What are the benefits and risks of each?

References and Further Reading

Australian Organic. 2015. "Wearing the Change." Accessed October 28, 2017. http://austorganic.com/news/wearing-the-change/

Australian Organic. 2018. "Profile of the Month: Bhumi Organic Cotton." Accessed October 7, 2018. https://austorganic.com/news/profile-of-the-month-bhumi-organic-cotton/

Barakvar, Vinita. 2014. "What I Didn't Know About Conventional Cotton." Nourish Melbourne. Accessed October 24, 2017. http://www.nourishmelbourne.com.au/organic-cotton/#.W-1WNMjRDcc

Baravkar, Vinita. 2015a. "Secrets to Success: Meet Vinita Baravkar of Bhumi Organic Cotton." *Women's Business School*, interview with Peace Mitchell. Accessed January 18, 2019. https://www.thewomensbusinessschool.com/secrets-success-vinita-barakvar-bhumi-organic-cotton/

Baravkar, Vinita. 2015b. "The Ethos Behind Bhumi Organic Cotton." *Earth LifeBalance* (blog), Bhumi, August 3, 2015. Accessed November 19, 2018. https://bhumi.com.au/blogs/earth-life-balance/53248899-the-ethos-and-inspiration-behind-bhumi-organic-cotton

Baravkar, Vinita. 2015c. "What Makes Bhumi Affordable? *Earth Life Balance* (blog), Bhumi, October 1, 2015. Accessed November 15, 2018. https://bhumi.com.au/blogs/earth-life-balance/67539843-what-makes-bhumi-affordable

Barakvar, Vinita. 2016. "Creating your Organic Sanctuary." *Earth Life Balance* (blog), Bhumi, February 1, 2016. Accessed November 15, 2018. https://bhumi.com.au/blogs/earth-life-balance/90401926-creating-your-organic-sanctuary

Baravkar, Vinita. 2017a. "Introducing Australia's 1st Fairtrade Yoga & Activewear." *Earth Life Balance* (blog), Bhumi, May 23, 2017. Accessed December 15, 2018. https://bhumi.com.au/blogs/earth-life-balance/introducing-australias-1st-fairtrade-yoga-activewear

Baravkar, Vinita. 2017b. "WhyChoosing Certified Organic Textiles Is Good For Your Skin." *Why Organic?* (blog), MademoiselleOrganic, February 5, 2017. Accessed October 29, 2017. https://mademoiselleorganic.com/about-organic-beauty/why-organic/why-choose-certified-organic-textiles-skin-bhumi-vinita/

Baravkar, Vinita. 2017c. "Why We Are So Excited About Our Yoga And Activewear Range? *Earth Life Balance* (blog), Bhumi, July 23,2017. Accessed November 15, 2018. https://bhumi.com.au/blogs/earth-life-balance/why-we-are-so-excited-about-our-yoga-and-athleisure-range

Baravkar, Vinita. 2018a. "Announcing The New Yoga & Activewear Soul Space Range." *Earth Life Balance* (blog), Bhumi, September 9, 2018. Accessed November 19, 2018. https://bhumi.com.au/blogs/earth-life-balance/soul-space-new-range

Baravkar, Vinita. 2018b. "It is Time for a Fashion Revolution." *Earth Life Balance* (blog), Bhumi, April 25, 2018. Accessed November 15, 2018. https://bhumi.com.au/blogs/earth-life-balance/its-time-for-a-fashion-revolution

Baravkar, Vinita. 2018c. "Top 3 Tips For Choosing Your Underwear." *Earth Life Balance* (blog), Bhumi, February 12, 2018. Accessed November 15, 2018. https://bhumi.com.au/blogs/earth-life-balance/top-3-tips-for-choosing-underwear

Benton-Collins, Kendall. 2017. "Bhumi Delivers Australia's First Fairtrade Yoga and Activewear Range." *Good On You*

Bhumi. 2017. "Bhumi." Accessed October 25, 2017. https://bhumi.com.au/pages/about-the-founder

Bhumi. 2018a. "FAQs." Accessed November 15, 2018. https://bhumi.com.au/pages/faqs

Bhumi. 2018b. "The Journey from Seed to Shelf." Accessed November 19, 2018. https://bhumi.com.au/pages/the-journey-from-seed-to-shelf

Bhumi Organic Cotton. 2017a. "Life's Essentials." YouTube, March 10, 2017. Accessed December 15, 2018. https://www.youtube.com/watch?v=FypZh31fdQc

Bhumi Organic Cotton. 2017b. "Thinking about Glamping? Don't Miss Out." Facebook, October 12, 2017. Accessed November 15, 2018. https://www.facebook.com/BhumiOrganic/posts/1722398601134864

Bhumi Organic Cotton. 2017c. "Yoga and Athleisure Range—Soul Space byBhumi." YouTube, April 5, 2017. Accessed December 15, 2018. https://www.youtube.com/watch?v=sc5jVGxxNpg

Guide to Organics. 2015. "Interview with Vinita Baravkar, Bhumi OrganicCotton." Accessed October 22, 2017. https://guidetoorganics.com.au/interview-with-vinita-baravkar-bhumi-organic-cotton/

Howlett, Caitlin. 2015. "OrganicCotton Basics With Bhumi." *Green Lifestyle Magazine*, April 8, 2015.Accessed October 23, 2017. http://www.greenlifestylemag.com.au/organic-cotton

Lawes, Lucy. 2016. "Back to Basics: Our New Arrivals!*Life Balance* (blog), Bhumi, November 5, 2016. Accessed November 15, 2018. https://bhumi.com.au/blogs/earth-life-balance/back-to-basics-our-new-range

Lawes, Lucy. 2017. "Beyond Skin: Protecting Our Largest Organ." *Life Balance* (blog), Bhumi, February 4, 2017. Accessed November 15, 2018. https://bhumi.com.au/blogs/earth-life-balance/beyond-skin-deep

Tranter, Jenny. 2015. "Interview: Founderof Organic Cotton Label Bhumi." (blog), State of Green, February 2, 2015. Accessed October 23, 2017. https://blog.stateofgreen.com.au/organic-cotton-bhumi/

Wholesale Investor. 2018. "Bhumi Announces Their New Yoga & Activewear Soul Space Range." September 21, 2018. Accessed November 15, 2018. https://wholesaleinvestor.com.au/bhumi-announces-their-new-yoga-activewear-soul-space-range/

Definitions

Brand extension: A strategy that expands the parent brand's coverage into new lines (e.g., Coke to Diet Coke to Cherry Coke) or new categories (e.g., Virgin Airlines to Virgin Gyms). Typically, brands are extended within the same product category (a line extension) or to new ones (category extension).

Category extension: Expanding the parent brand into a brand new product or service category. Examples would include Versace's shift from fashion to homeware to hotels.

Conscious consumerism: A consumer who considers the impact (social, environmental, ecological, political) of their buying decisions.

Line extension: The expansion of the parent brand within the same product or service category. This can involve expanding the product range or moving up and down the price curve.

Parent brand: The brand that is being extended in some way. Examples include Diet Coke—in this situation, Coke is a parent brand that is being extended.

Chapter 16

Digital Heritage Storytelling at Mulberry

Amanda Grace Sikarskie

The late 2010s have shown themselves to be years of cultural and financial uncertainty, with Brexit representing the tip of the iceberg in a sea of shifting political and economic alliances. Adding to this climate is the reality that the luxury market is becoming increasingly aspirational as housing prices soar and purchasing power stagnates, and that younger generations seem less interested in accruing possessions than even the Gen Xers before them. In this period of flux, luxury giants on both sides of the Atlantic—such as Chanel, Dior, Gucci, Halston Heritage, Mulberry, Saint Laurent, and Versace—must prioritize safeguarding their brand loyalty and recognition. To accomplish this, these and other luxury brands are increasingly turning to the cachet of their heritage, made accessible to a new generation of consumers through digital heritage storytelling on social sites like Instagram. Some brands have a much longer heritage upon which to draw than others, however. Whereas many luxury houses were founded in the nineteenth or early twentieth centuries, British luxury brand Mulberry was founded in the 1970s. To tell the story of its comparatively brief history, Mulberry inserts itself into the longer narrative of modern British history. This case study explores and evaluates the successes and failures of luxury brands' utilization of social media channels as a platform for digital heritage storytelling.

Learning Objectives

Upon completion of this case, students should be able to:

- Explain compelling brand storytelling grounded in heritage.
- Discuss how a brand story may be tied in with a larger narrative, such as a work of literature or art, or with a national story.
- Demonstrate how a brand story (and all the heritage implied therein) may be distilled into a few social media posts for digital heritage storytelling.

- Describe the role of hashtags in creating and perpetuating the heritage narrative online.

Introduction

If there is one commandment in luxury marketing right now, it is "honor thy heritage" (Doupnik 2017). Rolex's iconic slogan, "It doesn't just tell time, it tells history," speaks volumes to the importance of brand history and heritage in marketing luxury goods. This heritage is communicated to the consumer through storytelling, increasingly in 140 characters or less.

But what is a story? We may associate the word "story" with childhood fairy tales or some frivolous narrative, but stories are much broader than that. Quite simply, stories are how human beings logically structure narrative information. According to psychologist Susan Weinschenk, stories are such an effective communication strategy because they "allow us to break down events into smaller units so that we can better understand the information being communicated" (Weinschenk 2009: 116). In *Storytelling: Branding in Practice* (2005), Klaus Fog, Christian Budtz, and Baris Yakaboylu define storytelling as message, conflict, character, and plot. Founders, designers, models, muses, the consumer (or the consumer's parents or

FIGURE 16.1 From Mulberry's SS'18 collection representing heritage storytelling: "scattering of jewels - their placement recalls loose gemstones at the bottom of an heirloom jewelry box." © Victor VIRGILE/Gamma-Rapho via Getty Images

#BeyondHeritage is an effective hashtag for Mulberry's brand story, and the importance of hashtags in digital heritage storytelling cannot be overstated. Gucci, for example, used #utopianfantasy for the campaign discussed in the introduction above. Consider all that the phrase "utopian fantasy" conveys about the Gucci brand story. Tennis player Roger Federer, who has his own RF logo brand of athletic apparel, used the hashtag #RF20 after he won his record twentieth Grand Slam tournament at the Australian Open in 2018. His brand relies on communicating his unique—and still evolving—place in tennis history. Hashtags effectively function as the shorthand version of the brand story. Be purposeful and consistent in choosing hashtags and use them both online and in print.

Business Questions

Considering the case of Mulberry:

1 What are some other notably British brands? How does Mulberry's brand story compare to theirs?
2 Who are the characters in Mulberry's story?
3 What is the message, conflict, and plot of Mulberry's story?
4 How could the brand's story be tied in with a larger story—from literature, art, or religion, or with a national story? Brainstorm specific events in recent British history or British popular culture that could logically tie in with Mulberry products.
5 How can you solve the "instaproblem" of how this story can then be distilled into a single image or set of images suitable for posting on social media?
6 How would you hashtag the brand's story? Propose another compelling hashtag other than #BeyondHeritage.

References and Further Reading

Carr, Melissa G., and Lisa Hopkins Newell. 2014. *Guide to Fashion Entrepreneurship: The Plan, The Product, The Process*. New York: Fairchild.
Doupnik, Elizabeth. 2017. "British Brands Bank on Heritage for Future Growth." *WWD*, October 5.
Encyclopedia of Fashion. "Mulberry Company—Fashion Designer Encyclopedia" Accessed April 7, 2018. https://www.fashionencyclopedia.com/Mu-Pi/Mulberry-Company.html
Fog, Klaus, Christian Budtz, and Baris Yakaboylu. 2005. "Branding Through Storytelling." In Klaus Fog, Christian Budtz, and Baris Yakaboylu, eds., *Storytelling: Branding in Practice*, 12–25. Berlin: Springer.
Hoffmann, Jonas and Ivan Coste-Manière, eds. 2012. *Luxury Strategy in Action*. New York: Palgrave MacMillan.
Madsen, Suzanne. 2017. "Mulberry Gets Inspired by Britain, Bowie, and Princess Di." *Dazed*, February 22. Accessed April 7, 2018. https://www.dazeddigital.com/fashion/article/34841/1/ mulberry-get-inspired-by-britain-bowie-and-princess-diana-aw17-sloane
McRobbie, Angela. 1998. *British Fashion Design: Rag Trade or Image Industry?* London: Routledge.
Menkes, Suzy. 2018. "Spencer House is a Super-Glam Location for Mulberry Whose See Now Buy Now Collection Will Be on Offer All Weekend," *Instagram*, February 16. Accessed February 28, 2018, https://www.instagram.com/p/BfQ_Odsnwn5/?saved-by=sikarska
Mulberry. 2018a. "Shine On," *Instagram*, February 27. Accessed February 28, 2018. https://www. instagram.com/p/BftdB9YlURc/?saved-by=sikarska

Mulberry. 2018b. "The Marloes Satchel," *Instagram*, February 18. Accessed February 28, 2018. https://www.instagram.com/p/BfWP0n2Fouv/?saved-by=sikarska

Mulberry. 2018c. "The Rider's Lock," *Instagram*, February 23. Accessed February 28, 2018. https://www.instagram.com/p/BfjFa5dF6UR/?saved-by=sikarska

Weinschenk Susan M. 2009. *Neuro Web Design*. Berkeley, CA: New Riders.

Chapter 17

Epigram

Lifestyle Merchandising and Brand Management

GiHyung Kim and YoungJee Suh

Epigram is a men's casual wear brand that focuses on lifestyle merchandising. Epigram was created based on the approach that fashion items alone do not appeal to customers. With the concept "almost home," household items are arranged next to clothing to make it possible for customers to shop and feel as if they are in their own home or room. In 2015, Epigram was launched as a lifestyle brand with the themes of "man's room" and "man's kitchen" in major department stores in Korea. In its second pop-up store in 2017, Epigram collaborated with specialist companies to introduce lifestyle items. In this case study, students will analyze and present fashion lifestyle brand strategies based on Epigram. Students will be asked to identify and describe market research and lifestyle merchandising strategies and processes for effective brand management.

Learning Objectives

Upon completion of this case, students should be able to:

- Define and give examples of lifestyle merchandising for menswear.
- Describe effective market research needed for lifestyle merchandising strategies.
- Analyze advantages and disadvantages of merchandise assortments that include both nonfashion items and fashion items.
- Analyze advantages and disadvantages of companies adding/launching a separate lifestyle brand.
- Recommend brand management strategies for lifestyle fashion brands.

Introduction

Epigram is a men's casual wear brand operated through the fashion business division of KOLON Industries (KOLON Industries 2018). KOLON Industries is one of forty affiliated companies that belong to the KOLON Group. KOLON started by producing nylon in Korea in 1957. The group's name, KOLON, originated by combining the first syllable of Korea and the last syllable of nylon. Since then the company has become a leader in the Korean textile industry and takes great pride in its contributions to economic development of Korea.

The group has expanded into various business areas, including electronics, distribution, construction, chemical products, and pharmaceuticals and became a holding company in 2009. The total annual sales of the KOLON Group are approximately $10 billion, of which KOLON Industries accounts for 40 percent, KOLON Global accounts for 30 percent, and the other affiliated companies account for the remaining 30 percent. KOLON Industries previously belonged to the manufacturing division of the KOLON Corporation but separated to form a holding company in 2010. Each of the four business divisions of KOLON Industries—industrial materials, chemical, films, and electronic materials and fashion—holds a competitive position in its area. KOLON Industries employs approximately 3,700 people, and its annual sales total around $4 billion, with $200 million in net operating profits. The FNC Organization is the fashion division of KOLON Industries and manages twenty-seven brands in various categories ranging from outdoor, sports and golf, men's fashion, women's fashion, casual fashion, shoes and bags, premium fashion, and cultural space. The annual

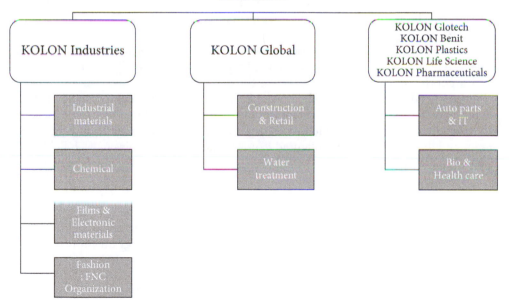

FIGURE 17.1 The breakdown of KOLON Corporation's enterprises. (Source: KOLON Industries, FNC Organization)

sales of the FNC Organization account for approximately \$1 billion and it employs more than 1,000 people.

Epigram started as one of the lines in the Series brand of men's casual wear. Traditionally, most Korean men's fashion brands have focused on formal suit items. However, since its launch in 2006, Series used a different merchandising and product category approach than other Korean menswear brands (KOLON Industries: Menswear 2018). It was a very attractive brand for trend leaders who pursued a new and original style. Over time, however, because of changing wants and needs of consumers, customer loyalty to Series began to decrease.

Epigram was launched in 2013 as a new brand to address these issues. In 2017, Series achieved sales of \$75 million in seventy stores through differentiated and refined brand concepts and product planning, merchandise allocation according to store characteristics, and visual merchandising

Business Problem

Challenges to the progress of lifestyle merchandising

Epigram has grown to become a lifestyle brand with the concept of "almost home" by offering various lifestyle products such as a women's line, food, and beverages (e.g., Korean agricultural products and traditional tea products) along with menswear. As can be inferred from the concept of "almost home," Epigram offers everything related to the home and Epigram's women's line offers various styles and daily wear with a comfortable silhouette, neutral colors, and simple designs. Epigram has also introduced various brands to suit different people's lifestyles.

In an interview with Han Kyung-Ae, executive director of the FNC Organization who manages Epigram, Ms.Han explained in detail the reasons Epigram was launched, the problems that occurred throughout the launch process, and the concept behind selling lifestyle items. The brand introduction documents and brand books were cited for further information.

Epigram started initially as a product line of Series. It was designed to attract new customers to Series by offering a more minimal style at a reasonable price. The Epigram line received a good response from customers in the Series stores who were more interested in their lifestyle products. Han wanted to make Epigram an independent brand but it was no longer enough to appeal to Korean customers through clothing alone; to construct Epigram's product merchandising Han decided to incorporate lifestyle items. In addition to clothing, cosmetics and living items were configured from specialized companies in each field. Lifestyle items were placed in spaces (e.g., a man's house, a man's room) and arranged in familiar and casual ways for customers.

Epigram was launched in department stores in fall 2015. Through the concept of "almost home," living rooms, kitchens, bed-rooms, and so on were designed, where clothing and lifestyle items were presented in the same space. The living room space in the middle of the store operated as a customized workshop classroom where Epigram coordinated events for men or families such as making candles with healing herbs, making socks, and art psychotherapy.

Epigram opened its first pop-up store with the theme "almost home 1" in Wonseo-dong, Jongro-gu, in May 2015 and tested the lifestyle concept for three months. The store was located next to the stone wall of Changdeok Palace, an important Korean historic place and UNESCO World Heritage Site. The Changdeok Palace and its surroundings, in natural and perfect harmony, aligned well with Epigram's concept of "almost home." The pop-up store represented a single-person household and consisted of three floors. It included a living room, kitchen, bathroom, and garden. It succeeded not only in representing someone's home but also in letting people experience a lifestyle. Lifestyle-oriented food and lifestyle brands were exhibited with clothes. There was also a brand selling products for dogs that had recently been launched by the FNC Organization's upcycling brand Re;Code, and a natural gentle detergent brand. Customers could experience how Epigram displays products to recreate the familiar space of home. During the opening, social dining, interior, and table setting classes were also held. Epigram's identity and concept was demonstrated to customers and people in the retail distribution industry. Of course, there were minor problems in the display of lifestyle items. For example, bottled jams and fruits were temperature sensitive, which caused some problems. These issues were taken into consideration in the design of the next pop-up store. Through the success of the pop-up store, Epigram became an independent brand, and its identity was established as a lifestyle brand. Because of the adequate testing process, there was no objection to Epigram being an independent brand.

FIGURE 17.2 One of the main concessions in the Hyundai department store, Pangyo branch with the concept of "men's bed-room," Seoul, Korea, 2017. (Source: Epigram Brand Introduction document/ KOLON Industries, FNC Organization)

References and Further Reading

Akim Mousterou. 2016 "United Arrows' Hirofumi Kurino Explains His Vision." Accessed November 2017. http://www.scmp.com/magazines/style/article/1975047/brains-behind-brand-united-arrows-hirofumi-kurino-explains-his

Amed Imran. "How do you create brand awareness?" *Business of Fashion* Accessed August 2015 https://www.businessoffashion.com/articles/basics/how-do-you-create-brand-awareness

Avery Jill and Gamze Yucaoglu. 2015. "Mavi: Fashioning a Path to Brand Growth." In *Harvard Business Review*, USA; Harvard Business School Publication Corp., May 03, 2017. Accessed November 2017. https://www.businessoffashion.com/articles/basics/how-do-you-create-brand-awareness

BySeries Epigram. Accessed June 2018, https://www.byseries.com/Brand/6031/SubMain

Johnson Noah. 2017 "How United Arrows Became Huge in Japan (And Ready for Global Expansion)." Accessed November 2017. https://www.gq.com/story/united-arrows-japan-global-expansion

KOLON Industries. 2018. Home. Accessed March 12, 2018. http://www.kolonindustries.com/Eng/main.asp

KOLON Industries: Menswear. 2018. Series. Accessed March 12, 2018. http://www.kolonindustries.com/Eng//Product/product05_02.asp

Definitions

Brand management: Analysis and planning strategies to determine how a brand is perceived in the market.

Lifestyle brand: A brand that offers a merchandise assortment that represents the interests, lifestyle, and attitudes of a particular target customer.

Market research: Strategies for gathering, analyzing, and interpreting data about consumers' wants and needs.

Chapter 18

Adoption of the "See Now Buy Now" Business Model in the Fashion Industry

A Fashion Calendar Revolution

Jennifer Kyungeun Lee

The Stella & Co. is a globally renowned designer and women's luxury apparel company that was established in 1992 and is currently based in New York City. There are two private labels directly owned and operated by the company, The Stella and The S, both of which are currently globally distributed through independent boutiques in fashion capitals such as New York City, Milan, and Paris. To ensure lower production costs without sacrificing product quality, the company has been dependent on its global supply chain partners to manufacture their products. Since 2012, the company has presented their collection via ready-to-wear runway shows, because 60 percent of wholesale orders are placed during the market weeks held right after the shows. Starting in 2016, the "see now buy now" business model, requiring immediate delivery after the runway show, began gaining popularity. The model has already been adopted by major luxury fashion brands such as Ralph Lauren, Tom Ford, and Burberry. Currently, there are increasing numbers of fashion brands fully or partially adopting this model and The Stella has been under pressure from consumers to do so as well.

Before adopting the "see now buy now" business model as a new venture of the company, The Stella must consider several issues, such as their heavy emphasis on wholesaling, their lack of mobile-commerce infrastructure, and their non-vertically integrated supply chain system. Now, The Stella has to make a decision on how best to react. How should the company respond to the market to create more positive responses from buyers towards the brands and to achieve larger sale volumes in future seasons?

Learning Objectives

Upon completion of this case, students should be able to:

- Analyze pros and cons in the revolution of the fashion calendar in the fashion industry.
- Understand relationships among brands, the supply chain, and mobile commerce in the "see now buy now" business model.
- Apply a case-based approach to learn about potential pitfalls to accepting the "see now buy now" business model.
- Identify how to proceed with a "see now buy now" business model for increasing in-season sale volumes.

Introduction

The Stella & Co.

The Stella & Co. is a globally renowned designer and luxury women's apparel company established in 1992 and based in New York City. The company originally started with The Stella, a private label brand targeting women in their thirties to forties in a high-end market. In 2017, a new line, The S, was launched that catered affordable luxury to consumers in their twenties to early thirties. Beginning with their the Fall 2002 show, The Stella and The S collection have been continuously presented to international retail clients during New York fashion week. Every year, during the market weeks occurring after their runway shows, approximately 60 percent of seasonal orders are placed by their global wholesale accounts from over twenty countries including the UK, France, Italy, China, and Japan. These orders are normally distributed to wholesalers' distribution centers within four to six months from the order dates. To manufacture products at lower costs without sacrificing quality, the company has collaborated with several global supply chain partners, mainly located in Asian countries such as China, Vietnam, and India. These partners normally require a production lead-time of at least three months to fulfill their orders from The Stella.

The "see now buy now" business model

In 2016, the emergence of the "see now buy now" business model, which made collections available to consumers immediately after their runway presentation, was considered to be a revolutionary phenomenon in the fashion industry. Many designer brands, such as Ralph Lauren, Tom Ford, and Burberry, adopted the "see now buy now" approach within their business model (Paton 2012). Using mobile phones while watching the runway shows, consumers can place an order in real time for items they like. There are three conditions required for fashion companies to successfully manage the "see now buy now" business model. First, a fashion company must be able to operate two different fashion calendars; one for the "see now buy now" merchandise and another for traditional retail. Until the "see now buy now" approach is proven as being sustainable for use as a long-lasting business model in the fashion industry, it is safer for fashion companies to run the model in addition to the traditional delivery schedule. Second, the "see now buy now" business model is a direct-to-consumer model that allows consumers to place an order for items in real time while watching them on the runway. Mobile commerce is one of the most frequently used purchasing tools for consumers enabling instant access to their selected items. Fashion companies must have a strong IT infrastructure in place to operate mobile commerce for their brands. Finally, consumers expect to receive their orders within one to two weeks from the dates that orders were placed during or after the runway shows. For immediate order fulfillment, a brand must manage vertically integrated production systems, which provide full access to controlling production lines and the calendar of the company's own factories or supply chain partners.

Recently, The Stella has been under pressure from consumers to adopt the "see now buy now" business model. There are several issues that the company must consider before they decide whether to go ahead with this as a new company venture.

Business Problem

Confusion of consumers

Due to a long-standing adherence to the traditional retail calendar, The Stella's wholesale buyers, as well as consumers, might be confused with the new fashion calendar of the "see now buy now" business model. Despite an increasing number of consumers in their twenties, a majority of The Stella's consumers are older and not accustomed to changes in the fashion calendar. These older consumers might still prefer to see the collections during fashion week and purchase items months later in stores after they have had a chance to consider them.

To minimize confusion of consumers not familiar with the new fashion calendar, some fashion companies are trying to modify the "see now buy now" approach as it fits between traditional seasonal fashion calendars. At present, it would be too early for The Stella to follow similar strategies of modification in their fashion calendar.

Supply chain capabilities

In the "see now buy now" model, one of the most important requirements is immediate delivery after the runway show, which generally works better for large fashion companies with a vertically integrated supply chain. For The Stella, a mid-size privately owned company, due to a heavy emphasis on wholesale to department stores, which needs at least a few months of delivery lead-time, there would be two separated production schedules operating; one for wholesale and another for the "see now buy now" model. This may overwhelm their supply chain, one not ready for such changes. Additionally, The Stella's supply chain partners work with multiple fashion companies. Normally, fashion companies with a larger order volume are a priority for the supply chain.

Direct to consumer model

The "see now buy now" model is a direct-to-consumer model that depends on an omni-channel approach—a multichannel approach to sales providing consumers with seamless shopping experiences online through a desktop computer or mobile device, or by telephone and bricks-and-mortar stores. A direct-to-consumer model is not aligned with The Stella's current retail channel strategy because rather than online platforms, the company currently retails mostly in department stores. Due to a lack of IT infrastructure, the company has not fully equipped mobile commerce. Hence, at this moment, an adoption of the direct-to-consumer model could put the company's long-standing vendor relationships in jeopardy.

Design, production, and retailing challenges

Regarding new fashion designs and production, "see now buy now" creates challenges for fashion brands as well as for retailers such as department-store buyers. In contrast to a traditional fashion retail cycle, "see now buy now" allows almost zero opportunities for fashion brands to try out new styles, instead, it requires fashion brands to produce only safe fashion items that some consumers might like and others might be bored by. As far as production in "see now buy now" is concerned, in order to avoid angering consumers, fashion brands must have sufficient quantities of merchandise with limited discount offerings. For The Stella as a well-known brand for innovative designs, committing to big production volumes of new styles without demand testing could have a huge drawback for their sales. Furthermore, since sales growth of department stores has been lower than single brand stores and e-commerce platforms, department-store buyers are losing their power and influence in the fashion industry.

The company's action

Despite the company's concerns, the "see now buy now" model has become more and more popular in the fashion industry. Now, The Stella has to make decisions about how best to react. Given its situation, should the company adopt a "see now buy now" model, or continue with its traditional design, production, and delivery schedule?

Business Questions

1   If you were an owner of The Stella, what would you do if your buyers continued to ask for your company to adopt the "see now buy now" model?

2   If you were one of the wholesalers purchasing from The Stella, what win-win strategies would you suggest The Stella operate to minimize potential risks of adopting the "see now buy now" model while satisfying consumer desire to use "see now buy now"?

3   Considering the current case, why would you consider adopting or not adopting "see now buy now" for the company's future growth?

References and Further Reading

Friedman, Vanessa. 2016. "How Smartphones Are Killing Off the Fashion Show." *The New York Times*, February 11. Accesed August 14, 2018. https://www.nytimes.com/2016/02/11/fashion/new-york-fashion-week-smartphones-killing-off-runway-show.html

Friedman, Vanessa. 2017. "These Three Hidden Omnichannel Costs Hurt Indie Retailers." *Apparel*, February 23. Accesed August 14, 2018. https://www.apparelmag.com/these-three-hidden-omnichannel-costs-hurt-indie-retailers

Paton Elizabeth. 2012. Fashion Shows Adopted a See-Now, Buy-Now Model. Has It Worked?*The New York Times*, February 7. Accesed August 14, 2018. https://www.nytimes.com/2017/02/07/fashion/see-now-buy-now-business-fashion-week.html

PART FOUR

Manufacturing, Supply Chain, and Technology

Introduction

This section includes case studies that focus on the challenges and opportunities that professionals in the fashion industry face in the areas of fashion manufacturing, supply chain management, and technologies used throughout companies' supply chains. Supply chain networks "include all of the interconnected individuals, businesses, and processes that are necessary to get a product to the ultimate consumer" (Burns and Mullet 2020, p. 2). Fashion brand companies use a variety of strategies to create supply chains that:

- Assure that the sectors within their supply chain work together.
- Enhance economic, environmental, social, and cultural sustainability.
- Create optimal time frames for meeting consumer demand.
- Are logistically managed in ways that result in effective and efficient flow of materials and products.

(Burns and Mullet 2020, p. 37)

Assuring effective, efficient, and sustainable supply chains poses numerous challenges and opportunities for fashion brand companies. Fashion brand companies must effectively coordinate all aspects of their supply chains to align with their companies' mission, objectives, and supply chain calendars. Professionals in the fashion industry must weigh the advantages and disadvantages of strategies associated with manufacturing, supply chain management, and technologies to best meet their companies' requirements. The case studies included in this section explore decisions of professionals around supply chain crises, supply chain transparency, sourcing decisions, and new technologies that affect supply chains.

References and Further Reading

Burns, Leslie Davis and Kathy K. Mullet (2020). *The Business of Fashion: Designing, Manufacturing, and Marketing*. 6th ed. New York: Fairchild Books/Bloomsbury.

Ha-Brookshire, Jung (2017). *Global Sourcing in the Textile and Apparel Industry*. 2nd ed. New York: Fairchild Books/Bloomsbury.

Londrigan, Michael and Jacqueline M. Jenkins (2018). *Fashion Supply Chain Management*. New York: Fairchild Books/Bloomsbury.

Chapter 19

Faux, Faux Fur

Responding to Supply Chain Crises

Myles Ethan Lascity

Fashion's use of fur has been contentious for decades. Starting in the 1990s, groups such as the Human Society International and People for the Ethical Treatment of Animals (PETA), led a revolution against using real fur in products through their famed "I'd rather go naked than wear fur" campaign. In 1994, Calvin Klein became the first major fashion designer to go fur-free, after PETA occupied the company's New York City headquarters. More recently, National Geographic noted a rise in fashion's use of fur and Karl Lagerfeld publicly defended it, even as designers like Michael Kors, Jimmy Choo, Armani, and Gucci have stopped the practice.

Another issue has sprung up, though, thanks to questionable supply chains. A Sky News and Humane Society investigation uncovered that products labelled as "faux fur" had been incorrectly labelled and contained real fur from rabbits, cats, and other animals. This has created both practical and ethical considerations for companies as consumers and governmental regulators have been upset by this discovery.

In this scenario case, students will be asked to see themselves as an executive for FauxBo Chic, a clothing and accessories company billed as fur-free but that had been inadvertently selling real products. Students will be tasked with outlining the company's response from better investigating their supply chain to a public relations campaign to restore faith in its faux-fur fashion

Learning Objectives

Upon completion of this case, students should be able to:

- Understand the business and ethical implications of supply chain decisions.
- Contemplate and justify business actions.
- Respond to business threats and public relations issues.

FIGURE 19.1 Luxury designer brands, such as Versace, have turned to faux fur. © JP Yim/Getty Images

Introduction

Picture it: New York City, two-thousand and something.

A young entrepreneur (you!) finally achieves their dream of striking out on their own to open a boutique clothing store. It took years of scrimping and saving as you worked as a personal shopper and buyer for a big, well-known fashion brand before you were able to make your own dream come true. Sure, it's not much—just a little storefront on a side street in SoHo, but it's *all yours*. Besides, you heard Tommy Hilfiger started out this way.

The best part: this new venture not only allows you to be your own boss and decide the type of boutique you want to own, but also allows you to free your conscience and be a 100 percent cruelty free shop. No animals are harmed in the making of your products, which means no leather and absolutely no fur.

You and your friends even decided upon the perfect name for the store one night while you were sipping on cocktails at your local haunt: FauxBo Chic. You love it—not only is it a riff off of boho chic, but it perfectly encapsulates the look you're going for and identifies the main selling point of your shop: selling cruelty-free fashions that look like the real thing.

Business Problem

Everything seems to be going swimmingly. After a few months in business, your clientele is growing and you have even been named as a "Store to Watch" by a prominent fashion blogger. You have been able to stop relying on friends to staff the store and currently have a small staff that takes care of the customer service, while you have been able to preoccupy yourself finding quality, ethical products and—at times—designing a few things of your own.

At first, you used local production venues for your products, but as your demands have picked up, you have started using a new overseas supplier. The man you talked to seemed nice enough and guaranteed the products would be ethically made of only the best synthetic fibers. And sure, the seller was vague about the production, but he *promised* it was all on the up-and-up.

Even better, the faux-fur movement seems to be gaining steam as none other than Donatella Versace has announced she is against using fur. Other designers such as Tom Ford and Michael Kors had disavowed fur, but the House of Versace seems like a whole other level (Bobb 2018).

"This really has legs," you say to yourself as you send off a press release announcing your inventory to the consumer reporter at *NY1*.

You didn't think much of it when the reporter showed up a few days later asking questions about your products and your ethical stances. You have dealt with reporters before and while her questioning didn't seem extensive, she picked up a few items you had recently received from your new supplier. Hopefully, she'll give you some good press, you continue on about your work and the interview fades to the back of your mind.

A few days later, the reporter drops by again and says she has a few more questions. With the camera rolling, she says the unthinkable.

"We had some materials experts test your products and found out that they actually *do* contain fur," she says as she stares you down. "Did you know?"

"What? That can't be!" you sputter and you feel your cheeks flush. "Of course they're not fur! The whole point of this store is to sell things that *aren't fur!*

"Our experts said that without a doubt, these," the reporter pauses for emphasis as she gestures to the products she had purchased during the last visit, "are definitely made of animal fur."

The reality quickly sets in that all the products the reporter is talking about are from your new supplier. You paused as you try to think of something to say. The big corporations like Neiman Marcus, Nordstrom, and Kohl's have had problems like this (O'Conner 2017), but this isn't supposed to happen to you. You aren't motivated just by profit, you really care about animals, and you would have never stocked these products had you known how they were made.

Business Questions

1 As the business owner being confronted with this news, how would you react to the reporter? What steps would you take immediately after the questioning? After the airing of the segment?

2 If you were in this scenario, is there anything you would have done differently?

3 How trusting would be you be of an overseas importer?

4 How much responsibility does a retailer have to investigate a supply chain?

5 Following this new information, would you trust this supplier again? Why or why not?

6 Imagine you are a customer who shopped at FauxBo Chic because of its ethical stances, but you have just seen the *NY1* report calling their products into question. Would you continue to shop there? Why? If they lost your business, what could they do to make amends?

7 In the above fictional scenario, the owner is a small business rather than a large corporation that has been found using real fur. Is the ethical onus different for large corporations who sell "faux fur" than for small businesses? Which should pay more attention to the supply chain?

References and Further Reading

Bobb, Brooke. 2018. "Donatella Versace Says Fur is Over." *Vogue*, March 14. Accessed July 27, 2018. https://www.vogue.com/article/donatella-versace-fur

Burns, Leslie Davis, Kathy K. Mullet, and Nancy O. Bryant. 2016. "Sourcing Decisions and Production Centers." In *The Business of Fashion: Designing, Manufacturing and Marketing*. New York: Fairchild.

Cline, Elizabeth L. 2013. *Overdressed: The Shockingly High Cost of Cheap Fashion*. New York: Portfolio.

Conniff, Richard. 2016. "Why Fur is Back in Fashion." *National Geographic*, September Accessed July 27, 2018. https://www.nationalgeographic.com/magazine/2016/09/skin-trade-fur-fashion/

Entrepreneur. 2013. "How to Find Suppliers for a New Business." *Entrepreneur Magazine*, February 19. Accessed July 27, 2018. https://www.entrepreneur.com/article/225774

Hajibagheri, Sarah. 2017. "More 'Fur Free' Retailers Found Selling Rabbit and Fox Fur, Sky News Finds." *Sky News*, December 20. Accessed July 27, 2018. https://news.sky.com/story/more-retailers-selling-real-fur-labelled-as-fake-sky-news-investigation-finds-11177979

Leitch, Luke. 2018. "Versace: The Resurrection." *1843 Magazine*, April/May Accessed July 27, 2018. https://www.1843magazine.com/style/versace-the-resurrection

O'Conner, Tamison. 2017. "Is Your 'Faux Fur' Really Fake?" *Business of Fashion*, December 21. Accessed July 27, 2018. https://www.businessoffashion.com/articles/intelligence/is-your-faux-fur-really-fake

Chapter 20

H&M Post-Rana Plaza

Can Fast Fashion Ever Be Truly Ethical?

David S. Waller and Helen J. Waller

In 2017, the Swedish-based global clothes retailer H&M was chosen as one of the World's Most Ethical Companies, for the seventh consecutive time, by the Ethisphere Institute. H&M is an example of a "fast fashion" retailer, which produces clothing that is designed quickly and produced cheaply to take advantage of the latest trend, which is then discarded for the next trend. Fast fashion has been heavily criticized for poor business practices, such as outsourcing production to factories overseas with unsafe working conditions, and a number of tragedies have been connected to its lower manufacturing and labor costs. On the other hand, ethical fashion, produced with environmentally friendly materials with workers making the apparel in safe conditions for fair wages, seems at odds with the fast fashion model. While there has been growing interest in ethical fashion among consumers, along with increasing awareness of environmental- and social-based ethically produced clothes, the collapse of the Rana Plaza factory in Bangladesh in 2013—which killed more than 1,000 garment workers—brought the world's attention firmly to this issue. Since the tragedy, H&M has spearheaded ethical reforms in the fast fashion industry. This case introduces the concepts of ethical clothing and fast fashion, and examines H&M's efforts to act ethically and sustainably since Rana Plaza, posing the question, "Can fast fashion ever be truly ethical?"

Learning Objectives

Upon completion of this case, students should be able to:

1 Understand the concepts of ethical clothing and fast fashion.
2 Identify H&M's ethical practices and policies since Rana Plaza.

3   Evaluate whether fast fashion can ever be truly ethical.

4   Propose future practices for a fast fashion company, such as H&M, to continue ethical and sustainable work.

Introduction

Managers in the fashion industry must often make decisions regarding appropriate and responsible actions in relation to the selection of raw materials, production, and marketing based on ethical considerations. While a particular action may be within the law or industry guidelines, it still may not be considered "ethical," and can therefore reflect badly on the brand. A lapse in ethical standards or judgment can result in actions that are highly visible and often very damaging to a company's reputation, leading to negative publicity, product withdrawals, or even consumer boycotts.

Ethical fashion

Interest in the manufacture and sale of "ethical fashion" has been increasing over the last twenty years. The concept of "fashion with a conscience" includes "fashionable clothes that incorporate fair trade principles with sweatshop-free labor conditions while not harming the environment or workers" (Joergens 2006, 361). The website Conscious & Chic (https://www.fashionwithaconscience.org) explains ethical fashion as "ethical = eco, thrift, vintage, charitable, local or fair trade."

The term "ethical" in a fashion context relates to "the positive impact of (1) a designer, (2) a consumer choice or (3) a method of production as experienced by workers, consumers, animals, society and the environment" (Thomas 2008). Haug and Busch (2016) expanded this idea with an "ethical fashion framework," identifying the relationships, roles, responsibilities, and influence of market and supplier regulators, consumers, mediators, designers, marketers, producers, suppliers, and workers in the fashion industry with the goal of creating an ethical fashion. In particular, this highlights the complexity of the process and the influence of consumer responsibility and fashion industry responsibility. Therefore, the process of supplying ethical fashion items means that there are roles and responsibilities from various stakeholders.

Fast fashion

Ethics and ethical practices are particularly pertinent for "fast fashion" retailers. Fast fashion is defined as low-cost fashionable clothing that has a high turnaround with a largely negative impact on the environment and people (Joy et al. 2012). H&M, Zara, and Topshop are seen as major practitioners of fast fashion. You might have shopped at a fast fashion store and noticed a quick turnover of clothes and accessories on display, the cheap prices and variable quality of products. You may have even bought something there and never worn it.

The "largely unregulated churn and burn of fast fashion" has been criticized for producing poorly made clothes, which are sent to landfills on mass, thereby increasing CO2 emissions. Fast fashion has also faced criticism for the environmental impact of large-scale cotton production and the disempowerment of women, with primarily female garment workers or underaged girls earning less than $3 per day for an average of 14 hours in sweatshops to produce clothes for fast fashion retailers (Barenblat 2017).

Rana Plaza

While there has been ongoing consumer interest in the making and purchase of ethically made clothing for many years, the fashion's industry's corporate responsibility was brought to the fore on April 24, 2013, when an eight-story garment factory, known as the Rana Plaza, in Dhaka, Bangladesh, collapsed killing 1,134 people and injuring around 2,500 more, many of whom were primarily garment workers. The building, which fell due to a structural failure, has been described as "the deadliest garment-factory accident in history" (Young 2013). This caused a number of well-known global brands, including several department stores, clothing specialists, and fast fashion brands, such as Benetton, Bonmarché, the Children's Place, Joe Fresh, Mango, Matalan, Primark, and Walmart (Guilford 2013), to be identified as companies using garment factories in Rana Plaza as suppliers, in addition to other factories that employed sweatshop conditions. The spotlight caused by this tragedy put pressure on these companies to change their supply chain and put policies and measures in place to prevent such a tragedy taking place again—and to manage their brand communication about ethics to the increasingly aware and conscious consumer.

In an environment of increasing interest and concern for ethically made clothes, what activities and company policies can fast fashion clothing manufacturers and retailers put into place to ensure that they not only do good, but are seen to do good by their customers? In many ways, ethical fashion is seen as a way of resisting the convention of "fast fashion," so is it possible for the two concepts to coexist in one brand?

FIGURE 20.1 Since the Rana Plaza tragedy greater attention has been given to ethical fashion. But is it enough? © MUNIR UZ ZAMAN/AFP via Getty Images

Business Problem

H&M, the Swedish-based global fast fashion clothes retailer, was not linked to any of the companies involved in the Rana Plaza disaster, but it nevertheless took a lead in encouraging ethical and sustainable practice in the fashion industry. In May 2013, H&M was one of the first globally influential brands to sign on to the "Accord on Factory and Building Safety in Bangladesh", which is a legally binding agreement between over 200 global clothing brands, retailers, and importers, two global and eight Bangladeshi trade unions, and four NGO witnesses, to ensure a safe and healthy working environment in the Bangladeshi ready made garment industry. Another agreement was signed in July 2013 when 17 major North American retailers, calling themselves the "Alliance for Bangladesh Worker Safety", announced the Bangladesh Worker Safety Initiative which included initiatives like factory inspections and safety commitment, establishing common safety standards for factories, worker training, and a worker voice.

H&M has become proactive in providing ethical product lines, launching organic collections, ensuring products are produced with environmentally friendly materials, stocking fair trade products where the makers are given a fair wage while working in safe conditions, and encouraging the collection of old clothes for recycling of the material. This reflects the trend in "ethical branding," where fashion brands and retailers target the environmentally aware market with specific offerings (Beard 2008; Manchiraju and Sadachar 2014).

H&M states on its website: "We want to make fashion sustainable and sustainability fashionable" (H&M 2017b). Its vision is "to use our size and scale to lead the change towards circular and renewable fashion while being a fair and equal company." For example, Arket is a brand in the H&M group that launched in August 2017, which "pushes transparency, which is vital to help keep corporations accountable, to a new level for mass-market fashion" (Bain 2017).

H&M has several policies throughout the organization and actions at the production and retail level to help it in its mission to be sustainable (H&M 2017c).

Some of the proactive ethically based activities that H&M undertake are as follows:

- H&M has some of the strictest standards for animal welfare, such as not accepting animal testing on cosmetic products or selling any real fur or angora wool.
- It is one of the world's largest users of organic cotton, with sustainably sourced cotton currently representing 43 percent of their cotton use, and recycled polyester.
- It does not accept child labor and has strict expectations for suppliers.
- It has clear guidelines for home working allowed by suppliers.
- All standard plastic bags are made from recycled plastic.
- As around "26% of the carbon emissions in a garment's lifetime occur after it has left the store" (H&M 2017c), H&M encourages caring for clothes in a sustainable way, and as part of their "Bring It" campaign, it aims to "close the loop" by providing customers with a way to hand in unwanted garments to be reused or recycled.
- Following the "close the loop" initiative, in 2014 H&M launched its first Close the Loop collection made with recycled textile fibers.
- Ninety-six percent of electricity used throughout H&M owned operations comes from renewable sources.

In 2015, H&M, IndustriALL, and Swedish trade union IF Metall signed The Global Framework Agreement, which is a collaboration to improve worker–employer dialogue at

H&M suppliers. However, there has been criticism of other agreements mentioned earlier, the "Accord on Factory and Building Safety in Bangladesh" and "Alliance for Bangladesh Worker Safety," even by the Bangladeshi government, which want to control and oversight of the industry (Kashyap 2017). These agreements were phased out in 2018 (Donaldson 2017) and the global retailers had to organize new arrangements and contracts with suppliers in Bangladesh. This will mean that different approaches will need to be taken with suppliers in the country by the fast fashion retailers in the future.

As the H&M group expands around the world with different brands, like COS, Monki, and Arket, it is important that there is a coordinated effort to ensure that ethical and sustainable policies are smoothly implemented. It can be difficult to ensure that corporate guidelines and expectations are strictly followed by suppliers and local managers in outlets worldwide. Can H&M guarantee that all stakeholders hold the same ethical values as the head office and still make a profit?

Finally, it is important for producers, outsourced manufacturers, retailers, media, and consumers to remember the ethical consequences of their actions and make an effort to produce, promote, purchase, and even dispose of affordable and accessible ethical fashion. However, in such a fast-paced part of the industry, this can be difficult to coordinate.

Despite H&M's efforts, criticism that fast fashion retailers are not doing enough to improve their ethical standards remains. Fast fashion calls for a quick turnover of inexpensive clothing, which can result in cost-cutting already underpaid factory workers, product oversupply and waste, and an increase in consumers' awareness of issues regarding ethically made clothing, particularly since the Rana Plaza tragedy. This leads us to question whether fast fashion retailers can ever truly be ethical in their practices.

Business Questions

1 What is "ethical clothing"? Give examples of how a clothing manufacturer can make its products more "ethical."

2 What are the advantages and disadvantages of focusing on being a sustainable fashion company?

3 What does transparency mean in the fashion industry? How does transparency improve sustainability?

4 Go the Sustainability section of the H&M website and review their ethical practices and policies. Which do you believe are the most important issues? Are there any issues you believe should be included in the future?

5 Do you believe that a fast fashion company can ever be truly ethical? Give reasons for and against your answer.

6 The case mentions the "Accord on Factory and Building Safety in Bangladesh" and "Alliance for Bangladesh Worker Safety," which are being phased out. What are the benefits of such initiatives? Who are the beneficiaries? What activities should be included in agreements in the future?

References and Further Reading

Bain, M. 2017. "H&M's New Brand, Arket, Names the Factory that Made Its Clothes. But the Name Isn't Enough." *Quartz*, August 30. https://qz.com/1064098/hms-new-brand-arket-is-fashions-transparency-conundrum-in-a-nutshell/

Barenblat, A. 2017. "Fast Fashion Is a Disaster for Women and the Environment." *Forbes*, July 26. https://www.forbes.com/sites/quora/2017/07/26/fast-fashion-is-a-disaster-for-women-and-the-environment/#589eaea11fa4

Beard, N. D. 2008. "The Branding of Ethical Fashion and the Consumer: A Luxury Niche or Mass-market Reality? *Fashion Theory* 12 (4): 447–467.

Clean Clothes Campaign. n.d. Rana Plaza: A Man-made Disaster that Shook the World." *Clean Clothes Campaign*. https://cleanclothes.org/ua/2013/rana-plaza

Diviney, E. and S. Lillywhite. 2007. *Ethical Threads: Corporate Social Responsibility in the Australian Garment Industry*. Melbourne: Brotherhood of St Laurence. Accessed July 22, 2015. http://library.bsl.org.au/jspui/handle/1/1727

Donaldson, T. 2017. "Accord and Alliance Will Leave Bangladesh Next Year." *Sourcing Journal*, October 24. https://sourcingjournalonline.com/accord-alliance-will-leave-bangladesh-next-year/

Guilford, Gwynn. 2013. "Here Are the Western Retailers that Source Clothes from the Bangladeshi Factories Where over 200 Workers Died." *Quartz Media Llc*. Accessed November 20, 2017. https://qz.com/78162/here-are-the-western-retailers-that-source-clothes-from-the-bangladeshi-factories-where-over-200-workers-died/

Haug, A. and J. Busch. 2016. "Towards an Ethical Fashion Framework." *Fashion Theory* 20 (3): 317–339.

H&M. 2017a. "H&M Named as One of the World's Most Ethical Companies." *H&M Press Release*, March 13. https://about.hm.com/en/media/news/general-2017/h-m-group-named-as-one-of-the-worlds-most-ethical-companies.html

H&M. 2017b. "How We Do It." http://about.hm.com/en/about-us/h-m-group-at-a-glance.html

H&M. 2017c. "Our Policies." http://sustainability.hm.com/en/sustainability/downloads-resources/policies/policies.html

Jägel, T., K. Keeling, A. Reppel, and T. Gruber. 2012. "Individual Values and Motivational Complexities in Ethical Clothing Consumption: A Means-end Approach." *Journal of Marketing Management* 28 (3–4): 373–396.

Joergens, C. 2006. "Ethical Fashion: Myth or Future Trend? *Journal of Fashion Marketing and Management: An International Journal* 10 (3): 360–371.

Joy, A., J. F. Sherry Jr., A. Venkatesh, J. Wang, and R. Chan. 2012. "Fast Fashion, Sustainability, and the Ethical Appeal of Luxury Brands." *Fashion Theory* 16 (3): 273–295.

Kashyap, A. 2017. "Bangladesh Textile Mill Burns, Yet Again: Government Should Publish Reports on Factories It Inspects." *Human Rights Watch*, September 21. https://www.hrw.org/news/2017/09/21/bangladesh-textile-mill-burns-yet-again

Kaufman, A. C. 2016. "Before Buying More Clothes at H&M, Read This." *Huffington Post*, September 20. https://www.huffingtonpost.com.au/entry/hm-ethical_us_57d6a8a1e4b00642712e45f0

Księżak, P. 2017. "The CSR Challenges in the Clothing Industry." *Journal of Corporate Responsibility and Leadership* 3 (2): 51–65.

Manchiraju, S. and A. Sadachar. 2014. "Personal Values and Ethical Fashion Consumption." *Journal of Fashion Marketing and Management* 18 (3): 357–374.

Reimers, V., V. Reimers, B. Magnuson, B. Magnuson, F. Chao, and F. Chao. 2016. "The Academic Conceptualisation of Ethical Clothing: Could It Account for the Attitude Behaviour Gap? *Journal of Fashion Marketing and Management: An International Journal* 20 (4): 383–399.

Shaw, D., G. Hogg, E. Wilson, E. Shiu, and L. Hassan. 2006. "Fashion Victim: The Impact of Fair Trade Concerns on Clothing Choice." *Journal of Strategic Marketing* 14 (4): 427–440.

Shen, B., Y. Wang, C. K. Lo, and M. Shum. 2012. "The Impact of Ethical Fashion on Consumer Purchase Behavior." *Journal of Fashion Marketing and Management: An International Journal* 16 (2): 234–245.

Thomas, S. 2008. "From 'Green Blur' to Eco Fashion: Fashioning an Eco-Lexicon." *Fashion Theory* 12 (4): 525–540.

Tseëlon, E. 2011. "Introduction: A Critique of the Ethical Fashion Paradigm." *Critical Studies in Fashion & Beauty* 2 (1–2): 3–68.

Young, Matt. 2013. "The Forgotten Tragedy: Six Months on from the Rana Plaza Factory Collapse in Bangladesh." News.com.au, October 29. http://www.news.com.au/world/the-forgotten-tragedy-six-months-on-from-the-rana-plaza-factory-collapse-in-bangladesh/news-story/189cca9f6defccf4c65b88ae1e95f171

Chapter 21

The Hiut Denim Company

Is One Product Enough?

Clare McTurk

Denim has dominated fashion markets for centuries making it one of the most widely used materials in the world. Established in 2012, Hiut Denim Co. is an exciting lifestyle denim brand that manufactures premium British-made jeans. Unlike most fashion brands Hiut Denim focus all their energy on one product "Denim Jeans." Hiut jeans use the very best raw materials, with handcrafted detailing and artisan processes, and benefit from a unique communication and sustainability strategy, including a free repair service. The mens and womens jeans sell for £100–£230 per pair, and are constructed in a former Marks and Spencer denim-manufacturing town in Wales.

This case study encourages students to discuss fashion business strategies where the focus is on product quality and craftsmanship quality rather than mass-market consumerism. Considering the risks and success factors of Hiut's one product strategy, students are encouraged to discuss the adjustments needed for marketing and communication techniques, consumer loyalty strategies and brand recognition to support UK and international expansion. Hiut Denim are a slow-fashion business, making products in the UK; students will examine the pricing structure of premium products in relation to UK costs and devise creative solutions to extend consumer choice.

Learning Objectives

Upon completion of this case, students should be able to:

- Discuss Hiut Denim Co.'s core values and corporate approach.
- Determine whether Hiut's approach to marketing and advertising can be sustained.
- Analyze the benefits and risks of Hiut's one-product strategy.

- Describe and evaluate the processes employed by Hiut to retain customers and encourage brand loyalty.
- Discuss and evaluate Hiut's brand recognition on a local and international scale.
- Propose creative strategic solutions to enhance consumer choice without extending the product range.
- Discuss Hiut's working environment and identify the benefits and costs of local production.
- Propose innovative solutions that will support UK manufacturing and the potential future skill shortages.

Introduction

Glance around a room; it will be no surprise that more than half the people will be wearing denim jeans, a globally recognized product and probably the most popular trouser of all time (Miller and Woodward 2010). The universal popularity of denim jeans has meant a significant growth especially with the discount sector pushing down prices and compromising on quality (Miller and Woodward 2010). The styling of a pair of denim jeans has evolved through technology and fabric, yet despite this, the key features found on jeans today are almost identical to the first ever pairs of Levi's made over one hundred years ago (Miller and Woodward 2010). Jeans are not considered as a high fashion product; however, contemporary brands where jeans have evolved from functional workwear into fashionable products associated with youth culture and expression have seen significant growth (Rahman 2011, Mintel 2016, Miller and Woodward 2010).

Mintel's October 2017 clothing retail survey reported that jeans were the most purchased product, stating that 43 percent of shoppers purchased a pair of jeans over a three-month period (June to August 2017). Recent studies have shown development in the use of authentic Japanese and American selvedge denim with designers Raf Simons and Tom Ford showing deep indigo jeans, straight-legged styles, and selvedge-style turn-ups in their SS18 collections (Conlon 2018).

Until 2002, Marks and Spencer maintained its UK jeans production, making up to thirty-five thousand pairs of jeans a week in their Welsh factory. However, increasing price pressures from fast-fashion producers meant that they could no longer compete. Overseas suppliers had the ability to rival the quality of products made in Britain (Penney 2013) forcing the closure of the last remaining denim plant in the UK. In search of a new opportunity, former advertising copywriter David Hieatt and his wife Clare had recently relocated to Wales having sold their ethical denim label, Howies, to retail giant Timberland. They were exploring UK denim manufacturing opportunities, and knowing that the Welsh town of Cardigan could supply a fully trained workforce, they developed a plan to bring jeans manufacturing back to Wales (Dehn 2012).

Business Problem

The company

Hiut Denim advertised in a local paper for skilled denim makers while importing twenty-four sewing machines from an old Wrangler factory in Poland. After a competitive interview process, they employed three "Grand masters," plus a cutter and a mechanic, totalling two hundred years of experience. Developing a slow-fashion approach, they began importing high quality organic denim from Turkey and the United States and handwoven selvedge denim from Japan. Hiut's core values are born out of quality and craftsmanship, informing their strategy to focus on "One" product. Slow fashion is not a new concept to the company founders, their previous label Howies, an outdoor ethical brand focused on product quality designed for longevity (Dehn 2012). Having a limited production and marketing budget, a yearly sales target of 2,500 jeans, and a production capacity of ten pairs per day they launched their new brand on social media with a series of tweets aimed at their Howie's connections. The results took them off-guard with articles in national media including the *Sunday Times* and *Independent*, and they were soon notching up multiple orders (Connor 2013). Social media was Hiut's main marketing strategy, and celebrity endorsements followed including the Manic Street Preachers, Cate Le Bon, and Ant and Dec who donned their Hiuts while presenting cult television show "I'm a Celebrity" and tweeting their loyalty to the brand out to their millions of followers.

Hiut Denim are an exception to the rule when it comes to its corporate approach. Going against the grain, they have a policy that all staff must leave on time or if possible early, they save every penny and they spend as little as possible on advertising and marketing. The strategy is to make the best quality product rather than the most products, there may be a

FIGURE 21.1 The Hiut Denim Factory. © Hiut Denim Co.

waiting time for products and it seems as though followers appreciate their honesty and transparent pricing policy. Hiut also include exclusive one-hundred-piece short production runs to keep the denim connoisseur energized, and advertise these through newsletters, social media, blogs, and YouTube videos. Their transactional website provides core product information and introduces their values, beliefs, and transparent business philosophy to the consumer. They have eighteen strategically selected UK stockists, two German outlets, and one outlet in Melbourne, Australia (https://www.Hiutdenim.co.uk).

The products

Hiut make denim jeans, and only denim jeans, and get great satisfaction out of making one product well. Prices start at £100, products are offered in several fits and fabric options including, 12oz organic, 14oz selvedge, and technical stretch denim. Men's are priced from £145 to £230 and offered in regular, slim, slim tapered, and skinny fit. Women's are priced from £100 to £195 with six options, skinny, skinny high waist, girlfriend, ultimate black, technical stretch, and a classic raw denim slim. In keeping with their core values, environmental factors are a high priority for Hiut and the global denim industry is known for its extensive use of water and chemical processing contributing to climate change (Ferrier 2014). Hiut have worked to develop innovative home-grown solutions to engage the UK denim enthusiast in sustainable alternatives to achieve the perfect jean.

The Denim Breakers Club

Products made from un-sanforized denim come with challenges often feeling uncomfortable and rigid. Many denim makers spend a lot of time and money making their products look pre-worn and pre-washed, a process that uses huge amounts of water (Siegle 2015). Hiut developed a sustainable solution in the "Denim Breakers Club." Selected jeans were allocated to denim breakers/wearers who would wear the jeans non-stop for six months without laundering. The jeans are returned to Hiut to be professionally laundered and auctioned online with the breaker taking a 20 percent commission (Ferrier 2014). All products including the pre-broken jeans come with a free repairs-for-life policy. However, not all denim lovers want to purchase a used item. Customers purchasing brand new products from Hiut are invited to join the "no wash Club."

The No Wash Club

Eighty percent of the environmental impact of jeans comes from laundering (Ferrier 2014). Hiut Denim have established their "No Wash Club." The "club" is a set of guidelines that will ensure the product lasts a lifetime, encouraging the customer to withhold laundering for six months. The process gives the jeans time to mould to the shape of the wearer, maintain their classic color and to fade naturally with everyday use. The club gives advice on how to keep jeans bacteria-free through freezing and to remove smells with fabric fresheners, contributing to their community and sustainability agenda, reducing water use and bringing denim enthusiasts together via the use of social media. Innovative use of online technology has been at the forefront of Hiut's success and Hiut jeans are the only products known to have a history tag.

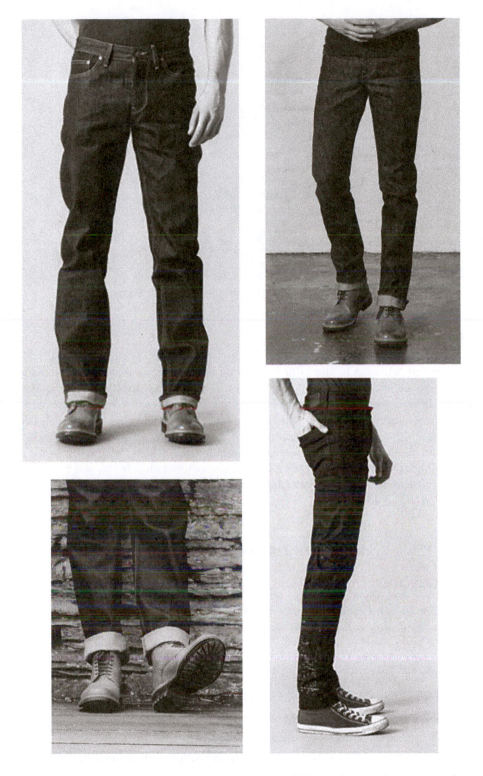

FIGURE 21.2 Examples of Hiut Demin's men's range. From left to right: Regular Organic, £145; Slim Selvedge, £230; Wide Leg Organic, £145; Slim Tapered Tech, £150. © Hiut Denim Co.

FIGURE 21.3 Internal pocket bag signed by garment maker. © Hiut Denim Co.

The history tag

The most recent addition to the Hiut Denim Co is the unique history tag (Benady 2014). The history tag provides a platform for wearers to create and save memories while wearing their jeans. Like a piece of art, the garment makers sign each pair of jeans at the same time allocating a unique number, which relates to the "History Tag App." The consumer downloads the app and then uploads images of themselves while wearing the products. The aim is to capture moments, create memories, and develop a story of the life of the product. The history tag stays with the product so if the consumer decides to sell their product or donate to a clothing charity the next user can pick up the history and continue the story (https://www.Hiutdenim.co.uk).

Business Questions

Major question

Is one product enough? Will Hiut have to extend their product range to remain financially viable and become a global denim player?

Study questions

1   What are the benefits and risks for a business of offering a single product?
2   How many different variations of jeans could they offer?
3   Would product variations expand their customer base?
4   Will followers tire and go to competitors to get a full-outfit experience?
5   There is a lot of competition in the premium jeans market. Do you expect brand lovers to have the finances available to purchase more than one pair?

6 How can Hiut continue to grow if they repair all products and what are the advantages to the business and to the consumer of customer programs such as lifelong repairs?

Further discussion

1 How can Hiut expand their brand recognition?

2 Discuss the positive and negative effects of the History Tag App. How likely are consumers to utilize the app or is it a marketing tactic?

3 To what extent is the No Wash Club a gimmick or a sustainable solution?

4 Does a local production strategy have longevity? How can Hiut ensure they have enough skilled workers over the next ten years given the UK skills shortage?

References and Further Reading

Benady, Alex. 2014. "Hiut's Clare Hieatt Acts Smart to Take on Denim's Big Boys." *PR Week*, September 10. Accessed August 18, 2017. https://www.prweek.com/article/1311208/hiuts-clare-hieatt-acts-smart-denims-big-boys

Bojer, Thomas Stege. 2016. *Blue Blooded: Denim Hunters and Jeans Culture*. Berlin: Die Gestalten Verlag.

Conlon, Scarlett. 2018. "It's in the Jeans: US Fashion Goes Back to Denim's Glory Days." *The Guardian*, January 19. Accessed April 10, 2018. https://www.theguardian.com/fashion/2018/jan/19/its-in-the-jeans-us-fashion-goes-back-to-denims-glory-days

Connor, Gary. 2013. "Jeans Manufacturing Returns to Small Welsh Town." *BBC*, April 24. Accessed August 18, 2017. https://www.bbc.co.uk/news/business-22246100

Dehn, Georgia. 2012. "Hiut Denim Co: The Jeans with the App that Tells Their History." *The Telegraph*, March 23. Accessed August 18, 2017. http://fashion.telegraph.co.uk/news-features/TMG9161337/Hiut-Denim-Co-The-jeans-with-the-app-that-tells-their-history.html

Ferrier, Morwenna. 2014. "The People Who Are Paid to Break in Your Designer Jeans." *The Guardian*, November 28. Accessed August 18, 2017. https://www.theguardian.com/fashion/fashion-blog/2014/nov/28/men-paid-break-in-designer-jeans-hiut-denim

Hiut, Denim. Accessed September 1, 2017. https://hiutdenim.co.uk/

Miller, Daniel. 2015. "Denim." *Consumption Markets & Culture* 18, no. 4: 298–300.

Miller, Daniel. and Sophie Woodward. 2010. *Global Denim*. Oxford: Berg.

Mintel. 2016. *Mintel Clothing Retailing Report UK*. October. Accessed August 5, 2017. http://academic.mintel.com.ezproxy.mmu.ac.uk/display/748789/

Penney, Loren. 2013. "How 'Made in Britain' Is Reinvigorating Our Industries." *Your Ready Business*, March 18. Accessed August 18, 2017. https://www.yourreadybusiness.co.uk/how-made-in-britain-is-reinvigorating-our-fashion-and-manufacturing-industries/

Rahman, Osmud. 2011. "Understanding Consumers' Perceptions and Behaviour: Implications for Denim Jeans Design." *Journal of Textile and Apparel, Technology and Management* 7, no. 1: 1–16. http://ojs.cnr.ncsu.edu/index.php/JTATM/article/viewFile/845/909

Siegle, Lucy. 2015. "The Eco Guide to Green Jeans." *The Guardian*, December 27. Accessed August 18, 2017. https://www.theguardian.com/environment/2015/dec/27/eco-guide-the-green-jeans

Smale, Will, and Greg Brosnan. 2017. "How a Welsh Jeans Firm Became a Cult Global Brand." *BBC*, December 13. Accessed April 10, 2018. https://www.bbc.co.uk/news/business-42237426

Styles, Ruth. 2014. "Would You Pay £200 for Jeans That Had Already Been Worn for Six Months?" *MailOnline*, December 1. Accessed August 18, 2017. https://www.dailymail.co.uk/femail/article-2855842/Would-pay-200-jeans-worn-SIX-MONTHS-Fashion-brand-hires-50-breakers-wear-artisanal-denim.html

West, Karl. 2014. "Selvedge Job: Jeans Company Helps Welsh Town Get Back In Its Stride." *The Guardian*, February 11. Accessed August 18, 2018. https://www.theguardian.com/business/2014/feb/11/selvedge-jeans-company-welsh-town

Chapter 22

Youngone Corporation

Global Sourcing and Corporate Social Responsibility

Yoon-Jung Lee and Yoori Chae

In this case study, corporate social responsibility (hereafter, CSR) programs at Youngone Corporation are examined to review the impact of economic activities of a clothing and textiles company on local communities. Youngone Corporation is a South Korea-based multinational company that was established in 1974. As a world-class manufacturer and exporter, it is the largest supplier of outdoor/athletic clothing, textiles, footwear, and gear for many globally known outdoor brands. Youngone operates its production facilities in countries including Bangladesh, China, Vietnam, and El Salvador. The company is known for hiring locals and providing benefits and welfare programs for its employees. Its CSR program includes various activities to serve the local community. One example is the Swiss Bangladesh Milk Project. In 2009, Youngone collaborated with Swiss specialists to implement a modern cattle breeding and dairy project in the Korean Export Processing Zone in Bangladesh in response to a shortage of high-quality pure milk for local residents. Another example is the restoration of a culturally significant residential site in Sonargaon, Bangladesh, which was the first attempt at preserving a cultural heritage site in Bangladesh. This case study reviews how the company developed its business in different countries including Bangladesh. Students will assess the economic and social impacts of the business on local communities and suggest strategies for a more socially responsible business model.

Learning Objectives

Upon completion of this case, students should be able to:

- Assess the economic and social impacts of the business on the society and the environment.

- Evaluate corporate social responsibility strategies of apparel manufacturing companies.
- Recommend strategies for socially responsible business models.

Introduction

The apparel manufacturing industry is known as a typical labor-intensive industry. Unlike rigid materials such as plastics and iron, fabric, the core material of apparel products, easily stretches and puckers. It also slides easily onto machines. Factory automation in the apparel industry lags far behind similar development in other industries, because the costs of developing machinery to substitute delicate human hands are too high. This is one of the reasons the apparel industry has long been a labor-intensive industry that depends on human labor. Accordingly, labor costs are a key factor in business performance in the apparel industry.

High labor costs are a huge burden on apparel companies. When labor costs in developed countries such as the United States increased, apparel companies turned their attention overseas where labor costs were lower, building manufacturing facilities in those countries or working with local contractors who had their own manufacturing facilities.

However, offshore manufacturing is not always a perfect solution, since there may be disadvantages and risks associated with it. In addition to difficulties caused by language barriers and cultural differences, most countries with low labor costs are less developed countries, which are risky in many ways for apparel companies. For example, a lack of transportation and communication infrastructure can cause various difficulties. Political instability can cause borders to be shut down, and strikes and revolts can stop manufacturing facilities. All these issues can cause failures to deliver products to the market at the right time, which results in tremendous losses for the companies.

Youngone Corporation

Youngone is a South Korea-based multinational company founded in 1974. As a world-class manufacturer and exporter, it is the largest supplier of outdoor/athletic clothing, textiles, footwear, and gear for many globally known outdoor brands, such as The North Face, Nike, and Puma. Youngone supplies over 40 brands/retailers around the world. The sales of Youngone in 2015 were *1,585 billon KRW (approximately 1.44 billion USD)* and currently more than 70,000 employees work for Youngone Corporation (Youngone Corporation 2018).

Initially, Youngone started as a simple trade brokerage company. However, in 1976, it built a manufacturing facility in Seongnam, Korea, and then became a manufacturer of outdoor/athletic clothing for apparel companies. The manufactured products are sold to consumers with the brand names of another firm (i.e., original equipment manufacturing, or OEM). In addition to the OEM business, the licensing business of US outdoor brand The North Face allowed Youngone to become a leading outdoor apparel company in South Korea. The licensing brand of The North Face in Korea was first introduced in 1997, but the brand did not receive a lot of attention until the early 2000s when the market for outdoor apparel exploded. With limited competition, The North Face dominated the Korean outdoor market with yearly sales records. The brand's sales in Korea rose from around 50 billion won in the early 2000s to around 500 billion won in 2010. Youngone also operated its own brand name, "Youngone", from 1991 to 2015. Recently, it launched a new outdoor clothing brand, Takhi.

Although the OEM business was initially successful, increasing labor costs in Korea posed a threat to the company. As an alternative, Youngone considered building offshore manufacturing facilities in countries with relatively low labor costs. In 1980, Youngone built its first offshore manufacturing factory in Chittagong, the second largest city in Bangladesh. It was the first garment manufacturing facility in the country. Since then, Youngone has built additional manufacturing facilities in Dhaka, the capital city, as well as in Chittagong. In 1999, Youngone purchased 2,500 ha from the government of Bangladesh and built a Korean Export Processing Zone (KEPZ). It was the first time that a private company had built an Export Processing Zone in Bangladesh. Youngone now has more than twenty factories in different countries, including China, Vietnam, and El Salvador, but about 70 percent of its factories are located in Bangladesh.

The population of Bangladesh is about 170 million, and the GDP per capita was US$1,532 in 2017 according to the International Monetary Fund. The minimum wage in Bangladesh is the lowest among Asian countries (Bangladesh US$68 vs. Vietnam US$112 per month, China US$261). In Bangladesh, two-thirds of the population is employed in the agricultural sector and the country is not fully industrialized. With sales of $28 billion in 2015, Bangladesh's garment industry accounts for 82 percent of the country's exports and employs 4 million people, mostly women. Youngone's manufacturing factories in Bangladesh provide the local people with jobs by hiring more than 50,000 workers.

CSR practices of Youngone Corporation

Youngone Corporation practices various CSR programs in countries where its manufacturing facilities are located. Youngone considers care for society one of its core values, along with honesty and integrity, excellence, agility, and accountability. The company is known to have spent 17.2 billion KRW, which accounted for 7.3 percent of its total operating income, on CSR activities in 2012. Youngone's CSR activities can be divided into the following six categories: donations; contributions to local communities; medical and health services; eco-friendly management; support for future professionals; and support for culture, arts, and sports (Youngone Corporation CSR 2018).

1) Donations
The Youngone Corporation makes in-kind donations and monetary donations to support marginalized peoples around the world. Youngone has donated clothes to non-profit organizations such as Warm Clothes for Children, World Vision, The Red Cross, and Good Neighbors. It also manufactures and sends relief goods, such as clothes, blankets, and shoes to disaster areas. For example, after the earthquake in Nepal in 2015, Youngone provided $100,000 worth of waterproof tents for people who had lost their homes. In terms of monetary donations, Youngone has focused on the value of education and donates to universities and schools. It has built seven schools and dormitories in Bangladesh to improve education facilities.

2) Contributions to local communities
The Youngone Corporation makes contributions to local communities. In Korea, employees from the head office visit local child and youth centers every week and share their skills and knowledge. They teach English, lead book clubs, and provide career advice to teenagers who visit the centers.

In Bangladesh, Youngone founded a dairy farm in 2009 after recognizing that there was a shortage of high-quality milk. The farm currently has over 100 animals that are crossbreeds of local cows and Swiss cows, to provide residents with high-quality milk. Youngone also provides technical and advisory support for a project that financially supports small businesses in Bangladesh.

3) Medical and health services

Youngone provides free medical and health services to people who are suffering from diseases and disabilities around the world. In collaboration with medical institutions, Youngone has sent medical teams to disaster areas that required medical services. Moreover, Youngone provides free medical treatment and counseling services for its employees. In the factory in Bangladesh, there are 70 medical teams and they introduced the first medical aircraft to Bangladesh.

4) Eco-friendly management

Youngone Corporation pays attention to environmental issues as well. Youngone recognized the problems of erosion caused by deforestation in the areas where their factories are located in Bangladesh. Youngone made a long-term commitment to carry out a large-scale planting project and built reservoirs to provide water for the local ecosystem. Over the past 16 years, Youngone has planted more than 2 million trees and built 17 reservoirs. It supports organizations that work to prevent the extinction of the Bengal tiger and to protect threatened wildlife habitats.

5) Support for future professionals

Youngone is devoted to training future professionals in the apparel industry through industry–university collaborations and providing internship programs to college students. Students participating in these programs have an opportunity to acquire hands-on experience. The programs include short internships in factories in Southeast Asia where students can experience diverse aspects of the field while interacting with local employees.

6) Support for culture, arts, and sports

Youngone supports culture, arts, and sports. For example, Youngone restored a significant cultural heritage site, Baro Sardar Bari in Sonargaon, Bangladesh. Youngone started this project after recognizing that the cultural heritage of Bangladesh was being lost due to lack of conservation. The Baro Sardar Bari is an important site where early Muslims settled. Through extensive research, Youngone restored the ornamentation, inner courtyard, and interior walls of the buildings. With local craftsmen, original furniture was reproduced and installed.

Youngone's active and diverse range of CSR activities has attracted the attention of many organizations and media. The recognition of Youngone's CSR activities has contributed to the positive image of the company. For example, the company was recognized in 2017 as the number one donating company in South Korea. Also, the former CEO, Ki-Hak Sung, received an award from World Vision International, a global non-governmental organization that helps people in need all over the world. However, there is a criticism that the company's pursuit of diverse CSR activities is meaningless unless it pays proper attention to its employees in developing countries.

Business Problem

Despite diverse CSR efforts, Youngone, along with other companies with factories in Bangladesh, has received negative publicity by the press abroad and in Korea in relation to labor protests in the Bangladesh garment industry.

In 2010, there was a violent protest in the Bangladesh garment industry. Workers protested for months because many factories failed to implement a new pay structure even though the government had officially announced a minimum wage increase (Al Jazeera 2010). Furthermore, skilled workers who were not eligible for the wage increase also demanded higher wages. Protesters occupied the streets and held up traffic. A bus was burnt, and two shopping centers were robbed. In the process of suppressing the protest, three people died and dozens were injured. During this same period, all 11 factories of Youngone in the Chittagong Export Processing Zone were shut down as a result (Bhuiyan 2013). Production for two days was lost, although Youngone implemented the new legal minimum wages as per the law.

Beginning in 2013, after the tragic collapse of the Rana Plaza Building, a series of labor protests took place in Bangladesh with the aim of improving wages and working conditions in the garment industry. A female worker was killed by the local police and at least 15 people were injured (Malay Mail 2014). The Youngone factory was vandalized (Malay Mail 2014).

Despite labor strikes, protests, and weak infrastructure, Bangladesh is still Youngone's major manufacturing site. The company has further expanded its operations despite the challenges in the country (Star Business Report 2014).

Business Questions

Major questions

1 How would you evaluate Youngone's business activities and CSR activities in Bangladesh? In general, do you think its operation of its manufacturing factories makes positive economic and social contributions to local communities? What additional information is needed to fully assess how socially responsible this company is?

2 Even though Youngone has put a lot of effort into CSR activities, the company still faces challenges while running its business in Bangladesh. From the company's perspective, do you think it is worth the investment to continue operating factories in Bangladesh?

3 How could Youngone overcome the criticism it has faced and improve its corporate image? Make recommendations regarding Youngone's relationships with its workers and buyers.

Study questions

1 What are the advantages and disadvantages of global sourcing?

2 What factors do apparel companies need to consider when making sourcing decisions?

3 What kind of CSR activities do companies in the apparel and other industries around the world conduct?

References and Further Reading

Al Jazeera. 2010, December 12. "Deadly Wage Protests in Bangladesh." Accessed March 2018. https://www.aljazeera.com/news/asia/2010/12/2010121212117750862.html

Bhuiyan, Mohammad Ismail. 2013, May. Reasonable Wages for Workers to Eliminate Unrest in Bangladesh's Ready-made Garments (RMG) Sector. Bangladesh Development Research Center. Accessed March 21, 2018. http://www.bangladeshstudies.org/files/WPS_no17.pdf

Burns, Leslie, Davis, Kathy K. Mullet, and Nancy O. Bryant. 2016. *The Business of Fashion: Designing, Manufacturing, and Marketing.* Chapter 11 Sourcing Decisions and Production Centers (pp. 254–288). New York: Fairchild Books/Bloomsbury Publishing Inc.

Ko, K.-J. and M.-J. Ji. 2014. "Corporate Social Responsibility of Outdoor OEM Company: Focusing on Youngone Corporation." *Journal of the Korea Trade Research Association* 39 (2): 1–21.

Kim, M. J. 2010. "The Status of CSR in Korea and Case Study of Success." *Global Issue Report (GIR); 10-010.* Accessed from http://125.131.31.47/Solars7DMME/004/88284.PDF

Kim, S. S. 2010. "Bangladesh Labor Force to Relieve Peace - A Case Study of Youngone Corporation." *KOTRA Global Market News.* Accessed from https://news.kotra.or.kr/user/globalBbs/kotranews/3/globalBbsDataView.do?setIdx=242&dataIdx=103185

Kunz, Grace, I., Elena Karpova, and Myrna B. Garner. 2016. *Going Global: The Textile and Apparel Industry.* New York: Fairchild Books/Bloomsbury Publishing Inc.

Malay Mail. 2014, January 9. One Shot Dead as Bangladesh Footwear Workers Riot. Malaymailonline. Accessed March 21, 2018. http://www.themalaymailonline.com/world/article/one-shot-dead-as-bangladesh-footwear-workers-riot

Sankar, S. and C. B. Bhattacharya. 2001. "Does Doing Good Always Lead to Doing Better? Consumer Reactions to Corporate Social Responsibility." *Journal of Marketing Research* 38 (2): 225–243.

Star Business Report. 2014, December 10. Youngone to Expand in Bangladesh. The Daily Star. Accessed March 21, 2018. http://www.thedailystar.net/youngone-to-expand-in-bangladesh-54610

Youngone Corporation. 2018. Home. Accessed February 26, 2018. https://www.youngonecorporation.com/

Youngone Corporation CSR. 2018. Corporate Social Responsibility. Accessed February 26, 2018. https://www.youngonecorporation.com/corporate-responsibility

Youngone Statement

Between the years 2010—2017, Youngone's export business has been growing at a Compound Annual Growth Rate (CAGR) of more than 6%, demonstrating the trust it had built with its business partners and the management strength of the company.

Definitions

Corporate social responsibility (from Burns et al. 2016): A philosophy whereby a company takes into consideration human rights, labor conditions, and environmental implications when making business decisions.

Sourcing (from Burns et al. 2016): Decision process of determining how and where a company's products or their components will be produced.

Chapter 23

Making Fashion Transparent

What Consumers Know about the Brands They Admire

Iva Jestratijevic and Nancy A. Rudd

In recent decades, tragic events in the fashion industry have led to increased expectations among consumers to know where, by whom, and under what conditions their clothing was produced. Although the need for supply chain transparency and accountability has grown, only 16 percent of fashion brands globally have publicly reported socially responsible efforts including disclosure of the full list of factories in their supply chain (Nimbalker et al., "The Truth Behind the Barcode," 2016). The Fashion Transparency Index reports and ranks fashion brands' business information across five key areas (policy and commitment; governance; tracking and traceability; audits and remediation; spotlight issues).

In this case study, students select and analyze one luxury brand and one mass-market brand listed in the Fashion Transparency Index. Using ratings and background material, students compare score differences across the categories for both their luxury and mass-market brands and identify the strongest and the weakest areas for each brand. Based on this comparison of the strategies, goals, and priorities of the two business sectors (luxury and mass), students address area(s) in which each brand need to improve in order to become more transparent and accountable. In addition, students provide recommendations as to how each brand might improve its transparency score, and describe and justify implementation priorities for differently positioned fashion brands.

Learning Objectives

Upon completion of this case, students should be able to:

- Describe why supply chain transparency can both strengthen/weaken brand image.

- Analyze the advantages and disadvantages of transparent communication for luxury versus mass-market fashion brands.
- Identify, describe, and justify improvement priorities for transparent and accountable communication for a luxury brand.
- Identify, describe, and justify improvement priorities for transparent and accountable communication for a mass-market brand.

Introduction

The Fashion Transparency Index is an annual review that ranks 100 of the largest global fashion companies according to the degree of information they publicly disclose about their products and business practices. Launched by Fashion Revolution, with *Ethical Consumer* creating the research methodology, the index annually ranks and compares available information across five areas: *policies and commitments* (social and environmental policies); *governance* (contact details of employees responsible for each key area); *traceability* (supplier list with factory contacts); *know, show, fix* (disclosing audit information and corrective action plans); *spotlight issues* (what the brand does to decrease negative impact). Whereas some mass-market brands release detailed supplier lists identifying products, services, and number of workers in each facility, some luxury brands disclose little or no business information.

Business Problem

Fashion supply chains of large fashion brands are typically complex global systems. Fashion companies work with farms, ranches, and textile companies that grow/raise/create, dye, weave/knit, and finish the materials. Most do not own their manufacturing facilities but instead work with hundreds of contract factories that cut, sew, and assemble garments. In a highly complex supply chain, ensuring sound human rights and sustainable environmental practices can be challenging.

The need for supply chain transparency has been triggered by several factors. During the last decade, numerous negative events have occurred in the fashion industry. Among the worst was the collapse of the Rana Plaza building in Bangladesh that killed 1134 workers (Khan et al. 2015). The building housed factories that produced clothing for well-known international mass-market brands, some of which never confirmed involvement despite their clothing labels being found in the rubble. In Cambodia, 284 factory workers fainted after inhaling heavy chemical dyes used in producing garments for Swedish fast fashion brand H&M (O'Carroll 2011). In addition to problematic working conditions in manufacturing, the fashion industry is acknowledged to be a major polluter of air and water.

Media attention of these events and issues has resulted in compromised consumer trust as a core feature of the business–customer relationship. Consequently, consumers are demanding greater transparency from fashion brands so that their purchases are not supporting companies known to contribute to environmental and human rights abuses.

Unlike mass fashion brands that outsource low quality fashion products in high quantities, luxury fashion brands are linked to expertise, quality, local culture, and heritage. Whereas one might presume that luxury brands are in a strong position to transparently promote workers' rights, sourcing practices, and production patterns, the competitive advantage of luxury goods is based on a vertical integration model where companies strengthen their production

TABLE 23.1 *Selected final brand scores, Fashion Transparency Index 2017 (Ditty 2017)*

Index 2017	Final Score 2017 (%)	Policy & Commitments (%)	Governance (%)	Traceability (%)	Know, Show & Fix (%)	Spotlight Issues (%)
See the full report for all brand scores and information on the scoring process and weighting methodology.	**Chanel**	**1**	**3**	**17**	**0**	**0**
0	Burberry	25	74	58	1	20
11	Hermes	22	57	0	29	1
0	Gucci	28	78	75	1	23
18	Dior	0	0	0	0	0
0	Nike	36	76	58	32	16
21	Zara	36	86	50	12	31
32	Gap	46	77	67	44	36
18	H&M	48	91	67	29	37
46	Levis	35	76	67	27	21
7						

FIGURE 23.1 The Fashion Transparency Index ranks fashion companies according to metrics including factory auditing and corrective action plans. © FADEL SENNA / AFP

chain by acquiring small and medium-sized suppliers (leather tanneries, reptile and crocodile farms, etc.). This need to guard proprietary design and manufacturing practices to protect the authenticity of their products requires that they do not disclose too much information about their supply chain. As such, the lack of public disclosure of business practices within their supply chain may not necessarily be an indicator of an unethical supply chain. In addition, experts describe this carefully controlled communication as a "mystical" allure of the luxury market (Kendall 2010; Tokatli 2014). Others explain obscure supply chain communication as a disadvantage of business delocalization, as luxury brands outsource precious materials and secure suppliers, production expertise, and authenticity (Kapferer 2012). With sustainable business initiatives, such as the Fashion Transparency Index, making transparency expected throughout the fashion industry, fashion companies are challenged to find optimal ways to communicate both negative and positive impacts on humans and the planet. How should mass and luxury brands react in order to improve their brand transparency?

Business Questions

1 What are the advantages and disadvantages of transparent business communications?

2 Go to the Fashion Transparency Index and select one luxury and one mass-market brand. Analyze and compare scores for each key business area.

3 Based on differences between a mass market and luxury brand, rank which of the five key areas is the most crucial for each sector and rank by importance the four remaining areas; discuss when and why limited information disclosure is acceptable.

4 Based on the comparison between different business sectors, strategies, and goals, indicate a potential area(s) of improvement for each brand.

5 Describe and justify implementation priorities.

References and Further Reading

Conca, James. 2015. "Making Climate Change Fashionable—The Garment Industry Takes on Global Warming." Accessed June 2017. https://www.forbes.com/sites/jamesconca/2015/12/03/making-climate-change-fashionable-the-garment-industry-takes-on-global-warming/#27be47f579e4

Dickson, A. Marsha, Molly Eckman and Suzanne Loker. 2009. *Social Responsibility in the Global Apparel Industry*. New York: Fairchild Books.

Ditty, Sarah. 2017. "Fashion Transparency Index, 2017." Accessed July 2017. https://issuu.com/fashionrevolution/docs/fr_fashiontransparencyindex2017?e=25766662/47726047

Ditty, Sarah and Bryony Moore. 2016. "Fashion Transparency Index, 2016." Accessed July 2017. http://fashionrevolution.org/wp-content/uploads/2016/04/FR_FashionTransparencyIndex.pdf

Fletcher, Kate. 2013. *Sustainable Fashion and Textiles: Design Journeys*. London: Routledge.

Gershon, Nimbalker, Jasmin Mawson, and Claire Harris. 2016. "The Truth Behind the Barcode: The Australian Fashion Report 2016." Accessed June 2017. https://baptistworldaid.org.au/wp-content/uploads/2016/05/2016-Australian-Fashion-Report.pdf

Julfika, Ali Manik, et al. 2013. "Western Firms Feel Pressure as Toll Rises in Bangladesh." *New York Times*. Accessed July 2017. http://www.nytimes.com/2013/04/26/world/asia/bangladeshi-collapse-kills-many-garment-workers.html

Kapferer, Jean-Noël. March–April 2012. "Why Luxury Should Not Delocalize a Critique of a Growing Tendency." *The European Business Review*. Accessed July 2017. https://www.researchgate.net/publication/282063651_Why_Luxury_Should_not_Delocalize_a_critique_of_a_growing_tendency

Kendall, Jonathan. 2010. "Responsible Luxury—A Report on the New Opportunities for Business to Make a Difference." Accessed June 2016. https://www.rapaportfairtrade.com/Docs/CIBJO-responsible_luxury.pdf

Khan, Reza Zeenath and Gwendolyn Rodrigues. 2015. "Human before the Garment—Bangladesh Tragedy Revised. Ethical Manufacturing or Lack Thereof in Garment Manufacturing Industry *World Journal of Social Sciences* 5 (1): 22–35.

Lund-Thomsen, Peter and Adam Lindgreen. 2014. "Corporate Social Responsibility in Global Value Chains: Where Are We Now and Where Are We Going? *Journal of Business Ethics* 123 (1): 11–22.

McLaughlin, Kathleen and Doug McMillon. Business and Society in the Coming Decades. Perspectives on the Long Term: Building a Stronger Foundation for Tomorrow. Accessed July 2017. http://www.mckinsey.com/business-functions/strategy-and-corporate-finance/our-insights/business-and-society-in-the-coming-decades

O'Carroll, Sinead. 2011. "H&M to Investigate after 300 Workers Faint at Cambodian Factory." Accessed June 2017. http://www.businessinsider.com/hm-to-launch-probe-after-workers-faint-at-cambodian-factory-2011-8

Smestad, Liat. 2009. "The Sweatshop, Child Labor, and Exploitation Issues in the Garment Industry." *Fashion Practice* 1 (2): 147–162.

Tokatli, Nebahat. 2014. "Made in Italy? Who Cares! Prada's New Economic Geography." *Geoforum* 54: 1–9.

Definitions

Supply chain transparency: This refers to public disclosure of business information that includes (but is not limited to) business standards and policies, structure of corporate governance and employees' responsibilities, resourcing, tracking, and traceability, business impact audits and improvements, human rights, and environmental protection.

Sustainable fashion: This refers to fashion manufactured, marketed, and used in the most sustainable manner possible, taking into account both environmental and socioeconomic aspects.

Vertical integration: The strategy used by a company to expand its business operations through purchase of the production and/or distribution chain.

Chapter 24

Gap Inc.'s Sourcing Dilemma

Stay or Leave China?

Sheng Lu

Like most multinational fashion companies, Gap Inc., a well-known iconic American clothing and accessories retailer, imports almost everything it sells from overseas. Currently China is Gap Inc.'s largest apparel sourcing base; in the 2017 fiscal year production from China accounted for 22 percent of the company's total sourcing value. However, with a fast-changing business environment, including an increasing cost of production in China, US consumers' higher expectation for speed to market, and the escalating US-China trade tensions, Art Peck, CEO of Gap Inc., believes it is time to reexamine the company's overall sourcing strategy. Critically, Art needs to decide whether Gap Inc. should continue sourcing from China or move sourcing orders elsewhere. Before Art can make up his mind, he needs to evaluate several key factors carefully, ranging from the competitiveness of China as an apparel-sourcing base, to possible alternatives to China, and the company's overall growth strategy.

Learning Objectives

Upon completion of this case, students should be able to:

- Identify the critical factors in fashion companies' sourcing decisions.
- Analyze the trade-offs in fashion apparel companies' sourcing and supply chain strategies.
- Evaluate the global nature of today's fashion apparel businesses.

Introduction

Gap Inc. is a well-known and iconic American clothing and accessories retailer established by Doris and Don Fisher in San Francisco, California, in 1969. As of December 2017, Gap Inc. operates 3,165 company-owned stores and 429 franchise stores across more than fifty countries worldwide and generates a total sales revenue of $15.5 billion per year (Gap Inc. 2017a). Currently, Gap Inc. manages five major brands that each have their own distinct portfolio and target market:

- *Athleta*: A premium-priced fitness and lifestyle brand, which focuses on creating versatile performance apparel to inspire a community of active, confident women and girls.
- *Banana Republic*: Focuses on clothing and accessories with detailed craftsmanship and luxurious materials. The styles represent versatile, contemporary classics that endure the test of time.
- *Gap*: Offers iconic apparel and accessories that are anchored in the optimistic, casual, and classic American style.
- *Intermix*: Styles on-trend pieces in unexpected ways and includes products from the most coveted established and emerging designers.
- *Old Navy*: Focuses on must-have and price-competitive fashion essentials for the whole family.

In 2017, the average unit retail price of these five brands ranges widely, from $28.32 (Old Navy) to as high as $244.95 (Intermix) (see Appendix 1). Excluding Intermix, Gap Inc.'s brands cover products in broad categories, from dresses, tops, bottoms, outerwear, and underwear, to accessories.

Business Problem

Like most US fashion brands and apparel retailers, Gap Inc. imports almost everything it sells from overseas. In the 2017 fiscal year, Gap Inc. sourced its products from approximately 800 vendors in fifty countries around the world (Gap Inc. 2017a). China is currently one of the largest apparel sourcing bases for Gap Inc.; products sourced from this country accounted for 22 percent of the company's total sourcing value in the 2017 fiscal year. However, with a fast-changing business environment, including increasing production costs in China, US consumers' higher expectation for speed to market, and the escalating US-China trade tensions, Art Peck, CEO of Gap Inc., believes it is time to reexamine the company's sourcing strategy.

Selecting an apparel sourcing base

While apparel manufacturing remains labor intensive, apparel sourcing is about far more than simply identifying places with the lowest wage level. Instead, apparel sourcing is increasingly about striking a balance between various factors, ranging from sourcing cost, speed to market, reliability, flexibility, to risk control (Berg, Berlemann, and Hedrich 2013; Ha-Brookshire 2017). Gap Inc., must also consider these factors.

First, for Gap Inc., production and sourcing cost remains one of the most critical factors in deciding where to source. Apparel retailing is a highly competitive business in the United States (S&P Global 2018). Ignoring the cost factor is often not a realistic option for fashion companies that target the mass market, such as Gap Inc. Price competition, in particular, is heated in the United States: as a reflection of this, in 2017, Gap Inc. sold 66 percent of its garments at a discounted price in the US market, of which about half were discounted by more than 50 percent (EDITED 2018).

Contrary to common perception, when breaking down the production cost of making a garment, only 12–20 percent of the production costs for making a garment goes on labor costs (which typically includes the cost for cutting, sewing, finishing, grading, and marking) whereas materials, including fabrics and trims, typically account for over 50 percent (Dinh 2014; Myers-McDevitt 2011). Because of the significant impact of the raw material on the final production cost of a garment, understandably, US fashion brands and apparel retailers are increasingly interested in sourcing from countries that have the capacity to provide locally supplied price-competitive textiles (Lu 2016, 2017). For example, in recent years, Gap Inc. has been leveraging its so-called "co-location" strategy in order to reduce production and sourcing cost. In this strategy, vendors need to cut and sew garments in the same country where raw materials are grown and processed (Abdulla 2018).

Besides labor cost and raw material, other main drivers of sourcing costs typically include shipping and logistics, foreign exchange rates, as well as the cost associated with compliance with trade regulations and social responsibility/sustainability requirements (Berg, Berlemann, and Hedrich 2013; Lu 2018a).

Second, speed to market is becoming an increasingly important sourcing factor for Gap Inc. With consumers' upgraded demand, US fashion brands and apparel retailers are under growing pressure to supply better quality products with greater innovation at a faster speed (Barrie 2018a). While the average lead time can take a year for many apparel retailers, Gap Inc. has set an ambitious goal to significantly cut its lead time to only eight weeks for many of its products (Abdulla 2018). Likewise, in a 2018 study conducted by McKinsey & Company, almost two-thirds of surveyed fashion brands and retailers said that improving speed to market was either a top priority or the highest priority for their company (Hunter, Marchessou, and Schmidt 2018).

The need for speed to market is gradually affecting where Gap Inc. is sourcing its products. For example, Gap Inc. is making particular efforts in growing partnerships with vendors in Central America and North America to lower the shipment time to US consumers (Abdulla 2018). Trade data also echoes the trend of apparel companies sourcing close to where their end products will need to be distributed: the value of US apparel imports from Mexico and Canada enjoyed a robust growth of 5.3 percent and 7.7 percent respectively in 2017 when compared to the figures from a year earlier; this growth is much higher than the world average of 1.4 percent (OTEXA 2018). Similarly, a 2018 survey of nearly thirty apparel sourcing executives suggested that near-sourcing from the western hemisphere, including members of the North American Free Trade Agreement (NAFTA) and the Dominican Republic-Central America Free Trade Agreement (CAFTA-DR), is growing in popularity among US fashion companies (Lu 2018a).

Third, supply chain risk and compliance with various environmental and social responsibility regulations also have a significant impact on Gap Inc.'s selection of sourcing destinations. Recent surveys of industry executives show that "unmet compliance (factory, social and/or environmental) standards," "labor disputes," "political unrest," and "lack of resources to manage supply chain risks" consistently ranked among the top challenges facing US fashion companies (Barrie 2018a; Lu 2017, 2018a).

Understandably, Gap Inc. is making increasing commitments to minimize the risks associated with sustainability and social responsibility in sourcing. For example, like many other US fashion brands and apparel retailers, Gap Inc. keeps records of the name, location, and function of all of the suppliers within their supply chain (Gap Inc. 2017a). Gap Inc. also regularly assesses its vendors overseas to ensure compliance with laws, environment and labor standards, occupational health and safety, and management systems (Gap Inc. 2017b).

In recent years, Gap Inc. has emphasized the use of "sustainable raw material" within its products. For example, Gap Inc. has instructed its suppliers to be in line with CanopyStyle, a company whose aim is to develop business practices to protect the world's forests, on the sustainable procurement of wood-derived fabrics, such as rayon, viscose, modal, lyocell, and Tencel, to eliminate the sourcing of wood pulp from ancient and endangered forests. Gap Inc. also encouraged all its suppliers to conduct the environmental footprint of their productions by using the Sustainable Apparel Coalition's Higg Index (Gap Inc. 2017b).

No sourcing destination is "perfect"

While almost all countries in the world make and export some apparel, it doesn't mean Gap Inc. has many options to choose from regarding where to source its products. Particularly, when Gap Inc. considers all the three primary sourcing factors—sourcing cost, speed to market, and risk of non-compliance, no sourcing base seems to be perfect. For example (see Appendix 2):

- *Asia* currently is the largest sourcing base for Gap Inc. and most other US fashion brands and apparel retailers (Gap Inc. 2017a; OTEXA 2018; USITC 2018). Top apparel producers and exporters from countries within the region, such as Bangladesh, Vietnam, Indonesia, and Sri Lanka, can offer very competitive prices. However, US fashion brands and retailers also say sourcing from Asian countries, in general, will incur a relatively long lead time because of the physical distance. A further concern for US fashion companies is that sourcing from some developing Asian countries involves high compliance-related risks (Barrie 2018b; USFIA 2018). For example, the high level of media and public attention to the social responsibility problems in the Bangladeshi garment industry, such as factory safety and treatment of workers, makes US fashion companies hesitant to source more from this country, despite "Made in Bangladesh" enjoying a prominent price advantage over many suppliers (Edmont 2018; Lu 2018a).

- *Western hemisphere*, includes members of NAFTA and CAFTA-DR as well as local sourcing from the United States. A new trade agreement, known as the United States-Mexico-Canada Agreement (USMCA), will also be implemented in 2020. Thanks to the geographic proximity, the western hemisphere enjoys notable advantages "in speed to market" compared to its Asian competitors (USITC 2018). US fashion companies also see sourcing from the western hemisphere as involving lower compliance-related risk compared with other regions in the world. However, the sourcing cost is a big disadvantage for the region as an apparel sourcing base; the special rules of origin in NAFTA and CAFTA-DR, which require that apparel is cut and sewn in Mexico and other Central American countries in order to qualify for duty-free benefits, often requires the use of expensive US-made yarns and fabrics (Platzer 2017). Moreover, the limited manufacturing capacity in the region often results in a lack of flexibility in sourcing textile raw material; this creates another concern for Gap Inc. and many other US fashion companies (Mesloh 2012; USFIA 2018). Given these disadvantages, in general, countries in the western hemisphere typically account for less than 10 percent of a US fashion brand and retailers' total sourcing value or volume for apparel products (Lu 2017, 2018a).

- *Sub-Saharan Africa (SSA) and Egypt* are also candidate sourcing bases for Gap Inc. The import duty-free benefits provided by the African Growth and Opportunity Act (AGOA) and the Egypt Qualifying Industrial Zone provide the main incentives for US companies to source from the region (Berg, Hedrich, and Russo 2015; Lu 2017). For example, AGOA's "third-country" fabric provision allows most SSA countries to export apparel to the US duty-free by using yarns and fabrics sourced from anywhere in the world. In comparison, most US free trade agreements adopt the strict "yarn-forward rules of origin," which, in general, require that all yarn spinning, fabric weaving, apparel cutting and sewing happen within the free trade agreement area (Lu 2018b). However, the poor infrastructure and very limited textile and apparel production capacity in SSA and Egypt make sourcing from there ideal for neither cost nor time saving. Restrained by the overall economic advancement level, apparel factories in SSA and Egypt do not have an impressive record of social and environmental compliance either (Berg, Berlemann, and Hedrich 2013).

Sourcing from China

China is one of the largest and most important sourcing bases for Gap Inc. In January 2017, Gap Inc. was sourcing from 234 vendors in China, compared with only 129 vendors in Vietnam, 120 vendors in India, and 51 vendors in Bangladesh (Gap Inc. 2017b).

As an apparel sourcing base, China enjoys two unique competitive advantages:

China's enormous production capacity and the completeness of its textile and apparel supply chain allows Gap Inc. to source almost any product in any quantity from the country. As shown in Appendix 3, in 2017 "Made in China" has no direct competitor within the US import market measured in value, textiles, and apparel (OTEXA 2018):

- Of the total eleven categories of yarn, China was the top supplier for three categories (or 27.3 percent);
- Of the total thirty-four categories of fabric, China was the top supplier for twenty-six categories (or 76.5 percent);
- Of the total 106 categories of apparel, China was the top supplier for eighty-seven categories (or 82.1 percent);
- Of the total sixteen categories of made-up textiles, China was the top supplier for eleven categories (or 68.8 percent)

Moreover, China was not only the top supplier for many textile and apparel products but also held a majority share of the market. For example:

- For the twenty-six categories of fabric that China was the top supplier for, China's average market share reached 40.5 percent, 22 percent higher than the second top suppliers for these categories.
- For the eighty-seven categories of apparel that China was the top supplier for, China's average market share reached 52.4 percent, 36 percent higher than the second top suppliers for these categories.

- For the eleven categories of made-up textiles that China was the top supplier for, China's average market share reached 58 percent, 43 percent higher than the second top suppliers for these categories.

China's overall status as a "balanced" sourcing base, regarding sourcing cost, speed to market, and the risk of non-compliance, makes it competitive compared with other sourcing destinations (see Appendix 1):

First, apparel "Made in China" continues to enjoy overall price competitiveness. In contrast with the popular view that "Made in China" is becoming more expensive, official trade statistics show that the unit price of US apparel imports from China actually dropped from US$2.68 per square meter equivalent (SME) in 2015 to US$2.38/SME in 2017, a decrease of 11.4 percent (OTEXA 2018). Similarly, the unit price of "Made in China" apparel in the US market was 80 percent of the world's average (US$2.96/SME) in 2017, down from 86 percent in 2015 (US$3.13/SME).

Second, industry sources say that sourcing from China overall will incur a shorter lead time when compared with other Asian suppliers, largely because apparel mills in China can easily get access to raw materials, trims, and accessories locally (Re:Source 2018). In comparison, many other leading apparel-exporting countries in Asia such as Bangladesh, Vietnam, Cambodia, and Indonesia, as well as countries in SSA, still heavily rely on imported textile materials that negatively affect their supply chain efficiency (Lu 2018a).

Additionally, Gap Inc. doesn't have to worry too much about the risk of non-compliance when sourcing from China. As of October 2018, 748 Chinese textile and apparel factories have been certified by the Worldwide Responsible Accredited Production program, which provides important assurances to US fashion brands and apparel retailers who are sourcing from the country. China also introduced its own Social Compliance 9000 for Textile & Apparel Industry Program (CSC9000T); strong support for the implementation of this program had been received from the local government from as early as May 2005 (Re:Source 2018).

However, continuing to source from China is not without its concerns. One major issue that Gap Inc., and many other US fashion brands and retailers, are facing right now is the escalating US-China trade war, which has created huge market uncertainties (AAFA 2018; USFIA 2018). On September 17, 2018, President Trump announced a levy for an additional 10 percent punitive tariff on US$200 billion worth of imports from China, which covers several textile and apparel-related products sold by Gap Inc. such as backpacks, handbags, purses, wallets, baseball gloves, hats, and fur apparel. Even worse, the Trump administration plans to increase the punitive tariff rate further to 25 percent starting from January 1, 2019, and apply it to all imports from China should a trade deal not be reached between the two countries (Lu 2018c). If Gap Inc.'s apparel sourced from China were to be hit with these additional tariffs it would affect their profit margin significantly.

As the Chinese economy becomes more advanced, the labor-intensive apparel manufacturing sector is no longer regarded as a pillar industry of strategic importance to the country. In recent years, a growing number of garment factories in China have been closing their businesses amid a mix of factors, ranging from fast increasing labor costs and competition from other lower-wage apparel-exporting countries, to the increasing value of the Chinese currency (Leng 2018). The US-China trade war is pushing more Chinese garment factories to move production overseas. This adds another layer of uncertainty to the future of China as an apparel sourcing base for Gap Inc.

Business Questions

1 Assume you are a sourcing manager for Gap Inc. How would you rank the following regarding importance when determining a sourcing destination:

   a. speed to market

   b. sourcing cost

   c. risk of non-compliance.

2 Is there another factor that you would rank more highly than these? Please specify. Why would you rank these as such?

3 In the 2017 fiscal year, Gap Inc. sourced its products from approximately 800 vendors in fifty countries around the world. What are the benefits of adopting such a diversified sourcing base? Is this necessary?

4 How should Gap Inc. adjust its sourcing strategy in response to the changing business environment as described in the case? Particularly, why or why not should Gap Inc. continue sourcing from China?

5 Which country or region could serve as the alternative to "Made in China" for Gap Inc. and why?

Appendices

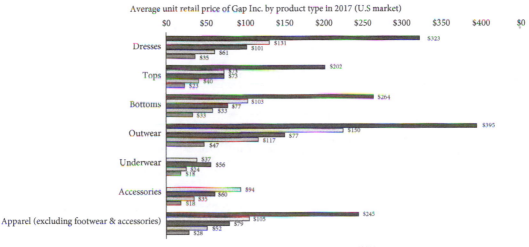

APPENDIX 1 Average unit retail price of Gap inc. by product type in 2017. *Data source:* EDITED 2018.

Region	Sourcing destination	Speed to market	Sourcing cost	Risk of non-compliance
Western hemisphere	USA	⬤ 5	◆ 1.5	⬤ 4
	Mexico	⬤ 4	△ 3	△ 3
	CAFTA-DR	△ 3.5	△ 3.5	△ 3
	Colombia	△ 3	◆ 2.5	△ 3
Asia	China	△ 3	△ 3.5	△ 3
	Vietnam	△ 3	⬤ 4	△ 3
	Bangladesh	◆ 2	⬤ 4.5	◆ 1.5
	Indonesia	◆ 2.5	△ 3.5	△ 3
	India	◆ 2.5	△ 3.5	◆ 2.5
	Sri Lanka	◆ 2.5	△ 3.5	△ 3
	Cambodia	◆ 2.5	△ 3.5	◆ 2.5
Others	AGOA	◆ 2	△ 3.5	◆ 2.5
	Egypt	◆ 2.5	△ 3	△ 3

APPENDIX 2 Comparison of leading apparel sourcing bases for US fashion companies. *Data source:* **LU 2018A.**

Note: The results were based on respondents' average rating for each country in a scale of 1 (much lower performance than the average) to 5 (much higher performance than the average). In the table, a circle means strength as a sourcing base (rating score between 5.0–4.0); a triangle means average performance (rating score between 3.0–3.9); a diamond means weakness as a sourcing base (rating score between 1.0–2.9).

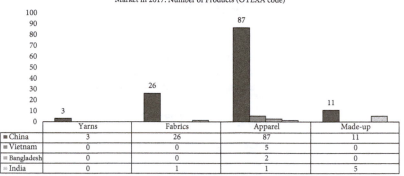

China, Vietnam, Bangladesh and India as a Top Supplier in the U.S. Textile and Apparel Import Market in 2017: Number of Products (OTEXA code)

	Yarns	Fabrics	Apparel	Made-up
■ China	3	26	87	11
■ Vietnam	0	0	5	0
■ Bangladesh	0	0	2	0
■ India	0	1	1	5

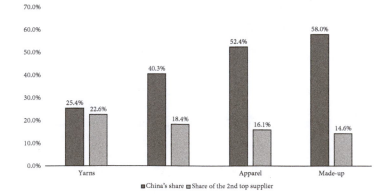

For Products that China was the Top Supplier in 2017 (by value): China's Average Market Shares vs Market Share of the 2nd Top Supplier

■ China's share ■ Share of the 2nd top supplier

APPENDIX 3 China's competitiveness as an apparel-sourcing base for US fashion companies. Top: China, Vietnam, Bangladesh, and India as a top supplier in the US textile and apparel import market in 2017: number of products (OTEXA code). Bottom: For products that China was the top supplier in 2017 (by value): China's average market shares vs. market share of the second top supplier. *Data source:* **OTEXA 2018.**

References and Further Reading

Abdulla, Hannah. 2018. "How GapInc is Using Scale to Speed Up Its Supply Chain." *Just-Style*, October 9, 2018. Accessed November 3, 2018. https://www.just-style.com/analysis/how-gap-inc-is-using-scale-to-speed-up-its-supply-chain_id134694.aspx

American Apparel and Footwear Association (AAFA).2018. "Companies OpposeTranche 3 of Section 301 China Tariffs." Accessed November4, 2018. https://www.aafaglobal.org/AAFA/AAFA_News/

Barrie, Leonie. 2018a. "Outlook2018—Apparel Industry Challenges and Opportunities." *Just-Style*, January 4, 2018. Accessed October 14, 2018. https://www.just-style.com/analysis/outlook-2018-apparel-industry-challenges-and-opportunities_id132514.aspx

Barrie, Leonie. 2018b. "The Top Sourcing Concerns for US Fashion Firms In 2018." *Just-Style*, July 19, 2018. Accessed October 26, 2018. https://www.just-style.com/analysis/the-top-sourcing-concerns-for-us-fashion-firms-in-2018_id134021.aspx

Berg, Achim, Benedikt Berlemann, and Saskia Hedrich. 2013. *The Global Sourcing Map—Balancing Cost, Compliance, andCapacity.* McKinsey & Company. Accessed October 12, 2018. https://www.mckinsey.com/~/media/mckinsey/dotcom/client_service/retail/articles/the_global_sourcing_map_balancing_cost_compliance_and_capacity.ashx

Berg, Achim, Saskia Hedrich, and Bill Russo. 2015. "East Africa: The Next Hub for Apparel Sourcing." McKinsey & Company. Accessed October 29, 2018. https://www.mckinsey.com/industries/retail/our-insights/east-africa-the-next-hub-for-apparel-sourcing

Dinh, Hinh T. 2014. *Light Manufacturing In Vietnam: Creating Jobs and Prosperity ina Middle-Income Economy.* Washington, DC: The World Bank.

EDITED. 2018. "Market Analytics Online Tool." Accessed September 30, 2018. www.edited.com.

Edmont, Jon. 2018. "A 2013 Collapse Killed 1,100 People. Bangladesh Factories Are Still Unsafe." *Wall Street Journal*, March 29, 2018. Accessed October 29, 2018. https://www.wsj.com/articles/five-years-after-tragedy-bangladesh-factories-remain-unsafe-1522324800

Gap Inc. 2012. *Annual Report in 2012.* Accessed October 1, 2018. http://www.annualreports.co.uk/HostedData/AnnualReportArchive/g/NYSE_GPS_2012.pdf

Gap Inc. 2016. *Annual Report in 2016.* Accessed October 1, 2018. http://www.annualreports.co.uk/HostedData/AnnualReportArchive/g/NYSE_GPS_2016.pdf

Gap Inc. 2017a. *Annual Report in 2017.* Accessed September 15, 2018. http://www.annualreports.co.uk/HostedData/AnnualReports/PDF/NYSE_GPS_2017.pdf

Gap Inc. 2017b. *Global Sustainability Report 2015–2016.* Accessed November 3, 2018. http://www.gapincsustainability.com/sites/default/files/Gap%20Inc.%202015%20-%2016%20Report.pdf

Ha-Brookshire, Jung. 2017. *Global Sourcing in the Textile and Apparel Industry*, 2nd edition. New York: Bloomsbury Publishing.

Hunter, Elizabeth, Sophie Marchessou, and Jennifer Schmidt. 2018. "The Need for Speed: Capturing Today's Fashion Consumer." McKinsey & Company, March. Accessed October 14, 2018. https://www.mckinsey.com/industries/retail/our-insights/the-need-for-speed-capturing-todays-fashion-consumer

Leng, Sidney. 2018. "China's Once-Booming Textile And Clothing Industry Faces Tough Times." *South China Morning Post*, April 30,2018. Accessed November 5, 2018. https://www.scmp.com/news/china/economy/article/2143938/chinas-once-booming-textile-and-clothing-industry-faces-tough

Lu, Sheng. 2016. *U.S. Fashion Industry Benchmarking Study.* Washington, DC: United States Fashion Industry Association. Accessed October 5, 2018. http://www.usfashionindustry.com/pdf_files/USFIA-2016-Fashion-Industry-Benchmarking-Study.pdf

Lu, Sheng. 2017. *U.S. Fashion Industry Benchmarking Study.* Washington, DC: United States Fashion Industry Association. Accessed October 5, 2018. http://www.usfashionindustry.com/pdf_files/USFIA-Fashion-Industry-Benchmarking-Study-2017.pdf

Lu, Sheng. 2018a. *U.S. Fashion Industry Benchmarking Study.* Washington, DC: United States Fashion Industry Association. Accessed October 10, 2018. www.usfashionindustry.com/pdf_files/USFIA-Fashion-Industry-Benchmarking-Study-2018.pdf

Lu, Sheng. 2018b. "KeyApparel Supply Chain Takeaways from Sourcing at MAGIC." *Just-Style*, August 28, 2018. AccessedNovember 2, 2018. https://www.just-style.com/comment/key-apparel-supply-chain-takeaways-from-sourcing-at-magic_id134301.aspx

Lu, Sheng. 2018c. "Timeline—Trump's Track Record on Trade—Update." *Just-Style*, December 4, 2018. AccessedNovember 4, 2018. https://www.just-style.com/analysis/timeline-trumps-track-record-on-trade-update_id133211.aspx

Margolis, Joshua, Paul McKinnon, and Michael Norris. 2015. *Gap Inc.: Refashioning Performance Management. HBS No. 9-146-019*. Boston, MA: Harvard Business School Publishing.

Mesloh, Debbie. 2012. *Towards 21st Century TPP Agreement for Apparel*. TPP Apparel Coalition, July 12, 2012. Accessed November 4,2018. http://www.tppapparelcoalition.org/uploads/120712aucklandpresentation.pdf

Myers-McDevitt, Paula J. 2011. *Apparel Production Management and the Technical Package*. New York: Bloomsbury Publishing.

Office of Textiles and Apparel. 2018. "U.S. Imports and Exports of Textile andApparel." Accessed October 14, 2018. https://otexa.trade.gov/msrpoint.htm

Platzer, Michaela. 2017. *Renegotiating NAFTA and U.S. Textile Manufacturing*. Washington, DC: Congressional Research Service. Accessed October 29, 2018. https://fas.org/sgp/crs/row/R44998.pdf

Re:Source. 2018. "Apparel Sourcing Database." *Just-Style*. Accessed November 4, 2018. https://resource.just-style.com

S&P Global. 2018. "Textiles, Apparel & Luxury Goods Industry Survey." Accessed October 11, 2018. www.capitaliq.com

United States Fashion Industry Association (USFIA).2018. *Sourcing Trends and Outlook for 2018*. Washington, DC: USFIA.

United States International Trade Commission (USITC).2018. "Shifts in U.S. Merchandise Trade 2017—Textiles and Apparel (Investigation No. 332–345)."Washington, DC: USITC. Accessed October 26, 2018. https://usitc.gov/research_and_analysis/trade_shifts_2017/textiles.htm

Definitions

Higg Index: A self-assessment standard for social and environmental sustainability within the supply chain of a fashion brand.

Lead time: The time gap between designing a garment and making the garment available in the retail store.

Chapter 25

Growth of Green Apparel Manufacturing Strategies in Bangladesh

The Sustainable Road Ahead

Maher Anjum and Lynne Hammond

This case study explores the changing competitive environment influencing the shift towards responsible and clean production in Bangladesh by global retailers after the Rana Plaza tragedy in March 2013. The case explores the concept of "green" and clean manufacturing in supply chains through analyzing and evaluating the approach adopted by one organization: Plummy Fashions Ltd. (PFL) in Bangladesh. The manufacturer is a leader in delivering apparel production that is ethical and environmentally friendly, giving them a strong competitive advantage over their rivals in these areas. They are ranked as Platinum in LEED (Leadership in Energy and Environmental Design), the highest level rating globally.

The case study offers an in-depth analysis of the key supply chain decisions that PFL have to consider when managing continuous and competitive growth of global apparel production, while at the same time trying to maintain a strong commitment to sustainability values. The case is taken from the authors' consultancy work and provides examples through rare expert interviews and context mapping of best practices related to strategic sustainable leadership, particularly environmental approaches. PFL has allowed the development of this case study through sharing their sustainable approaches and providing the authors with visits and access to their green factory environments. This case study is problem based and is suitable for graduate and postgraduate students seeking to critically explore, analyze, and evaluate the challenges of balancing responsible sourcing with competitive growth strategies for the global apparel manufacturing sector.

Learning Objectives

Upon completion of this case, students should be able to:

- Develop insights into one Bangladesh knitwear manufacturer with sustainable and green factory conditions and environment.

- Evaluate one Bangladesh manufacturing facility in order to identify critical success factors that contribute to competitive advantage through environmental sustainability.

- Explore the concepts of clean production and the sustainability agenda in Bangladesh apparel and knitwear manufacturing and the links to retailer/buyer demands.

- Analyze the apparel supply chain process and how responsible supply chain measurements are being used to enhance sustainable practices in Bangladesh.

- Develop arguments that explore the balancing of responsible supply chains with low-cost products and goods from both retailer and manufacturer perspectives.

- Evaluate similarities and differences of manufacturing business models to enable sustainable goals to be integrated into the apparel supply chain.

- Analyze the consumer role in driving supply chain transparency and how this type of commitment is influencing consumer buying behavior.

- Develop awareness of compliant global sourcing strategies and what solutions can be used to support clean and responsible production.

- Evaluate how the sharing of data and information using digital platforms can improve the sourcing teams and vendors/suppliers' performance.

- Develop a set of tools and methodologies that can be used to measure and monitor the environmental and social impacts across the value chain from preproduction to production stages.

Introduction

According to the Pulse of the Fashion Industry report (2017) the fashion industry has been an engine for global development.

> One of the world's largest consumer industries, generating €1.5 trillion in annual apparel and footwear revenues in 2016, it employs around 60 million people along its value chain. To continue the growth trajectory, the fashion industry needs to address its environmental and social footprint. The earth's natural resources are under pressure, and the fashion industry, although not the most obvious contributor, is a considerable one. Social conditions also in the fashion industry are far from those set forth in the United Nations' goals for sustainable development. With current trajectories of production and consumption, these pressures will intensify by 2030 to the point of threatening industry growth itself.

With increasing globalization, the apparel industry is often dispersed geographically with manufacturing, distribution, and retail operations located across several different countries and continents. Retailers have to work hard to ensure that transparency and labor standards are monitored on a regular basis and that sustainable goals are aligned to their business vision.

Apparel supply chain transparency and responsible sourcing are important business objectives for the global fashion industry. Köksal et al. (2017, 2–3) cite Seuring and Müller's definition of sustainable supply chain management as "the management of material, information and capital flows as well as cooperation among companies along the supply chain while integrating goals from all three dimensions of sustainable development, i.e., economic, environmental and social, which are derived from customer and stakeholder requirements."

Today's consumers are becoming more aware of the need to protect the environment and desire that their clothes are made in a more responsible way throughout the production process from design, production, and logistics to distribution and disposal. The challenge for the apparel supply chain is to address how clothing can be made in a more sustainable way to combat damage to the environment and, furthermore, that people employed in the sector have socially acceptable working conditions and are paid a living wage.

Key issues facing a shift towards sustainable manufacturing in Bangladesh

The Dhaka Apparel Summit has become an important driver of change through dialogue and discussions with international professionals in order to develop the textile and apparel industry in Bangladesh. The first summit was held in 2014 and started the process of sharing and developing future strategic planning for the sector. The 2017 summit brought together leading experts in the field to share experiences and ideas in order to discuss ways in which the ready-made garment industry could achieve sustainable growth into the twenty-first century for better and more responsible supply chains. The 2017 theme was exploring how partnerships and working together for the future could lead better social and labor practices alongside environmental challenges during the textile and garment manufacturing process (Preuss 2017, Dhaka Apparel Summit 2017).

In 2021, Bangladesh will be fifty years old and has set an objective to become a middle-income country from a low-income country. To achieve this development, Vision 2021 (Bangladesh Government 2012) was developed and adopted in 2006 alongside a plan to achieve its goals. It has eight key goals. Of these:

- Goal 3 is "To become a poverty-free middle-income country";
- Goal 6 is "To become a globally integrated regional economic and commercial hub"; and
- Goal 7 is "To be environmentally sustainable."

According to Vena (2013):

Remarkable results have been noted in achieving the UN Millennium Development Goals (MDGs). The biggest improvements have been experienced in MDG 1 (poverty alleviation), MDG 2 (universal primary education), MDG 3 (gender equality) and MDG 5 (reducing maternal mortality) … In the area of women's empowerment, Bangladesh has made extraordinary improvements as well. Women now occupy key high-level positions in the government, high and supreme courts, police and the armed service.

The Vision 2021 goals are developed further in the perspective plan and more specifically as, "Addressing globalization and regional cooperation," "Establishing a knowledge based society," and "Mitigating the impacts of climate change." As a measurement of success it aims to: change the sectorial composition of output, with the shares of agriculture, industry, and services approximating 15 percent, 38 percent, and 47 percent respectively by 2021.

Growth and development of Bangladesh's apparel sector

Bangladesh is a highly important manufacturing destination for fast fashion due to the benefits of low-cost labor, large-volume capacities, extensive production experience, and good trading agreements with European countries. It currently employs four million people, mostly women, with over five thousand factories servicing the global export market (Nagaraj 2018). It is ranked as the second largest manufacturing industry and has experienced year-on-year growth since 2007. In fact "Textile Today" (Akter 2017) says the average growth in 2007–2016 was 12.8 percent though slowing down to 8.47 percent over the last five years. In 2016 the 7.76 percent year-on-year growth had an estimated value of US$28.67 billion.

Reasons cited for sourcing from a country in general are: cost cutting, flexibility, shorter lead times, and quality. Thus, there is never assurance that retailers will source from the same manufacturer/country year on year. Therefore, it is significant that retailers continue to source from, and increase the amounts of sourcing from, Bangladesh.

In the "State of Sourcing Survey 2017—Supply Chain Shifts," a survey carried out annually by *just-style* (Barrie 2016), asked the question: which sourcing markets do you expect to grow in importance in the next five years? Bangladesh has been placed in second place with 50.8 percent, up from 41 percent in 2016. Similarly, the question: do you expect to source more or less from Bangladesh in 2017? The response of 38.6 percent of those surveyed says that they intend to source more from Bangladesh in 2017 (versus 35.6 percent in 2016).

The growth of the sector is partly due to the fact that the Bangladeshi apparel manufacturers have been able to, and continue to, meet the requirements for sourcing. The growth and development in sustainable practices is related to more efficient machinery as well as manufacturing processes and practices that have also assisted in making Bangladesh the choice for sourcing. This development in the Bangladesh apparel industry has been supported through training and skills development funded externally by international organizations, such as the International Finance Corporation, alongside private sector funding acquired by manufacturers. International funding in the form of aid has been received from the European Union, Netherlands, Germany (GTZ), United Kingdom (Department for International Development, or DFID), US (USAID), and Norway (Norad) amongst others to support new knowledge, practice, and training for sustainable practices in the apparel sector.

The key players that are driving change and leading the way are the apparel and textile industrial associations at a national level, the BGMEA (Bangladesh Garment Manufacturers and Exporters Association) and the BKMEA (Bangladesh Knitwear Manufacturers and Exporters Association). The role of these industrial associations is to provide a coordinated body that works with retailers, national government, trade associations, and international NGOs directly and who provide a unified voice to managing change. The BGMEA is investing in a new university campus to upgrade and develop international curricula and educational approaches to compete with other manufacturing countries such as India, Myanmar, Vietnam, Cambodia, and China.

The key perspective and context for change

There are several challenges the apparel sector faces to ensure professional business models are embedded into the manufacturing sector. Ongoing education and training needs to address some of the weaknesses in the supply chain strategies such as labor relationships between owners and workers, health and safety regulations of factories, and low adoption of environmental practices, such as water, energy, and waste management.

In particular, fast-fashion retailers face challenges to ensure that their supply chains are addressing future sustainable approaches. Fast-fashion retailers such as H&M have over five hundred factories in Bangladesh and the fashion retailer is a driving force to ensure that sustainable standards are embedded into the apparel supply chain.

H&M is part of the Accord program, which was set up by European retailers after the Rana Plaza accident to monitor and carry out audits/checks to ensure social and environmental standards are being met by the factories that they source from. According to Accord (Bangladesh Accord Secretariat 2017) it has completed remediation visits in more than sixteen hundred factories in Bangladesh to ensure they are compliant and provide better sustainable standards. It is reported (Aktar 2017) that the combined visits of Accord and ALLIANCE to apparel factories in Bangladesh found less than 2 percent of them to be at risk of fire and health and safety breaches compared to 4 percent globally. In November 2013, H&M set up a Centre of Excellence in Bangladesh to support textile workers at their supplier factories to have access to education and skill development, and to ensure they are employed at a level matching their skills.

Fashion's need for raw materials and labor intensive production processes make it an industry particularly vulnerable to environmental disruption, as are the profit margins of businesses that operate within it. The fashion industry has evolved using a linear model when it comes to raw materials, often expressed as take, make, and waste (Mellery-Pratt 2017). Increasing awareness of the environmental and social concerns surrounding the fashion industry and the Rana Plaza industrial accident has led to major changes to building health and safety developments.

The Rana Plaza building collapse in 2013 was one of the worst ever industrial accidents, and has been the catalyst for change for building safety requirements and driving better corporate responsibility practices in Bangladesh. More inspections into factory conditions have been undertaken by international experts and the BGMEA have been working with the International Labor Organization to ensure that the improvements are carried out with remediation actions.

One trend that is being adopted by Bangladesh manufacturers is the movement towards "green factories" to address the environmental damage caused by apparel and textile production. In addition, Bangladesh is moving towards clean and lean manufacturing models to improve their supply chain reputations. Clean production is defined by the United Nations Environment Programme as the "continuous application of an integrated preventative environmental strategy to processes, products and services to increase efficiency and reduce risks to humans and the environment" (UNIDO 2010).

Business Problem

Circumstances contributing to the business issue

The Bangladesh Bank, the central bank responsible for overseeing and maintaining monetary and financial stability of the country, makes its commitment to Vision 2021 in its 2015 report "Designing a Sustainable Financial System in Bangladesh":

[Bangladesh] is seeking to transform from a low-income economy to the first stages of a middle-income economy over the decade from 2010, through enhanced and sustainable agricultural production, accelerated industrialization and increasing integration into the global economy. At the same time it must address critical energy supply and infrastructure gaps, handle rapid urbanization and address vulnerability to floods, cyclones, storm surges and drought. The nation's aspirations are based on a vision of increased investment (targeted to rise from 24% to 38% of GDP over the decade). While some of this will be public investment to address infrastructure gaps, the greatest rise is in private investment, from 1.2 trillion Taka (US$15 billion) in 2010 to 4.8 trillion Taka (US$61 billion) by 2021.

In order to understand the complexities of apparel supply chains and manufacturing in developing countries such as Bangladesh, it is important to provide a framework of how global, national, and local forces are driving competitiveness for both the retailers and the manufacturers.

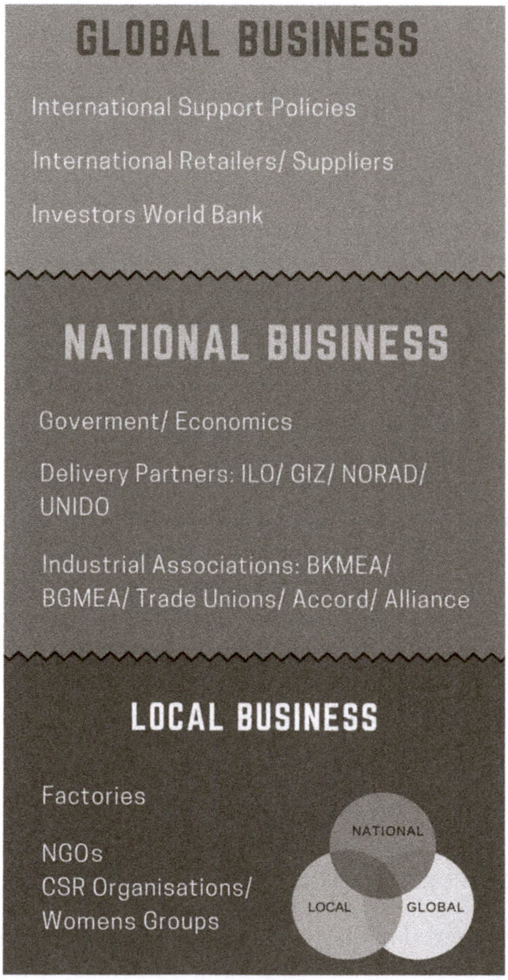

FIGURE 25.1 Sustainable apparel business framework diagram (developed by the authors based on experience of working with international and external agencies providing funds and grants to Bangladesh). © Maher Anjum, Lynne Hammond.

The growth of the Bangladesh apparel and textile manufacturing industry has been driven by the ever-increasing consumer demand for cheap clothing that puts pressure on buyers to achieve highly competitive price points. To manage the increase in demand from retailers for value-added products, investment into environmental and ethical systems has been slow and impact assessments limited and not strategic. Adoption of sustainability, clean production, and social responsibility has largely been initiated by external agencies and international projects. Figure 25.1 indicates the international support, initiatives, and investment that contribute to the Bangladesh apparel industry, combined with the national investment by governments and industrial associations that provide strategies and direction to shape new agendas. At the local level, it is the investment and new production models that are now emerging to provide new green and sustainable factory environments. Extensive industry projects have been undertaken with organizations, such as the United National Industrial Development Organization (UNIDO), the British Council, and Green Grade, to support business growth in the Bangladesh apparel industry.

A Survey Report by Social Responsible Asia, titled "CSR: The Present Status of Bangladesh & Way Forward" (2017), states that, till now, most of the businesses in Bangladesh are family owned and first generation businesses. They are involved in community development work in the form of charity without having any definite policy regarding the expenses or any concrete motive regarding financial gains." If the industry is to compete in the future and achieve its Vision 2021 goal of US$50 billion, the challenges that should be addressed are based on stronger sustainable, responsible, and clean production methods with better work practices. Bangladesh, although the second largest manufacturing industry globally, still needs to develop and implement long-term policies and innovation to control unregulated expansion of factories that are non-compliant and non-regulated.

Since 2014 there has been a considerable shift towards fit-for-purpose manufacturing facilities that are newly constructed with high environmental and best practice building regulations. The Bangladesh apparel sector has had to address the challenges of embedding ethical, environmental, and sustainability concerns into their business models to ensure that responsible and clean production are core values. The circumstances contributing to the business problem are based on four areas:

1 There is a lack of a long-term strategic roadmap and vision to inform change in the Bangladesh apparel sector. Questions such as how government, industry, and international stakeholders can collaborate better to improve competitive advantage and achieve the Vision 2021 target are ongoing.

2 There is still limited understanding of the changing demand by consumers towards responsible clothing. There is a long way to go before consumers will change their buying habits and want to pay more for their clothing. Retailers are under pressure to limit a damaged reputation and to ensure that their supply chains are ethical and environmentally strong, but to also keep prices low. This is a difficult balancing act to ensure profit margins can be maintained with low-cost fashion products.

3 There has been a slow adoption of "home-grown" sustainable leadership developments in the supply chain in order to explore new business opportunities for win–win scenarios for both retailers and manufacturers. With limited progress made in areas such as establishing research centres, for example, university education and management training programs, the majority of the existing knowledge centers are mainly led by international experts, not by national, regional, and local professionals and experts.

4   There have been low levels of investment to build sustainable innovation and initiatives into the apparel and textile industry. Bangladesh Bank allocated 5 percent of finance to sustainable and green sector agricultural and manufacturing. It has requested that local banks report, as part of their annual reports, on their financial lending to sustainable manufacturing (UNEP 2015). In spite of this and the funds available from the International Finance Commission, the evidence shows that take-up by the sector has been slow.

Introduction to Plummy Fashions Limited Company history and operations

Plummy Fashions Ltd. was established in 2006 as a direct supplier to UK and European high street retailers. Plummy was set up as a specialist volume knitwear producer competing on low-cost apparel manufacturing of basic products such as T-shirts and polo shirts to supply mass-market retailers. The company is led by Mr. Mohammed Fazlul Hoque who has been active in the apparel industry for over twenty years and was president of the BKMEA for six years. He was also president of the Bangladesh Employers Federation and director of the International Apparel Federation. Other directors also have a minimum of fifteen years' experience in the knitwear business. The company employs professional experts to manage production, quality assurance, and industrial engineers to ensure excellence in the manufacturing of knitwear.

In 2013, as a response to the Rana Plaza tragedy, Fazlul Hoque began to explore the building of a green factory complex. He recognized the need for the Bangladesh apparel industry to change and become more responsible towards ethical and environmental practices, and for safe and clean production environments to become common practice.

In September 2015, the new factory opened its doors on the outskirts of Dhaka, in the district of Narayanganj. Part of the required investment was supported by the Bangladesh Green Industry fund. The US Green Building Council LEED certification scheme awarded the PFL complex a high score of 92 out of 110, a platinum rating level (US Green Building Council 2018).

There are seven categories used to score the building based on: sustainable sites; water efficiency; energy and atmosphere; material and resources; indoor environment quality; innovation; and regional priority credits.

TABLE 25.1 *Plummy's LEED Scorecard—Platinum, 92/110*

Category	Score
Sustainable Sites	25 of 26
Water Efficiency	10 of 10
Energy and Atmosphere	31 of 35
Material and Resources	7 of 14
Indoor Environmental Quality	10 of 15
Innovation	5 of 6
Regional Priority Credits	4 of 4

In 2015, the company employed 1,250 people in total with 14 managers. On average, Plummy produces roughly 200,000 to 240,000 pieces per week or 866,666 to 1,040,000 per month. The garments produced are mainly T-shirts, polo shirts, sweatshirts, and trousers. Plummy supplies value retailers and brands, such as Zara, Pull & Bear, Next, Debenhams, Kappa, Aldi, Falabella in South America, Tailor Vintage in the USA, and is exploring developing orders with PVH, Levi's in the USA, and Next in the UK. In an interview with the CEO, Fazlul Hoque, in Dhaka in April 2017, Hoque stated that the company's turnover in 2017/2018 was US$30 million.

In 2016, Plummy was awarded a National Award on Environments from the Bangladeshi prime minister Sheikh Hasina. The building is one of only three factories in the world that have been recognized as being centers of excellence for green apparel manufacturing.

Mission and sustainable supply chain practices

Plummy outline their mission for better manufacturing environments and being the greenest knitwear factory in the world on their website. The company is committed to driving sustainability into their preproduction and production processes to ensure both ethical and environmental practices are of a high level and standard. The supply chain is compliant with the certification and accreditation systems listed in Table 25.2.

Although Plummy's sustainable strategies have a long way to go to arrive at the high levels of compliance demanded by leading international brands and retailers, the company does demonstrate a desire to drive responsible supply chains and embed competitive advantage into their business model for future manufacturing developments.

Plummy's CEO, Fazlul Hoque, demonstrates a strong commitment to sustainable leadership strategies through his mission and investment to improve Bangladesh's reputation and image as an apparel manufacturing base. He has pioneered and innovated new green factory environments that are both built and operate in a safe and clean manner. He is a

TBALE 25.2 *Plummy Fashion Ltd Certification Bodies and Accreditation Systems*

Name	Website	Description
BSCI	https://www.bsci-intl.org/content/what-we-do-0	Business Social Compliance is a leading supply chain system that drives social compliance improvements.
SEDEX	https://www.sedexglobal.com/about-us/	A non-profit making organization that is one of the largest collaborative platforms for sharing responsible sourcing data on supply chains.
Oeko Tex 100	https://www.oeko-tex.com/en/business/certifications_and_services/ots_100/ots_100_start.xhtml	Independent testing and certification system for textile products at all processing levels.
GOTS	https://www.global-standard.org/certification/how-to-become-certified.html	Global organic textile standards and certification.
BCI	https://www.thebci.org/index.php/get-bci-certified	The Business Community Institute is a leading institute for the business community.
WRAP	http://www.wrapcompliance.org/	Gold Certificate of Compliance

member of Social Responsible Asia (SRAsia), indicating his sustainable values and actions towards achieving responsible supply chains (SRAsia 2012). The company does not as yet publish an annual report on their sustainable activities and actions but have their own key performance indicators in place to measure sustainable performance.

Figure 25.2 is a sustainable apparel production framework diagram developed by the authors from reviewing various manufacturers' websites that show the level of commitment towards sustainable, clean, and responsible principles. It indicates four pillars that can be used to monitor sustainable apparel performance, which has been used in this case as a tool to assess PFL's sustainable practices. The four pillars of ethical, environmental, product development, and retailer engagement have been developed as a way of understanding and organizing the complexities of sustainable apparel production. The diagram demonstrates the many layers required to achieve high levels of compliance and sustainability in the supply chain.

Return on investment into sustainable manufacturing is now attracting new customers such as Aldi and Lidl. These retailers new into the apparel market are wanting low-cost, high-volume products but with a high sustainable performance in their supply chains. In addition, the company is investing in people management through better training and development of their teams. Plummy has adopted a change management program and is ensuring that workers are being trained on better workplace practices and in addition building a professional management team that can implement sustainable and CSR practices. The CEO

FIGURE 25.2 Sustainable apparel production framework diagram. © Maher Anjum, Lynne Hammond.

has been open and transparent about the reasons for moving towards green manufacturing. He has outlined information and data that give insights into the sustainable manufacturing processes, methods, and environments providing in-depth knowledge and understanding of the complexities of supplying and producing fast-fashion and value-fashion products.

Besides Mr. Hoque, the team is made up of experienced, motivated, and skilled production experts, industrial engineers, quality assurance managers, technicians, and specialists. However, the need to improve training of mid- and top-level managers, and not relying on manpower coming from India or Sri Lanka are two of the challenges to achieving a long-term competitive advantage. The team oversees the implementation of lean manufacturing production systems for better supply chain management. Lean manufacturing is an operational strategy oriented towards achieving the shortest possible cycle time by eliminating wastes. The benefits of such a system are the focus on productivity and efficiencies during the production process.

The following section is organized based on the four pillar model headings (Figure 25.2).

Product development

Plummy has a style development department equipped with modern instruments and software to work with various buyers' design groups. They are well-aware of modern fashion trends and capable of fulfilling major buyers' requirements across all types of knitted products. Lean manufacturing processes with strong follow-up ensures on-time production with the correct quality of the product. Quality assurance teams with foreign experts follow up the quality from yarn stage to the final product.

Plummy offer two types of circular knitwear production: cut-and-sew and fullyfashioned knitwear. In circular knitwear Plummy produces a wide variety of products for women, children, and men. Plummy are familiar with various products from very low GSM (grams per square meter or gm/2) women's wear to heavy winter wear. Plummy has a modern knitting and dyeing facility with a well-equipped laboratory to produce different types of high quality fabrics. Plummy produce all types of fabrics such as single jersey, rib, interlock, fleece, terry, plated, pointel, etc. In addition to 100 percent cotton PFL also produce cotton mixed with elasthane/lycra, polyester, viscose, modal, melange, neppy fabrics, etc. with different kinds of finishing.

Plummy has installed machineries with high performance in all sections of the factory. In the cuttingsection they have auto cutters from Topcut Bullmer, Germany, supported by software-based pattern making. All sewing machines are equipped with auto-trimming devices. For the finishing section Plummy selected vacuum tables, irons from Veit, Germany, and metal detectors from Hashima, Japan. In the knitting-section the famous Fukuhama brand machines have been installed to ensure the highest quality knitting is produced. The dyeing section is fitted with top-quality machinery ensuring minimal shrinkage and smooth finishing.

The most advanced Bus Bar Trunking System from Graziadio, Italy, has been installed to avoid electrical hazards. Plummy has equipped the factory with a high-quality fire protection system; besides fire-fighting equipment, the factory is monitored by a fire detection system with more than two hundred and fifty smoke and heat-detecting devices installed. In addition, the training center provides a fire training and awareness program for workers and a dedicated fire-fighting unit has also been set up.

There is an in-house quality assurance team which oversees each stage of the process of production. Plummy is pioneering both a competitive advantage through offering sustainable production to fast-fashion retailers, and embedding social responsibility and environmental practices into their business model. Köksal et al. (2017) describe this to be a normative strategy or a "Sustainable Supply Chain Management (SSCM) strategy by focal companies to counteract supply chain disruptions by the implementation of supplier management systems such as environmental and social standards, e.g., ISO14001 and SA8000."

Ethical manufacturing

Plummy, through its LEED certification provides a good quality working environment for their workers. This includes training rooms, rest rooms, a Lifestyle Centre which includes a medical center and childcare facilities, and employee committees. Plummy offers safe and comfortable working conditions: an evaporative cooling system has been installed along with high standard toilets and shower facilities and locker facilities, a spacious dining area, and bicycle parking has been offered for the workers. These are important socially responsible practices that indicate that the company has sustainability and social ethical compliance practices embedded into their business model.

Environmental manufacturing

The LEED-certified green manufacturing unit is made up of a three-building complex that houses both knitting and garment production plants. The site is 5.5 acres, landscaped with a combination of award-winning designed buildings and three acres of garden spaces. A key sustainability feature is Plummy's world-class natural water management system through which they can recycle and reuse both rainwater and surface water. An auto sensor for urinals, dual-flush water closets, and faucets with a flow rate of 1.5 liters per minute have been installed to comply with the US-EPA (US Energy Policy Act) and Plummy's efficient water fixtures reduce water use by up to 60 percent. A natural lake located inside the factory premises ensures a balanced ecosystem.

In addition to the water-management strategies, the factory makes use of solar energy, has a CFC-free cooling system, an LED lighting system, low energy consuming machines, etc. to minimize its carbon footprint, all with the required industry certifications and accreditations (LEED Platinum, BSCI, SEDEX, Oeko Tex 100, GOTS, and BCI). Plummy has also obtained accreditation from the Accord and Alliance in Bangladesh in 2015/2016 and established a well-equipped training center to train workers with the key objective to increase workers' efficiency for high-quality production methods. In addition, various training programs have been implemented on health, sanitation, fire safety, and labor laws.

Retailer engagement

In April 2017, Fazlul Hoque outlined why he is investing in sustainability:

Business return is the primary purpose. In this instance however it was not all about Return on Investment. I wanted to do something that was about improving the image of the country and image of the sector. Personal satisfaction that something good has been done. People come to visit every week. I want people to come. I want everyone to see the place. I want to be transparent. I want to share. I want to get the message out.

He states that trying to achieve the balance between paying more for production and keeping a strong sustainable strategy embedded into the business model is not an easy path. He also comments that the Bangladesh ready-made garment sector has a bright future as they are achieving a competitive advantage and getting orders from China.

Taking PFL's situation as a value manufacturer, balancing responsible and clean production with competitive pricing of low-cost goods is clearly a challenge for any business. Given the complexities of the issues, how can Bangladesh move towards more sustainable apparel production? And, furthermore, how can the global apparel manufacturing industry address these issues to ensure that people, plant, and profit are aligned to retailers' and consumers' demands?

Business Questions

The case study could be used as a resource to support essay questions that explore:

- Circular economy/closed-loop systems versus traditional linear supply chain models
- Transparency versus opaque supply chains
- How technology can support the sustainable supply chain and apparel production
- The risk management scenario of not embedding sustainable, ethical, and environmental strategies into a retailer's/brand's business values.

1. In the global supply chain, there is a need for mutually beneficial and responsible business practices and actions by all stakeholders to ensure sustainability is embedded into the manufacturing processes.

- Consider the extent to which supply chain transparency can play an important part in a fashion retailer and/or fashion brand's mission statement and value proposition.
- Find examples of how H&M are embedding sustainable production in Bangladesh.

2. Ensuring that common values and shared knowledge is part of a transparent supply chain will require closer cooperation between buyers and suppliers. These issues are being focused on by various global forums such as the United Nations, OECD, and G7.

- Discuss and develop a set of tools that can be used to support a critical evaluation of the sustainable manufacturing model.
- Develop a list of sustainable certifications that could be implemented into the manufacturing model to ensure factories meet international standards of compliance.
- Discuss the role of industrial associations such as the BKMEA and BGMEA in driving sustainable change to the apparel and knitwear industry.

3. At a local level, Bangladesh needs to respond to changing pressures and demands to manage competitiveness to build meaningful sustainable agendas and roadmaps that demonstrate globally that there are long- and medium-term solutions in place.

- What factors and procedures need to be considered when creating a compliant global sourcing strategy for a fashion brand?
- What Corporate Social Responsible (CSR) practices are currently being implemented in Bangladesh?

- List the Key Performance Indicators (KPIs) that could be implemented to measure the impact of sustainable apparel production.

4. On their website Plummy outlines its vision for better manufacturing environments and being the greenest knitwear factory in the world. Can transparency disrupt entrenched supply chain processes and provide an opportunity for change?

- Develop a SWOT of PFL's 'sustainable approach. How can PFL monitor compliance with its ethical ambitions? (Refer to the key certification and accreditations used by Southeast Asian manufacturers to indicate transparency in the supply chain.)
- What are the gaps in PFL's 'green manufacturing strategy and their production processes?
- Develop a production map of PFL that indicates the key stages of knitwear production and explore the environmental impact of each of these stages.

5. Is value fashion at odds with sustainability and clean production?

- Discuss the extent to which sustainable apparel production can be cost effective and create competitive advantage? Propose alternative manufacturing business models that can support the attainment of sustainable development goals.
- Consider the influence of other stakeholders, e.g. government, NGOs, and consumers.

References and Further Reading

Accord. 2017. Accessed July 9, 2018. http://bangladeshaccord.org/

Asian Development Bank (ADB). Accessed July 9, 2018. https://www.adb.org/about/main

Akter, A. 2017. "An Overview of Bangladesh RMG 2016." *Textile Today*, Febuary 15. Accessed August 18, 2017. https://www.textiletoday.com.bd/overview-bangladesh-rmg-2016/html

Bangladesh Accord Secretariat. 2017. "Quarterly Aggregate Report." *Accord*, May 8. Accessed July 9, 2018. http://bangladeshaccord.org/wp-content/uploads/Accord-Quarterly-Aggregate-Report-May-2017.pdf

Bangladesh Garment Manufacturers and Exporters Association (BGMEA). Accessed July 9, 2018. https://www.bgmea.com.bd/

Bangladesh Knitwear Manufacturers and Exporters Association (BKMEA). "BKMEA At a Glance." Accessed July 9, 2018. https://www.bkmea.com/BKMEA-at-a-glance

Christopher, Martin. 2005. *Logistics and Supply Chain Management*. Financial Times/Prentice Hall.

Clean Clothes. "Transparency." Accessed July 9, 2018. https://cleanclothes.org/transparency

Deutsche Gesellschaft fur International Zusammenarbeit (GIZ). Accessed July 9, 2018. https://www.giz.de/en/worldwide/351.html

Dhaka Apparel Summit. 2017. "Dhaka Apparel Summit 2017." Accessed July 9, 2018. https://www.dhakaapparelsummit.com

Fashion Revolution. "Transparency." Accessed July 9, 2018. https://www.fashionrevolution.org/about/transparency/

Goworek, Helen. 2011. "Social and Environmental Sustainability in the Clothing Industry: A Case Study of a Fair Trade Retailer" *Social Responsibility Journal* 7, no. 1: 74–86.

Haque, Mohammed Mozammel. 2008. "Corporate Social Responsibility in Apparel Industry in Bangladesh: A Labour Standard Perspective." *BRAC University*, December. Accessed August 10, 2017. http://dspace.bracu.ac.bd/xmlui/handle/10361/230

H&M Group. "Our Supplier Factory List." Accessed July 9, 2018. http://sustainability.hm.com/en/sustainability/downloads-resources/resources/supplier-list.html#cm-menu

Hammond, Lynne, and Maher Anjum. 2015. "Will Green Growth Bolster Bangladesh Garment Exports?" *just-style*, December 8. Accessed August 18, 2017. https://www.just-style.com/analysis/will-green-growth-bolster-bangladesh-garment-exports_id126674.aspx

International Finance Commission (IFC). Accessed July 9, 2018. https://www.ifc.org

International Labour Organisation (ILO). Accessed July 9, 2018. https://www.ilo.org

Barrie, Leonie. 2016. "State of Sourcing Survey 2017—Supply Chain Shifts" *just-style*, December 23. Accessed July 9, 2018. https://www.just-style.com/analysis/state-of-sourcing-2017-survey-supply-chain-shifts_id121233.aspx

Köksal, Deniz, Jochen Strähle, Martin Müller, and Matthias Freise. 2017. "Social Sustainable Supply Chain Management in the Textile and Apparel Industry—A Literature Review." *Sustainability* 9: 100.

Leadership in Energy and Environmental Design (LEED). Accessed July 9, 2018. https://www.usgbc.org/leed

Masud, Abdullah Al, A.A.M. Arfanul Hoque, M. Shakhawat Hossain, and M. Rezwanul Hoque. 2013. "Corporate Social Responsibility Practices in Garments sector of Bangladesh, A Study of Multinational Garments, CSR view in Dhaka EPZ". *Developing Country Studies* 3, no. 5: 27–37.

Mellery-Pratt, Robin. 2017. "5 Sustainable Threats Facing Fashion." *Business of Fashion*, May 26, 2017. Accessed August 18, 2017. https://www.businessoffashion.com/articles/intelligence/5-sustainability-threats-facing-fashion

Norwegian Agency for Development Cooperation (Norad). 2014. "Bangladesh." August 29. Accessed July 9, 2018. https://www.norad.no/en/front/countries/asia-and-oceania/bangladesh/

Nagaraj, Anuradha. 2018. "More Women Are Taking Charge in Bangladesh's $28 Billion Garment Industry" *Global Citizen*. Accessed July 28, 2018. https://www.globalcitizen.org/en/content/women-bangladesh-unions-workers-rights/

Porter, Michael E. and Mark R. Kramer. 2006. "Strategy and Society: The Link Between Competitive Advantage and Corporate Social Responsibility." *Harvard Business Review* 84, no. 12 (December): 76–92.

Preuss, Simone. 2017. "Dhaka Apparel Summit Focuses on RMG Industry's Sustainable Future" *Fashion United*, March 3. Accessed July 9, 2018. https://fashionunited.com/news/business/dhaka-apparel-summit-focuses-on-rmg-industry-s-sustainable-future/2017030314935

Pulse of the Fashion Industry Report. 2017. "Copenhagen Fashion Summit Conference." Accessed August 10, 2017. https://www.copenhagenfashionsummit.com/pulse/

Raturi, Birendra. 2017. "CSR—Present Status of Bangladesh and Way Forward." *SRAsia*, May 2017. Accessed August 16, 2017. https://www.sr-asia.org/images/survey_2017.pdf

SEDEX. Accessed July 9, 2018. https://www.sedexglobal.com

Social Responsible Asia (SRAsia). 2012. "Professional Networking Organisation on Social Responsibility in Asia." Accessed July 9, 2018. https://www.sr-asia.org/images/publication/conference%20proceedings%20may%202017%202012%20dhaka%20bangladesh.pdf

Social Responsible Asia (SRAsia). 2017. "CSR: The Present Status of Bangladesh & Way Forward." May.

Sustainable Apparel Coalition. "The Higg Index." Accessed July 9, 2018. https://www.apparelcoalition.org/the-higg-index/

United Nations Environment Programme (UNEP). 2015. "Designing a Sustainable Financial System in Bangladesh, Summary Briefing." October. Accessed July 9, 2018. https://www.greengrowthknowledge.org/sites/default/files/downloads/resource/Designing_a_Sustainable_Financial_System_in_Bangladesh__Summary_Briefing_UNEP.pdf

United Nations Industrial Development Organization (UNIDO). 2010. "Taking Stock and Moving Forward." *UNIDO* and *UNEP*. April. Accessed July 9, 2018. https://www.unido.org/sites/default/files/2010-11/Taking%20stock%20and%20moving%20forward-November2010_0.pdf

US Green Building Council. 2018. "LEED is Green Building." Accessed July 9, 2018. https://www.usgbc.org/leed

Vena, Celeste Montera. 2013. "CSR in the Bangladesh Textile Industry: Responsible Supply Chain Management, European Institute for Asian Studies." *EIAS November Briefing Paper*. Accessed July

9, 2018. https://www.eias.org/briefing-papers/csr-in-the-bangladesh-textile-industry-responsible-supply-chain-management-november-2013/

Bangladesh Government. 2012. "Perspective Plan of Bangladesh 2010–2021: Making Vision 21 a Reality." *General Economic Division, Planning Commission, Government of the People's Republic of Bangladesh*, April. Accessed August 10, 2017. https://www.plancomm.gov.bd/perspective-plan/

Wilson, John P. 2015. "The Triple Bottom Line." *International Journal of Retail & Distribution Management* 43, no. 4/5: 432–47.

Definitions

Accord: An independent, legally binding agreement between brands and trade unions designed to work towards a safe and healthy Bangladeshi ready-made garment industry.

Asian Development Bank (ADB): Conceived in the early 1960s as a financial institution that would be Asian in character and foster economic growth and cooperation in one of the poorest regions in the world.

Bangladesh Garment Manufacturers and Exporters Association (BGMEA): One of the largest trade associations in Bangladesh.

Bangladesh Knitwear Manufacturers and Exporters Association (BKMEA): The Apex Trade Body solely representing the knitwear sector of Bangladesh; it stands out in the global panorama with its distinct identity and stature.

Deutsche Gesellschaft fur International Zusammenarbeit (GIZ): Has around 260 national personnel and 18 seconded staff in Bangladesh.

International Finance Commission (IFC): A member of the World Bank Group; the largest global development institution focused exclusively on the private sector in developing countries.

International Labour Organisation (ILO): The only tripartite UN agency. Since 1919, the ILO has brought together governments, employers, and workers representatives.

Leadership in Energy and Environmental Design (LEED): A US Green Building Council certification and the most widely used third-party verification for green buildings, with around 2.2 million square feet being certified daily.

Norwegian Agency for Development Co-operation (Norad): A directorate under the Norwegian Ministry of Foreign Affairs. Acts in matters regarding Norway's International Climate and Forest Initiative (NICFI).

Chapter 26

New Technology Acceptance in the Global Fashion Industry

Fashion ERP (Enterprise Resource Planning), SCM (Supply Chain Management), and CAD (Computer-Aided Design) Systems

Jennifer Kyungeun Lee

Laura & K Fashion is a well-known global sportswear company with excellent brand recognition that was established in the 1980s and is based in the United States. The company currently includes 21 private-label brands and 17 imported brands that are domestically distributed as well as globally, to 23 countries worldwide. Laura & K Fashion has been working with over 100 global supply-chain partners, including original equipment manufacturing (OEM) companies, mainly located in Asian countries, to produce fashion products such as apparel, bags, and accessories. Laura & K is one of the fashion industry's leaders in incorporating advanced technologies, such as enterprise resource planning (ERP), supply chain management (SCM), and computer-aided design (CAD) systems, which enhance efficiencies in product development and global sourcing processes. Last year, the company reestablished its IT infrastructure and updated its ERP and SCM systems to the latest versions to fit new product development and global sourcing processes suggested by IT specialists from an outside consulting firm. Six months after adoption, many system users at Laura & K did not want to use the new systems anymore due to associated inconveniences and inefficiencies caused by multiple system issues. Global supply-chain partners also complained that Laura & K's new technological systems caused problems that reduced their own manufacturing efficiencies. Laura & K must now make a decision on how best to respond to the company system users and global supply-chain partners in the face of the claimed inconveniences and inefficiencies, all of which could continuously occur and will potentially decrease the company's profits and product quality for next year.

Learning Objectives

Upon completion of this case, students should be able to:

- Analyze the advantages and disadvantages of adopting new technologies in global fashion companies.
- Understand relationships between process innovation, new technology adoption, and user acceptance toward new technological system(s).
- Identify and evaluate potential barriers to accepting new technologies according to user perspectives.
- Determine how to proceed with a hypothetical new technology adoption project for enhancing user acceptance toward new technological system(s).
- Propose strategic solutions for resolving issues of user resistance toward new technologies.

Introduction

Anderson and Laura & K

William Anderson is founder and CEO at Laura & K fashion, a large well-established global sportswear company. Anderson has successfully managed his company, creating superior brand recognition, since the company was established in the 1980s. Laura & K is a highly globalized company that sells products from twenty-one private-label brands in twenty-three countries around the globe. In addition, the company operates import-buying businesses from seventeen European brands in the United States. To produce the company's private-label merchandise with high quality at more competitive pricing, Laura & K has been aggressively increasing the number of global supply-chain operations in the last five years. Currently, the number of global supply-chain operations working with Laura & K is over 100, including original equipment manufacturing (OEM) companies, textile mills, and functional material research and development companies. These companies are specialized in manufacturing apparel, bags, and accessories and are mainly located in Asian countries, such as China, Vietnam, Bangladesh, and India.

Laura & K's new technologies

To facilitate efficient collaboration across departments in Laura & K and their global supply chain, in the early 1990s, Laura & K adopted enterprise resource planning (ERP) systems, and then added other systems, such as supply-chain management (SCM) and computer-aided design (CAD). ERP is a business management system that integrates multiple functional areas within an organization such as finance, planning, purchasing, inventory control, and human resources (Mayeh, Ramayah and Mishra 2016). SCM coordinates and incorporates workflows among materials, information, and finance with and across organizations (Lin and Lin 2014). CAD is drafting software used for the automatic processing of design and design data documentation in two-dimensional (2D) or three-dimensional (3D) views (Md 2017). Since then, the company has been continuously updating these systems to the latest versions. To foster efficient collaboration, the company also has supported their supply-chain partners in adopting and maintaining these systems in their companies. Because of Laura & K's constant investment in the latest technologies, the company has emerged as one of the foremost fashion industry leaders with an advanced IT infrastructure. Using ERP, SCM, and CAD systems, users both in Laura & K and those working for the supply-chain partners have been able to quickly communicate with one another, sharing data and monitoring work processes in real-time, and all using reduced paper-based methods. Additionally, Laura & K's product development and manufacturing lead-times have been at least two to three weeks shorter and production costs 10 percent to 20 percent lower than their competitors. Beyond this, the biggest return to Laura & K in adopting new technologies has been the ability to promote quick managerial decision making via enhanced data visibility. Results show the company's sales volume and profits have grown constantly in the last 20 years.

New system adoption

From 2016 to 2018, there have been two major changes related to Laura & K's business functions. Firstly, the number of global supply-chain partners in different countries has dramatically increased. Secondly, in response to an increasingly globalized business environment, product development and global sourcing processes were changed. Anderson considered 2017 to be the appropriate time to again update the company's technology systems to the latest versions. Upon his request, the founder and CEO received a proposal written by a group of IT specialists temporarily hired from an outside business consulting firm for the company's new technology advancement plan for upcoming years. The proposal stated that it was necessary to reestablish the company's IT infrastructure and update current ERP and SCM systems, adapting to innovations in product development and global sourcing processes. The detailed proposal also suggested investing one year doing the following: a company-wide process innovation (PI) project for three months, IT infrastructure reestablishment, system updating for six months, pilot tests with selected system users from all departments in the company and supply chain for two months, and system deployment to all users in the company and supply chain for one month. Traditionally, in new technology adoption, the PI project is an essential step for identifying problems associated with current work processes and systems as well as user needs of new systems. PI also assists in creating optimal solutions to resolve identified issues and address user needs. It is important to precede with PI steps before adopting new technologies. Based on PI results, IT specialists analyze existing IT infrastructures and systems and reestablish them to align with optimal solutions. Pilot tests are conducted to ensure that the changed IT infrastructure and systems function as planned, to receive feedback from users to guarantee their needs are fulfilled and to prevent potential errors in the future. After pilot testing, the new system is deployed to all system users.

Business Problem

Reduced project time and budget

For the next three years, Anderson has allocated a portion of the budget to new brand extensions that target consumers in the global market. Considering the finances required by these new ventures, Anderson requested that the IT consulting group reduce the budget in the proposal for new technology advancement by approximately 50 percent. When executing new IT projects, Anderson normally operates a special task-force team consisting of insiders from across departments in the company and an outside IT consulting group. Because of time constraints for this project, however, he decided to only allocate outsiders to the task in order to expedite the progress. Even though Anderson never dramatically reduced the new IT project's timeline or budget and depended only on outsiders' perspectives, he thought that the project was workable, since his company's previous IT projects had been successful and already had stabilized systems. Additionally, the IT consulting group said they should be able to work within the given time limits and budget. To satisfy Anderson's requests, a small group of IT specialists and a reduced number of system users completed the project within six months instead of one year, as originally proposed. For example, the PI project was completed in two months instead of four months; pilot tests were accomplished in one month, not two months. Only limited system users from a few select departments in Laura & K participated in pilot tests for one month, even though it had previously been suggested that users from all departments both in Laura & K and the supply chain should be involved for two months. In addition, mainly for cost-saving purposes, SCM systems were changed to a different company's systems instead of upgrading previous SCM, absorbing more maintenance costs. During the one-month system deployment, two weeks of new system training sessions were provided to system users.

Issues with the project

Because of the reduced project time and manpower input, several issues occurred that affected the success of the new IT advancement project of Laura & K. First, due to the reduced timeline for PI, only users from a few particular departments in the company participated in the system review meetings to identify user needs and the current systems' issues. Hence,

FIGURE 26.1 To avoid frustrations and lost productivity, pilot tests of new technology systems must include adequate time and input. © JGI/Tom Grill/Getty Images

Laura & K's system users who had not participated in PI did not have a chance to express their important system needs to the IT consulting group. For example, system needs and usage were different between users in the product development department and those in the import-buying department, since the import-buying department only deals with products already manufactured by other companies. Users in the import-buying department were not using nearly half of the processes and functions in previous SCM systems and barely used the CAD systems. Second, during the pilot tests, only a fraction of potentially problematic issues were discovered and resolved in view of the limited number of users. In particular, because of the short time period, users from the global supply chain were not able to participate in the pilot tests. In previous systems, their urgent issues delayed data changes across systems. For example, if a designer at Laura & K changed information in her or his designs, the change was only reflected across systems between half a day and one day later, meaning the supply-chain partners were unable to instantly see modified design information. Delayed data changes across systems caused increased product development and manufacturing lead-times. Subsequently, new systems' capabilities in real-time data changes were not able to be completely tested. Third, new SCM systems, requiring a lower maintenance budget than previous ones, required extensive hours for testing to ensure compatibility with other systems existing within the company's IT infrastructure. Unfortunately, limited time for system testing was allotted to work within the given project times and budgets. Potential errors related to incompatibility between new SCM and other systems were not able to be completely prevented before system deployment. Fourth, regarding the user training, two-week sessions were not enough for users to learn how to use the new system, nor were the transition times from using previous systems to new systems sufficient for users. Finally, when the proposed project time frame and budget were reduced, the IT consulting group members did not provide honest feedback to Anderson pertaining to the potential issues that might occur throughout the project, since they were only responsible for completing the project within the given time and budget as outside contractors for the company.

System users' responses toward new systems

At the beginning of the new system adoption, most of the system users were not aware in advance of changing from previous systems to new ones, since a limited number of users were involved in the new system adoption project. Their initial responses were of confusion due to such short notice. Additionally, some users felt that the company's management ignored them by not giving them a chance to express their needs and feedback regarding new systems. During the two-week training sessions, many users felt that there was a lack of training time. At the end of the training, users started complaining that the new systems were difficult to learn and use. One month after the deployment of the new systems, a negative climate surrounding their use had already started emerging throughout the company. Soon after, multiple users continuously expressed various complaints with the new systems. For instance, a major user need for the new systems involved including all changed product development and global sourcing processes in the systems that were partially missing in previous systems. In the new systems, some of the changed processes were still missing or not accordingly functional. Users in the import-buying department mentioned that the new system structure was complicated and contained unnecessary functions only used by users in product development departments. Users in the accessories department noted that global sourcing processes partially contained unnecessary management approval steps that were only required by the apparel department, and these steps increased overall production lead-times in nonapparel departments. Users in the global supply chain identified that reflecting data changes across systems was often delayed instead of being completed in real time. In other words, users were able to see changed data in ERP systems, though the SCM systems still showed previous, unchanged data. Unless constantly comparing data between the ERP and SCM, it was difficult for users to discern data discrepancies among different systems. Additionally, there were communication barriers between users in design departments and the supply chain, due to delayed data changes across the systems. Furthermore, users in the finance departments found that partial data could not be sent from the ERP to new SCM systems. It was later discovered that the new SCM was not fully compatible with the existing IT infrastructure of Laura & K. Users continually reported other errors during execution of product development and global sourcing processes in the new systems.

User acceptance toward new technological system(s)

After six months of new system adoption, due to multiple issues occurring in the new systems, a majority of system users held unfavorable attitudes toward using the new systems. Interestingly, users who used previous systems for a longer period of time presented stronger resistance to switching to the new systems. Furthermore, older users held stronger loyalty to previous systems than younger users did. Overall, the majority of users, both in Laura & K and the global supply chain, claimed that the new systems were inefficient and inconvenient to use. In the end, they refused to use the new systems.

Project failure and Anderson's actions

Anderson received feedback about the new systems' performance as well as system users' poor acceptance toward the new systems. He was also notified that product development lead-time for some items started to increase by one to two weeks, causing delays in the introduction of new products on the market. In addition to an extended manufacturing lead-time, claims by buyers of lowered product quality had become an issue. Anderson was embarrassed that his new technology investment turned out to be a failure unlike any he had previously experienced. He began to critically evaluate why this venture was not successful with the goal of determining how he could respond to the company system users and global supply-chain partners. It was clear to Anderson that the newly adopted systems' inconveniences and inefficiencies claimed by the users must be resolved as soon as possible, since these issues could continue to occur and potentially decrease the company's profits as well as product quality for the next year. He truly regretted that he had overlooked the importance of user acceptance toward new technological systems for a successful technology investment.

Business Questions

1   If you were Anderson, what would you do if your employees refused to use the new systems in which you had invested?

2   If you were one of the IT consulting group members, what would you do if you heard about the reduced project timeline and budget before the project began?

3   In the globalized market environment in the fashion industry, what should be the main priorities for adopting new technologies in a company?

4   Considering the current case, why do you think user acceptance toward a new technological system(s) is important for successful adoption by a company?

5   If you were a system user of Laura & K, instead of refusing to use the system, what alternatives would you suggest to the company if you felt like the new systems were inefficient and inconvenient?

References and Further Reading

Cantamessa, Marco, Francesca Montagna, and Paolo Neirotti. 2012. "Understanding the Organizational Impact of PLM Systems: Evidence from an Aerospace Company." *International Journal of Operations & Production Management* 32 (2): 191–215.

Hur, Hee J., Ha K. Lee, and Ho J. Choo. 2017. "Understanding Usage Intention in Innovative Mobile App Service: Comparison between Millennial and Mature Consumers." *Computers in Human Behavior* 7: 353–361.

Lin, Tsan-Hwan and I-Ching Lin. 2014. "Factors for Information Technology Acceptance Willingness and Adoption in Logistics Industry from Supply Chain Perspectives." *International Journal of Electronic Business Management* 12 (3): 167–177.

Mayeh, Maral, T. Ramayah, and Alok Mishra. 2016. "The Role of Absorptive Capacity, Communication and Trust in ERP Adoption." *The Journal of Systems & Software* 119: 58–69.

Md, Tabraz. 2017. "Importance of Fashion Cad Computer Aided Design Study for Garment Industry in Bangladesh." *International Journal of Scientific & Technology Research* 06 (10): 26–28.

Azevedo, Susana Garrido and Helena Carvalho. 2012. "Contribution of RFID technology to better management of fashion supply chains." *International Journal of Retail & Distribution Management* 40 (2): 128–156.

PART FIVE

Merchandising Management and Retailing

Introduction

This section includes case studies that focus on the decisions that professionals in the global fashion industry make in the areas of merchandising management and retailing. Merchandising includes the "the management processes related to buying and selling fashion products; that is, product assortment planning, acquisition, pricing, presentation, and sales to fulfill a company's financial goals" (Burns and Mullet 2020, p. 3; Kunz 2010). These management processes are often said to have an overall goal of getting the right product:

- *in the right quantity*
- *at the right price*
- *to the right place*
- *at the right time.*

Professionals in the fashion industry involved with product assortment planning, retail buying, pricing, presentation, and sales are often faced with challenges and opportunities around courses of action to best meet the needs of their consumers as well as their companies' financial, environmental, and social goals and objectives.

The case studies included in this section focus on merchandising management processes associated with retailing fashion products. Retailers are "the businesses that make a profit by selling goods and services to the ultimate consumer" (Burns and Mullet 2020, p. 10). Today's fashion retailing environment includes numerous formats and channels for presenting and selling merchandise to consumers, such as bricks-and-mortar stores, online retailers, mobile technologies, small pop-up shops, and kiosks. As fashion business professionals evaluate the most effective retail formats for their target customers, they must weigh the advantages and disadvantages of strategies associated with these multiple channels. Case studies in this section focus on the challenges and opportunities fashion retailers are facing and how they are adapting to the ever-changing fashion retail environment.

References and Further Reading

Burns, Leslie Davis and Kathy K. Mullet (2020). *The Business of Fashion: Designing, Manufacturing, and Marketing*. 6th ed. New York: Fairchild Books/Bloomsbury.

Koumbis, Dimitri (2019). *Fashion Retailing: From Managing to Merchandising*. New York: Bloomsbury.

Kunz, Grace I. (2010). *Merchandising: Theory, Principles, and Practice* (3rd ed). New York: Fairchild Books.

Chapter 27

ALAND Retail Store

Assortment Planning: Product Categories and Lines

Chanjean Jung

ALAND is a multi-brand lifestyle store in the moderate price zone, targeting the mass market. ALAND sells lesser known brands in Korea, which include emerging young Korean designer brands, social responsibility brands, and other emerging domestic and overseas brands. Recently, ALAND has encountered a problem—it has not been profitable even though it is popular with young consumers. The CEO of ALAND needs to revise categories and product lines, and develop a private-label brand that can increase net profits. This case study challenges students to devise product categories and lines which reflect the target consumer's fashion choices and lifestyles.

Learning Objectives

Upon completion of this case, students should be able to:

- Discuss how ALAND might plan merchandise assortment as a fashion lifestyle store.
- Analyze the advantages and disadvantages of a private-label brand (PB).
- Propose categories or product lines for PB development at ALAND retail stores and give reasons for your choices.

Introduction

ALAND opened in 2005. It demonstrated the possibility of success as a new retail business format in Korea. Since the early days of the Korean fashion market in the 1970s, retail shops selling a single manufacturer's brand have dominated the fashion industry. ALAND is a multi-brand lifestyle store which offers a variety of products in addition to fashion clothes for women and men, such as bags, accessories, shoes, books, stationery, tableware, storage boxes, and traveling kits.

ALAND is a leading multi-brand retailer in the moderate price zone, targeting the mass market. ALAND distributes about 570 brands, with a broad product line breadth in various categories. It features lesser known brands in Korea, including emerging young Korean designer brands, social responsibility brands, and other emerging domestic and overseas brands. The overseas brands are especially popular since they are sold at lower prices than through other fashion distribution channels in Korea. ALAND attracts young Asian tourists who prefer K-Fashion (Korean Fashion), as well as young Korean consumers, who are seeking new and unique items. Its target consumers consider ALAND to be a special shopping place featuring new and stylish items at a reasonable price.

In 2017, ALAND had thirteen stores, mainly in commercial districts and shopping malls, in Seoul and Gyeonggi-do, Korea. According to INCRUIT (http://www.incruit.com/company/9468387), ALAND had sales of $3.7 million and employed 189 people. ALAND also opened stores overseas; three in Hong Kong and one in Thailand. ALAND is about to open a large store, with a total area of about 10,600 square feet across three floors, in Brooklyn, New York.

FIGURE 27.1 The ALAND shop building at Hongdae (Hongik University) shopping street, Seoul, South Korea. Source: YOORAN PARK/Alamy Stock Photo.

Business Problem

The CEO of ALAND is always working to stay current with contemporary trends and make changes at the ALAND stores that appeal to young consumers who are seeking new things. She has been facing a problem recently: ALAND isn't profitable even though it is still popular with young consumers. ALAND's sales and net profits had continued to increase since the company was founded in 2005, but their performance was negative for the first time in 2016.

The CEO of ALAND needs to update product lines and put more emphasis on fashion products (such as women's and men's apparel, footwear, accessories, beauty, and skincare) than has been done previously. She has withdrawn or reduced low-profit product lines such as books, traveling kits, and tableware, and instead added cosmetics that are of Korean origin, under Asia's market conditions. ALAND now offers various cosmetic brands, including its own private-label brand (PB): "LAND MUSEUM." In 2017, one of ALAND's stores tested a coffee shop as a new product line, which caters to young consumers' lifestyle in Korea.

The CEO of ALAND decided to emphasize "strengthening the online channel" and "expanding globally" as growth keywords in 2017. She reinforced the PB line as one of the ways to improve profits under this condition. ALAND plans to increase the number of PBs rather than domestic and overseas manufacturer brands, on a vendor basis, because PBs are expected to increase net profits.

ALAND already has one PB: "3.3 FIELD TRIP" and has actively adjusted the PB based on market conditions since 2016. For example, 3.3 FIELD TRIP added a new category of yoga outfits for women, based on yoga's growing popularity. In addition, ALAND has continuously collaborated with current hot brands or new emerging designers within various categories, such as bags, watches, glasses, and stationery as well as clothing.

Business Questions

Major question

How should ALAND update its merchandise assortment and develop a PB at a time in which net profits are declining? The main task is to discuss how ALAND should plan new product lines and categories, including development of a new PB.

Study questions

1   Why do you think ALAND attracts young consumers in Korea?
2   What are the difference between merchandise assortment at ALAND, a lifestyle store, and IKEA?
3   Analyze why PBs can be more profitable than other domestic or overseas brands.
4   What is your opinion of the addition of a coffee shop as a new product line at ALAND stores?
5   Suggest categories or product lines for a new PB which would provide a new atmosphere in ALAND stores and give reasons for your choice.
6   Suggest how ALAND should respond to the growing community of mobile and online shopping customers.

References and Further Reading

ALAND. 2018. Accessed June 19, 2018 http://www.ALAND.co.kr/

Design Jungle. 2017. "ALAND, MMMG, Promens, etc." Accessed June 19, 2018. http://magazine.jungle.co.kr/designnews/daily/view_new.asp?idx=29747&cate=19

Hong Seung Hae. 2017. "ALAND's Growth Engine This Year? An 'Online and Global' Focus." Accessed June 19, 2018. http://www.fashionbiz.co.kr/TN/?cate=2&recom=2&idx=158760

Hong Seung Hae. 2017. "ALAND's 'PB'." Accessed June 19, 2018. http://www.fashionbiz.co.kr/TN/?cate=2&recom=2&idx=160147

Hong Seung Hae. 2017. "ALAND & Wonder Place Strengthen Global Business.". Accessed June 19, 2018. http://www.fashionbiz.co.kr/TN/?cate=2&recom=2&idx=159655

Incruit. 2017. "ALAND Company Information." Accessed June 19, 2018. http://www.incruit.com/company/9468387

Korean Fashion + Tex News. 2017. "ALAND to Acquire Asian Market." Accessed June 19, 2018. http://www.ktnews.com/sub/view.php?cd_news=103798

The Korea Times. 2017. "Famous Korean Store 'Aland' Opens in Brooklyn." Accessed June 19, 2018. http://www.koreatimes.com/article/1047053

Definitions

Merchandise assortment: The variety of products that a retailer presents to the consumer. In determining the product assortment retailers need to decide on product line breadth—the number of product lines or variety offered by the retailer—as well as product line depth, the number of categories within a specific product line.

Private-label brand (PB): A brand designed, produced, controlled by, and carrying the name of the store or a name owned by the store.

Chapter 28

Department Stores and the "Retail Apocalypse"

How Might American Retailer Macy's Survive?

Priscilla Martinez and Lorynn Divita

The "retail apocalypse" is a term that was coined to describe the significant number of bricks-and-mortar retail stores closing; the phenomenon has plagued many retailers in recent years. Bricks-and-mortar retail is going through transformative changes and, as a result, not all retailers are able to stay alive in the face of new and emerging competitors. E-commerce has shaken the retail world, but while it is a contributing factor to the retail apocalypse it is not the only cause. Those retailers that do survive will be flexible and ready to respond to market conditions and proactively implement changes when necessary in order to remain viable. Successful retailers will need to focus on the customer experience, better trained associates, and creating a seamless experience across channels. In this case study, students are introduced to the concept of the retail apocalypse and will analyze the ways in which one department store retailer, Macy's, might succeed in today's retail environment.

Learning Objectives

Upon completion of this case, students should be able to:

- Identify factors that have contributed to the "retail apocalypse."
- Describe factors that have contributed to Macy's challenges in today's retail environment.
- Evaluate strategic alternatives for Macy's to improve its performance in today's retail environment.

Introduction

The "retail apocalypse" describes the phenomenon of a significant number of closings, bankruptcies, and reduced inventories of traditional bricks-and-mortar retail stores. There are many potential reasons why a retailer can fall victim to the "retail apocalypse." Just as the Industrial Revolution changed production and manufacturing, the digital revolution has immersed itself in our daily lives and has irreversibly changed retail (Bader 2017). The online shopping experience has become just as important as that of the bricks-and-mortar store, and as technology continues to speed up sales cycles and reshape the overall shopping experience, many believe it has been the primary cause of the retail apocalypse (Bader 2017). The digital age has allowed consumers to have access to unlimited amounts of data on products and goods, including the ability to compare prices. According to analysts, department stores gravely underestimated the popularity of online sales for apparel. Consumers were more willing to purchase clothing and accessories online than retailers anticipated, which caused department store retail space to be less significant. Concurrently, stand-alone stores, off-price retailers, and big box stores increasingly took more market share, which itself has taken a chunk out of department store sales (White 2016). As fashion trends have also started to change at a faster pace, it has become imperative for bricks-and-mortar retailers to stay ahead of fashion trends to remain relevant. In addition, the belief that the customer is king is more applicable than ever, as consumer opinion can spread like wildfire via social and digital media. Therefore, company mistakes become known quickly, so elevated customer service is expected and necessary. These factors along with the increased availability of fast fashion at low cost and the Great Recession of the late 2000s have all contributed to the shift in consumer behavior to search for a bargain.

Despite some consumers' belief, the internet is not the only culprit of the "retail apocalypse." Millennials have become the largest consumer group (outnumbering the baby boomers) and department stores have found themselves lacking in appeal to this demographic. Undervaluing customer service and not keeping up with current trends has resulted in negative revenues for some major department stores, such as Sears, who were forced to close 142 unprofitable stores and file for bankruptcy protection in October 2018 (BOF Team 2018).

Another factor contributing to the "retail apocalypse" is that many loans that retailers were forced to take out during the recession are now due for repayment, and many retailers have maxed out their refinancing options. According to Bloomberg, between 2019 and 2025 the total value of maturing loans will reach US$5 billion in high-yield borrowings, which many retailers are not equipped to handle. This has caused a surge in bankruptcies and store closings (Meza 2017).

Perhaps as a consequence of the "retail apocalypse" shopping malls have been struggling recently and it is said that by 2023 half the malls in the United States will close. This is another major cause for concern for department stores such as Macy's that have traditionally been anchored to shopping malls rather than being stand-alone stores (Meza 2017; Rushe 2017). Shopping malls were once the heart of American retail, yet in 2018 many former booming malls are increasingly becoming empty or housing businesses other than retailers. Ironically, America's largest shopping mall, The Mall of America, celebrated its twenty-fifth anniversary in August 2017 and has proved to be an exception to the mall crisis (Rushe 2017). The increased department store closings due to oversaturation and overexpansion have hurt shopping malls, just as mall closures have affected major department stores and other retailers. According to Green Street, 800 department store locations would need to close in order to regain their pre-recession health. That means that 20 percent of shopping mall anchors would need to close—this would be devastating for already struggling malls (White 2016). By analyzing current market and consumer trends, and comparing retailers that have growing success or stable profits, retailers can formulate a strategy to survive the "retail apocalypse."

Business Problem

Macy's and the American retail landscape

In 2017 Macy's was considered by analysts to be on the losing end of the "retail apocalypse." The company had experienced a sales decline across every financial quarter for the past eleven quarters (almost three financial years). Macy's blamed the hurricanes in Florida and Texas for causing a 3.6 percent drop in same-store sales for the third quarter of 2016 (Berfield and Rupp 2017). During the biggest shopping day of the year in 2017, Black Friday, Macy's encountered yet another setback as "over-capacity" caused their credit card processing to slow. This mishap gave the already vulnerable store a reputation for not being ready for major retail events (O'Shea 2017). In the three years prior to 2017, revenue fell from US$27.5 billion to US$24.6 billion with profits cut by nearly half and market value down by around two-thirds (Berfield and Rupp 2017).

Much of the blame for falling profits of department stores such as Macy's has been directed toward Amazon. However, Amazon, or e-commerce in general, is not the only one to blame for the department store or bricks-and-mortar decline. In addition to e-commerce, off-price retailers including Marshall's and TJ Maxx (TK Maxx in the UK) have also been successful. Since 2015, Macy's revenue has fallen whilst e-commerce and off-price retailers have continued to rise (Howland 2017). Off-price retailers' approach of avoiding poor service (sometimes by offering no service at all), combined with affordable prices, convenience, speed, and a modern feel is what makes these retailers more appealing (Berfield and Rupp 2017).

Although competition has taken business away from Macy's, one of their earliest mistakes according to Nick Egelanian, president of a retail consulting firm, was to buy so many already failing department stores instead of reinventing themselves. As Egelanian noted, "They were buyers when they should have been sellers" (Berfield and Rupp 2017). Macy's recognizes that it needs to make major changes in order to survive this phenomenon and has decided that now is the time to act.

Business Questions

Major question

What strategies should Macy's implement in order to survive beyond the current retail apocalypse?

Study questions

1   What is the "retail apocalypse" and what factors have contributed to this phenomenon?

2   What factors and/or characteristics have contributed to Macy's challenges in today's retail environment?

3   Identify three strategic initiatives that Macy's could develop and implement to successfully compete in today's retail environment? What are the advantages and disadvantages of each? Which one would you recommend they implement first, second, and third, and why?

References and Further Reading

Bader, Eric. 2017. "The Retail Apocalypse: A Survival Guide." *The Secured Lender* 73 (8): 18–20. Accessed December 10, 2018. http://www.thesecuredlender-digital.com/thesecuredlender/october_2017?pg=20#pg20

Barfield, Susan and Lindsey Rupp. 2017. "Macy's Has a Plan to Survive the Retail Apocalypse." *Bloomberg Businessweek*, November 21 Accessed December 10, 2018. https://www.bloomberg.com/news/features/2017-11-21/macy-s-plan-to-survive-the-retail-apocalypse

BOF Team. 2018. "Avoiding the Fate of Sears." *Business of Fashion*, October 19. Accessed December 7, 2018. https://www.businessoffashion.com/articles/professional/avoiding-the-fate-of-sears

Gara, Antoine. 2017. "The Retail Apocalypse and Mall Die-Off Goes from 'Big Short' to Contrarian Buy." *Forbes*, November 17. Accesed December 10 2018. https://www.forbes.com/sites/antoinegara/2017/11/17/the-retail-apocalypse-and-mall-die-off-goes-from-big-short-to-contrarian-buy/#2d0095cd4c52

Howland, Daphne 2017. "Nordstrom and Macy's: A Lesson in Surviving the Retail Apocalypse." *Retail Dive*, August 17. Accessed December 10, 2018. https://www.retaildive.com/news/nordstrom-and-macys-a-lesson-in-surviving-the-retail-apocalypse/449051/

Kline, Daniel B. 2017. "Changing Retail: Is Everything You Know about 'Retail Apocalypse' Wrong? *USA Today*, September 21. Accessed December 10, 2018. https://www.usatoday.com/story/money/business/2017/09/21/is-everything-you-know-about-the-retail-apocalypse-wrong/105809518/

Meza, Summer. 2017. "America's 'Retail Apocalypse' Comes From Bigger Problems Than Amazon." *Newsweek*, November 9. Accessed December 10, 2018. http://www.newsweek.com/retailers-closing-too-much-debt-707560

O'Shea, Dan. 2017. "Macy's, Lowe's Hit by Black Friday Technical Glitches." *Retail Dive*, November 27. Accessed December 10, 2018. https://www.retaildive.com/news/macys-lowes-hit-by-black-friday-technical-glitches/511606/

Poggi, Jeanine. 2008. "A Roller-Coaster Ride: Retail Shares in Tizzy Over Recession Fears." *WWD*, January 10. Accessed December 10, 2018. https://wwd.com/wwd-publications/wwd/2008-01-10-2117516/

Rushe, Dominic. 2017. "Big, Bold ... and Broken: is the US Shopping Mall in a Fatal Decline? *The Guardian*, July 23. Accessed December 10, 2018. https://www.theguardian.com/us-news/2017/jul/22/mall-of-america-minnesota-retail-anniversary

White, Martha C. 2016. "Is the Heyday of Malls Past As More Department Stores Close? *NBC News*, April 30 Accessed December 10, 2018. https://www.nbcnews.com/business/consumer/heyday-malls-past-more-department-stores-close-n565021

Chapter 29

The Botanical Store: Urban Outfitters' Expansion into Plants as a Lifestyle Statement

Jo Hurley

Urban Outfitters is a global youthful consumer brand that sells clothing as well as houseplants largely to millennials who have an aesthetic lifestyle. The brand uses plants as part of their visual merchandising strategy. This case study examines the experiential impact of plants in a store environment alongside whether there is an ongoing market for houseplants as part of the brand's development strategy. The business topic of this case underpins the analysis behind Urban Outfitters' expansion into houseplants alongside the advantages and disadvantages of this concept. The case study will also look to question the maintenance of selling houseplants in stores, alongside the role that social media plays in lifestyle purchasing decisions.

Learning Objectives

Upon completion of this case, students should be able to:

- Define the changing consumer behaviors and generational demographics of millennials and Generation Z.

- Explore the advantages and disadvantages of a traditional fashion retailer developing lifestyle products.

- Critically review Urban Outfitters' process, promotion, and concept of introducing plants in a fashion environment.

- Evaluate the opportunities that plants can provide for retail environments especially within experiential retail.

- Analyze the longevity and consumer markets of lifestyle products alongside looking further into wellness trends and experiential retail.

Introduction

Urban Outfitters is a global mass-market brand situated across major cities in the UK, Europe, the USA, and most recently the Middle East. They are one of six brands owned by parent company URBN: Anthropologie, Free People, Terrain, BHLDN, and the restaurant chain the Vetri Family (URBN 2018a). As some retailers in the youth fashion sector are forced to close stores, Urban Outfitters continues to open new stores with expected growth in Dubai as part of a franchise partnership in 2019 (Singh 2018). Urban Outfitters' business model is based on creating experiential events in their global stores, from Instagram influencer meetings to in-store gyms in US stores. Products range from vintage inspired fashion for men and women, to sportswear, homeware, houseplants, books, and records.

The URBN group first started selling houseplants in the United States in 2008 when it started the house and garden company Terrain (URBN 2018c). When launching Terrain, Richard Hayne, the CEO and cofounder of Urban Outfitters, was inspired by the idea of merging garden and home space into one. Since 2014, Urban Outfitters' stores have expanded into selling cacti and succulents. The benefits of consumers purchasing houseplants include enhanced air quality, which falls into the larger contemporary wellness trend.

The year 2014 also marked the launch of the brand's concept store Space Ninety-Eight in the hipster village of Williamsburg, Brooklyn. Local designers' products were installed in the marketplace with surrounding plants being a key feature of the visual merchandising. The space is still open and continues to promote local creatives and workshops in the community. Trend websites such as LS:N Global promoted the idea as an exciting concept of this time. The brand is keen to be the leader within innovative retail thought.

Dependent on the space available in the store and natural lighting, Urban Outfitters today sells plants globally, ranging from large ferns, succulents, cacti, and terrariums to smaller houseplants. The price of the plants includes an aesthetically pleasing ceramic planter; as of 2018 these retail for between £8 to £12 dependent on the size of the plant. The popular "Grow it" (grow your own) kits are priced at £15.

Urban Outfitters' competitors, other lifestyle-geared brands such as Cos and Other Stories, have yet to enter into the houseplant market. In this sense, the brand has pioneered the extension of a traditional fashion brand by selling plants as a lifestyle product extension. The store is well known within its target market age group for selling plants as a cool added product. Houseplants are adaptable to apartment living and are promoted by interior magazines as ways of brightening up a short-term home. Botany writer Kimberley Aston states: "bringing the outside in or creating an urban jungle could be a way to reconnect with nature that many feel is missing from their lives in modern cities" (Kimberly Aston, personal interview, November 2018). Additionally, as the millennial generation are increasingly having children later in life, there has even been speculation as to whether houseplants are replacing children and pets: "Houseplants offer younger people a chance to nurture a living thing without the responsibility of caring for a pet or child. They are much more widely available then they were in the past and the internet means people can track down pretty much any plant they desire" (Jane Perrone, personal interview, November 2018).

Consumers are also looking for collectible and exotic varieties of plants, as seen on both the visual social media platforms Pinterest and Instagram, with a vast number of hashtags popularizing cacti such as #houseplantsofinstagram. Independent plant sellers such as Prick LDN, Geo Fleur, and Botanique, and global plant websites like Cactusland are popular with consumers who want exotic varieties of houseplants.

Business Problem

The first Urban Outfitters store was opened in 1970 located on the US campus of the University of Pennsylvania (URBN 2018b), highlighting the brand's early connection with a youthful target audience.

The lifestyle of the consumer is a factor in why Urban Outfitters has introduced houseplants as purchasable products within their stores. The Urban Outfitters stores are in key cities across the globe and attempt to mirror the consumer who lives in these demographics.

Store aesthetic

Since Urban Outfitters expanded both regionally and internationally into houseplants, there has been a strong impact on their store aesthetic. London's Oxford Street store has recently introduced a devoted houseplant emporium between the first and second floor. The space has been styled with hanging lanterns, oriental style rugs, and popular terrariums to simulate the desired lifestyle of the consumer. The space is also made of wood, offering the viewer a natural message. Lettering on the stand, captioned "Happy plants for Happy Spaces," functions as a lifestyle quote and creates an instagrammable scene. The hashtag #UOHome is also communicated to the customer within the store; this hashtag had over 150,000 posts

FIGURE 29.1 Plant displays can be seen in Urban Outfitters stores, both for sale and as part of the stores' visual merchandising. © Jo Hurley.

FIGURE 29.2 Urban Outfitters November 2018. A cactus display can be seen with rose gold watering cans and other planting accessories. © Jo Hurley.

as of November 26, 2018. Further promotions for consumers to purchase their houseplants online and through the Urban Outfitters app are also present. Plants are present throughout the store, often within visual merchandising stands, though there is a significantly strong presence at the till/cashier points in the form of hanging planters that are available for purchase.

At the UK Birmingham store, a cacti collection is placed downstairs as part of the window display and to allow for natural light. Other products, such as books and rose gold watering cans, are also positioned with the houseplants.

In the United States, Urban Outfitters has started to sell faux flowers, such as artificial Yucca plants and banana trees complete with matching pots. Urban Outfitters showed a 13.7 percent sales growth in the second quarter of 2018 according to FashionUnited (2018); while they do not report breakdowns specifically for their houseplant sales, one might make assumptions that this indicates that the lifestyle brand is stocking the "correct" merchandise for its target market.

Digital and social media

Urban Outfitters' sales continue to increase; one of the factors contributing to this is the group's use of e-commerce and social media platforms. As of November 2018, the brand has 8.2 million followers on Instagram. In comparison, Urban Outfitters' largest competitors—

the fashion and lifestyle stores Cos and Other Stories—had amassed 1.4 million and 1.3 million followers respectively as of November 26, 2018; Urban Outfitters are consequently leaders within this area.

Urban Outfitters started to sell its plants to online customers in 2017. It also sells houseplant accessories such as planters and books on houseplants and terrariums. Consumers can now shop the look via Instagram by searching for UOHome. Items such as "Grow it" bonsai and cactus kits are very popular and have been known to sell out online.

Problems and risks

The houseplant project was not without its problems. For example, during the early stages staff did not always know how to advise customers on how to look after the plants. Kimberley Aston raised concerns about this, because customers could be put off from buying plants in the future: "Without the knowledge of how to care for these plants from store staff there's a risk that consumers will be buying a dying plant" (Kimberly Aston, personal interview, November 2018). To rectify this, from November 2018, the brand introduced a promotional poster next to the products within Urban Outfitters' stores, showing how the consumer should look after their plants at home (see Figure 29.2).

Another issue was in the limited packaging provided to support the plant for its post-purchase journey home. Packaging options were anything from plants being wrapped in brown paper, to being placed free standing in a paper bag. Both of these options could be problematic for the health of the plant. Urban Outfitters encourages sustainable recycling of all of its packaging and thus might struggle to implement packaging suitable for the support of these plants that meets these requirements.

#Houseplants

One of the reasons houseplants have enjoyed a peak in popularity has been thanks to the growth of visual social media platforms such as Pinterest and Instagram. The hashtag #houseplants boasts 1.2 million posts, whilst #cactus had 9.4 million posts as of November 2018. Houseplant enthusiasts and specialists have also become more involved with showing the health benefits of nature in our homes via social media channels. On Instagram Kimberley Aston, known as @kingstreetjungle, describes herself as a "botany enthusiast of the Instagram generation." The plant writer Jane Perrone also feels that "Instagram has played a huge role in popularising certain plants that look good and are easy to care for" (Jane Perrone, personal interview, November 2018).

Key issues

The key issue is whether the introduction of houseplants as consumer products for Urban Outfitters has a big enough appeal for millennial and Generation Z consumers as first time or repeat purchases. Another problem to rectify is the in-store care of the plants by retail staff, while further issues may begin to arise from the lack of packaging to support the plants' journey to a customers' home, and a lack of after-care instructions for the consumer.

Business Questions

1 How does the introduction of houseplants align with the URBN group's brand identity?

2 Which demographic aspects of Urban Outfitters' consumer have played a major part in buying houseplants?

3 How might different social media platforms influence the Urban Outfitters consumers' purchasing habits?

4 Given their target demographic, how could Urban Outfitters extend the range of houseplants that they currently offer?

5 What other brand extensions could Urban Outfitters offer that align with the lifestyle of their Generation Z and millennial consumer?

6 How could Urban Outfitters incorporate houseplants in their store environment without jeopardizing the health of the plants they sell?

7 What solutions can Urban Outfitters instigate to ensure the health of the houseplants they sell and ensure the consumer can get their plants home safely and sustainably?

8 What is the potential for retailing houseplants online?

9 Does the brand offer enough variety of their houseplant collection to encourage repeat purchasing or gifting?

10 Is the trend for houseplants part of a larger trend around sustainability and wellness for the consumer?

References and Further Reading

FashionUnited. 2018. "Urban Outfitters Q2 revenues increase 13.7 percent." 22 August. Accessed 22 March, 2019. https://fashionunited.uk/news/business/urban-outfitters-q2-revenues-increase-13-7-percent/2018082238420

Singh, Prachi. 2018. "Urban Outfitters Partners with Azadea Group to Expand Presence in the Middle East." *Fashion United*, October. Accessed November 29, 2018. https://fashionunited.uk/news/retail/urban-outfitters-partners-with-azadea-group-to-expand-presence-in-the-middle-east/2018103139710

URBN. 2018a. "Who We Are." Accessed November 29, 2018. https://www.urbn.com/who-we-are

URBN. 2018b. "History." Accessed November 29, 2018. https://www.urbn.com/who-we-are/history

URBN 2018c. "Terrain." Accessed December 12, 2018. https://www.urbn.com/our-brands/anthropologie/terrain

Definitions

Generation Z: Consumers born after 1996 and before 2012.
Millennials: The generation born between 1981 and 1996.

Chapter 30

John Smedley

Transforming a British Luxury Family Business

Bethan Alexander

John Smedley is a 234-year-old family business based in the UK. It specializes in knitwear within the premium-luxury sector and still operates from its original manufacturing location in Lea Mills, Derbyshire. The management of change in order to cope with continuous market shifts has been a key feature of the firm since its inception, as evidenced in John Smedley's business sustainability over three centuries. These transformations include shifts from a manufacturer to brand perspective, and from mono- to multichannel wholesale, to sustain growth whilst retaining private family ownership. Business environment change presents both a challenge and an opportunity for John Smedley, which today is faced with a need to adapt to a business landscape that is being disrupted by global e-commerce, extensive global outsourcing, and increasingly connected consumers. For John Smedley, navigating this new world is critical to sustaining future business expansion.

Family business research has been growing over the past two decades yet is still considered an emergent field of study with there being a greater need for specific research into addressing the complexity of decision-making in family businesses and how this differs to nonfamily organizations. This case study highlights some of the characteristics and issues unique to family business decision-makers and asks students to consider how family firms should approach business transformation. Students will discuss the core competencies and capabilities that are required to identify and overcome the challenges within a family business and how these might be distinct from nonfamily businesses

Learning Objectives

Upon completion of this case, students should be able to:

- Understand the need for integration between shared vision and implementation within a family business.

- Identify the distinct differences between family businesses and nonfamily businesses.

- Evaluate John Smedley's product and marketing strategies in relation to their brand principles.

- Explore strategies for John Smedley to sustain competitive advantage in a volatile market.

- Assess the key competencies and capabilities required to engineer business transformation within a family firm.

- Analyze the issues in leading and managing family businesses and how to overcome them.

Introduction

Knitwear specialist John Smedley is an idiosyncratic company within British luxury fashion, claiming to be the "oldest manufacturing factory operating from its original site in the world" (Ian Maclean, managing director [MD] of John Smedley and family member, interview with author 2015) (see Figure 30.1). The company was founded in 1784 in Derbyshire, UK, when Peter Nightingale and John Smedley opened a mill near a brook in Lea Mills. The mill then specialized in producing muslin and spinning yarn but by the end of the eighteenth century it had evolved to knitting and hosiery manufacturing. Today, John Smedley remains a family-owned business, managed by the eighth generation of the founding Smedley family, and is renowned for its fine-gauge knitwear, which was recognized with the receipt of a royal warrant in 2013 (Wright 2013). It produces *c.* 400,000 knitted garments each year, 70 percent of which are exported to over thirty-five countries and are shown during London Collections: Mens (Mirza 2018; Palmieri 2016). John Smedley have around 200 UK and 500 overseas stockists (Spybey 2015) with wholesale prices ranging from £20 for knitted accessories to £95 for cashmere jumpers.

Reported turnover in March 2018 was £18 million, a growth rate of 6.4 percent year on year, and a profit (before tax) of £582,000, a decrease of 8.6 percent year on year (Fame 2018). The business currently employs 350 staff (see Appendix 1 for key financials 2014–18). Over its 234-year history, John Smedley has encountered significant moments of change as shown in the timeline (see Figure 30.2). The John Smedley brand bible has six core brand values that drive the business, some of which can be found stenciled onto the walls of the factory to remind and reinforce (See Figures 30.3 and 30.4).

The John Smedley brand values are:

1 *Britishness:* "There is a real sense of pride knowing that after more than 230 years we still celebrate true British craftmanship and make every single product within Britain."

2 *Quality:* "I trust the product. I feel reassured in what I am wearing as I know it has been made with care, with the highest quality materials."

3 *Design:* "Our customers feel our dedication to design through subtle touches and details that speak to them."

4 *Craftmanship:* "Fashion can be seen as becoming too throwaway. We are here to make knitwear that goes beyond trends where true craftmanship is everlasting."

5 *Color:* "Color is emotive and powerful and helps to communicate our design expression to our audience."

FIGURE 30.1 The John Smedley factory, Lea Mills, Derbyshire, 2015. © Bethan Alexander.

FIGURE 30.2 John Smedley timeline. © Bethan Alexander.

6 *Community:* "We reach out to our worldwide customers and partners to build a community of trust for our garments."

It aims to keep steadfast to these values whilst navigating business model transformation from: "predominantly wholesale to predominantly retail" (Maclean interview with author, 2015).

FIGURE 30.4 John Smedley brand value stencils. © Bethan Alexander.

process, our suppliers, customers and consumers trust in us and building trust through our relationships is really important" (Maclean interview with author, 2015).

Operating in a competitive market

Increased market opportunities and fierce competition are challenging the foundations of family businesses (Pounder 2015) and it is posited that new entrepreneurial practices may be important for family businesses to succeed in everchanging marketplaces. Research shows that corporate lifespans are decreasing rapidly (Gilbert et al. 2012; Leavy 2017), suggesting that as companies grow they require more effective ways to manage change, an efficient process that enables them to adjust.

Many traditional UK manufacturers have offshored production to Asia due to lower material and manufacturing costs, with China alone commanding a 32 percent share of garment production supplying Europe (Hounslea 2016c). UK manufacturing costs have doubled but volumes have halved over the last decade. However, price competition is not a business choice for John Smedley, as this opposes the premium quality values on which the firm was founded, and it takes pride in still maintaining. "This is a very big cultural and business challenge for the business, demanding different skill sets, different challenges, but that is the strategy" (Maclean interview with author, 2015). Growth to date has been achieved organically, with cash flow potentially inhibiting growth potential and future transformation.

FIGURE 30.5 John Smedley factory machinery. © Bethan Alexander.

Achieving and sustaining competitive advantage

John Smedley recognizes that most of its manufacturing competencies can be replicated offshore—raw materials, manufacturing processes and efficiencies, even quality—but what cannot be imitated is the John Smedley brand, the heritage, the importance of location, the brand stories associated with product, place, and people from the past, present, and future. Indeed, the role and importance of provenance to heritage luxury brands has received much attention in scholarly research (Aaker 1991; Collins and Weiss 2015; Okonkwo 2007), emphasizing the key drivers of product narrative, authenticity, and place in communicating it. Moreover, the notion of brand origin, defined as the overall perception consumers form of products from a particular country, is also important, with research demonstrating that this has a positive impact on consumers' evaluations and purchase intention (Magnusson et al. 2011). This is borne out in a UK luxury market study that found that 60 percent of the 2,000 consumers surveyed would buy a luxury product if it was made in the UK (Brooks 2013). Thus, provenance and brand origin has been a key differentiator for many British luxury brands.

The need for John Smedley to compete differently is compelling.

I have to build a brand, I have to find ways to add value to the product—intangible value—that will enable us to charge a higher price to cover our very high manufacturing costs in the UK, but at the same time, remove some of the margin elements I pay to others and retain some for myself. I can do that by retailing. (Maclean interview with author 2015)

This is in response to the seismic shifts happening in the retail landscape, with digital disrupting traditional routes to market and the onset of a consumer centric omnichannel environment (Grewal et al. 2017). John Smedley has responded by putting greater emphasis on multichannel distribution—own e-commerce and physical stores—expanding their store base from one in Brook Street to two with the opening of their Jermyn Street, Mayfair, London, store in 2016. They have developed strategic partnerships, in terms of overseas retail and distribution networks (e.g., their partnership in Japan with Bigi Group in 2018) and through product collaborations with leading designers to showcase British craftmanship and UK design talent (e.g., Holly Fulton, Claire Barrow, Phoebe English, Ashley Williams, 1205, and Lou Dalton, launched at London Fashion Week [LFW], autumn/winter 2016). They have also cemented their premium positioning by showcasing at LFW since 2013 (Cvetkovic 2017; Hounslea 2016a, 2016b). Today retail represents around 20 percent of turnover, contract manufacturing 10 percent, and wholesale the remaining 70 percent.

The future family business challenge

John Smedley faces multiple business challenges going forward:

1 the unique family owned and operated business structure and the associated decision-making tensions and trade-offs between doing what is right for the business versus family that this often raises;

2 the rapidly changing business landscape challenge, with the demise in UK manufacturing, growth of digital channel proliferation, shift to direct-to-consumer business models, importance of brand experiences and consumer centricity; and

3 the cash-flow challenge that comes with operating a 100 percent family-owned business centered on a manufacturing-distribution business model with no external investors to provide further capital injection.

Research asserts that the continuity of family businesses would be more effective if they would behave more like nonfamily businesses, rather than decision-making being anchored by family traditions and legacy (Stewart and Hitt 2012). However, as a business deeply rooted in family, John Smedley has strived to cultivate a culture that accepts continuous change, especially so in today's volatile market. They have done this whilst maintaining their family value system—centered on credibility, honesty, respect, and modesty—and reflected this in their brand values. The focus has been on leading business transformation and, in doing so, raises awareness around the importance of leadership, engaging innovation, and challenging current products and practices.

Often the success of a family business relies heavily not only on workforce capabilities but also on the impact of social and economic factors and the potential to fit with the enabling business environment (Pounder 2015). John Smedley's future strategy is clearly focused on maintaining private family ownership, achieving business growth through the direct to consumer model whilst reinvesting in the firm for the future. How they will achieve this in a competitive and disruptive fashion market, running a capital-intensive business will be challenging. These challenges are compounded with the distinct issues that family firms face regarding balancing family and business activities and, from a management perspective, conflict and tensions between family members; succession planning; governance; access to finance to fund growth; and attracting new and maintaining talent given traditional restrictions on upward mobility for nonfamily members (Boyatzis and Soler 2012; Pounder 2015; Stewart and Hitt 2012).

John Smedley's MD highlights two key challenges for the business going forward. First, its vision to remain a privately-owned family business, which is inherently capital intensive, results in little working capital to reinvest in the business. "Access to finance and ensuring what we choose to invest in has the biggest return on business growth is important. We are very restricted financially compared with a nonfamily business that has investors" (Maclean interview with author 2015). Second, "how to achieve business model transformation, maintaining our wholesale business whilst growing our direct to consumer without incurring high overheads associated with physical retail."

The priority is to remain a small independent privately owned family business. This raises common issues associated with family businesses involving ownership, governance, management, succession and/or employment, as fundamental business motivations are different. Are the challenges identified by John Smedley the only ones, or given the rapidly shifting business landscape, are there other priorities that should take precedence to sustain competitive advantage and achieve future growth?

Business Questions

Analyze the challenges and opportunities arising from the multiple transformations presented in the case and make recommendations for strategizing sustainable expansion:

1 How has John Smedley demonstrated sustainable competitive advantage over its lifespan?

2 Give examples of how John Smedley has/could undertake business transformation.

3 What are the components of John Smedley's shared vision? Create a diagram to visualize these. What does this say about the business values?

4 What are the opportunities and challenges of managing a family business in today's fashion marketplace?

5 What are the distinct differences between family and nonfamily businesses and how does this impact strategic decision-making?

6 What are the key competencies and capabilities required to engineer business transformation within a family firm?

7 Given the two key business challenges cited by John Smedley, what are your strategic recommendations for achieving sustainable growth?

8 As a business owner and manager, what might you learn from John Smedley in terms of operating and growing a business in a dynamic fashion market?

Appendix

Appendix 1. Key financials and employees 2014–2018 (£ sterling)

	2018 (31 March)	2017 (31 March)	2016 (31 March)	2015 (31 March)	2014 (3 March)
Turnover	18,000,000	16,912,000	15,916,000	16,362,000	17,249,191
Profit (Loss) Before Tax	582,000	637,000	413,000	709,000	1,507,340
Net Tangible Assets (Liabilities)	11,301,000	10,989,000	10,614,000	8,926,000	8,539,348

	2018 (31 March)	2017 (31 March)	2016 (31 March)	2015 (31 March)	2014 (3 March)
Shareholders Funds	10,883,000	10,673,000	10,261,000	8,926,000	8,539,348
Profit Margin	3.23	3.77	2.59	4.33	8.74
Return on Shareholders Funds	5.35	5.97	4.02	7.94	17.65
Return on Capital Employed	5.15	5.80	3.89	7.94	17.65
Liquidity Ratio (x)	2.43	2.61	2.71	1.95	1.79
Gearing	4.73	3.93	4.36	-	-
No. Employees	350	350	354	399	396

Source: Fame, "John Smedley Ltd Financial Results" (2018).

References and Further Reading

Aaker, David. 1991. *Managing Brand Equity: Capitalizing on the Value of a Brand Name*. New York: The Free Press.

Anthony, Scott. 2016. "What do you Really Mean by Business Transformation?". *Harvard Business Review* 29 February: 2–4.

Ashkenas, Ron. 2015. "We Still don't Know the Difference between Change and Transformation." *Harvard Business Review*, January 15: 2–4.

Beastall, Chris. 2017. "In Conversation with Ian Maclean, Managing Director of John Smedley." September 29. Accessed July 9, 2018. https://www.apetogentleman.com/conversation-ian-maclean-managing-director-john-smedley/

Boyatzis, Richard E. and Ceferi Soler. 2012. "Vision, Leadership and Emotional Intelligence Transforming Family Business." *Journal of Family Business Management* 2 (1): 23–30. https://doi.org/10.1108/20436231211216394

Brooks, David. 2013. "Luxury Focus: Selling the Story Behind the Brand." *Drapers*, November 16. Accessed July 31, 2018. https://www.drapersonline.com/business-operations/luxury-focus-selling-the-story-behind-the-brand/5054939.article

Collins, M. and M. Weiss. 2015. "The Role of Provenance in Luxury Textile Brands." *International Journal of Retail & Distribution Management* 43 (10/11): 1030–50.

Cvetkovic, Alecs. 2017. "The Factory Floor: John Smedley." *The Jackel Magazine*, June 30. Accessed July 9, 2018. https://www.thejackalmagazine.com/factory-floor-john-smedley/

Ebeltoft. 2018. *Global Retail Trends and Innovations—Welcome to the New Normal*. Ebeltoft report, 13th edn. Retail Innovations.

Fame. 2018. "John Smedley Ltd Financial Results." Accessed July 9, 2018. https://www.bvdinfo.com/

Gilbert, Clark, Matthew Eyring, and Richard N. Foster. 2012. "Rebuild Your Core While You Reinvent Your Business Model: Two Routes to Resilience." *Harvard Business Review*, December: 66–73.

Grewal, Dhruv, Anne L. Roggeveen, and Jens Nordfält. 2017. "The Future of Retailing." *Journal of Retailing* 93 (1): 1–6.

Hounslea, Tara. 2016a. "John Smedley to Open on London's Jermyn Street." *Drapers*, March 1. Accessed July 9, 2018. https://www.drapersonline.com/news/john-smedley-to-open-on-londons-jermyn-street/7005317.article

Hounslea, Tara. 2016b. "John Smedley to Launch Six Designer Collaborations at LFW." *Drapers*, February 19. Accessed July 9, 2018. https://www.drapersonline.com/news/john-smedley-to-launch-six-designer-collaborations-at-lfw/7004996.article?search=https%3a%2f%2fwww.drapersonline. com%2fsearcharticles%3fkeywords%3dJohn+Smedley+to+Launch+Six+Designer+Collaborations +at+LFW

Hounslea, Tara. 2016c. "Textiles Special 2016: Sourcing." *Drapers*, February 12. Accessed July 31, 2018. https://www.drapersonline.com/business-operations/textiles-special-2016-sourcing/7004738. article

Leavy, Brian. 2017. "Two Strategies for Innovating in the Face of Market Disruption." *Strategy & Leadership* 45 (4): 9–18, https://doi.org/10.1108/SL-05-2017-0051

Magnusson, Peter, Stanford A. Westjohn, and Srdan Zdravkovic. 2011. "Further Dlarification on How Perceived Brand Origin Affects Brand Attitude: A Reply to Samiee and Usunier." *International Marketing Review* 28 (5): 497–507.

Mirza, Khabi. 2018. "Icons of British Fashion." *Drapers*, April 4. Accessed July 9, 2018. https://www. drapersonline.com/product-and-trade-shows/icons-of-british-fashion/7029734.article

Neff, John. 2011. "Non-financial Indicators of Family Firm Performance: A Portfolio Model Approach." Unpublished PhD qualifying paper, Weatherhead School of Management, Case Western Reserve University, Cleveland, OH.

Okonkwo, Uché. 2007. *Luxury Fashion Branding: Trends, Tactics, and Techniques*. New York: Palgrave Macmillan.

Palmieri, Jean E. 2016. "John Smedley." *Women's Wear Daily* 211 (3): 24.

Pounder, Paul. 2015. "Family Business Insights: An Overview of the Literature." *Journal of Family Business Management* 5 (1): 116–27, https://doi.org/10.1108/JFBM-10-2014-0023

Prahalad, C. K. and Gary Hamel. 1990. "The Core Competence of the Corporation." *Harvard Business Review* 68 (3): 79–91

Spybey, Kat. 2015. "Homemade: Knitting it Together." *Drapers*, July 21. Accessed July 9, 2018. https://www.drapersonline.com/business-operations/home-made-knitting-it-together/5076985. article

Stewart, Alex and Michael A. Hitt. 2012. "Why Can't a Family Business Be More Like a Nonfamily Business? Modes of Professionalization in Family Firms." *Family Business Review* 25 (1): 58–86.

Wright, Ian. 2013. "Close Up: Ian Maclean, John Smedley." *Drapers*, January 19. Accessed July 9, 2018. https://www.drapersonline.com/close-up-ian-maclean-john-smedley/5044822.article

Definitions

Competitive advantage: Defined as what makes a business entity better than its competitors. A key challenge for business strategy is to find a way of achieving sustainable competitive advantage over other competing products and firms in a market.

Family business: Defined by Pounder as "a business which is owned and or managed by a family" (2015, 1187).

Chapter 31

Indochino: The Customer Experience from Online to Bricks-and-Mortar

Shopping of the Future: Customization and Personalization in Menswear

Flora Brunetti

In the changing retail environment, the path to purchases and customer interactions with brands have become a challenge, with competition offering both experience and service. With a blend of personal interaction and technology, a retail business can offer a lot more to their customer in the hopes of creating a lifelong relationship with them. Technology has become more advanced and in order to survive, apparel brands have to keep up with the speed and functionality of not only their competition, but consumers as well. Consumers today are armed with enough data to make purchase decisions and brand judgements before they even visit a physical retail location or browse a website. They are influenced by the mass amounts of user generated content, and advice from online review forums. This case study outlines the business operations of one made-to-measure menswear brand which hopes to change the way men shop for customized suits. Students will provide suggestions regarding how this company can successfully continue to build their business by reinventing traditional customer service and marketing models both in online and bricks-and-mortar shopping.

Learning Objectives

Upon completion of this case, students should be able to:

- Describe and analyze technology-based tools for apparel brands.
- Explain how customer service is changing in an age of online shopping.

- Evaluate customer loyalty marketing strategies for an apparel brand.
- Develop a customer journey tool for businesses to use for online consumers.

Introduction

How to buy a suit

The traditional suit buying experience dates back to the beginnings of Savile Row, a street in Mayfair, London, that developed a reputation for its traditional bespoke tailoring for men in the eighteenth century. Suits from Savile Row were renowned for costing thousands; a lot has changed over the intervening years, however, and a new generation of consumers who are looking to spend less than $500 for a suit now control a large proportion of the markets' target consumer. The suit industry has consequently adapted, and suit buyers are faced with three options when it comes to their purchase, which significantly vary in price:

- Bespoke suits are tailor-made to a specific individual and produced exactly as a customer requests. They sit at the higher end of the price margin.
- Custom, made-to-measure suits provide a cheaper alternative to bespoke suits and allow consumers to choose from a selection of styles—the suit will then be made according to their measurements.
- The third and cheapest option is to purchase an off-the-rack suit that has been made to factory measurements which can be tailored to an individual following purchase.

One retailer out to change how men shop for suits is Vancouver-based made-to-measure menswear brand, Indochino. Indochino was created so that customers can create the suit to their measurements, and then build the style with certain customizations. Its custom, made-to-measure business model allows customers the option to build a personalized suit without the high price tag of bespoke tailoring. This is perfect for a man who wants to put his individual style into his wardrobe without spending a lot of money. The company started life ten years ago as a business that solely operated on e-commerce: men were able to sign up to the website, submit their body measurements to their profile, choose their customizations, such as label size, extra buttons, and fabric, and receive their custom suit at their door within one month.

However, with the help of new CEO Drew Green, who felt that a physical showroom is the key to success, the company started opening physical locations across North America. Indochino continues to grow, and the brand now has over twenty locations in major markets. By visiting a showroom customers can get a full experience of shopping for suits with styling options that they otherwise would not be able to attain by just strictly shopping online.

Whilst an Indochino customer is able simply to submit their measurements through the company's website and build their custom, made-to-measure suit, customers who visit the showroom are able to receive professional advice from style guides. Once in the showroom, a customer has the opportunity to work with a style guide who will take their measurements and help them choose fabric and customize their suit or shirt. Within three weeks, they will have their personalized product delivered to their door. Once the suit is adjusted with the right specifications, the customer no longer has to update measurements and can order another suit anytime, anywhere. Innovations in technology and production capabilities have enabled Indochino to offer this experience to its consumers at a fraction of the cost of other companies, and therefore has enabled the much cheaper purchase of made-to-measure apparel. CEO Drew Green has stated that through this model: "We've redefined custom clothing for a new generation and disrupted the fashion industry by offering tailored suits and shirts at a price comparable to ready to wear alternatives. Today's consumers are increasingly demanding products personalized to them, and innovation and technology is finally allowing them to access this at a price they can afford" (*World Retail Congress* 2017).

This case discusses customer service in a business model that is driven by technology and online purchase. By the end of the case, students will critically analyze how a business maintains a large number of customers who order a suit but do not have any follow-up after the initial purchase, and evaluate how to attract and maintain customers who do not have physical proximity to a style guide.

The made to measure experience is bringing people back to bricks-and-mortar

According to Lin Grossman, the future of shopping will be that of convenience, experience, and options. "Retailers will constantly need to evolve, innovate and unify their omni-channel efforts so shoppers' paths to purchase are as frictionless as possible" (Grosman 2017).

In the modern, hyper-connected world, consumers have been able to become keen researchers of products—they are not only able to locate retailers that will offer them the best price online but, regarding the physical show room, are also able to find the one that will offer the best experience. Consumer shopping behavior today, therefore, often requires that retailers provide convenience, speed, entertainment, and good customer service, while also being competitively priced. The success of a brand or retailer will depend on the dynamic story they can tell through their marketing, the experience they give to their customer, and the personalization that sets them apart from the competition. If a retailer doesn't deliver or offer an acceptable consumer experience, a consumer will likely seek out a different brand that they know will offer it.

Whilst it is assumed that most individuals today complete their shopping online, physical retail has been proven to remain an important touchpoint for consumers. Overall, "only 21 percent of consumers are primarily online shoppers, purchasing more than half of their items online. The majority (79 percent) typically buy half or less of the items they need online. How consumers shop has been shown to vary significantly depending on the what they're buying." (NRF 2017)

It can be difficult to sway consumers to not shop conveniently online, however younger consumers show they can be convinced to visit stores more frequently when offered the chance to have a new experience or pick up items that they had already purchased online. The National Retail Federation's Fall consumer view found that "half of Millennial/Gen Z respondents say they are shopping in stores more than they were a year ago" (NRF 2017). Much of this increase is due to the changes that brands and retailers are making to attract this generation of consumer.

Indochino is, thus, focusing its efforts on developing the quality of their showroom experience in order to attract a greater portion of these customers. Although they may carry higher costs, consumers today are generally willing to pay more for customization (Brannon and Divita 2015) and, indeed, many desire customization services. By understanding the need for this new generation of consumer to get as much personalization as possible, Indochino's showrooms are set up to only include fabric and samples of the type of suit a customer can buy, rather than offering physical products to be bought. For example, aside from some shirts and the suits on the mannequins, there are no physical products offered in the stores. Customers are paired with a style guide who will take their body measurements, then place a sample suit on them to determine the best fit—this style guide then helps them to decide on customizations (such as the style of the pocket, monogram, lapel, vent, button, and whether they require pants) for their suit and select their fabrics. Once the customer receives the suit about three weeks later, they then have the option to get their suit adjusted and tailored to even more of their liking and specifications.

Mass customization represents future opportunities for the apparel industry. The payoffs for mass customizations include higher customer satisfaction, stronger loyalty to the brand, the ability to gather more information about the consumer, and the potential for better forecasting because of the relationship between the core consumer and the company (Zimmermann 1998).

> At Indochino, the highly engaging personalized experience that our customers enjoy in our showrooms is a part of our overall product. Upon arrival, they are designated their own personal stylist who consults and assists them in designing their suit and building their custom wardrobe. This VIP treatment paired with what was traditionally seen as a luxury product, is something the majority of our customers have never had the opportunity to experience before. We believe this emphasis on creating personalized experiences over impersonal transactions will be the saviour of retail. (*World Retail Congress* 2017)

FIGURE 31.1 Made-to-measure menswear brand Indochino uses their physical showroom to enhance the customer experience. © Rich Polk/Getty Images for Indochino

Business Problem

Today, men are finding more options when it comes to personalizing their style and are becoming more fashion forward than ever before. This is where an engaged customer service strategy can really work. By offering recommendations about an individual's style, a brand may be able to develop a sense of trust and loyalty with its consumers, thus allowing it to excel in omnichannel retail. Indochino's showrooms, and the personal style guides who are present within them, offer a significant opportunity to develop an engaging customer service strategy by developing a personal relationship between style guides and consumers. However, building this relationship would rely upon consumers returning to the Indochino showroom following their first purchase. This is a challenge for the company as, once a customer is taken through their entire experience at Indochino's showroom and their measurements have been saved online, there isn't much reason left for a customer to return unless they want to look at the fabric choices in person or to receive further assistance from a style guide.

One could argue that Indochino are not currently capitalizing on the use of their in-store style guides, as they do not remain in contact with their customers following them leaving the store. Though the company targets the millennial generation who value experience and quality to a significant extent, one consumer stated that he would feel much closer to a brand if his style guide followed up after he wore his suit to the event he purchased it for. It is important to remember the significance of after-purchase service, which is the main focus of relationship marketing. Resultantly, working on their postpurchase consumer engagement may be a way to build connections between Indochino and consumers; by providing each customer with a personal style assistant who is interested in and wants to help them look their best, both before and following a purchase, customers may be encouraged to return to a showroom just to seek further advice from this person and purchase more items. Turning every consumer into a loyal Indochino customer is a brand's ultimate goal—loyalty is probably one of the best measures of a brand's success.

If Indochino's strategy is to draw in first-time customers through emphasizing the experience that one has within the store, the only logical way to get them back in shopping again would be to offer the best possible service from the style guides from the beginning. This means that Indochino need to work on customizing and personalizing their style guide experience within their showrooms too in order to encourage repeat custom.

Promotions and marketing strategy

The key for Indochino to acquire new customers is for it to ensure that it is creating the right marketing strategy and building a more prominent online presence. The rest of the experience comes after the customer walks in the door. Indochino currently focuses their efforts on social media advertising, digital adverts online, email marketing, and podcasts. They are also reliant on gifting sports players, media professionals, and influencers in major markets across Canada and the United States as part of their public relations tactics and to build some organic reach. The company targets their efforts to the millennial generation who are looking to purchase their first or second suit.

Our marketing budget is spread across the transactional focus as well as driving appointments to our showrooms," Green said. "Indochino's data also shows the company is establishing deep relationships with its customers. Nearly 50 percent of Indochino's transactions are return customers, which is the company's second-largest channel for customer acquisition. Although Indochino's showroom strategy is growing in scale, Indochino is also looking at ways to enhance its online experience, and will launch those enhancements in phases throughout the year. (*World Retail Congress* 2017)

As the competition continues to grow in the customizable apparel business, keeping the customer engaged and continuing to shop with your brand becomes an even bigger challenge. How to maintain a relationship is key to successful customer relations. If Indochino wants to be the face of the changing retail environment and the leader in menswear customization and made-to-measure, they will need to keep up with advancements in shopper expectations and technology.

Business Questions

1   If you were to look at the technology that Indochino is currently using, how could you make it better? How could the company sell more product with an updated digital platform as simple as a website? Can you think of any tools or technology in the market that would be a good fit for a company like Indochino?

2   How does a brand like Indochino continue to gain customers back to their showroom?

3   What can the style guides do to keep repeat customers coming back?

4   How can the brand track their customer journey? Utilizing the tools necessary to keep up with traditional retail and e-commerce, what would you add to their existing strategy? Describe an effective customer journey tool or map for Indochino.

5   How does an e-commerce business integrate with a showroom experience successfully?

6   How does the company further integrate personalization?

7   In the age of data is everything Indochino are doing all they can to acquire and utilize the data they are receiving in terms of future business or for effective, personalized, and interactive marketing campaigns?

References and Further Reading

Brannon, Evelyn L. and Lorynn Divita. 2015. *Fashion Forecasting*, 4th edn. New York: Bloomsbury Publishing.

Burns, Leslie, Kathy Mullet, and Nancy O. Bryant. 2016. *The Business of Fashion: Designing, Manufacturing, and Marketing*. New York: Fairchild Books/Bloomsbury.

Grosman, Lin. 2017. "The Future of Retail: How We'll Be Shopping in 10 Years." *Forbes*, June 20. Accessed July 21, 2018. https://www.forbes.com/sites/forbescommunicationscouncil/2017/06/20/the-future-of-retail-how-well-be-shopping-in-10-years/3#

Indochino. 2018. "Home." Accessed August 3, 2018. https://www.indochino.com/

National Retail Federation (NRF). 2017. "The Customer Channel." Fall. Accessed July 21, 2018. https://nrf.com/resources/consumer-research-and-data/consumer-view/the-customer-channel

Sudo, Chuck. 2018. "Omnichannel Marketing is Helping More E-Retailers Like Indochino Understand The Need For Storefronts." *Bisnow*, February 14. Accessed July 21, 2018. https://www.bisnow.com/national/news/retail/the-key-to-e-retailer-indochinos-explosive-growth-the-past-three-years-brick-and-mortar-85015?rt=54623?utm_source=CopyShare&utm_medium=Browser

World Retail Congress. 2017. "An Interview with Drew Green, Chairman and CEO INDOCHINO." *World Retail Congress*, February 22. Accessed July 21, 2018. https://www.worldretailcongress.com/news/interview-drew-green-chairman-ceo-indochino

Zimmermann, K. A. 1998. "Mass-produced for Individual Looks." *Women's Wear Daily*, December 9: 24.

Definitions

Bespoke fashion: merchandise custom-made to an individual's specifications; typically suits and specialty items (Burns, Mullet, and Bryant 2016).

Customer journey: The full experience a customer goes through when interacting with a fashion brand including all possible touchpoints.

Made-to-measure: A customized design and production process whereby a garment/product is made specifically for one individual based on their measurements and preferences (Burns, Mullet and Bryant 2016).

Off-the-rack: Ready-to-wear made with mass-production techniques using standardized sizing (Burns, Mullet and Bryant 2016).

Relationship marketing: A type of marketing that focuses on customer loyalty rather than shorter term acquisitions and individual sales.

Chapter 32

The Lime-Green Colored Glove

Product Design and Development, and Buyer Liaison

Valerie Wilson Trower

A cross-functional collaboration and an exercise in human resource (HR) management, this case explores an example drawn from a UK accessories manufacturer's business to detail the consequences of the practical difficulties of sampling given a relatively small end-use. The designer for a large specialist supplier was required to determine if she should risk challenging her line manager—one of the owners of the company—and endure the adverse comments of other directors and senior colleagues, by showing a sample which they believed had no commercial value to a long-standing client. The case study raises questions about buyers' expertise; a buyer's ability to imagine the possible success of another color way; and the perceived value of the designer's input. The case also examines assumptions about the nature of the accessories market.

Learning Objectives

Upon completion of this case, students should be able to:

- Understand the operations of the accessories market.
- Explore cross-functional collaboration in the fashion business and its contribution to developing design and business opportunities.
- Evaluate human resource management and issues around maintaining personal integrity in a commercial environment.
- Discuss the role of the designer in fashion business by exploring the design and production process.

- Develop an understanding of the role of the buyer in fashion businesses by exploring the design and production process.
- Gain an appreciation of the opportunities and threats for UK-based, traditional, established accessory and garment businesses.
- Understand the persistence required to challenge and change established norms.
- Consider and discuss professional behavior in the workplace.

Introduction

Accessories manufacturing is a world apart from mainstream fashion supply and retailing, but often provides a season's key fashion look. Using specialist machinery and construction techniques, accessories manufacturers are relatively small and unimportant customers of fabric suppliers. Nevertheless, for many retailers, without seasonal accessories, one season would look much like another. Many accessories manufacturers remain family-owned businesses: regionally located, employing generational expertise, and intent on maintaining stability rather than significant growth. This can sometimes result in a relatively narrow view of business opportunities as they continue to make private-label merchandise, often manufacturing workwear and civil and military defense items to help smooth fashion's seasonal production demands. Many supply their near-competitors, with whom they have long-standing relationships, who do not have capacity or expertise to fulfil a particular merchandise requirement, e.g. offering fabric gloves to a leather glove business.

This case study documents an opportunity for And Sons Ltd. to offer a new design to BCC, a long-standing, private-label customer with their own accessories brand name. Commercial constraints required the initial sample be made in a non-viable color. Persuing the sample in defiance of senior management proved a challenge for the designer and an example of human relations in an industry setting.

And Sons Ltd., as a glove manufacturer and leather processor, supplied accessories to the UK high street; civil and military defence; and workwear client markets—with an annual turnover of, then, £6 million. Unusually, And Sons Ltd. employed a Design and Development Manager, Kay, the only female member of the senior management team of six, three of whom were directors and shareholders in the family business.

Kay developed seasonal ranges of men's, women's, and children's fashion accessories, mostly gloves, for large high street customers, occasionally contributing to civil and military defense projects. Kay had persuaded the Managing Director (MD) to allow her to offer production to well-known UK luxury design names, including Paul Smith, Betty Jackson, and Osprey. Although the volume of these orders did not significantly contribute to the company's turnover or profitability, they more than covered her annual salary and expenses and she believed that completing orders for these well-known brands was an endorsement of the design capacity and production quality of the company.

Business Problem

And Sons Ltd.'s long-standing customer, BCC

And Sons Ltd. had long supplied BCC, the only well-known brand name in the UK gloving world, with private label merchandise. The relationship was friendly and And Sons Ltd.'s MD and his fellow directors knew BCC's senior management well, usually inviting BCC's MD and his team to lunch at a local country restaurant before discussing business, when they visited to consider seasonal ranges twice a year. BCC's buyer, John, then in his late fifties, had worked for BCC all his life, commencing as a junior and rising to become an experienced buyer.

Comparison of And Sons Ltd. and BCC's customer base

And Sons Ltd. had just two salespeople, members of the senior management team who were also responsible for materials, supplies, and work-wear development respectively, although two of the directors also handled several specific significant accounts themselves. BCC operated concession spaces in London department stores, and supplying them, rather than approaching the stores directly, was an effective use of And Sons Ltd.'s sales resources.

Professional relationships

Kay found John, BCC's buyer, rather difficult to deal with, and perhaps he found her relative youth (she was thirty years old) to be something of a threat. She tolerated a number of comments about her appearance, for example her pale green Max Mara suit—it was the 1980s!—provoked a comment from him about a "green costume," as though she was some 1940s film star. Kay felt it was pointless to complain about his behavior towards her to the MD as, although he would have listened, he would have observed that BCC were clients, and told her, judging correctly, that she was well able to deal with the comments.

The uneasy professional relationship with John continued for some years, until Kay developed a lime-green colored glove as part of a seasonal range to show BCC's team.

And Sons Ltd.'s sourcing and manufacturing requirements and sampling

And Sons Ltd. regularly sourced from a Leicester-based trim supplier, who supplied the shoe trade and also offered garment trims. Many knit fabrics are unsuitable for gloves unless they are simplex-knitted, because they are prone to "ladder" at either the top or the bottom of the thumbhole, resulting in a high level of seconds or returned merchandise.

The lime-green glove sample

For the Spring/Summer 1989 season Kay sampled a mesh frill, about 3 inches wide, finished with a metallic-silver stitch at each edge, which was possible to use for glove-making. Unfortunately, it was only available in lime-green. Sampling a meter of lime-green fabric mesh from another regular supplier, Kay asked one of the factory's sample hands to make a plain wrist-length (1BL), fabric-mesh glove using an overlocker set up to stitch very closely together—almost like a Brosser machine stitch—and stretching the frill flat as they zig-zag stitched it across the hemmed edge of the wrist end of the glove, on the top of the ruched elastic stitching. The lime-green glove was then "closed" or made, and the raw edges of the frill caught in to the side-seam. After ironing, the glove was presented with a former—(a cardboard, hand-shaped stiffening)—and placed in an appropriate-sized cellophane bag.

Range review

Reviewing her proposed selection of approximately twenty glove samples for BCC, including fabric, leathers, and suedes, in a wide range of men's and women's formal and casual styles, a few days before their scheduled visit, Kay showed the lime-green colored glove to her MD and other members of the senior management team, and was immediately met with derisive comments and laughter.

It is a truth that most customers purchase gloves for warmth or protection in cold weather, therefore the predominant men's and women's colors sold are black; browns/ochres; navy blue for women; and to a lesser extent, for women: red, purple, and orange. The proportion of fabric gloves—white for wedding or Confirmation use, or black or metallic for evening-wear—is much smaller. Lime-green colored gloves would be almost unheard of unless they happened to become a novelty fashion for a season.

Kay's response

Kay chose to risk annoying her MD and patiently explained that when the glove went into production it could be black, (which she knew had a small but significant market), but that she had been unable to source the sample in black. Rather grudgingly, her MD agreed it should remain in the selected range to be shown to BCC.

BCC's response

The BCC team arrived; the company's senior management team and BCC's team had lunch and returned to the office and Kay started to show the samples, explaining how they might fill a merchandise category. When she passed the lime-green glove to John, her MD and the two other directors present began to laugh. As she began to explain to John that she had been obliged to sample it in green, he finished the sentence for her and they both said at the same time: "It would work in black." Kay was pleased at his understanding of the purpose of the sample, and they both smiled. Exceptionally, he had the experience to imagine a small item in another color way. From that day onwards, she found John treated her with professional respect, and she never had to endure another comment about her appearance.

Buyer's decision

BCC purchased the glove and a number of other styles: a small order—around 200 dozen pairs—and retailed them in Liberty, Selfridges, and other UK premium department stores across the country that winter. Kay noted with satisfaction, the lime-green glove was not amongst the marked-down merchandise in the New Year sales.

Business Questions

Issues for Kay

1 Should she withdraw the sample?
2 Should she risk missing the selling season and delay sampling until the trim is available in black at a future date?

3 Could she have insisted that the supplier make a black sample? She required one meter and the likely buy, should the glove be selected, would only be a few hundred meters.

4 Should she have risked a disagreement with her MD by showing the sample in lime-green, or just accept his view that no one would buy a lime-green glove?

HR questions

5 How might And Sons Ltd.'s MD have felt about his employee showing an uncommercial sample to BCC?

6 Was it better to let Kay show the glove than to veto it? If so, why?

7 Should buyers be able to imagine other color ways?

Broader industry questions

8 And Sons Ltd.'s MD vetoed samples that were likely to cause problems in making (e.g. limited production capacity) or produce unacceptable returns (e.g. if a trim could be pulled off). Was the lime-green glove sample either?

9 Can UK-based manufacturing businesses rely on the seasonal fashion market?

10 How might And Sons Ltd. and BCC have furthered their businesses to satisfy customers' needs and wants?

References and Further Reading

Bean, Roger, and Russell Radford. 2000. *Powerful Products: Strategic Management of Successful New Product Development.* New York: Amacom.

Best, Kathryn. 2015. *Design Management.* London: Fairchild/Bloomsbury.

Sowrey, T. 1987. *The Generation of Ideas for New Products.* London: Kogan Page.

Ulrich, Karl, and Steven D. Eppinger. 2016. *Product Design and Development.* 6th ed. New York: McGraw Hill.

Definitions

Brosser machines: Used to produce a dense, miniature version of an over-locked stitch using only two threads—an over-locker uses three. Used by the fur and leather trades

Button Length (BL): The length of any glove measured from the seam at the base of the thumbhole nearest the top (the finished edge of the glove, near or above, the wrist) to the top edge in inches. Each inch is a "button length," and written as "BL," deriving from the spacing between buttons on the long, above-elbow length Victorian and Edwardian period gloves. A glove with one inch of finished fabric between the base of the thumbhole and the top edge of the glove after making (sewing) is termed 1BL

Closed/Made: The process of "making" for all gloves. After the thumb is set on to the flat cut-out glove shape, the fittings (the strips between the fingers) are sewn on to the palm side of the glove. The glove is then closed and finally the top edge is finished. Occasionally, as described, the top edge is finished first then the glove is made

Dozen(s): Most merchandise purchased by volume retailers is purchased in dozens rather than single units. Before computer-generated ordering systems, this reduced the number of zeros that a large order required and reduced numerical mistakes

Chapter 33

Depop the Social Shopping Platform

Developing the Business Model for International and Physical Expansion

Helen Beney

This case explores Depop, a social shopping platform founded in 2012 that operates in the UK, Italy, and the USA. The business developed as a digital vintage and streetwear fashion resale marketplace and has gained high awareness amongst individuals between 14 and 24 years of age in the UK. Designed for the Instagram generation, the platform allows users to buy, sell, and amass followers, and develop retail personalities.

In January 2018 Depop announced that it had secured US$20 million in series B funding. These funds were raised in order to support Depop's growth in the US market. Depop hoped to do this through both developing the functionality and user experience of the digital platform and establishing physical spaces that would facilitate creative conversations and retail experiences for users in key American cities. This case study can be used to explore business strategy, international expansion, and experiential retail spaces. By considering the founder's vision and the business' current operating model, customer base, and market contexts, this case study provides students with a basis upon which to explore the potential value proposition for bricks-and-mortar expansion, and to evaluate the digital and physical business model and opportunities for growth in the United States and internationally.

Learning Objectives

Upon completion of this case, students should be able to:

- Identify users' aims, needs, and motivations to explore Depop's creative and cultural positioning.

- Discuss and appraise the potential business challenges presented by having two categories of customers: buyers and sellers.
- Assess Depop's key business activities, skills and resources, partners and relationships as strategic devices to deliver customer value in a highly competitive and growing marketplace.
- Conduct a macro analysis to review the risks and opportunities associated with the US market, with specific reference to the competition, sector growth, and business channels.
- Analyze the effectiveness of Depop's current customer value proposition, that gives equal focus to socializing and selling.
- Evaluate the current Depop business proposition through the lens of the business model canvas (Osterwalder 2010; Strategyzer n.d.).
- Develop a customer value proposition for Depop that could drive scale in the United States over the next two to five years.
- Discuss the opportunities for experiences, content, and collaborations that could effectively drive brand awareness and user engagement for Depop.
- Evaluate the opportunity to develop physical spaces as part of Depop's business development strategy.
- Research, design, and justify solutions for the physical spaces proposed in the United States.
- Discuss the opportunity to bridge the gap between online and offline retail.
- Explore the resources and relationships required for Depop's development relative to the potential impact on scale and revenue generation.
- Assess the business functions, processes and relationships required to support a value proposition for growth in the United States.
- Review strategic business model options for operating and driving revenue at scale internationally.
- Analyze whether the relative scale of the funding Depop have received could support the growth strategy you have identified.

Introduction

Background and business development

In 2011, Simon Beckerman was living in Italy where he had cofounded a lifestyle magazine, *PIG* (a younger version of *Dazed and Confused*, the provocative British style and culture magazine), and a sunglasses brand "Super Sunglasses." He recognized that the rise in the internet required that he move online in order to generate further revenue. He consequently had the idea to combine the creative vibe and insight of *PIG* with a digital sales platform that would host the unique items that featured in the magazine. He believed that the site should be mobile and social so that its users (creatives, influencers, designers, and brands) could see what their friends were buying and liking. Before long, Beckerman realized that this online platform required a selling platform as well and thus re-envisioned the app as a social selling

FIGURE 33.1 Depop logo. © Depop.

marketplace under the name of Depop. In launching Depop, Beckerman's mission was to help creative people not only to sell but also to be "discovered."

Beckerman secured initial seed funding of €2 million (approximately US$2.4 million) in October 2012 from H-Farm, an incubator campus and venture capital firm based in Italy that specializes in start-up investments in the digital and innovation sectors (Crunchbase n.d.). Following this, Depop moved their headquarters from Italy to London for the business' international launch in April 2013 and quickly generated a user base that was 50,000 strong and who were selling around 350,000 items. At this time Depop had only fourteen employees. Depop describe their philosophy and style as:

> a global conduit of connection, not only in m-commerce, but culture, design, and creative communities around the world. (Depop n.d.-a)

Beckerman recognized that most decision-making within fashion buying was based on social factors and thus designed the app with features that were typically reminiscent of social media channels such as Instagram; users are able to "like" and "follow" other sellers in order to encourage buyer and seller interactions. Engaging with Depop is simple—sellers download the app, make a profile, and upload photos and copy for the items they want to sell. Users can scroll through the "explore" page of items that are recommended by the Depop team, search for specific items, or browse the stores they follow. Sold items remain on the site and therefore build followers who add to the brand and store's personality and profile.

Depop are aware that being creative and pushing boundaries are intrinsically related to success. They aim to create and maintain strong community connections, with their fundamental customer value proposition giving equal focus to socializing and selling. The product offer is deliberately progressive and inclusive. Whilst vintage and street style items are dominant, the product mix allows for an eclectic curation such as street style items adjacent to fabulously styled drag outfits, and "plus" models mixed with size eights. Depop engaged with users to encourage great styling and strong photography and contact those with good stock but bad photos to help them develop their profile. By valuing curation in the app and creating fresh editorial content, Depop is determined to keep its core integrity and personality.

FIGURE 33.2 @inthejunkyard/Alex Lee. © Depop.

Services: Buying and selling

Sellers on Depop are responsible for packaging and postage in the UK; "shipping integration" with a one-click printable mailing label available in the United States from 2017 (Depop n.d.-b). Money changes hands through PayPal and 10 percent of the transaction is paid to Depop. The comparative costs for sellers using resale sites depends on the service model offered. Depop, like eBay and Etsy, charges a 10 percent commission from all sales for the basic sellers service. Direct competitors to Depop such as Poshmark in the United States charge up to 20 percent but manage the financial transactions and provide sellers with prepaid packaging materials. In the luxury sector the basic costs vary from 20 percent (Tradesey) to 25 percent (Vestiare Collective). Vestiaire Collective provide options for sellers who can choose a basic or concierge service that authenticates, values, photographs, wraps, and dispatches sales for a fee.

By the end of 2015 the app, operating under the motto "hello we're open," had been downloaded some 3 million times, with a third of its users selling items. The app was beginning to get significant recognition, British *Vogue* described it as "a thrift-shopping oasis for millennials combined with an interactive interface that references the double tap attention grabbing sinkhole of Instagram" (Satenstein 2016). Owing to its success Depop was able to launch in the United States in 2015. Los Angeles became the second most popular city for use of Depop only after London and, whilst growth in the app use had been slower there, Beckerman saw the United States as the next phase in the brand's journey.

The customer: Buyers and sellers

At its initial launch in Italy in 2011, the Depop customer profile initially followed that of *PIG* magazine, "cool" millennials, whilst in the UK the brand resonated more strongly with a younger generation aged between 16 and 24 years old. The United States also followed the UK profile, which meant that there was a large crossover of Generation Z and millennials that dominated Depop's international market: 80 percent of users were under 25, 70 percent were female, and 60 percent of the app's users both bought and sold (Knowles 2018). Most of Depop's buyers were into streetwear or vintage, and many sellers identified themselves as creatives, stylists, or curators.

For Generation Z, buying into the authentic voice of "culture curators" and the eclectic product mix is seen as aspirational; there is fun in the discovery that they do not just have to follow the taste set by traditional fast fashion brands and high street stores. For Depop, the community interface is key for "a buy-and-sell space that's far more fun than sitting at home alone on your computer waiting to snap up something from eBay" (Banks 2017). "We are really hands-on when it comes to discovering and empowering creativity at an early stage," said Depop's senior marketer, Tainá Vilela. "That's what sets us apart." The communication style of the app also resonates with the "authenticity-first mindset of the digital generation" (Banks 2017) where sellers are encouraged to personally engage with products and cultural conversations.

The Depop team are always on the hunt for people and brands to include on the platform that embody the "Depop style" and, when producing content, the priority goes toward showcasing those who shape or would shape culture. Beckerman said;

> in a sort of way the magazine we were creating before is inside Depop. We see ourselves much more than a marketplace but also going towards media somehow in a more—if I may use this word—modern way. (Banks 2017)

With further funding throughout 2016 and 2017, Depop was able to secure its place as the resale app of choice for younger millennials and teenagers in the UK. Beckerman described this as "gradual lean growth [which was] picking up very fast" (Banks 2017).

By 2018, Depop was able to segment its creatives (sellers) into four levels; the level that their sellers sat at was dependent on their level of activity and number of followers. This ranged from one-time sellers, through to beginners, to active, and finally to top sellers, who frequently had 400,000 followers on Depop and could (but not necessarily) have in excess of 100,000 on Instagram. An example of one of these top sellers is Isabella McFadden, "@internetgirl," who personifies the style of social communication that is so successful on the site. MacFadden, 22, a college dropout from Toronto with a flair for retro and "thrift-shop" fashion began "monetizing" her social media presence on the app in 2016. By 2018, she had almost half a million followers (placing her consistently in the platform's top global sellers), employed two assistants, and had opened her own website selling unworn second-hand stock and her own fashion line (Whatling 2018). Over time, Depop has become well known as a hub for Generation Z creative entrepreneurs.

Consumer lifestyles

Raga and Beckerman identified that the app tapped into the millennial future work-scape; millennials did not want nine-to-five desk jobs but hoped to combine "social self-presentation" with "numerous activities, pulling revenues from all corners of the physical

FIGURE 33.3 Isabella McFadden @internetgirl/Brigita Žižyt. © Depop.

and digital worlds" (Remsen 2017). "They're much more entrepreneurial," Raga said in an interview with the *Financial Times* (Remsen 2017). For many users, Depop was their first experience of buying and selling; some quickly graduated to top 500 seller status where monthly sales of between $600 to $10,000 was common. Beckerman observed that many of their sellers were "savvier" than traditional fashion outlets, some of which are struggling to adapt to mobile selling. Even established online clothes brands such as Monki sold one-off or customized items on the app as a way to reach a younger audience (Whatling 2018).

Marketing and promotion

Unlike other resale apps, such as Austrian start-up Shpock, Depop spends very little on traditional marketing, such as television advertisements. Instead, it uses the social aspect of its community to spread the word by showcasing up-and-coming designers and referencing

FIGURE 33.4 Depop homepage. © Depop.

magazines and bloggers that feature the brand. They have developed a number of partnerships with brands and individuals that had developed a sense of authenticity with its consumers, such as Converse and the blogger Chiara Ferragni, who reflect their creative and cultural values. Influencers such as Shaq O'Neal and Dita von Teese were also amongst the first to start using the app; the presence of popular influencers on Depop greatly raised public awareness.

In 2017 Depop rebranded its site focusing on the "attitude" and "confidence" of its buying and selling community. Beckerman said, "we are curating now a proper editorial team and we will treat Depop not only as an app but like a proper magazine" (Banks 2017).

The Depop team

Sellers, buyers, employees, and investors are considered important stakeholders who, Depop feel, believe in the business and share their resources with others, whether that is their capital, time, or passion. However, as a relatively new entrepreneurial venture the vision of Beckerman was key in driving that strategy. When Beckerman first received investment, he recognized that he needed a strong team to work with him, including the need for a CEO to run the company, which would allow him to focus on the vision and direction. In 2016 Beckerman became Creative Director, and Maria Raga, previously VP of Operations, became the CEO. Together, their aim was to become the most loved and inspirational marketplace for creatives all over the world.

> "I am thrilled to be leading Depop, it's an exciting time for us as we are becoming a truly global platform," said Raga …. We are becoming part of the youth culture and a place for people and brands to inspire and get inspired by each other. (Terrelonge 2016)

By 2017 there were over 100 staff internationally, working across PR, photography, marketing, design, technology, finance, and community (seller) development and support. Many of the young Depop team were attracted to working for the company as they were initially users of the app and, unlike many digital start-ups, they came from both technological and creative backgrounds. They embodied the brand philosophy when working with sellers not only by giving them insights on their sales but also by producing original "media" content and stories, showcasing their shops, and distributing PR.

The growth of Depop

Depop grew from 5 million users in 2016 to 8.5 million users by the start of 2018; a growth of 103 percent globally and 130 percent in the United States. At the beginning of 2018 they had 100 staff across four offices in Italy, the USA, and the UK. The business had developed in the UK as a vintage and streetwear fashion resale site with high awareness amongst 14-to-24-year-olds, and by 2017 annual transaction values were in excess of US$230 million.

With the ambition to expand the US business, Depop identified that they would need to drive brand awareness in order to expand their buyer and seller base. They felt they could do this predominately through word of mouth and by curating an exceptional social buying and selling experience. They also believed they needed to drive original content to strengthen the brand and develop physical spaces to achieve their ambition. However, in planning to do so Raga and Beckerman were moving away from Depop's core activity of managing an online marketplace. They also needed to quickly identify which skills and technologies to invest in to enhance their digital functionality and user experience. Whilst challenging, they felt that a combination of the physical and digital was key to competing and driving scale in the United States.

Business Problem

The marketplace and competition

With some three quarters of purchase decisions identified in 2017 as being influenced by social networks, combining social with shopping via mobile devices was widely recognized as a highly attractive market area. Mobile (M) commerce was the fastest growing sector globally, and the number of sites and apps for users to resell garments had grown significantly. eBay was launched in 1995, and with it the resale market grew. In 2017 ThredUP, another US fashion resale website, estimated the value of the US "re-commerce" market at US$18 billion annually (n.d.) and IBISWorld (2018) calculated it was worth around £700 million in Britain. Looking at resale across all channels it was forecast to reach 11 percent of the market by 2027, and therefore outselling fast fashion globally (ThredUP n.d.).

Whilst eBay dwarfed all other players, generating *circa* US$9 billion in revenue per annum (Datafox n.d.), the market sector was growing fast with Tradesy, ThredUP, Vestaire Collective, Vinted and the RealReal, and Poshmark all actively pursuing growth strategies in the US market. "Poshmark," arguably Depop's closest competitor in the United States, launched in 2011 and reportedly had 3 million sellers, and sales of US$500 million in 2017. Poshmark was successful in raising US$87.5 million in funding in 2017, led by Temasek, which is also an investor in Farfetch (Sherman 2016), and planned to expand and enter new countries, starting with additional English-speaking regions and then moving into Western Europe and Asia. They also planned to make the shopping experience more immersive; for example, partnering with Amazon on "Poshmark Stylist Match" to link the Alexa artificial intelligence tool to their app (Sherman 2016).

In China, where Wechat dominated, the resale market was valued at US$60 billion annually (2018) with Alibaba spending US$15 million in 2016 to acquire Xian Yu, a social commerce app. In Europe, the Austrian flea market app Shpock claimed 10 million users and launched UK television advertisements during 2017 to increase awareness and attract users.

Due to the highly competitive nature of the market and the low conversion of product on offer to sales revenue, it has proven hard for businesses to translate activity into profit (Sherman 2016). This has already led to some consolidation with Covetique (backed by ASOS) closing and Tradesy acquiring luxury reseller Shop Hers in 2015.

The Depop ambition

Between 2015 and 2017 Tradesy, ThredUP, Vestaire Collective, and Vinted and the RealReal (all active in the US resale market) alone raised over US$240 million in funding, leading to what has been described as a "winner-takes-all" battle for second-hand clothing start-ups (DiNinzio in Sherman 2016).

Raga and Beckerman believed that they too needed scale to compete with these start-up brands. They intended to continue with their strong "mostly organic growth" by tapping into the next generation's entrepreneurial, community driven, and creative spirit. They felt that growth in the United States was essential before they could consider other market opportunities. They understood that the quality and volume of sellers and the attractiveness of their "product" was key to driving the business, not least because the percentage of goods sold relative to the volume on offer via social commerce were often "as low as fifteen percent" (Azeez 2015).

> Fashion re-sale is a challenging business, not least because it requires a high level of consumer participation. (Sherman 2016)

Their ambition was to create a natural extension of the app where the Depop community could get together and inspire each other, providing multifunctional spaces to help bridge the gap between online and offline (Chitrakorn 2018). From the start Depop had always welcomed the user community into its offices. Beckerman had identified that encouraging creative conversations and supporting "culture shapers" digitally and physically was a key pillar of the brand, and he and Raga wanted to be active and visible in both domains.

At the end of January 2018, Simon Beckerman and Maria Raga of Depop sat down to discuss the next stages in building the company. Raga had recently announced in an interview that they had secured US$20 million in series B funding, Raga stated:

> The investment will support the global growth of the platform, particularly in the US, and scale the business. This will include the opening of bricks-and-mortar beta spaces, which will help us get even closer to our users and experiment with new formats. (Terrelonge 2018)

Beckerman and Raga needed to firm up their plans regarding these beta physical spaces and to drive their strategy for growth.

Raga and Beckerman agreed on two locations that reflected their creative and cultural positioning, and in which they hoped to open bricks-and-mortar spaces for Depop: New York's China Town and the Silver Lake area of Los Angeles. Now they need to make decisions on the value proposition that will determine how they will design and use the spaces for launch.

Back in 2015 Beckerman had said that he would like Depop to be a new and more modern version of eBay; he hoped that Depop would do so by tapping into millennials' enthusiasm for influencers and social media, as well as by considering their desire for a more personal and social shopping experience. Indeed, by 2018 the resale market, with its retail appeal for Generation Z and millennials who frequently hunt for value, vintage, and unique items was starting to be seen by many investment companies as a major opportunity and was generating considerable funding from investors, especially for digital marketplaces. In the United States, there are already a number of medium-to-large players across all levels of the market and the volume of investment has increased the intensity of competition where businesses are engaged in a race for growth and market share. Depop feels that focusing on the United States will present the best opportunity to deliver international scale. They also recognize that in order to scale internationally they will also need to drive brand awareness and engagement. Could creating physical experiences contribute to widescale US brand awareness? How could the planned spaces help them get closer to their customers, bridging the gap between online and offline retail? What propositions, products, functions, and services would inspire more US customers to explore Depop and become loyal users of the app; both as buyers and sellers? What value propositions and business model opportunities would best enable them to compete in the United States and ultimately globally?

Business Questions

1 Is venturing into physical space a wise move to aid Depop's community development and brand awareness in the United States, or could it represent a costly diversion from their core activity of running a digital marketplace and scaling the online transactions through growing their user base?

2 If physical spaces were to prove a key element of the growth and market penetration strategy, what should the customer value proposition be? What should the spaces look like? What cultural and retail-based experiences could they host and curate, and how could they bridge the gap between online and offline and reach a wider audience?

3 From Depop's perspective, the fundamental business issue is how to grow across the US market.

   • Depop has a distinct brand personality that effectively taps into the teenage and millennial zeitgeist in the UK. How could they develop this to achieve a high level of brand awareness across the United States, driving the number of users and transactions quickly?

   • What would inspire more US customers to explore and become loyal users of the app? What customer value could Depop add?

4 The market has been described as a "momentum business" where the resale markets are only as attractive as the sellers and users that they represent. Is Beckerman and Raga's focus on "cool community engagement" sufficient to compete with larger established businesses in the United States and Europe and those who have generated larger sums in various rounds of funding?

   • Could the stated aim for largely organic growth compete in a potentially "winner takes all" environment and one where the social media giants could still enter the market?

5 The millennial desire for "friction free" transactions means that functions, services, and security need continuous improvement from in-house or collaborative research and development teams.

- What features might provide a competitive advantage for Depop and how might these be developed?

- How important is brand trust in developing the number of buyers and sellers? How could Depop drive brand trust in the United States?

- We have already seen collaborations between Poshmark and Amazon; what are the opportunities and risks for Depop? Make specific reference to the competition for growth in the United States?

References and Further Reading

Azeez, Walé. 2015. "Depop: We're all Shopkeepers Now." *Politico*, October 27. Accessed July 20, 2018. https://www.politico.eu/article/depop-were-all-shopkeepers-now/

Banks, Emma. 2017. "Simon Beckerman Talks What's Next for Depop." *Milk XYZ*, April 24. Accessed July 20, 2018. https://milk.xyz/articles/simon-beckerman-talks-whats-next-for-depop/

Brignall, Miles. 2017. "It's Part-eBay, Part-Instagram, but is Depop Safe for Your Teenagers? *The Guardian*, June 3. Accessed July 20, 2018. https://www.theguardian.com/money/2017/jun/03/depop-ebay-instagram-teenagers-buy-sell-risks-fraud

Chitrakorn, Kati. 2018. "Depop Secures $20 Million for US Expansion." *Business of Fashion*, January 23. Accessed July 20, 2018. https://www.businessoffashion.com/articles/news-bites/depop-secures-20-million-for-us-expansion

Christy, Sophie. 2015. "Fed up with eBay? Sell on Etsy, Depop and Folksy instead." *The Telegraph*, March 30. Accessed 20 July 2018. https://www.telegraph.co.uk/finance/personalfinance/money-saving-tips/11490640/Fed-up-of-eBay-Sell-on-Etsy-Depop-and-Folksy-instead.html

Crunchbase. n.d. Depop." Accessed July 20, 2018. https://www.crunchbase.com/organization/depop

Crunchbase. n.d. Overview, Seed Round." Accessed December 7, 2018. https://www.crunchbase.com/funding_round/depop-seed–e8009314#section-overview

Datafox. n.d. Depop." Accessed July 20, 2018. https://datafox.com/competitors/depop

Depop. n.d.-a. "Buy. Sell. Discover." Accessed December 29, 2018. https://www.depop.com

Depop. n.d.-b. Shipping Guide US." Accessed December 7, 2018. https://depophelp.zendesk.com/hc/en-gb/articles/360001790787-Shipping-guide-US

IBISWorld. 2018. *Second-Hand Goods Stores - UK Market Research Report*. February. Accessed July 20, 2018. https://www.ibisworld.co.uk/industry-trends/market-research-reports/wholesale-retail-trade/except-of-motor-vehicles-motorcycles/second-hand-goods-stores.html

Knowles, Kitty. 2018. "Depop CEO: Solving 3 Big Problems For Young Cool Shoppers." *Forbes* April 26,. Accessed December 3, 2018. https://www.forbes.com/sites/kittyknowles/2018/04/26/depop-ceo-solving-3-big-problems-for-young-cool-shoppers/#46cfb7be7b40

Made in Shoreditch. n.d. Start Up in Shoreditch: Interview with Simon Beckerman Founder of Depop." December 10. Accessed July 20, 2018. http://madeinshoreditch.co.uk/2013/12/10/startup-in-shoreditch-interview-with-simon-beckerman-founder-of-depop/

Morrison, Emma. n.d. In Conversation with Depop founder Simon Beckerman." *Artefact*. Accessed July 20, 2018. http://www.artefactmagazine.com/2015/01/14/in-conversation-with-depop-founder-simon-beckerman/

Osterwalder, Alexander and Yves Pigneur. 2010. *Business Model Generation*. Hoboken, NJ: Wiley.

Remsen, Nick. 2017. "How the Clothes-selling Platform Depop is Creating Young Entrepreneurs." *Financial Times*, March 2. Accessed July 20, 2018. https://www.ft.com/content/67de4da6-fed4-11e6-8d8e-a5e3738f9ae4

Satenstein, Liana. 2016. "All Those Millennials Can't Be Wrong: Why Depop Just Might Change the Way You Shop." *Vogue*, March 31. Accessed July 20, 2018. https://www.vogue.com/article/depop-millennial-friendly-shopping-app

Sherman, Lauren. 2016. "Resale Sites Prepare for Battle." *Business of Fashion*, May 11. Accessed July 20, 2018. https://www.businessoffashion.com/articles/fashion-tech/resale-sites-recommerce-online-vintage-real-real-thredup-vestiaire-collective-tradesy-poshmark

Strategyzer. n.d. Canvases, Tools and More." Accessed July 20, 2018. https://strategyzer.com/canvas

Terrelonge, Zen. 2016. "New CEO takes Helm at Depop as Social Shopping Platform Secures $8.25m Investment." *RealBusiness*, October 3. Accessed August 8, 2018. https://realbusiness.co.uk/funding/2016/10/03/social-shopping-platform-depop-gets-new-ceo-and-investment/

Terrelonge, Zen. 2018. "Depop Pockets $20m Series B Investment to Drive US Growth." *RealBusiness*, January 23. Accessed July 20, 2018. https://realbusiness.co.uk/funding/2018/01/23/social-shopping-service-depop-pockets-20m-series-b-investment/

Thredup. 2018. *2018 Resale Report*. Accessed July 23, 2018. https://cf-assets-tup.thredup.com/resale_report/2018/2018-resaleReport.pdf

Whatling, Eve. 2018. "Mobile Magnates." *The Economist 1843*, February/March. Accessed July 20, 2018. https://www.1843magazine.com/style/mobile-magnates

Definitions

Customer value proposition: The benefits that a company provides to a consumer in order to encourage them to use their service.

Seed funding: The initial round of capital financing to support the early development of a business, offered in exchange for equity.

Series B funding: The second round of capital financing for a start-up business. At this stage the product/service is usually already being sold to the market.

Chapter 34

Ellistons Department Store

Merchandising Strategies for a Multichannel Retailer

Anthony Kent, Justine Davidson and Ruby Fowler

Retailing in physical stores and digital channels, online and mobile, has become increasingly important but also more complex. Distribution and communication channels need to be integrated to make shopping easier through a seamless customer experience of the brand. This case demonstrates how organizational management and the operational function of merchandising can cause major problems in achieving these objectives. In particular, it focuses on the location of inventory and how it is managed to avoid "stock outs" in different channels. The case is based on an anonymized fashion retailer with multiple physical stores and a strong online presence. It shows how this retailer has created a competitive advantage with its "endless aisle" inventory management strategy whose aim is to make shopping easier. Nevertheless, increasingly demanding customers who want access to more merchandise, immediate availability, and fast delivery to convenient delivery points, raise questions about the location of the inventory, who manages it and how. The case asks students to consider whether retailers should set limits on merchandise assortment and its availability and whether merchandise managers in the future will have to be "informed editors of choice."

Learning Objectives

Upon completion of this case, students should be able to:

- Critically assess how the management of multichannel retailing determines the operational integration of different distribution channels. The case illustrates how a seamless approach to managing different channels increases consumer satisfaction.

- Analyze the organization of multichannel retailing and explain its contribution to creating a competitive retail position.
- Examine the role of merchandisers and their contribution to successful multichannel retailing.
- Explain the operational functionality of merchandising and inventory management in the context of multichannel retailing.
- Identify and develop future scenarios for merchandising in multichannel retailing.
- Analyze and learn from industry practice and consider strategies for developing seamless customer experiences across retail and communication channels.
- Examine the dynamic between online business and store management and how it poses a fundamental incentive problem.

Introduction

This case explores merchandise management and its contribution to successful multichannel fashion retailing. With the development of e-commerce, online retailing has become increasingly important but also more complex. For fashion retailers, merchandising and sales in physical stores, website and mobile channels require close attention to product range planning and stock control. Customers shopping in online channels now have high expectations about product availability and retailer communications about the product, i.e. they want to buy what they can see online. Satisfaction levels are worryingly low: over a third of UK retailers who claimed to offer a multichannel service experienced an increase in customer complaints.

Central to multichannel retailing is a "one brand—one message" strategy. The emergence of this integrated approach to multichannel management is rooted in the need to ensure the recognition of a single brand across multiple channels in the eyes of the customer. These efforts focus on the relationship between retailers and their customers, and the need to maximize the potential of each channel by creating a seamless experience across all channels. This unity, however, is often missing in decentralized and nonintegrated companies where products differ between online stores and bricks-and-mortar stores and the look and feel of a brand can be quite different depending on the channel.

Examples of different approaches are evident across the fashion sector. For example, at UK department store John Lewis, all "click and collect" orders are dispatched from a warehouse, which customers like because they know they will get a new, untouched item. Marks and Spencer have made similar improvements to their fulfilment strategy, implementing a "buy online and collect in store" strategy. In this case, if the distribution center is out of stock, there is a selection of larger stores which can fulfil the order from their own stockholding.

Although multichannel opens up new views of retailing, for many companies implementing the required changes is not an easy process. Despite the call for integration across channels, the relationship between them remains suspicious or even hostile in some instances. This history of competition between store and e-commerce functions is firmly rooted in the notion that e-commerce is cannibalizing the business of traditional stores, which remain burdened with individual sales targets and managing their own profit and loss without considering online revenues. The dynamic between the online business and the stores poses a fundamental incentive problem: Why would a store manager suggest to a customer that they can find an item online if it detracts from that manager's individual targets? And why would a Sales Associate direct a customer online if their earnings derive partly from a commission?

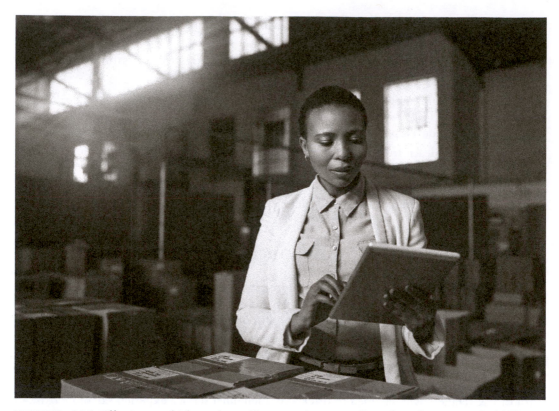

FIGURE 34.1 Effective multichannel retailing requires coordinated and integrated fulfillment strategies. © Hiraman/E+/Getty Images

This antagonistic relationship poses a significant challenge to retailers in terms of their long-term customer relationship management. Research has demonstrated that customer engagement with retailers across more than one retail channel leads to higher levels of loyalty (Fernández-Sabiote, and Román 2012). In the words of one retail manager:

> each channel takes part in a virtuous circle in each promoting the other ... every customer lost to e-commerce is a customer who spends less in every other channel and with the company.

In response to these developments, multichannel retailers have adopted a variety of organizational strategies to engage with consumers, ranging from a "silo" approach to a fully integrated model, with most companies falling in between these two extremes. A typical operational strategy for entrants into multichannel retailing, based on a store-based channel and online website, is through organizational "silos;" independent teams working in different functions. These maintain a distinction between channels: an online group of merchandisers and distribution specialists manage the new business separately from the team in the retail stores. In the early stages, an online business often gets overshadowed as traditional retail activities dominate the organization's attention.

Most retailers, however, have moved away from this organizational structure and have progressed towards integrating their online business with other departmental and operational functions. For some companies the business as a whole reaches a point where the benefits of integrating the online and the retail store operations outweigh maintenance of a separate online business. Others identify the potential to reduce expenses through shared buying of inputs and the promise of shared knowledge and expertise through integrated channel management. For many companies, a major challenge is the middle management and its organization to achieve the acceptance of integrated services.

Pressure on resources and rapid advances in technology influence the relationship between different departments and teams including strategy, operations, and IT to form a barrier to integrated planning and practices. Investment in IT is needed to match the rate of change in the online environment and that in turn determines organizational integration. The challenge of multichannel retailing lies in the speed of technological change and the need to integrate everybody with new systems and ways of working.

In addressing these obstacles, the retail sector has developed a hybrid organizational model that integrates some strategic and operational aspects of the business while maintaining distinct functions in other respects. Some companies have practices that maintain separate stock systems for online and offline retail stores, despite a high level of integration with other functions such as marketing and buying, because their systems lack the operational capacity to ensure accurate "down-to-the-last-one" stock management. This inhibits the introduction of "click and collect" programs or the utilization of online kiosks in stores. Despite these operational challenges, many retailers have achieved an integrated approach to the practices of marketing and branding on their websites. However, they have yet to fully develop an ability to manage their merchandise across different channels.

Business Problem

Ellistons is a large department store retailer in the UK, with a large international presence in nearly thirty countries. It has a strong heritage in fashion, on which it has focused since the 1980s and it is well known for its collaborations with fashion designers that contribute a fresh and distinctive "look" to its fashion business. Womenswear forms the largest sales category, accounting for over 17 percent of the company's turnover: £2.3 billion with profits of £126 million in 2016. Its importance is expected to drive future growth through increased market share and improved profitability. However, the retailer's performance in this sector has been modest as fashion retailing has faced a number of challenges.

The retailer's strategy is based on four objectives: to focus on the UK, to deliver a compelling customer proposition, to increase merchandise availability and choice through multichannel retailing, and to expand the international accessibility of the brand. The multichannel strategy, in the view of the company's CEO, is all about making shopping easier for the consumer and in part this will be achieved by having more accurate and appropriate stockholdings across all channels. The strategy should provide more choice and availability by extending the number of brands and fashion categories to customers, while increasing the variety of delivery options. With more ways to shop, the company plans to extend the design and content of its mobile, website and in-store points of contact. The result of this more integrated approach should improve the company's customer experience and brand loyalty. In the meantime, while some progress has been made to achieve these aims, the company still retains a "horizontal" approach to its operational organization, with its focus on layers of management and distinctive functions.

Ellistons' multichannel strategy

Ellistons' multichannel strategy is to increase availability and choice through multichannel operations, specifically to grow the online business. Customer focus is particularly important in womenswear, as it is a mature and highly competitive market. With "time-poor" customers seeking ways of saving shopping time, they no longer want to be dependent on opening hours or location and 24/7 availability has become the norm. As over 60 percent of Ellistons' customers have used an online channel in the previous twelve months, this is an important function. Moreover, online is estimated to grow to 30 percent of their business by 2020 mostly coming from the mobile channel. In the past, online sales have demonstrated an annual growth rate of nearly 40 percent as customers have increasingly turned to multiple channels to buy fashion clothing. However, app usage on mobile devices lags behind and this is an area where Ellistons has identified a development need and has prioritized device specific content and usage in store.

A distinctive strategic innovation for Ellistons which has set it apart from other retailers is the "endless aisle" strategy. The strategy addresses the problem of having the right merchandise in the right place to maximize online, offline, and mobile sales. For some retailers, such as US company Macy's, the strategy is used to hold stock offsite and customer orders are fulfilled direct from the supplier. In this case "endless aisle" makes a big difference in terms of order fulfilment by enabling the company to deliver online orders from stock held for distribution to stores. The initiative not only offers customers a more seamless channel experience, but it also reduces the risk of having inventory in the wrong location; fewer "out of stocks" lead to higher sales and ultimately profit. It has revolutionized the ways orders are fulfilled and led to the company winning the "Retail Technology" initiative of the year award in 2013.

A second element of their multichannel fashion strategy is the enhancement of customer experience. Ellistons has been criticized for poor customer service with perceptions of poor staffing levels and attitude to customers. Although the company was ranked in the top 10 percent of retailers in a consultancy report on multichannel retailing, it was the only major department store not to make it into the actual top ten. It performed relatively weakly due to its absence of real-time stock information and site navigation tools, and for having too many out of stock products. These problems are contextualized by a view of the future of retailing as a consumer-centric model that is "total retail."

A third key element is order fulfilment, with increasing pressure to deliver products more quickly as companies race to achieve same day "click and collect" while minimizing their costs. The long-term goal for retailers should be to drive this process within a timeframe of as little as two to three hours. However, this is only really achievable with fulfilment from store stocks. Following the success of its "endless aisle" format and the lack of similar services from their competitors, Ellistons had the opportunity to create a faster fulfilment service and made some progress in this direction with orders taken and collected within the store, known as self-fulfil. The process benefits both the retailer in terms of cost-to-service, and the customer, as it is inherently faster. Notably, customers prefer the "view availability in stores" function to "click and collect" in their shopping journey. While the first steps in this faster and more customer-focused initiative have been taken, there is still scope for improvement.

A key issue is lack of availability with some 45 percent of retailers failing to supply products that had been searched for online and overall, around 10 percent of online users are not satisfied with their customer experience. Key problems highlighted were online orders being cancelled without warning, poor customer service, and late delivery. This is a serious issue for Ellistons as the consumer falls back on "generalizations from experience" to determine their responses next time round without undertaking any additional learning. It can lead to the consumer condemning a whole range of products and implicating the brand as well.

More broadly, online users now know exactly what they want and are using search engines to find specific items but find that retailers offer other services, or worse, annoy them by showing them items they cannot have because they are out of stock. There appears to be a mismatch between the retailer's priorities and consumer expectations: while retailers respond to the demand for faster deliveries, consumers really want to ensure that what they see on the screen is actually in stock. This all suggests that consumers seek control of their shopping experience and to be able to browse and order in the fastest possible way, across all devices. They are increasingly intolerant of not having control and being forced to choose company-determined paths in their shopping journey.

A further consideration in stock management and availability for Ellistons and its competitors has been the consumer's changing sequences for product searching and purchasing. They may undertake their search online before visiting stores or at the same time, using a mobile device. This can take the form of "showrooming," with consumers researching in store, for example, trying on clothes and shoes for fit, and buying the same product more cheaply online. However, the majority of customers still want to go to a store to try on and feel the product before purchasing and the use of online services in store has become much more established. Kiosks, interactive screens and devices enable customers to look up items online and order into the store if, for example, the right size is not available. As one store executive commented "we get a lot of people who have browsed online and then come into store expecting to see the full range … and that is why it is good that we have kiosks to order from, and they can get next day click and collect instore." And as consumers become more expert in making choices, the pressure on management responses can only increase.

Range planning

Ensuring the availability of merchandise in each channel is a key role of Ellistons' merchandisers. Their function is to develop range plans to determine the extent of the range, with the number of different lines and SKUs (stock keeping units), the amount of each product to be bought, and its delivery to store. The process begins with sales analysis, the development of a sales plan, and finally an assortment plan. It involves the review of current seasonal sales, space and sales planning, financial parameters and category plans, and typically, analysis of past sales performance to inform future trend and sales forecasts.

At Ellistons, past sales performance is not analyzed by channel but at product level across all channels. Moreover, online analysis is not necessarily undertaken at the planning stage but takes place later in the merchandising process. This means that a range with a high level of online sales at around 22 percent of the sales mix is managed in the same way as ranges with lower online sales. Other managers see the problem as one of data analysis, comparing in-store and online sales and the speed of reaction needed to respond to changes. At least one of Ellistons' competitors has developed their sales plan through online and like-for-like physical store channel "building-blocks."

Online performance is analyzed for its fit with strategy, budgeting, range planning, and stock management. The assortment planning process varies by retailer and by the merchandiser's preferences. However, it must balance style, color, core and fashion, size, and price point, with sufficient stock to meet sales targets. At Ellistons, merchandisers discuss these dimensions in terms of category planning (products) and stock phasing (quantity and time) but spend less time on decision-making about the locations and processes to improve order fulfilment through all of the channels.

After assortment planning, a second key role for merchandisers is stock management, which involves responsibilities to manage intake and commitment to accommodate the stock requirements of the business and to manage the stock distributions to stores optimizing customer demand, available selling space, and seasonal selling opportunities (Jackson and Shaw 2001). The process is normally managed by a team comprising the merchandiser, logistics manager, and operations manager. However, multichannel introduces a high degree of complexity. Each combination of service and destination requires a different fulfilment process to be in place with the role of logistics and merchandising being predominantly day-to-day management of orders.

Inventory management

Despite the "endless aisle strategy" one issue highlighted at Ellistons is the difficulty of moving stock between "free stock" available to stores and the online stock holding. As a manager observed "there shouldn't be any reason to prevent online stock that is not selling to be sent out to store if needed. There needs to be one place for stock to service both online and stores." At present when stock goes from different DCs (distribution centers) it cannot be recalled and it should be possible to feed the retail store stock from online stockholdings if particular lines are not performing well. Alternative solutions to this problem are seen at retailers Next and Sainsbury's, which both have a virtual online warehouse within the main warehouse, which means stock can be easily and freely moved between channels. As a result, it can be switched between online and stores at any time, so the stock is used to its full potential.

Ellistons' operations team have challenged the limitations of their stock movements: moving stock between online and store can be achieved in twenty-four hours but the managerial sign-off and agreement to fund the costs of the movement is perceived as the cause of delays. Stock management should not incur costs to the company because as a competitor explained "a single stock pool warehouse solution is the utopia of multichannel retailing. Moving stock between different fulfilment warehouses is margin erosive." However, Ellistons has three major distribution centers, which serve different purposes. This means that stock has to be physically moved between them. Merchandise does not always go to the DC where the online fulfilment takes place and so time can be lost in processing the goods out of the DC and sending them back to the online DC before being made available to customers.

The role of online merchandisers is to manage the coverage of departments and promotions via the website and emails, and manage stock for key lines and events. Online merchandising is undertaken in a separate division from the merchandising to stores due to the different requirements of the team and to allow the company to focus on more in-depth analysis of online trading. An important part of their analysis is customers' shopping habits across the web and mobile channels. They respond by updating and evolving the website to create additional categories based on current trends or seasons and track customers' engagement with these. Moreover, they access a lot of information and analysis that other merchandisers do not. This points to their findings being used at the planning stage, especially as the target for online sales is a quarter of the total sales mix. Senior managers would like them to be more involved in the merchandising strategy and to feedback and contribute to the online strategy for the whole department.

Although separate to the core womenswear buying and merchandising division, it is seen as very important that the team are aware of all merchandising decisions so they can trade effectively across sites and channels. However, the relationship between core merchandising and online is not as effective as it should be to deliver operational efficiencies. The merchandisers thought they definitely could do with more communication, as they don't see each other regularly enough, probably only once or twice a season. Other retailers demonstrate differing approaches to merchandiser integration; George at ASDA have integrated their online merchandisers into their core teams so they sit amongst the main team and liaise regularly rather than as separate dot-com merchandisers. At John Lewis, organizational integration is performed by an online merchandise assistant in the core merchandise teams who can micromanage the online business through detailed performance analysis and offer practical support. However, online merchandisers do not have any input into order quantities at the planning stage, although they should be more involved in suggesting online quantities to be added to store volumes. The company finds it just does not have sufficient time to do this type of analysis for every brand. Having someone to do this could deliver a huge benefit.

Another key area of online merchandising growth is the concept of the online platform being a retailers' flagship store, offering more options and width of ranges than any of the physical stores. As one retailer explained, "the real benefit to the customer is that he or she has access to the broadest offer possible when shopping online." Ellistons do offer some online exclusive lines and some extra sizes, and the merchandisers feel there is room to develop these further, finding from their analysis that bigger sizes sell better online than in store. This led them to trial size 24s online and later offer petite sizes in at least one of the ranges. Lines sold exclusively online provide a more attractive proposition to the customer, something the merchandisers are always looking to expand. However, there is evidence from both customers and store managers that they would prefer to see more options in store. In fact, the CEO feels that it could be easy to give too many online options, because online sites—unlike physical stores—are perceived as limitless. Instead, merchandisers should be "informed editors of choice" offering the customer the product they truly believe in rather than every possible option, as a means to grow customer loyalty.

The emergence of an integrated approach to multichannel management is rooted in the need to unify all channels under one business for the customer and to ensure the recognition of a single brand across multiple channels. For many fashion retailers, customer experience is an increasingly important success factor and its successful management may make the difference between future success and failure.

Business Questions

This case raises questions that look beyond the strategy of multichannel retailing to the often neglected operational problems that arise from its organization and implementation.

1 Although Ellistons has made progress in responding to the challenges of multichannel retailing, it must continue to develop its order fulfilment strategy to maintain its competitive position. Which is the most feasible and acceptable option?
2 The multichannel strategy, in the view of the company's CEO, is all about making shopping easier. What are the key resource and organizational elements needed to make this happen?
3 The analysis of online performance should be central to the merchandising plan, rather than separately managed. How and when should it be integrated—and who should make the decisions?
4 In what ways does the merchandising function contribute to consistent customer satisfaction across the channels? This question addresses a fundamental problem of

accessibility and availability of merchandise in store and through digital channels; to what extent is this a critical element of online service?

5 Explain multichannel customer experience and how it can be managed. The customer expects a seamless service across all channels; this question can be used to explore experience, part tangible (merchandise, the store itself, retail staff) and part intangible (the sensory environment, the quality of service). It is often difficult to manage intangible experiences, and students should explore the case study to understand how experiences can be holistically managed.

6 How can Ellistons effectively build their assortment plans to integrate the different channels and manage their stock effectively? This is a more detailed question appropriate to a merchandising or operational management course. What are the implications of the "endless aisle"? Consider the locational issues of inventory and the need to provide fast and accurate delivery to customers.

7 What organizational change is required to allow Ellistons to achieve efficient omni-channel retailing and how will it be implemented and managed? Omni-channel is proposed as a completely integrated form of multichannel retailing, from both retailer and customer perspectives. What further integration needs to take place, what changes need to be made, who will manage the channels and where will they be positioned in the organization?

8 Online sites can be seen as presenting "limitless" merchandising opportunities but what are the problems with this perception? What should the boundaries be?

9 Develop a plan to enable merchandisers to be "informed editors of choice" which also strengthens control over stock and finances. "Informed editors of choice" deserves detailed discussion; what sort of knowledge do editors need to make informed choices? How will they know what are the right choices and how will the retailer manage them?

References and Further Reading

Fernández-Sabiote, Estela, and Sergio Román. 2012. "Adding Clicks to Bricks: A Study of the Consequences on Customer Loyalty in a Service Context." *Electronic Commerce Research and Applications* 11, no. 1 (January–February): 36–48.

Frasquet, Marta, and Maria-José Miquel 2017. "Do Channel Integration Efforts Pay-Off in Terms of Online and Offline Customer Loyalty?" *International Journal of Retail & Distribution Management* 45, no. 7/8: 859–873.

Jackson, Tim, and David Shaw. 2001. *Mastering Fashion Buying and Merchandising Management.* Basingstoke: Palgrave.

PART SIX

Entrepreneurship and Fashion Law

Introduction

This section includes case studies that focus on the decisions that professionals in the fashion industry make in the areas of entrepreneurship and fashion law. Fashion entrepreneurship is the process of creating new businesses within the fashion industry, including businesses related to design, branding, marketing, technology, and/or retailing. Starting a new fashion business is a common goal for many students in fashion-related programs and courses. Fashion entrepreneurs are the individuals who start these new businesses, and they are faced with multiple decisions as they launch their businesses. Case studies on entrepreneurship focus on fashion entrepreneurs weighing the advantages and disadvantages of alternative courses of action in launching and sustaining their new businesses.

Fashion law is "that area of law that deals with the day-to-day business problems of the fashion industry" (Jimenez and Kolsun 2010, p. 3). Fashion professionals are faced with challenges and opportunities related to legal aspects of running their businesses. Case studies related to fashion law focus on decisions that fashion professionals must make to ensure that their businesses are complying with regulations associated with:

- Forms of business ownership (e.g., sole proprietorship, partnership, corporation).
- Ownership and licensing of intellectual property (e.g., trademarks, tradenames, patents).
- The operation and management of their fashion businesses.

(Burns and Mullet 2020)

References and Further Reading

Burns, Leslie Davis and Kathy K. Mullet (2020). *The Business of Fashion: Designing, Manufacturing, and Marketing*. New York: Fairchild Books/Bloomsbury.

Granger, Michele M., Tina M. Sterling, and Ann Cantrell (2019). *Fashion Entrepreneurship: Retail Business Planning*. 3rd ed. New York: Fairchild Books/Bloomsbury.

Jimenez, Guillermo C. and Barbara Kolsun (2010). *Fashion Law: A Guide for Designers, Fashion Executives, and Attorneys*. New York: Fairchild Books.

Chapter 35

Kickstarting a Brand

Using Crowdfunding to Launch a Brand

Eda Sanchez-Persampieri and Marie Segares

After splitting with his long-time business partner, John Grimes is seeking a new entrepreneurial venture. He is unsure of the direction to take in terms of product development but is confident his entrepreneurial mindset will lead him to a successful idea. After a significant amount of research and sampling, John creates an apparel product with a great marketing story. He does not have the resources to self-fund (bootstrap) his idea and attempts to obtain investor funding. He pitches his idea to several investors, but each scoff at the feasibility of it. As a last-ditch effort, he decides to use the crowdfunding platform, Kickstarter, to obtain funding and launch his idea. He sells nearly $300,000 of merchandise in less than thirty days to more than 5,500 customers or, in Kickstarter parlance, "backers." His innovative concept breaks all apparel funding records on Kickstarter but what did this mean? Can John build a scalable company around his innovative idea? Or was this just a one-off project?

Learning Objectives

Upon completion of this case, students should be able to:

- Identify challenges associated with transitioning and scaling from a crowdfunding project to a men's lifestyle brand with multicategory product offerings.
- Understand the role of funding and sourcing and production in the entrepreneurial process.
- Comprehend the importance of developing an entrepreneurial mindset and developing an effective, collaborative team.
- Analyze entrepreneurial business situations and demonstrate a working knowledge of the planning and strategy processes that lead to a sustainable startup enterprise.

Introduction

In 2011, after an acrimonious and financially damaging split with his business partner, John Grimes was looking for the "next hot thing." John was unsure how to proceed but was confident his entrepreneurial skills would lead him to an innovative and scalable idea. His previous business was product-driven and focused on differentiated versions of a multiuse product that was sold within the gift industry sector. John beta-tested a few different products with the goal of duplicating his previous business model and building a startup enterprise around a single product. John's research, rapid prototyping, and testing quickly yielded many possible product ideas.

After additional targeted market research, John focused on innovating men's premium underwear. John had no fashion industry experience but did have extensive media and brand launching experience. He named his new venture Chert and Char (CAC) and used his Brooklyn loft as CAC's offices. John did not have the resources to bootstrap his idea and attempted instead to obtain venture capital or angel investor funding. He pitched his idea to several investors but was rejected by all of them, many scoffed at the feasibility of his idea. As a last-ditch effort, John decided to use the crowdfunding platform, Kickstarter, to obtain funding and launch his idea. He received pledges to the value of nearly $300,000 in less than thirty days from more than 5,500 "backers."

Entrepreneurial mindset

There is much debate centered around the nature versus nurture aspect of entrepreneurship. Some believe the skills and inclination for entrepreneurship cannot be learned and one must be a born entrepreneur. Others believe entrepreneurship is a mindset and can be learned. The entrepreneurial mindset is a set of attitudes, skills, and behaviors that include initiative and self-direction, risk-taking, flexibility and adaptability, creativity and innovation, critical thinking, and problem solving. John Grimes possesses, whether innately or learned, the entrepreneurial mindset.

Crowdfunding and important platforms

Crowdfunding is considered a nontraditional, alternative technique to raise the funds needed to launch and/or sustain a project idea, cause, or startup company. Capital is raised through a collective pool of individuals who invest small amounts. The concept of crowdfunding can be traced back through the centuries, and one well-known example is the eighteenth-century author Alexander Pope, who crowdfunded the publication costs for his translation of *The Iliad* (Strähle and Bulling 2018). The concept of crowdfunding evolved and many attribute the modern-day launch of online crowdfunding initiatives to the rock band Marillion, who in 1997 solicited fan contributions to fund a record and concert tour (Strähle and Bulling 2018).

Since 1997, crowdfunding models have further evolved and developed distinct categories with specific end goals. The categories include rewards-based, donation-based, equity-based, peer-to-peer lending, and hybrids of the four main categories. John utilized the rewards-based crowdfunding category for his project. To broaden the exposure of his crowdfunding initiative, John leveraged his own social media networks as well as funder networks associated with the crowdfunding platforms.

Business Problem

Overnight success

John was initially quite sceptical of crowdfunding his idea and anticipated his campaign would not achieve the funding goal of $30,000. He was quite surprised when the funding goal was reached within a week and grew exponentially to reach $300,000 within thirty days. CAC became the new record holder for the most funded apparel project on Kickstarter, far surpassing the previous record by nearly a factor of five. John created a public relations goldmine by leveraging CAC's Kickstarter success with his extensive network of media connections. He was touted as the upstart outsider who was disrupting a stagnant business sector; top press outlets such as *WWD, Forbes, FastCompany, Sourcing Journal*, and *Entrepreneur* uniformly praised him for innovating the sector through his method of sale, reshoring techniques, and marketing approach. Even John's fractious ex-business partner, Peter, called to congratulate him. Why, then, had John been waking up in a cold sweat since day fifteen of the campaign?

Empathize, define, ideate, prototype, and test

During his rapid prototyping stage, John sourced a local New York City sample maker and contracted for samples costing $75 each, plus over $1,000 (and counting) in pattern-making fees. John quickly learned that men's underwear is very complicated to sew and requires more construction precision than other apparel. John had no idea how to mass produce nearly 30,000 total units of underwear within the thirty- to sixty-day delivery timeframe. Worse yet, he had sold his underwear for $15 per unit or, in Kickstarter parlance, he "owed" backers a "reward" for each $15 funded. His sample maker offered two factory recommendations and John immediately made appointments with each.

At each appointment, the factory owner was distrustful of John. Neither of the factory owners had heard of Kickstarter and wanted to know which retailers were buying all this underwear. They could not understand John's distribution channel strategy. Both factory owners were nonplussed by John's expectations to deliver so many products within thirty days and asked him a battery of questions for which he was unprepared, including whether he already owned the fabric, if he had production patterns and a cutting room and demanding to know specifics about his logistic arrangements. Each factory quoted him around $10 per unit but the quote covered only sewing and packing and did not include fabric and other material costs, cutting, or logistics. John was frantic, feeling like a victim of his own success.

The first hire

After meeting with the factory owners, John stopped at a café to relax and think about his problems. During this break, he caught snippets of a conversation between the café owner, Chloe Beauchamp, and another patron. He couldn't believe his luck. Chloe was speaking about her experience as part of the team that launched Jonathan Kean, a mega-successful apparel brand. Perhaps, she could help him somehow. John quickly explained his situation to Chloe and asked if she would be willing to work with him. Chloe was a fashion-industry veteran with nearly twenty years in brand building, product development, and sourcing experience. She was intrigued by the concept of using Kickstarter as a customer-acquisition tool and to share apparel as "rewards" to the community of backers. She agreed to help John with the sourcing and production, but could only devote fifteen to twenty hours each week to working on the project. Chloe explained to John that a sixty- to seventy-five-day production-logistics cycle was a realistic goal.

The team dynamics

With his sourcing and production problems somewhat under control, John focused on building a small team. John recognized the urgent need for someone to assist with overseeing the website buildout, package development, customer service inquiries, and media and marketing related tasks. He placed an ad on Craigslist (an American classified advertisement website) and after interviewing a few candidates, he hired Monica Formosa. Monica was a graduate of a fashion college with nearly three years of marketing and digital media experience, but her apparel industry expertise was limited. John believed she would apply innovative approaches to the challenges faced by CAC.

After extending the offer of employment to Monica, he asked Chloe to meet with Monica after telling Chloe that he will rescind the job offer if she doesn't like Monica. Chloe was a little confused by this statement, as John had already offered Monica the job. Chloe was concerned that Monica might have already resigned from her current employer, and wondered how the situation would play out if she in fact did not like Monica. Chloe thanked John for including her but suggested that he should have included her in the initial interview process rather than post-hire. The interaction was uncomfortable for both of them. Chloe began to doubt John's leadership abilities, and John felt reprimanded by Chloe.

CAC needed to fill an accounting and operations role. Again, John placed an ad on Craigslist and, after several interviews, selected Rob Morton as the best candidate. After the previous encounter, John decided that Chloe and Monica should meet with Rob prior to any employment offer. Chloe did not have much time to meet with Rob because she was busy finalizing the factory negotiations and running her café. After meeting very briefly with Rob and finding him "competent enough," Chloe hastily gave her approval as she did not have any extra time to meet with additional candidates. Monica, who had no experience with making hiring decisions, was unsure of Rob but deferred to Chloe's opinion.

A big growth idea

During their second weekly team meeting, Chloe asked John if he knew how Ralph Lauren started his empire. He did not, so Chloe explained that the multibillion-dollar apparel behemoth started off by selling ties—just ties. Monica remembered this story from her *Introduction to Fashion* textbook and stated John should do the same but with underwear. John was shocked at the apparent suggestion that he could launch a multibillion-dollar company. The idea of scaling his idea into an international industry leader was incredibly exciting, but John knew he couldn't bootstrap that type of growth in the present business environment. He would need significant capital to achieve a similar growth trajectory but obtaining funding would be a major challenge.

Growth potential and opportunities

The following week, John approached the investors that had previously rejected his funding request, confident one or two of them would be eager to invest in CAC, as he considered his

Kickstarter success as proof-of-concept and his media strategy was garnering CAC significant press coverage. Within a day, one of the investors offered John a debt deal of $250,000 at 12 percent interest with monthly interest-only payments and a balloon payment due within forty-eight months. As an extra incentive, the investor offered additional bridge funding of up to $350,000 based on CAC achieving certain revenue metrics within the first eighteen months.

Soon after the investor's offer, Jesus Wu contacted John and wanted to discuss his potential involvement with CAC. Jesus Wu, a well-known angel investor and CEO of a billion-dollar e-commerce site, had been cited by many industry experts as a "rockstar" entrepreneur and guru of customer service. Within a few days, John met with Jesus and his team. Jesus immediately recognized in John a kindred spirit with an entrepreneurial mindset, and offered John a handshake equity investment deal of $500,000 for 35 percent ownership of CAC.

At the next weekly team meeting, Monica suggested crowdfunding should become CAC's business model, confident the feature could be run through the CAC website. Rob immediately objected and explained, in a berating-tone, the operational problems created by this model, but Chloe cut him off, stating that crowdfunding is a viable idea and that preselling all items to order would reduce CAC's liquidity problem by significantly reducing inventory needs.

Business Questions

John realizes CAC has the potential and opportunity to develop into a multimillion—possibly multibillion—dollar lifestyle brand. Now John must decide which funding opportunity will be the most effective, and he needs to rethink the structure of his team and the team members.

1 Scalability:
   a. How can John build a scalable company around his innovative idea? By focusing on product extension? Brand extension? Innovating other stagnant apparel products?
   b. Can a fashion startup achieve financial sustainability by focusing on a single product, such as men's premium underwear, or should John evolve from a product-driven business model to a lifestyle-driven business model?
   c. Do the 5,500 backers represent brand equity? How can John leverage this to scale?

2 Financing:
   a. Should John seek equity or debt financing?
   b. Which type of investor is most feasible for CAC's growth?
   c. Should John consider crowdfunding as a business model?

3 Team building:
   a. Describe John's leadership style. Is it effective? Explain.
   b. Founder-CEOs are frequently replaced within the scaling phase of a company's existence. There are many reasons this might occur but often it is because of weak or inconsistent leadership skills and an inability to effectively lead the scaled organization. How can John revise his leadership approach and build his skillset to avoid this fate?
   c. Should John reconsider his current team members' roles within the company? Which roles does he need to fill or replace to build out his team? Who should be John's next new hires?

References and Further Reading

Barnett, Chance. 2014. "Crowdfunding Tips Proven To Raise Funding." *Forbes*, July 3. Accessed June 1, 2018. https://www.forbes.com/sites/chancebarnett/2014/07/03/7-crowdfunding-tips-proven-to-raise-funding/#1ae42b502a9d

Belleflamme, Paul, Thomas Lambert, and Armin Schwienbacher. 2014. "Crowdfunding: Tapping the Right Crowd." *Journal of Business Venturing* 29 (5): 585–609.

Chan, Jonathan. 2018. "16 Crowdfunding Experts Share Their Top Tips and Advice on How to Crush Your Next Crowdfunding Campaign." *Foundr.com*. Accessed June 1, 2018. https://foundr.com/crowdfunding-experts/

Fernandes, Clare, Madalena Pereira, José Lucas, Rui Miguel, and Manuel Santos Silva. 2016. "Entrepreneurship in the Fashion Industry: The New Paradigm." Global Fashion Conference, Stockholm University, October 21–22. Stockholm, Sweden.

Indiegogo. 2015. "8 Crowdfunding Tips from Crowdfunding Experts." *YouTube*, December 11. Accessed June 1, 2018. https://youtu.be/kec22Ng366U

Investopedia. 2018a. "Bootstrapping." Accessed June 1, 2018. https://www.investopedia.com/terms/b/bootstrapping.asp

Investopedia. 2018b. "Debt Financing." Accessed June 1, 2018. https://www.investopedia.com/terms/d/debtfinancing.asp

Investopedia. 2018c. "Equity Financing." Accessed June 1, 2018. https://www.investopedia.com/terms/e/equityfinancing.asp

Investopedia. 2018d. "Friends and Family Shares." Accessed June 1, 2018. https://www.investopedia.com/terms/f/familyandfriends.asp

Investopedia. 2018f. "Scalability." Accessed June 1, 2018. https://www.investopedia.com/terms/s/scalability.asp

Investopedia. 2018g. "Venture Capital." Accessed June 1, 2018. https://www.investopedia.com/terms/v/venturecapital.asp

Ireland, R. Duane, Michael A. Hitt, and David G. Sirmon. 2003. "A Model of Strategic Entrepreneurship: The Construct and Its Dimensions." *Journal of Management* 29 (6): 963–89.

Jalie Sewing Patterns. 2013. "How to Make Men's Trunk Underwear (Jalie Pattern 3242)." *YouTube*, June 11. Accessed June 1, 2018. https://youtu.be/HOOWQMaElNw

McGrath, Rita Gunther and Ian MacMillan. 2000. *The Entrepreneurial Mindset: Strategies for Continuously Creating Opportunity in an Age of Uncertainty*. Cambridge, MA: Harvard Business School Press.

Mollick, Ethan. 2014. "The Dynamics of Crowdfunding: An Exploratory Study." *Journal of Business Venturing* 29 (1): 1–16.

Mues, Fredrik. 2017. "A Guide to Success: How To Raise Capital Online via Crowdfunding." *Brandba*, January 31. Accessed June 1, 2018. https://www.brandba.se/blog/2017/1/31/a-guide-to-success-how-to-raise-capital-online-via-crowdfunding

Roos, Dave. n.d. "10 Ways to Finance a New Business." *Money*. Accessed June 1, 2018. https://money.howstuffworks.com/10-ways-to-finance-new-business.htm

Strähle, Jochen and Lena Bulling. 2018. "Case Study: Marillion." In *Fashion & Music*, ed. Jochen Strähle, 245–64. Singapore: Springer Singapore.

Definitions

Angel investors: Investors in small startups or entrepreneurs. The capital provided may be a one-time investment to help the business propel, or an ongoing injection of money to support and carry the company through its difficult early stages.

Bootstrapping: When an entrepreneur attempts to found and build a company from personal finances or the operating revenues of the new company.

Debt financing: When a firm raises money by borrowing money or selling debt instruments. In return for lending the money, the creditors receive a promise that the principal and interest on the debt will be repaid.

Donation-based crowdfunding: "Donors" or "supporters" (terms differ from platform to platform) pledge funds to causes, such as an earthquake; fundraising events, such as a walkathon; or for personal projects, such as a student's study-abroad tuition. Unlike rewards-based crowdfunding, there is no reciprocal expectation of a reward. Donation-based platforms include Go-Fund-Me and Crowdrise.

Equity crowdfunding: Through this modality, individuals can make direct equity investments into startups with hopes of investing in the next Facebook or AirBNB. Investing in startups is high risk as typically only one or two out of every ten startups survive to produce some profits, and fewer offer profitable return on investment. The US government strictly regulates equity crowdfunding to protect the novice and low-net-worth investor. Equity platforms include AngelList and Our Crowd.

Equity financing: The sale of an ownership interest to raise funds for business purposes.

Friend and family financing (FFF): Friends and family shares are often regarded as the very first sources of capital for a young business entity.

Peer-to-peer lending crowdfunding: This modality enables borrowers to crowd-source loans. Individual investors (lenders) can select one or a portfolio of loans to fund based on relevant but anonymized financial criteria including FICO scores. According to Prosper, a leading peer-to-peer lending platform, this type of lending offers people a way to invest in each other that is both financially and socially rewarding. Another key lender within this modality is Lending Tree.

Rapid prototyping: The quick execution of product samples for testing and revision purposes. Rapid prototyping enables a quicker product launch.

Rewards-based crowdfunding: The modality most familiar within the spectrum of crowdfunding. In rewards-based crowdfunding, people act as "backers" or "funders" (terms differ from platform to platform) and pledge money that is used to produce creative projects or products in return for receiving some sort of reward. The pledge amount determines the reward and may range from an emailed thank you letter to an actual product. Rewards-based platforms include Kickstarter and Indiegogo.

Scalability: A scalable company is one that can maintain or improve profit margins while sales volume increases.

Other variations of crowdfunding: These include hybrids of the four main modalities. Examples of leading platforms include Kiva, which organizes interest-free peer-to-peer lending; Realty Mogul, which crowdfunds real estate investments; and Patreon, which organizes subscription funding for creative artists and makers.

Venture capital firm (VC): is an investment firm who either provides capital to startup ventures or supports small companies that wish to expand.

Chapter 36

Shoes of Prey: Design Custom-Made Shoes

Identifying Opportunity within the Global Fashion Industry

Caroline Swee Lin Tan

This case study focuses on Shoes of Prey, a fast-growth online retailer that disrupted the footwear industry in 2009. By 2014, the company reported sales growth rates of approximately 250 percent. The case describes how Shoes of Prey started their fully customizable shoe venture and follows the entrepreneur's start-up and growth process. The business expanded into the bricks-and-mortar environment by establishing a physical presence in an upmarket department store in Australia in 2014 and the United States (through Nordstrom department stores) in 2015. As of October 2016, the company decided to scale back and focus on a pure e-commerce strategy due to the lack of profitability and increasing costs in physical retail. Shoes of Prey continues to disrupt the industry by entering the growing athleisure market in late 2017, introducing customizable fashion sneakers.

Students will learn how the entrepreneurial team discovered that their idea was a good business and market opportunity, and the different issues faced throughout their entrepreneurial journey. This case study is targeted at students undertaking fashion business courses focusing on fashion entrepreneurship, entrepreneurial process, entrepreneurship and innovation, small business management, or entrepreneurial strategy and growth.

Learning Objectives

Upon completion of this case, students should be able to:

- Understand that new opportunities for innovation can be derived internally or from industry.

- Identify the sources of opportunity entrepreneurs draw on to get business ideas.
- Analyze potential business opportunities through understanding market trends.
- Identify issues fashion businesses face when starting a new venture.

Introduction

Jodie Fox, cofounder and chief creative officer of Shoes of Prey (Figure 36.1), grew up in Lismore, New South Wales, a small country town in Australia. Being the first to attend university in her family, Jodie studied law and international business. However, upon starting her law career in the banking and finance industry, she quickly realized that she was not passionate about law. She remembers, "My heart was not in law to be honest. I was doing amazing work, working with incredible people, but it was not something that was making my heart sing." She then made a list of things that made her happy in life. Having a strong interest in branding, she decided to pursue a career in an advertising agency and learnt the art of brand-building.

FIGURE 36.1 Jodie Fox trying on different shoes. (Source: Shoes of Prey)

During this time, Jodie was always on the lookout for the perfect pair of shoes. She could not find suitable colors, heel height or comfort levels in the correct style, shape, or size. Typical sizes varied from a size 35 to 41, with many brands not offering half sizes or different widths for the feet. "I started to commission shoe design after I discovered a store in Hong Kong where customers could custom design footwear just as how customers would commission a tailor to make a dress, suit or shirt. I wanted to make shoes that were both comfortable and stylish."

After Jodie's own collection of custom-made shoes grew, her friends started noticing: "When I started wearing new and interesting shoes, my girlfriends always asked where my shoes were coming from and when I explained, they asked me to design shoes for them or commission their designs."

Teaming up with friends she met at university in Queensland, Michael Fox and Mike Knapp, the cofounders embarked on a journey to put together a business plan from their lounge room. Jodie explains, "Starting Shoes of Prey was like the meeting of three passions between the co-founders. The boys, who were former Google employees, were really excited about online retail and looking for a really great novel idea that they would be able to use." Jodie realized that this could potentially be a disruptive business opportunity.

All three founders possessed unique skills and expertise—Jodie focused on brand-building and public relations while Michael Fox concentrated on business development and established the supplier processes. Mike Knapp, the chief technology officer, designed the website to include 3D software. However, as the team were still working full-time when they started Shoes of Prey, they could only dedicate their free time to work on the business. This was rather difficult. As the business grew, Mike was the first to quit his job at Google as a software engineer to concentrate on Shoes of Prey. Shortly after, Michael and Jodie followed suit. With an entrepreneurial spirit and lack of fashion or shoe-industry experience, they were determined to pioneer this space. Capitalizing on the growing trend of mass customization in the women's footwear industry, customers design their own shoes based on available

FIGURE 36.2 Shoes of Prey web-based 3D design platform. (Source: Shoes of Prey)

design templates, colors, and materials on the Shoes of Prey web-based 3D design platform (Figure 36.2). Jodie elaborates, "We test the things we think might work, and when they don't, we adapt and move on with that much more understanding."

Business Problem

Shoes of Prey: The beginning

Shoes of Prey was funded from personal savings, bootstrapping the company for the first 2 ½ years with an initial capital injection of A$50,000. Start-up costs were minimal because they did not have to purchase inventory beforehand. The business model required customers to pay for their products upon designing their shoes. Orders were then placed with the factory. The supplier's invoice was not due until several months after delivery to the customer. This was important for the cash flow of the business, helping Shoes of Prey break even within two months of operation, obtaining multimillion dollar revenues in under two years.

To acquire customers as a young start-up, the founding team emailed their entire personal network to explain their new business. Friends were incentivized with a discount to place an order. They also wrote a blog so that family and friends were always up-to-date with the latest news. "We gained attention by entering a start-up competition in January 2010 and was a finalist for the Best Bootstrapped Startup at the Crunchie Awards. We also communicated with the public by issuing press releases to provide validity to the brand in the customer's mind."

Within five months of inception, Shoes of Prey launched their first online campaign by engaging with juicystar07, a famous 16-year-old YouTube vlogger who provided online make-up tutorials with a following of 500,000 viewers for each video she uploaded. Juicystar07 spoke about making custom-made shoes on the Shoes of Prey website, ending her video with encouraging viewers to enter a competition to design a pair of shoes, with the best design winning a pair of shoes. When the video went live, half a million viewers visited the Shoes of Prey website. 90,000 people entered the competition. As the website went viral, the team had to be sure that "share" buttons were placed at various points on the website to make Shoes of Prey shareable. Even though the website had increased traffic from their regular 200,000 visitors to 500,000 viewers, sales volumes did not change.

Jodie remembers, "We made an assumption that increased traffic would impact sales. Upon further investigation, we realised that we did not think of our target customer, who was primarily a professional woman, aged 25–35 years old, and loves fashion." Juicystar07's target audience were mainly 14–16-year-olds who could not afford to spend $250 on a pair of shoes. Feeling disappointed, this experience taught the three founders a valuable lesson about the differences in their target market.

Jodie and her team then wrote about the brand's experience in the form of a case study on their website. "We pitched it out to the press and received an email from the Wall Street Journal requesting to write a story on Shoes of Prey. When this article went live, the business tripled in sales because the Wall Street Journal reader is more aligned with the Shoes of Prey's offering."

The key to engaging with customers is to design a business that is unique and interesting to encourage press coverage. Jodie found that the most effective way to reach customers revolved around "below the line" marketing, with a particular emphasis on public relations via magazines, direct e-mail campaigns, search engine marketing, Google adwords, remarketing, and social media such as Facebook and YouTube. Existing customers connect with Shoes of Prey not only through email but by actively participating on Twitter, Instagram, and Facebook. Online users of the Shoes of Prey page are also sent a Net Promoter Score Survey while browsing the website, which asks one question, "Would you recommend Shoes of Prey?" with an option to make comments. This not only gives customers the opportunity to communicate with the brand but provides Shoes of Prey with valuable customer feedback.

With the goal of making customers happy, Shoes of Prey has managed to attract a large customer base by emphasizing a customer focus. Jodie emphasizes,

> It in our culture. The name of our service team is called Customer Happiness Wonder People. We are constantly talking about what it is to give great customer service. We want to give customers what they want, when they want it. I think it's just so core to what we care about—the way we treat each other really flows over to the way we treat our customers as well.

For example, employees are encouraged to look for ways to streamline customer processes and continuously ask themselves, "Will this make customers smile?" This has resulted in Shoes of Prey ranking 1st place in the Customer Happiness Awards 2015, receiving the highest rating average in Australia and New Zealand.

Expansion into bricks-and-mortar

As customers would often ask "What would the shoe be like in real life?", Shoes of Prey decided to showcase their products by opening a concession store in David Jones, an upmarket Australian department store in Sydney, and a stand-alone store in Bondi Junction in 2013. Although customers enjoyed the interaction and online experience, they still wanted to try shoes or feel the leather on their feet in real life.

> You obviously can't make every single pair of shoes that is designed. It could go into the millions. We hit 4 million shoe designs the other day. The thing we can do is make them understand the real life product. I think that people still want an interaction and they want to try something on—particularly if it's a brand that they hadn't spent a lot of time with.

In the store environment, swatches of more than 170 materials were available to enable shoppers to interact with and get a feel for how the different shades and textures work in combination.

Shoes of Prey was then able to use the retail environment to evoke happiness by utilizing music and a Shoes of Prey scent. As customers sat comfortably in store, they used iPads provided to design their shoes. This "design center" was created in collaboration with The General Store, a retail strategy and innovation firm. As a result, Shoes of Prey became the only Australian finalist to qualify and win the store design of the year category <1200 sqm at the World Retail Awards in Paris (Figure 36.3), beating companies such as the Puma flagship store in Osaka and the Karl Lagerfeld concept store in Paris.

Growing Shoes of Prey

After the success of their first physical store in Sydney, Shoes of Prey decided to venture into the North American market. Jodie says, "We always saw Shoes of Prey as a global business. There was great organic growth in the US. As a retailer, the company needed to be based in its biggest market, the United States, because of the critical mass."

FIGURE 36.3 Award-winning Shoes of Prey store design. (Source: Shoes of Prey)

They received an initial cash injection of A\$3.2 million in 2012 and another \$US15.5 million in 2015 to help accelerate the growth and expansion into the US market. In total, Shoes of Prey has raised \$US24.6 million in venture capital from venture funds in Australia and the United States.

Entering this market alone would be rather challenging because of the lack of established networks in the United States. Therefore, they penetrated the market by establishing a partnership with Nordstrom, one of the largest North American department stores with similar company values. Jodie emphasizes, "It is important to find the right partner to aid the growth of Shoes of Prey." By June 2015, Shoes of Prey was available in six Nordstrom outlets in Chicago, Los Angeles, New Jersey, San Francisco, Seattle, and Washington DC, with a view to expand into the Asian and European markets. To expand upon their traditional online user experience, the team developed an iPad app used in Nordstrom boutiques. The design studios had samples of each style and types of leather (snake skin, fish skin, soft leather, vegan, metallic, etc.).

Returning to its roots as a pure online retailer

Although omni-channel retail had been extremely important in fueling the growth of Shoes of Prey, by October 2016, Shoes of Prey decided to shut down its physical retail operations, focusing solely on a new e-commerce strategy. The label has since learnt that bricks-and-mortar was not driving profitability, with physical retail operations only accounting for 15 percent of sales. Despite this setback, Jodie says, "The physical stores helped us connect with customers, engaging them in conversations, provided brand exposure, and insights into future growth opportunities. The biggest opportunity for Shoes of Prey right now is pureplay online."

The future of Shoes of Prey

While Shoes of Prey has been successful at leading the custom shoe e-commerce space since inception, there are still many opportunities for exploration. For example, in May 2017, Shoes of Prey introduced a one-week express production capability as part of an ongoing plan to shrink the gap between order and delivery. Jodie explains, "We're heading to a future where customized product is the norm, and so the immediacy of that product is extremely important." This is just an example of the company adapting to customer demands.

Moreover, by observing fashion-market trends and consumer demand from millennials and Gen-Z, the company identified a rapidly growing women's athletic footwear market. With the growth of athleisure and "hyper personalized" trends in recent years, Shoes of Prey launched a fully customizable sneaker in September 2017. According to Edited, a fashion forecaster and retail technology company, the sneaker trend has increased by 159 percent since 2013.

While many businesses focus on mere monogramming or basic color choice, Shoes of Prey customers are able to select from fabrics, including contrast panels, sole thickness, platform heights, custom lining, eyelets, and lace tips (Figure 36.4). Jodie says, "I believe that this move into the sneaker market is a logical brand expansion given that large high fashion brands such as Alexander Wang have continued to collaborate with Adidas with new collections."

FIGURE 36.4 Shoes of Prey customized sneakers. (Source: Shoes of Prey)

With the growth rate of technology, Jodie believes that in the future customers would own a screen or hologram that says, "'Good morning, what shoes would you like today?' By connecting to one's calendar, the local weather and other data—like what one has worn recently and what everyone else is wearing at today's team meeting—the device will find shoes that match, and a shoe will print out while showering!"

All things considered, Jodie reiterates that the Shoes of Prey brand is not about shoes. "It is about the ability to get you exactly what you want, when you want it. The vision is to democratize fashion by creating a world where anyone can be their own designer … We believe it's about a bigger movement that moves us towards more sustainable businesses that is not reliant on guessing what people want."

In 2009, Shoes of Prey started as a dream. The company currently has five offices globally, located in Los Angeles, Sydney, China, Tokyo, and Manila. The shoes are made in their 4,000-square-meter company-owned factory in Dongguan, China, and shipped globally within one week. They have achieved sales volumes of over A$5 million and grown rapidly since inception. The team has managed to identify a market niche (e.g., affordable custom-designed women's footwear), utilizing online channels while providing an engaging and delightful customer experience online (e.g., user-friendly 3D shoe design software).

To date, shoppers have designed 6 million shoes on their website with 5 million unique viewers visiting shoesofprey.com in 2016. With a team of almost 200 employees, Shoes of Prey ships to over 100 different countries on a monthly basis and hopes to ship 1,000 shoes per day by the year 2021. The future of online fashion retail relies on analyzing metrics to help companies understand the gaps in the market.

Business Questions

Opportunity evaluation

1　How did Jodie Fox discover that her idea would be a good business opportunity?

2　How did Jodie evaluate the success of her idea?

3　How did Shoes of Prey find new opportunities to take their business to new markets and growth levels?

4　How did Shoes of Prey identify opportunities in market trends?

5　What future opportunities might there be for Shoes of Prey?

6　As an entrepreneur, what might you learn from Shoes of Prey in identifying opportunities for innovation (both from their mistakes and their successes)?

Business growth

1　How did Shoes of Prey overcome their credibility problem or liability of newness, which is an issue faced by most new start-ups?

2　As a first mover who revolutionized the footwear industry, how did Shoes of Prey grow so quickly?

3　As an entrepreneur, what might you learn from Shoes of Prey about growing a business (both from their mistakes and their successes)?

References and Further Reading

Carballo, Charlie. 2017. "How Shoes of Prey Co-Founder Jodie Fox Turns Challenges into Opportunities." *Footwear News*. Accessed August 2017. http://footwearnews.com/2017/business/power-players/shoes-prey-jodie-fox-women-power-careers-380818/

Fitzsimmons, Caitlin. 2013. "Shoes of Prey Co-founder Jodie Fox Runs 3km in High Heels for Promotional Video." *Business Review Weekly*. Accessed August 2017. http://www.brw.com.au/p/marketing/shoes_high_prey_heels_founder_jodie_GZueQKKc441zo0T60BXjdM

Fitzsimmons, Caitlin. 2015. "Shoes of Prey Walks, New HQ is Los Angeles." *Business Review Weekly*. Accessed August 2017. http://www.brw.com.au/p/entrepreneurs/shoes_of_prey_walks_new_hq_is_los_joXbC0mGWJBgvhwhOZnHYJ

Hochman, David. 2017. "Losing a Deal at Nordstrom Helped This Shoemaker Become a Millionaire." *CNBC*. Accessed August 2017. https://www.cnbc.com/2017/07/24/losing-a-deal-at-nordstrom-helped-this-shoemaker-become-a-millionaire.html

Kimmorley, Sarah. 2014. "Here's How Shoes of Prey Built Its Astounding Business by Getting to Know Its Customers." *Business Insider Australia*. Accessed July 2017. http://www.businessinsider.com.au/heres-how-shoes-of-prey-built-its-phenomenal-business-by-simply-getting-to-know-its-customers-2014-9

Kimmorley, Sarah. 2015. "In Good Company: How Jodie Fox Took Shoes of Prey beyond the Digital World into Physical Stores." *Business Insider Australia*. Accessed August 2017. http://www.businessinsider.com.au/in-good-company-how-jodie-fox-took-shoes-of-prey-beyond-the-digital-world-into-physical-stores-2015-4

Martinkus, Angela. 2013. "My Small Business: Jodie Fox, Shoes of Prey." *The New Daily*. Accessed August 2017. http://thenewdaily.com.au/money/2013/11/14/small-business-jodie-fox-shoes-prey/

Addendum

After ten years of operation, Shoes of Prey collapsed into liquidation in March 2019. Even though they achieved fast growth with little investment, the company started to decline when attempting to target mass-market fashion consumers. They entered this market after conducting market research with Nordstrom and David Jones, learning that customers were willing to buy customized shoes if Shoes of Prey could simplify the design process, expand their distribution at a cheaper price, and reduce lead time. Despite the evidence, they realized that mass-market customers actually want the latest trends, styles and brands that were worn by celebrities and influencers. Shoes of Prey then decided to pivot and focus on customers with size issues: small, large, wide and narrow feet. They also undertook short manufacturing runs for other companies. However, because of the high operational costs and ethical benchmarks that Shoes of Prey stands for, this meant that the new target markets were unfeasible, resulting in the business' downfall.

Chapter 37

Louis Vuitton Versus My Other Bag

Luxury Brand Protection

Agnieszka Witońska-Pakulska

The fashion industry is a serious sector of the global economy. Fashion is a dynamic business; trends change fast and companies need to react fast. Having a fashion brand requires not only good taste and a love for fashion, but also good business, financial, and strategic skills. It is crucial for fashion companies to be aware that the brand they have is their most valuable asset and, as such, it needs to be protected. Having a clear, comprehensive, and effective brand protection strategy from the very beginning will save nerves, time, and money if and when trouble comes.

In 2014, Louis Vuitton, the Paris-based fashion house, filed suit in the Southern District of New York against the Los Angeles-based company—My Other Bag (MOB). Louis Vuitton based its suit on the claim that MOB designs not only infringe Louis Vuitton federally registered trademarks and copyrights, but that MOB was diluting its famous trademarks and raised the claims of false designation of origin/unfair competition.

Using the case between Louis Vuitton and My Other Bag students will analyze firstly, what assets of business enterprise can be protected by the brand, and secondly the steps that the brand owner can undertake to protect their brand.On the basis of the case students will be able to explore when and why fashion brands need to take legal action, and analyze and reflect on whether taking legal action always makes good business sense.

Learning Objectives

Upon completion of this case, students should be able to:

- Understand how the assets of a fashion brand can be protected from copyright infringement.
- Describe how third parties can infringe fashion brand assets.

- Evaluate the measures Louis Vuitton has taken to protect its trademark against My Other Bag and propose other strategies.
- Analyze the social media role in brand protection and propose the actions that can be taken using social media to protect the brand.
- Define the consumer role in building brand value from the point of view of both Louis Vuitton and My Other Bag customers.
- Propose a fashion brand strategy for a luxury fashion brand and draft the procedure that should be taken in case of an infringement.
- Identify the consequences of not taking legal actions to protect a brand.

Introduction

Louis Vuitton is a luxury fashion house known for its high-quality handbags and other luxury goods. The average Louis Vuitton bag costs around 1,000 EUR or more (Louis Vuitton 2018b). Louis Vuitton invests in marketing and high-quality materials not only to create and maintain a sense of exclusivity and luxury but also to protect its brand assets. Due to the close management of the brand, many of Louis Vuitton's designs and trademarks are famous and well-recognized symbols of high fashion and wealth worldwide. As stated on the Louis Vuitton website: "Louis Vuitton's Intellectual Property Department is managing over 12,000 intellectual property rights including trademarks, designs and copyrights with support of 250 agents around the world" (Louis Vuitton 2018a).

As the court in Louis Vuitton Malletier, S.A. v. My Other Bag, Inc. (2016) noted:

> In particular, Louis Vuitton's Toile Monogram design … a repeating pattern featuring the interlocking, stylized letters "L" and "V" and three stylized flower designs … —has become the defining signature of the Louis Vuitton brand. Louis Vuitton has registered trademarks in the Toile Monogram and in the component stylized flower designs. Two other iconic Louis Vuitton designs, the Monogram Multicolore and the Damier, have achieved comparable levels of recognition and are also registered as trademarks.

My Other Bag (MOB) was founded in Los Angeles, California, in 2011 by Tara Martin (Lipstick Sister 2016). MOB produces and sells canvas tote bags bearing caricatures of iconic designer handbags on one side and the text "My Other Bag … " on the other.

> "the name 'My Other Bag' was inspired by novelty bumper stickers, which can sometimes be seen on inexpensive cars claiming that the driver's 'other car' is an expensive, luxury car, such as a Mercedes." MOB's "website and other marketing play up the idea that high-priced designer bags cannot be used to carry around, say, dirty gym clothes or messy groceries, while its casual canvas totes can." (Louis Vuitton Malletier, S.A. v My Other Bag, Inc. [2016])

Several of MOB's tote bags display images designed to evoke classic Louis Vuitton bags:

> "MOB markets its bags as [e]co-friendly, sustainable tote bags playfully parodying the designer bags we love, but practical enough for everyday life. Whereas Louis Vuitton handbags sell for thousands of dollars apiece, MOB's totes sell at prices between thirty and fifty-five US dollars." (Louis Vuitton Malletier, S.A. v My Other Bag, Inc. [2016])

Business Problem

Louis Vuitton brand assets and their protection

Louis Vuitton is a French luxury fashion house which was founded in Paris in 1854. Since the beginning, Louis Vuitton has invested a lot of money in its brand protection. It has registered trademarks and designs worldwide (Louis Vuitton 2018c). Since Louis Vuitton is a well-know fashion brand other market players undertake actions that constitute an infringement of Louis Vuitton's intellectual property rights, which mainly constitute counterfeits aimed at reaping the benefits of Louis Vuitton's trademark.

Louis Vuitton's aim is to protect the brand's reputation and the associated sense of exclusivity and wealth. But most importantly Louis Vuitton needs to maintain the registration of trademarks by protecting against their dilution. Therefore, the Paris-based fashion house has to decide what actions should be taken and against which parties in order to effectively protect its brand assets.

One of the latest trends in fashion is the "trademark parody." Famous luxury brands' trademarks are altered in such a way that they are meant to be funny, for example, the "LV" of Louis Vuitton as Lord Voldemort on t-shirts (Colman 2014).

But parody is also a defense to trademark infringement. The reasoning behind it is that there is no likelihood of confusion because a parody will not be taken seriously. The parody must initially bring to mind the original, but on the other hand it must be clever enough that it is not the original nor connected with the original. In order for it to be a parody it needs to be clear that it is a humorous take-off of the original (Kobulnick and Bernet 2017).

My Other Bag products and their use of Louis Vuitton brand assets

My Other Bag, started selling simple canvas tote bags with the text "My Other Bag ..." on one side and drawings meant to evoke iconic handbags such as Louis Vuitton, on the other. My Other Bag canvas totes grew in popularity mainly because of the drawings of the iconic bags and received a lot of publicity from bloggers and media. My Other Bag totes were meant as a joke and were meant to be taken in jest. They are made of canvas and are meant for everyday use and their price is around 35 EUR.

Louis Vuitton reaction to My Other Bag totes

In 2013 Louis Vuitton sent a cease and desist letter to My Other Bag, but as Louis Vuitton claims, not only did MOB not comply with the Louis Vuitton demands but they also introduced new products that in the luxury brand's opinion infringed and diluted their trademark (TFL 2014).

As a result of MOBs reaction to the cease and desist letter, Louis Vuitton Malletier, S.A. decided to bring a case against My Other Bag. In 2014 Louis Vuitton filed a suit in the Southern District of New York. The case was brought with respect to MOB totes that were concededly meant to evoke iconic Louis Vuitton bags. More specifically, Louis Vuitton brought claims against MOB for trademark dilution and infringement under the Lanham Act, 15 U.S.C. § 1125(c); a claim of trademark dilution under New York law; and a claim of copyright infringement (Louis Vuitton Malletier, S.A. v My Other Bag, Inc. [2016]).

FIGURE 37.1 Louis Vuitton's intellectual property includes its iconic trademark of interlocking letters and stylized flower designs. © Edward Berthelot/Getty Images

Louis Vuitton argued that My Other Bag's marketing strategy was based on the association of its totes with the Louis Vuitton bags and that as a result My Other Bag's totes were likely to create a confusion in the market. In Louis Vuitton's opinion the confusion would be caused by the fact that consumers might believe that MOB designs were created in collaboration with Louis Vuitton. Furthermore, Louis Vuitton alleged that MOB's use of its trademarks was likely to blur the distinctiveness of those marks; being more specific, Louis Vuitton claimed that by MOB using its trademarks they would appear less exclusive than they actually were (TFL 2014).

My Other Bag's reaction to the suit

The basic defense undertaken by My Other Bag was the parody defense. My Other Bag argued that its use of Louis Vuitton trademarks was necessary because its bags were clearly a parody of more expensive ones; in particular the Louis Vuitton bags. In My Other Bag's opinion, no customer buying My Other Bag's totes would think they were buying a Louis Vuitton bag or a bag that was made in collaboration with Louis Vuitton. Furthermore, My Other Bag totes are not a substitute for Louis Vuitton handbags. My Other Bag emphasized that its tagline is a clear play on the "My other car is ..." bumper sticker gag and the tagline is meant as a joke and not to be taken seriously (Louis Vuitton Malletier, S.A. v My Other Bag, Inc. [2016]).

Possible outcomes of the case

In bringing the case, Louise Vuitton was confident of a positive outcome, however this was not guaranteed.

If My Other Bag lost the case it would mean that the parody defense was ineffective, with the result that other companies offering products that are meant to parody luxury brands could be at risk of lawsuits from luxury fashion houses.

If Louis Vuitton lost the case it would be obliged to pay My Other Bag's attorney fees. My Other Bag could continue selling the canvas bags using the Louis Vuitton trademark, and any other companies parodying famous trademarks would be less concerned about potential trademark infringement claims. Furthermore, in such a case Louis Vuitton would have to make some strategic decisions as to its reactions to such trademark parody, and would have to find other ways of protecting its intellectual property rights against dilution.

Business Questions

1 What assets can be protected by the fashion brand? Is it only the design or only a trademark?

2 What intellectual property rights can fashion brands use in protecting their brand? Which rights are most effective in the fashion industry?

3 What legal actions can the fashion brand undertake against companies that use their intellectual property rights such as trademarks? And why is it important to take legal action?

4 Imagine working for Louis Vuitton on its legal team—what would you recommend in the next case concerning parody? Would you bring claims in court or would you take any other steps? Think of a means of addressing the issue other than litigation, and draft a series of recommendations for Louis Vuitton as to what actions should be taken and the reasoning behind them.

5 Do you think big fashion companies such as Louis Vuitton should fight competition in general or only focus on fighting counterfeits? What are the benefits and risks of each approach?

6 Do you think that if a brand is an aggressive enforcer of its intellectual rights it has an impact on how it is seen by its customers?

References and Further Reading

Colman, Charles E. 2014. "Trademark Law and the Prickly Ambivalence of Post-Parodies." 163 U. Pa. L. Rev. Online 11. Accessed June 11, 2018. https://www.pennlawreview.com/online/163-U-Pa-L-Rev-Online-11.pdf

Conlon, Louis. 2016. "Vuitton's Counterfeit Crusade." *Vogue*, January. Accessed May 31, 2018. https://www.vogue.co.uk/article/louis-vuitton-sues-taobao-alibaba-counterfeit-users

The Fashion Law (TFL). 2014. "Louis Vuitton Slapped My Other Bag with a Major Lawsuit." June. Accessed May 31, 2018. https://www.thefashionlaw.com/home/louis-vuitton-slapped-my-other-bag-with-a-major-lawsuit

TFL. 2016a. "'My Other Bag' Appeal Not Looking Promising for Louis Vuitton." December. Accessed May 31, 2018. https://www.thefashionlaw.com/home/my-other-bag-appeal-not-looking-promising-for-louis-vuitton?rq=my%20other%20bag

TFL. 2016b. "My Other Bag Victorious in Louis Vuitton 'Parody' Battle." December. Accessed May 31, 2018. https://www.thefashionlaw.com/home/my-other-bag-victorious-in-louis-vuitton-parody-battle?rq=my%20other%20bag

TFL. 2017a. "Supreme Court Denies Louis Vuitton's Appeal Over 'Parody' Tote Bags." October. Accessed May 31, 2018. https://www.thefashionlaw.com/home/supreme-court-denies-louis-vuittons-appeal-over-parody-tote-bags

TFL. 2017b. "What are the Chances that the Supreme Court will Agree to Hear Louis Vuitton's Case?" August. Accessed May 31, 2018. https://www.thefashionlaw.com/home/what-are-the-chances-that-the-supreme-court-will-agree-to-hear-louis-vuittons-case?rq=my%20other%20bag

Kobulnick, Jeffrey A. and Michael A. Bernet. 2017. "Parody Products: When Should Brand Owners "Smile or Laugh" and When Should They Sue?" August. Accessed May 31, 2018. https://www.americanbar.org/publications/landslide/2016-17/july-august/parody-products-when-should-brand-owners-smile-or-laugh-and-when-should-they-sue.html#45

Lipstick Sister. 2016. "Wonder Woman: Tara Martin, Founder of My Other Bag." January 26. Accessed September 18, 2018. https://www.lipsticksister.com/single-post/2016/01/26/Wonder-Woman-Tara-Martin-Founder-of-My-Other-Bag

Louis, Vuitton. 2018a. "Brand Protection." Accessed June 11, 2018. https://uk.louisvuitton.com/eng-gb/la-maison/brand-protection#

Louis, Vuitton. 2018b. "Handbags." Accessed June 11, 2018. https://uk.louisvuitton.com/eng-gb/women/handbags/_/N-2keomb

Louis, Vuitton. 2018c. "Legendary History." Accessed June 11, 2018. https://uk.louisvuitton.com/eng-gb/la-maison/a-legendary-history#centennial

Louis, Vuitton Malletier S.A. v. Haute Diggity Dog, LLC, 507 F.3d 252 (4th Cir. 2007). Accessed May 31, 2018. https://www.law.berkeley.edu/files/louisvuitton.pdf

Louis, Vuitton Malletier S.A. v. My Other Bag, Inc., 156 F. Supp. 3d 425 (S.D.N.Y. 2016).

Louis, Vuitton Malletier S.A. v. My Other Bag, Inc., No. 16-241-cv (2nd Cir. 2018). Accessed May 31, 2018. https://caselaw.findlaw.com/us-2nd-circuit/1762991.html

Rodulfo, Ikea. 2017. "Issues Brilliant Response to Balenciaga's $2,145 Look-Alike Bag." *Elle*, April. Accessed May 31, 2018. https://www.elle.com/fashion/news/a44804/ikea-response-balenciaga-bag/

United States District Court. 2016. "Southern District of New York, Louis Vuitton Malletier S.A. v My Other Bag, Inc." *Opinion and Order*, June. Accessed May 31, 2018. https://pl.scribd.com/document/294867656/Louis-Vuitton-v-My-Other-Bag-decision-pdf

Definitions

Trademark parody: For trademark purposes, parody is defined as a simple form of entertainment. Parody must convey two contradictory messages—that the new product *is* the original, but also that it is clearly not the original and is instead a parody.

Chapter 38

Cultural Appreciation or Cultural Appropriation

Native American-Inspired Jewelry Design

Celia Stall-Meadows

A fictional fashion accessories business, Reflections, has expanded its line of fashion jewelry into an uncharted area of Native American-inspired designs. The new jewelry collection, Tribal, is inspired by beautiful Native American culture and art, such as feathers, arrows, and dream catchers. Reflections' Tribal jewelry collection generates only marginal success in sales, until a popular Hollywood celebrity is photographed wearing one of the Tribal pieces. The red-carpet runway images circulate on social media. Within a few days, sales spike for all the pieces in the Tribal collection. Reflections is pleased with the publicity and the increase in sales. Prior to the celebrity sighting, Native American tribes had been unaware or unconcerned with the Native American-inspired jewelry by Reflections, but social media propels the issue of cultural appropriation—profiting from minorities' cultural artifacts—into the public eye. The tribal leaders criticize Reflections' promotion of cultural stereotypes and call for a boycott of the fashion jewelry manufacturer and the retailers who sell the merchandise. How should Reflections respond?

Learning Objectives

Upon completion of this case, students should be able to:

- Explain the concept of cultural appropriation.
- Compare the conflicting viewpoints between cultural appropriation and cultural appreciation.

- Apply knowledge of similar problems of cultural appropriation or appreciation in recent history.
- Reconcile the need for a company to be profitable and culturally sensitive.

Introduction

You are the creative director for a well-known domestic fashion jewelry company in the United States called Reflections. The twenty-five-year-old company makes moderately priced fashion accessories for department stores. In an effort to boost flagging sales, your company recently expanded into a sixth collection, which is a line of Native American-inspired fashion jewelry, to add to the company's other five brands. The original five are as follows:

- Meteorites and Metals: A collection inspired by futuristic and high-tech materials, including glass beads, stainless steel, and clear acrylic.
- Crazy Daisy: A collection of colorful sixties retro jewelry, made of metals and plastics, in avocado green, harvest gold, and burnt orange.
- Pompeii: A collection inspired by the ancient Greek and Roman civilizations.
- Queen Nefertiti's Jewelry: Reminiscent of ancient Egypt, this heavily bejeweled collection is of gold electroplate, with faux precious gemstones or semiprecious gems, like lapis lazuli and cultured pearls.
- Awesome Reflections: The company's religious artifacts collection, with crosses, ankhs, yin–yang symbols, and other world religion symbols.

When the company launched its line of Native American-inspired fashion jewelry, Tribal, the American Indian population took little notice. Among other indigenous looks, the jewelry included dream-catcher pendants, arrow necklaces, trade bead bracelets, chunky petroglyph-inspired bracelets, and chandelier-style feathered earrings. The Tribal collection sales during the first season were profitable, but modest. Sales remained steady into the second quarter until an event occurred that no one expected. Reflections' top management reacted with excitement and hopefulness.

Business Problem

The publicity came in the form of an unexpected celebrity endorsement of one of the pieces in the Tribal collection. The Native American-inspired collection piece became an overnight sensation when the necklace was photographed on an A-list celebrity at a high-profile Hollywood event. The clasp on the actress's necklace came unhooked and the Tribal necklace by Reflections clattered to the floor. With poise under pressure, she held up the necklace to the paparazzi and made a light comment about it. Photographers snapped shots and the image was quickly circulated through several social media channels. Within days, customers flocked to the department stores looking for the infamous piece. The inventory of the particular necklace style, as well as several related pieces, sold out in record time.

The serendipitous publicity generated attention from several major Native American tribes and the tribal leaders spoke out against the jewelry designs, saying they exemplified "cultural appropriation" and "theft of the cultural significance of the symbolic designs." The tribal leaders called for a boycott of all the merchandise made by Reflections, as well as a

FIGURE 38.1 Cultural appropriation is considered disrespectful, demeaning, mocking, or downright theft of a minority's cultural icons and ideas. © Pascal Le Segretain/Getty Images

boycott of the retailers who stock the brand. In spite of the spike in sales revenue, the top management for Reflections needs to react quickly to the negative publicity and make tough decisions. You are called on the hot seat and senior management is demanding answers and solutions. Time is of the essence.

Business Questions

What recommendations for action should you make to the company executives? Before you propose any action, your boss demands that you conduct research about a similar event, when a special-interest group has boycotted a brand or company. Your boss believes that analyzing historical facts is a way to make an educated decision about future actions.

    You have many options for a response to the boycott, but the response you choose will likely affect sales. Response options include an orchestrated press conference and press release; an institutional advertising campaign; a social media campaign; a live forum that gives voice to both the tribal leaders and Reflections' executives; a lawsuit against the tribes; or no response at all, in hopes that the whole thing blows over. Weigh up the pros and cons of each of these options and give a detailed justification for the one you think will be the most effective. Explain how your own belief system, as well as the research on another boycott, influenced your recommendation for Reflections' executives.

References and Further Reading

Arewa, Olufunmilayo. 2016. "Cultural Appropriation: When 'Borrowing' Becomes Exploitation." The Conversation, June 20. Accessed June 13, 2017. http://theconversation.com/cultural-appropriation-when-borrowing-becomes-exploitation-57411

Calmese, Darío. 2017. "Op-Ed: Fashion Does Not Need Cultural Appropriation." *Business of Fashion*, June 6. Accessed July 17, 2017. https://www.businessoffashion.com/articles/opinion/op-ed-fashion-does-not-need-cultural-appropriation?utm_source=Subscribers&utm_campaign=2372e5c073-what-donna-karan-did-next-the-realreal-raises-50-m&utm_medium=email&utm_term=0_d2191372b3-2372e5c073-419443797

Oxford Reference. "Cultural Appropriation, Quick Reference." Accessed June 2017. http://www.oxfordreference.com/view/10.1093/oi/authority.20110803095652789

Chapter 39

Approaching CSR with a New Kind of Transparency

How E-commerce Retailer Everlane Set New Industry Standards in Brand Communication

Nina Bürklin

Founded in 2010, the e-commerce retailer Everlane shook the apparel industry with its innovative concept of transparent pricing. According to the company's corporate social responsibility (CSR) strategy, founder and CEO Michael Preysman and his team aim at new forms of brand communication, including openness about their supply chain and prices. Furthermore, the San Francisco-based online retailer counters fast fashion cycles with its timeless and high-quality products that range from menswear to womenswear and accessories. Building on modern forms of strategic communication like Twitter and Instagram as well as temporary pop-up shops, Everlane has managed to establish a stable customer base. Exploiting the inefficiencies of bricks-and-mortar retail, the e-commerce start-up incorporates quick prototyping with small order numbers that allow the team to test new products regarding fit, materials, and colors, thus improvements are made based on feedback from its clientele. Hence, Everlane empowers customers to be informed and involved with their purchase and binds them emotionally to the company. Despite Everlane's current success, the question arises of how to handle a growing customer base worldwide. The scalability of the business model focusing on close customer relationships and a limited product portfolio needs to be examined. Recommendations for current and future transparency, marketing, and distribution strategies need to be defined. Furthermore, although the social enterprise has received considerable amounts of attention and praise for its courageous corporate strategy, the future will be determined by its consistency and credibility. Strategies to maintain Everlane's credibility in the long run need to be developed.

Learning Objectives

Upon completion of this case, students should be able to:

- Analyze the concept of e-commerce as a web-based distribution model in contrast to conventional supply chain management of bricks-and-mortar retailers.
- Grasp the concept of corporate transparency as a means of a corporate social responsibility strategy and founding principle of a social enterprise.
- Learn about innovative ways of brand communication and marketing strategies, such as social media or guerrilla marketing.
- Understand the importance of specifying a particular target group and the according product range and company's positioning in the market.
- Critically revise and evaluate future risks and opportunities of a so-far very successful social enterprise and its public perception, especially with regard to consistency and credibility.

Introduction

Quitting his job in venture capital to pursue his dreams of starting his own business, Michael Preysman founded the e-commerce retailer Everlane in 2010. Producing high-quality clothing, the San Francisco-based company has shaken the industry with its pioneering concept of transparent pricing. Following his passion for great design and fighting his frustration with the lack of innovative retail, then 25-year-old entrepreneur Preysman founded the online retailer focusing on luxury products with minimalist design at reasonable prices.

Despite the highly competitive and saturated market, the idea of ethical clothing and a transparent supply chain resonated well with investors, too. According to *Inc.* magazine, Everlane has raised some $US5 million in venture and angel funding. While the company declined to share figures, *Women's Wear Daily* reported in October 2015 that revenues would hit $US30 million. The same year, founder Preysman was included in Forbes' "30 under 30" list for his work on the company in reinventing retail and e-commerce. Following its corporate social responsibility (CSR) with openness and transparency at the core of its strategy, the creative retailer was included in the Fast Company's "50 Most Innovative Companies" list in 2016.

While a general trend toward transparency becomes visible across different industries and company sizes, Everlane's focus on transparency was a founding principle that has been held up until today, as stated by CEO and founder Preysman: "The transparency message is at the core of what we stand for" (Britt 2016). Even though there is general consensus among the majority of stakeholders in the apparel industry that transparency is highly relevant, the majority of companies show only limited efforts to provide information to all relevant stakeholders. Hence, Everlane seemingly fills a void in an industry that is characterized by opaqueness in the supply chain. Specifically, the e-commerce retailer provides customers with detailed information about the price of materials, hardware, labor, duties, and transport and compares it with conventional margins.

Business Problem

Supply chain management and e-commerce

Everlane's business model of "Radical Transparency" aims to exploit the market inefficiencies of bricks-and-mortar retail to deliver high-quality fashion basics at a fraction of department store prices. To do this, the e-commerce retailer circumvents capital and labor expenditures associated with traditional stores. Espousing a solely web-based distribution model, Everlane adheres to a low inventory policy to minimize working capital costs, often leading to stock outs. Before a launch, it deliberately orders fewer products than its demand forecasts imply. Through these small batches it gains feedback, then redesigns to produce stronger versions of its products. This rapid feedback loop is facilitated by its direct relationship with factories. Everlane designs in-house and works directly with factories, from Vietnam and Spain to the United States.[1] Not only does this relationship with manufacturers allow Everlane to pass on savings to the consumer, it also allows the social enterprise to more easily ensure that factories comply with its labor and ethical sourcing. Moreover, this prototype-build-pilot model also heightens consumer hype around product restocking. For instance, the launch of Everlane pants led to a 12,000-person waitlist.

Transparent pricing

Everlane's core strategy is to break down the "true cost" of each item. From the design phase to transport, Everlane sheds light on the costs of its business, thereby highlighting

FIGURE 39.1 Michael Preysman, CEO of Everlane, founded the company around the ideas of ethical fashion and transparency. © Lars Ronbog/Getty Images for Copenhagen Fashion Summit

the differences between its model and the "traditional retail" model. While most retailers obscure production costing, Everlane actively promotes it: the company explains the price for everything from materials to transport; the cost is then approximately doubled to create the retail price. For example, the men's city jacket[2] sells for $US88, and on the website you can see an infographic at the bottom of the page that breaks the true cost down: materials $US10.17, hardware $US4.93, labor $US11.84, duties $US1.91, and transport $US0.90 for a total cost of $US30. By Everlane's reckoning, an equivalent product would cost $US150 in traditional retail. The founder launched Everlane with itemized costs for a t-shirt, and applied the same transparency to sweaters, shoes, and bags as the number of products grew. Preysman and his team believe they can deliver everyday basics to men and women at around half the cost of traditional retail.

On the website, you can also find information on the specific factory where each item is made, read about the factory's owner, and view images of the production process. For overstock products, there is even an option to "choose what you pay," where consumers are offered three staggered prices to choose from: the lowest of the three prices, 10 percent of the profits go to Everlane, for the middle price, 20 percent, and for the highest price, 30 percent. Moreover, Everlane never discounts products as part of holiday weekend promotions, and goes as far as shutting down its site on Black Friday. The e-commerce retailer's prices are fixed, contrasting with traditional retailers such as JCrew and Gap who run steep and frequent promotions.

Brand communication and marketing strategy

Everlane has created a brand that represents a particularly strong ideology. Its notion of "Radical Transparency" has high importance when it comes to empowering its customers. From showcasing its content, gathering feedback, and hosting cool events, the Everlane customer ultimately becomes part of the company. It empowers its consumers to be informed and involved with its purchases. Lastly, Everlane's customers shoulder a lot of the marketing burden—most of the company's growth is due to word-of-mouth.

Everlane largely markets through social media platforms such as Instagram with no print campaigns or television advertising. The marketing strategy is creatively adapted to build intimate relationship with customers. Some examples include sending out surveys to explore why people didn't purchase an item or hosting happy hours across the United States with talks and parties tailored around the theme of Transparent Cities. In addition, it initiates events called "room-service" that take place in hotels during which selected customers get an exclusive preview of the new collection and are invited to spread the word on their own social media channels. This guerrilla-style marketing approach allows Everlane to spend less on marketing in comparison to other retailers, passing on the savings to its customers. Furthermore, the e-commerce retailer has active Twitter, Instagram, and Snapchat accounts that encourage user-generated content.[3] Streaming stories that direct followers to secret pop-up locations, show tours of the factories, provide random acts of kindness, and easy-to-digest retail production facts allow Everlane to establish a good relationship with its customers. Everlane's use of user-generated content and hashtags is another example of how it cements the relationship: #DearEverlane is a hashtag used on its Instagram account to showcase recent reviews from satisfied customers. The stories are informative, real, and Everlane usually responds with humorous information about a special product relating to the customer's story.

Additionally, Everlane has engaged in cause-related marketing several times. In cooperation with the American Civil Liberties Union (ACLU), it launched the "100 % Human Collection" which comprised mainly t-shirts and sweaters. Since the ACLU has existed for 100 years to defend the civil rights provided in the constitution of the United States, this campaign aimed to encourage people to take a more active interest in human rights. For every 100% Human item sold, Everlane donates $5 to the not-for-profit organization. The collection has sold out twice, and, obligingly, been restocked twice—an achievement that likely elicits some pride in Everlane's customers, the company itself, and the ACLU.

Target group and product portfolio

Price transparency aside, on the heels of garment manufacturing-related tragedies in recent years there is a greater demand for more ethically produced garments, particularly from younger generations. Nowadays, Everlane is considered a go-to for hip millennials with money and a conscience when it comes to their clothes. These are young people born between 1981 and 1995 who follow the baby boomer generation and have differing values regarding sustainabilityand work-life balance, and place value on experiences instead of just possession. When Everlane needs to hire new employees in San Francisco or New York, its recruitment strategy is to send an email to the customer list. Preysman describes the typical Everlane customer as having "an entrepreneurial, intellectual, Millennial mindset" (Britt 2016)—a person who wants to know where her food comes from, why things are the way they are, essentially a knowledge-based consumer. Targeting those who reflect Everlane's values through the products they buy has led to huge success. But Preysman adds that reaching that consumer still means hitting all the right notes of easy shopping, accessible price, and a clear aesthetic.

It turns out that transparency, if the company is truly committed to it, impacts product strategy, too. Everlane is item based vs. collection based, which means products are well made and styles are designed to be timeless. A plain black tee, if it's well made and comfortable, will be in customers' closets for a long time. Aiming for shelf life over seasonality means that Everlane avoids the aggressive discounting cycles inherent in retail collections. Constantly focusing on minimalist design, Everlane has since expanded into womenswear, menswear, leather accessories, and children's wear. Due to its solely web-based distribution, it has become the industry leader in high-quality design while curtailing overhead costs, which allows Everlane to deliver a luxury product without a luxury price tag.[4]

Future risks and opportunities

As of June 2018, there are approximately 200 employees and the company has plans to expand into the building next door in the next few months while continuing its relentless rollout of new products. However, it must be careful that its growth does not undermine the brand equity it has so skillfully developed. Everlane would do well to consider the effect of deliberately low inventory on missed sales and earnings opportunity. While its current cult following may be willing to wait months for its Petra Bag, new customers may not be as "sticky" or forgiving. Everlane's rapid proliferation of products may also jeopardize its simple and easy shopping experience. While scaling, Everlane must ensure that it continues to aggressively manage factories to ensure compliance with its ethical standards and sustain its high brand equity. Lastly, Everlane's goal must be not to lose credibility and, thus, sales among its customer base.

Business Questions

1 What are the potential benefits of corporate transparency as a pricing strategy and in which areas are the benefits visible? How consistent is the concept of "Radical Transparency" with Everlane's CSR? What kind of risks might be related to the rather drastic concept of transparency?

2 What are the key strengths of Everlane's supply chain management? Analyze and explain the mechanisms of the e-commerce retailer's underlying business model including potential advantages and disadvantages. How can this model be maintained in the future?

3 What does it mean for a social enterprise like Everlane to be consistent and credible? Think about strategies by which Everlane can move forward with consistency and credibility.

4 Develop a target customer persona that reflects the personality, goals, behavior, and lifestyle that Everlane is targeting.

5 Are Everlane's marketing activities consistent with the target market needs?

References and Further Reading

Bhaduri, Gari and Jung E. Ha-Brookshire. 2011. "Do Transparent Business Practices Pay? Exploration of Transparency and Consumer Purchase Intention." *Clothing and Textiles Research Journal* 29 (2): 135–149.

Britt, Aaron. 2016. "Everlane Expands Its Reach." Accessed June 2017. http://www.sfchronicle.com/style/article/Everlane-expands-its-reach-6204937.php

Everlane. 2017. "About Everlane." Accessed June 2017. https://www.everlane.com/about

Kang, Jiyun and Gwendolyn Hustvedt. 2014. "Building Trust between Consumers and Corporations: The Role of Consumer Perceptions of Transparency and Social Responsibility." *Journal of Business Ethics* 125 (2): 253–265.

Lieber, C. 2015 "Can Everlane Really Become the Next J.Crew?" Accessed June 2017. http://www.racked.com/2015/10/8/9442455/everlane-expansion

Simintiras, Antonis C., Yogesh K. Dwivedi, Geetanjali Kaushik, and Nripendra P. Rana. 2015. "Should Consumers Request Cost Transparency?" *European Journal of Marketing* 49 (11/12): 1961–1979.

Notes

1 The image of Everlane's garment-dyed tee factory in Los Angeles, USA can be viewed at: https://www.everlane.com/factories/tees-sweatshirt

2 This jacket can be viewed at: https://www.everlane.com/products/mens-city-jacket-black

3 An example of Everlane's Instagram's account can be viewed here: https://digitalstrategysolutions.wordpress.com/2015/12/11/how-to-use-instagram-for-your-business/

4 An example of Everlane's product portfolio for women including shirts, dresses, pants, jackets, and shoes can be viewed at: http://www.refinery29.com/2016/11/129678/everlane-limited-edtion-party-capsule#slide-10

Chapter 40

Patagonia: Creative Sustainability Strategy for a Reluctant Fashion Brand

Rosemary Varley, Natascha Radclyffe-Thomas, and William Webb

This business strategy case revolves around the marketing activities of the outdoor apparel brand Patagonia; specifically, the clothing product category. Patagonia was founded as a performance-wear brand designed for adventurous outdoors spirits who enjoy nature and respect the environment. Developing high-performance functional products and integrating sustainability give Patagonia authenticity amongst its consumers and form the core of its business and brand identity. The case study highlights the socially responsible aspect of the company, both in its product offer and operations, and the distinctive management culture is touched upon. The case study presents comprehensive information about marketing, advertising, and retailing activities, including the famous 2011 reverse marketing campaign when Patagonia used a full-page ad in The New York Times and implored Black Friday shoppers: "Don't buy this jacket." Background context and information about the company's founding principles and business philosophy are provided for students to analyze past brand marketing strategy within the overall context of the strategic aims of the corporation. Patagonia has adopted a slow growth business model but its own success and the increasing athleisure segment offers Patagonia potential to expand internationally, and to reconsider whether its focus should be on performance or its fashion offer. The case provides an interesting company context in which to consider marketing activities, given its brand values of high quality and performance and corporate responsibility, and enables the discussion of business ethics and sustainability issues in the wider fashion industry through the detailed examination of an iconic sustainable fashion brand.

Learning Objectives

Upon completion of this case, students should be able to:

- Analyze and evaluate key concepts of sustainability and environmental and social responsibility and how these are enacted through Patagonia's product development and strategic marketing activities.
- Identify and discuss the importance of business ethics in relation to the management structure and practices of Patagonia.
- Develop insights into Patagonia's application of business theory, for example, the STP (segmentation, targeting, positioning) model, by conducting an evaluation of past, current, and future customer targeting.
- Apply core marketing theories, for example, using Ansoff's matrix to evaluate potential growth strategies for Patagonia.
- Evaluate the current retail strategy including experiential marketing and use of flagship and bricks-and-mortar stores.
- Identify and evaluate the potential advantages and risks of reverse marketing and viral marketing; evaluate how viral marketing aligns with the brand's core values and business philosophy.

Introduction

Patagonia was founded in 1972 by the then thirty-four-year-old French Canadian rock-climbing pioneer Yvon Chouinard. Chouinard's founder story of his personal journey from intrepid rock climber to leader of a multimillion-dollar outdoor-clothing company is integral to the brand's identity and is showcased on the Patagonia website (see "Company History" sections on https://www.patagonia.com). It relates how his passion for nature and outdoor activities led to his starting his first business, Chouinard Equipment, selling innovative high-quality climbing equipment designed for minimal environmental impact. Now in his seventies, Chouinard heads a prosperous global apparel business with an environmentally focused business philosophy in tune with twenty-first-century lifestyles and values. This business philosophy is articulated in two books. *Let My People Go Surfing* (first published in 2005 and reissued in a ten-year anniversary edition) is a memoir and manifesto of sustainable business practices which has become something of a bible for the sustainability movement; his second book, *The Responsible Company* (Chouinard and Stanley 2012) further articulates Chouinard's principles and mission.

The Patagonia outdoor clothing and activewear brand was created as Chouinard leveraged its reputation as the largest supplier of climbing equipment in the United States. The new brand name, Patagonia, was selected for its universal air of adventure and mystique, and ease of pronunciation in many languages. On their website Patagonia affectionately refer to their customers as fellow "dirt-bags"—athletes, travelers, and adventurers, and their product positioning focus is on healthy lifestyles rather than the competitive spirit of brands such as Nike or the fashion focus of others such as Elle Sport. As the company's website explains: the company "makes clothes for climbing—as well as for skiing, snowboarding, surfing, fly fishing, paddling and trail running. These are all silent sports. None require a motor; none deliver the cheers of a crowd. In each sport, reward comes in the form of hard-won grace and moments of connection between us and nature" (Patagonia 2018b).

Nevertheless, the extensive range does bring the company into competition with some large companies in the sports and outdoor leisure market as well as independent specialist retailers. In the United States the market leader REI (Recreational Equipment Inc.) has approximately 50 percent market share, with Eastern Mountain Sports and Columbia Sportswear significant competitors in this segment as well as The North Face (owned by the VF Corporation), which is growing fast from a low market share. Further competition is provided by discounters such as Target and Wal-Mart, from mainstream brands such as L L Bean and Timberland (at the style end of the serious market), and companies such as lululemon exploiting the athleisure market. In addition, Patagonia products can be found on generalist online retailers such as Amazon and eBay, and the more fashion focused ASOS.

Consumer and lifestyle trends are providing a growth impetus to the outdoor leisure market which is expected to show an annual growth rate of 9.8 percent, resulting in a market value of $84,238 million by 2022 (Statista 2018). Publicity given to the importance of health and fitness are encouraging outdoor activities and the large baby-boom demographic have increasing leisure time as they reach retirement. Recent years have also seen the emergence of the ecotourism market, while the stress and pollution characterizing continuing urbanization is encouraging people to enjoy nature when they can.

Performance is the key selling point for Patagonia products and the brand's marketing emphasizes product features and benefits. Patagonia runs its own product and fabric development laboratory which is guided by the three overriding principles of quality, innovation, and environmental impact. Patagonia's Product Lifecycle Initiative aims to make their garments more multifunctional ensuring customers get increased value from them, that environmental impact is minimized, and the total product range reduced. For example, materials for outdoor clothing include durable, sustainable cotton and high-tech nylons and synthetics, and clothing items are lightweight, breathable, water and wind resistant, or warm. Products are frequently recognized for their quality by their peers. For example, in 2014 *Outside Magazine* named *Patagonia's* nano-air jacket and hoody for their Gear of the Year award.

The Patagonia range has expanded to cover many kinds of outdoor sports and leisure activities and now sells clothing, bags and backpacks for men, women, children, and babies; the online shop showcases the complete range, with jackets, causal tops, and trousers being the dominant product categories. The product range now extends to over 1,000 product lines, selling internationally to customers who aspire to the brand's adventurous associations even though they may not personally pursue them, and its iconic fleeces have become the "uniform" of San Francisco area venture capitalists. In 2014, it was reported that Patagonia had a 14.4 percent share of the $4 billion US core specialist outdoor leisure market, and although Patagonia seems to be an unlikely and maybe even reluctant fashion brand, there are a number of factors that point to the appeal of this iconic brand in a fashion context.

Business Problem

Patagonia did not set out to be a fashion brand; however, the core appeal of Patagonia products, their authenticity as functional attire, and the quality of the materials used has resulted in the brand having a considerable following from fashion-aware consumers. Patagonia-branded product is not only sold through the mass-market online fashion retailer ASOS, but is heralded by trend-led fashion destinations, such as *Hypebeast*, a Hong Kong-based online retail and editorial source for contemporary men's fashion. In 2015, fleece jackets reminiscent of Patagonia styling appeared on the runway of women's brand Altuzarra and Louis Vuitton's men's collections, and up-and-coming menswear designer Patrik Ervell cited the Californian "normcore" style as his inspiration to include fleece in his range that year (Sherman 2015). More recently *GQ* magazine published a feature article on Patagonia entitled "How Patagonia Became Fashion's Favorite Outdoor Brand," in which the author suggests "Authenticity, thoughtful design, strong ethos—wait, isn't that everything a brand needs to be cool in 2017?" (Hine 2017a). In another *GQ* article Hine (2017b) writes, "Patagonia has spent the last few decades making corporate responsibility look cool, and in the process has made their classic products look even cooler."

Retail strategy

Physical distribution is handled from a 342,000-sqare-foot (32,000m²) warehouse in Reno, Nevada. It serves as the global distribution hub for Patagonia, shipping some seven million units annually to the company's US retail stores; online and catalog customers; and its wholesale network of more than 1,000 dealers around the world. As in all things, Patagonia was sensitive to environmental concerns when establishing its facility, equipping it (like its head office) with solar panels to provide power (Troy 2015).

Patagonia operates a multichannel strategy, which is partially under its direct control and partially run in partnership with a network of dealers varied between a version of franchising where stores operate under the Patagonia brand and traditional wholesalers. According to Dun and Bradstreet in 2015 Patagonia had 900 accounts in the USA. It is not easy to identify exactly how many Patagonia-branded stores exist and their split between company owned and dealer outlets as no overall directory is provided. In 2017, their own stores included thirty-one in the United States, twelve in Japan, four in Chile, two in Australia, and one each in Argentina and Canada (according to the Patagonia website in 2017). According to an article published in the *Telegraph* (Cave 2015) twenty-four stores in Europe bear the Patagonia name; however, in 2017 the website appeared to indicate only three were fully owned.

Stores tend to be located near to centers of key sports—mountains for climbing and skiing, rivers for fishing, and the sea for boarding. For example, the company's mainland European stores are all in the Alpine region. There is a flagship "Iron Works" store adjacent to the company's headquarters at Ventura, although Patagonia's largest store, with 750 m² of selling space, is in Portland, Oregon. The most recent US store is a three-floor, 14,000-square-foot outlet opened in an old warehouse in the Soho district of Manhattan in July 2015. Amongst its many innovations is a 3,500-square-foot community workspace which nonprofit environmental organizations can book for meetings and events. Reclaimed materials are used throughout, including material salvaged from the refurbishment of the New York Museum of Modern Art. Customers can sign up for yoga classes and other activities. An on-site Worn Wear repair station fixes customers' old Patagonia clothes for them. The company designs each store as a one-off; as Jim Little the vice president of global retail, explains in a 2011 blog post:

> Cookie cutters are not part of the toolbox. Each store has its individual flair and flavor spiced with vibrant colors, one-of-a-kind displays and amazing sports images installed by our visual design team. We like historic buildings when we can find them and like a good marriage prospect, we like them unattached—that is, freestanding … We use existing building materials whenever we can to preserve the integrity of each store. We also use repurposed, recycled and sustainably produced materials. (Little 2011)

In many ways, Patagonia's website appears more like the website of an environmental nongovernmental organization (NGO) than a mainstream retailer. The company has continent-specific websites which are informative and visually stunning. Pro.patagonia.com serves Patagonia professional customers, jp.patagonia.com serves Japan and eu.patagonia.com serves Europe. The sites are available in five languages: English, Japanese, German, Italian, and French. In July 2014, Dmitri Siegel, Patagonia's global executive creative director and VP for global e-commerce led a team that relaunched the website. A range of short videos embedded against most products highlight key product features and provide information about materials. The site is mobile optimized and Patagonia also has a mobile app to help facilitate e-sales, but still devotes 50 percent of its space to images and editorial rather than shopping. The site receives around three quarters of a million visitors monthly in the USA.

Patagonia sustainability initiatives and supply-chain management

Patagonia's mission is stated on its website as: "Build the best product, cause no unnecessary harm, use business to inspire and implement solutions to the environmental crisis" (Patagonia 2017). All Patagonia products carry its "ironclad guarantee," that the company will repair their products at a reasonable price or if an item is defective, offer a rebate or refund. Chouinard passionately believes that this concern for quality and sustainability does not need to pose a conflict with running a highly successful business and this is embodied in the company's involvement in a range of initiatives. "Every time we do the right thing, our profits go up ... I look at this company as an experiment to see if we can run it so it's here 100 years from now and always makes the best-quality stuff," he says (Hamm 2006).

Patagonia has worked independently and in collaboration with peer and competitor businesses, as well as suppliers and industry bodies, to ensure its own standards of sourcing and production whilst influencing policy and practice at an industry level. In 2008 Patagonia was awarded the Eco Brand of the Year at the Volvo Eco Design Forum and Patagonia is one of the founding partners of the Sustainable Apparel Coalition. Patagonia was an early adopter of organic cotton, using it exclusively in all cotton products since 1996. They subsequently launched Patagonia Denim in 2015 which uses organic cotton and less impactful dyeing and production processes. Many of its garments rely on bird down to provide their insulation, and Patagonia has been at the forefront of ensuring its down supply chain meets the highest industry standards (for more details of Patagonia's social and environmental initiatives see Table 40.1).

Committed to making its products landfill-free, the company's entire product range is recyclable and the introduction of childrenswear, rather than being a response to an identified market opportunity, was a solution to the problem of wasted scraps of material from the production process for adult garments. Launched in 2016, Patagonia's Re\\\ ten-piece collection of jackets, vests, and pants are made from 100 percent reused down, wool, and polyester, and even the labels, zippers, and buttons are made using between 50 and 80 percent reclaimed materials.

The corporate responsibility section of Patagonia's website includes a link to their "Footprint Chronicles" a world map detailing the social and environmental impact of each of their products and giving locations and brief details of the farms, textile mills, and factories involved in their supply chain. Patagonia was forced to reexamine its wool supply chain following a 2015 exposé of animal cruelty at one facility which diminished their reputation for ethical sourcing embodied in the Patagonia Wool Standard. New guidelines for each

TABLE 40.1 Examples of Patagonia's Social and Environmental Initiatives

Initiative	Details
Recycled Polyester, 1993 (https://www.patagonia.com/recycled-polyester.html)	Patagonia was the first outdoor-clothing manufacturer to recycle plastic bottles into fleece fabric.
1 percent For The Planet, 2002 (https://www.onepercentfortheplanet.org)	Cofounded with Craig Mathews of Blue Ribbon Files and originating from Patagonia's established policy of contributing 1 percent of all sales (or 10 percent of profits—whichever is greater) to environmental organizations since 1985. 1,486 members in more than 60 countries contribute 1 percent of their total sales as an "Earth Tax" to environmental organizations.
Common Threads Initiative, 2005	A garment recycling program that encourages Patagonia and its customers to reduce, repair, reuse, recycle, and reimagine Patagonia products.
Patagonia Traceable Down, 2007 (https://www.patagonia.com/traceable-down.html)	Traces down from parent farm to apparel factory to help ensure the birds that supply it are not force-fed or live-plucked. Since 2017, Patagonia virgin down is certified to Global TDS (Traceable Down Standard).
Sustainable Apparel Coalition, 2010 (http://apparelcoalition.org)	Cofounded with Wal-mart to work collaboratively with peers and competitors in the apparel, footwear, and textile sector to develop a universal approach to measuring sustainability.
Worn Wear, 2013	The Patagonia subsidiary Worn Wear encourages recycling of Patagonia unsold and discarded products which are laundered and resold. As well as annual tours in the United States the first Worn Wear tour in Europe took place in 2016.
Tin Shed Ventures, 2013 (previously $20 Million & Change)	Patagonia's corporate venture capital fund used to invest in environmentally and socially responsible start-ups.
DamNation, 2014 (https://www.damnationfilm.com)	Patagonia produced a documentary exposing the environmental damage done by America's 80,000+ dams.
Patagonia Denim, 2015 (https://www.patagonia.com/denim.html)	100 percent organic denim collection manufactured using environmentally friendlier dye, Fair Trade certified sewing practices, and 100 percent organic cotton.

stage of wool supply were drafted and the supply-chain details were linked to products in the online shop, helping make Patagonia's supply chain one of the most transparent in the clothing industry. Patagonia updates its supplier list twice a year. In 2018, the company stated it was working with seventy-nine finished good suppliers located in thirteen countries across Asia and the Americas, namely Bangladesh, China, Colombia, El Salvador, Hong Kong, India, Vietnam, Mexico, Nicaragua, the Philippines, Sri Lanka, Thailand, and the USA. Patagonia regularly audits its garment production factories, scoring them on how they measure up to social responsibility and environmental goals. For its materials suppliers (mills) further down the supply chain Patagonia has environmental and health and safety requirements as well as a raw materials social responsibility program, under which suppliers must measure whether they comply with safety, social responsibility, and environmental criteria as well as citing areas for improvement.

Although it could be argued that Patagonia's main sustainability thrust is concerning the environment, their significant recent growth in Fair Trade certificated garments indicates the company's deep concern for social well-being. On the company website (Patagonia.com 2017) it states that 30 percent of the entire product range is now Fair Trade and the company showcases its commitment in a twelve-minute film *Fair Trade: The First Steps*, found in the "Corporate Responsibility/Fair Trade" section of the company website. In January 2017, a Patagonia press release announced that the company had won the World Economic Forum Accenture Strategy Award for Circular Economy (Byars 2017).

People management

Aside from Chouinard himself, president and CEO of Patagonia Inc. and Patagonia Works, Rose Marcario is one of the most significant figures in the organization. Other board positions are managing director, treasurer, and vice president of human resources and head of shared services, which includes the finance and legal departments. Chouinard's wife Malinda is also listed as company director and is a major shareholder in the business.

The functional structure of Patagonia provides for a high level of centralization that helps to ensure integration and control over the firm's activities and functional areas. Although top-level management is not structured by product category, there is a team leader for each of the eight major product areas to oversee the design and creation of a range appropriate for all of Patagonia's markets. The number of people working in the organization has grown steadily as the business has grown but remains slim. In 2016, it was reported that 866 women and 862 men worked in the business and its family-friendly policies including maternity and paternity benefits are reported to have positively impacted productivity and resulted in a 100 percent return to work of new mothers (Chhabra 2016).

In his book *Let my People Go Surfing* Chouinard extolled the virtues of "Positive Leadership," by which he means decisive, proactive decision-making. Although Patagonia has a reputation as an outstanding and enlightened employer, anyone who does not embrace its culture or values, or who fails to perform does not last long as the company demands hard work, creativity, collaboration, and results. That said, employee turnover rates are well below the US industry average. In keeping with the company's values sales associates receive no commission on the items that they sell—unusual in the retail sector.

The boundaries between work and personal time are blurred for Patagonia employees and the company embraces flexible working hours—just as long as the job gets finished! In the words of Chouinard: "I think flexitime has worked really well … nobody cares when you work as long as the work gets done. The surf comes up—you go surfing" (Chouinard quoted in Wieners 2012). It is unsurprising that employees appear to be closely engaged with the brand's values and mission. As Nicholas Ind states (2007) "Patagonia is a standard bearer for an 'employee centric approach' that stresses the value of engaging people with the organization they work for and stimulating them to live the brand." A taste of the culture of the company can be found in the Jobs section of the website under the "Culture/Life" section (Patagonia 2018a).

Marketing

Apparel businesses make decisions on product type and market level to make the most efficient use of their resources. This process of segmentation and targeting helps them to determine where to position themselves in relation to competitor brands so they can best appeal to their target customers. Patagonia's focus on quality design, materials, and production, and its pricing strategy means their customers tend to be fairly affluent and discerning buyers. Some cynics have questioned whether Patagonia is in fact a luxury brand, and coined the nickname "Patagucci" for the business. In 2006, the director of Patagonia's catalog operations, Paul Miller, reported that Patagonia had identified three customer typologies based on a detailed analysis of purchasing patterns from the company's catalog:

- casuals: one-time buyers new to the brand, 64 percent of whom don't repeat purchase

- loyalists: become avid customers and understand Patagonia's core values, appreciate the durability and performance of the clothing; 50 percent of these buyers are lost after two years

- cheerleaders: avid buyers who begin by identifying with Patagonia's core values and its socially conscious business practices. Ninety-five percent of cheerleaders recommend the company to friends and family, often online. (Miller 2006)

Targeting such a niche market, Patagonia has sought to reinforce its sustainability positioning through superior technical knowledge, customer service and services, events, courses, advice and information, and its garment repair service. Company records indicate that Patagonia recycles about 20,000 pounds of gear per year (roughly equal by weight to twenty thousand R2 jackets) and repairs some 40,000 garments; their Reno repair shop is the largest facility of its kind in North America. This service marketing initiative has created a sustainable dimension of competitive differentiation, as well as decreasing the company's ecological footprint and enhancing its reputation.

The company's view is that "Building a brand is not about marketing. It's about having authenticity" (Reinhardt 2003). Marketing is not seen by the company as a "promise," but rather a campaigning "call to action." The company had sales of $800 million in 2016 (double its 2010 sales), and despite the company's ambivalent attitude towards marketing, in March 2015, the American Marketing Association inducted Chouinard into their Hall of Fame. The famous "Don't buy this jacket" campaign in November 2011 encapsulates the brand authenticity. The very simple and clear message was made in a full-page advertisement taken in *The New York Times* on Black Friday, probably the world's busiest shopping day. This created controversy because of the apparent contradiction of the message and the use of an advertisement to broadcast it. A clothing company with retail stores whose ultimate aim is to earn money asking its customers not to buy its own products is very provocative. Sales assistants were even told to ask customers presenting at the checkout "Do you really need this product"? The campaign met with two kinds of reaction: total rejection (from noncustomers) of the exhortation, thinking it is pure hypocrisy; and total adherence (from loyal and potential customers) because the message was in line with the set of values of the brand and its followers. Discussions in the marketing community since 2011 have come up with the term *reverse marketing* to describe what Patagonia did, but at the time the company certainly did not employ the technique as an instrument of sales generation. It did, nevertheless, generate an enormous amount of discussion in the media and precipitated a growth of 40 percent in jacket sales in the following two years.

Joy Howard, who joined Patagonia as vice president of marketing in 2013 explains the company's reluctance to use conventional advertising: "We have a mission to solve problems in the world. That's very much a part of how we engage with consumers, and that engagement puts a low priority on advertising. It's the 'dead last' thing Patagonia wants to do" (Berg 2013). Word of mouth is central to the brand community. Patagonia is a company about whom stories are told—on the website, in the advertising, in the Head Office and stores, out in the field.

Patagonia's communications strategy has principally revolved around publicizing its many environmental initiatives and much of the budget goes into photography and filmmaking. The 2011 *Worn Wear* film has already achieved classic status as an icon of the sustainability movement. Like any activist organization, Patagonia is expert at generating PR, both in the physical and digital worlds. By creating a relevant and compelling social media presence, the company has been able to grow its consumer base by targeting new demographic markets and promoting organized activities. Its various websites have extensive sections explaining its initiatives and providing journalists with copy for publication. In July 2014, Adam Fletcher, director of PR and communications, launched a company blog that can be filtered by subject sections (*The Cleanest Line* n.d.) to share news with editors and the wider Patagonia community including customers.

International development

Patagonia is heavily concentrated in its home market. Most international sales are achieved via relationships with local partners, and as such will be entered into Patagonia's accounts at a value considerably less than retail price depending on the nature of the relationship. Japan is Patagonia's largest overseas market where they enjoy a long-term relationship with the Japanese menswear business BEAMS. Free standing Patagonia stores operate in the main cities (fifteen outlets in Tokyo alone), and the product is also distributed to independent stores. In June 2014, a new flagship branch opened in the Marunouchi district of Tokyo. Most of the materials were procured from old buildings and reused at the store in keeping with Patagonia's values and philosophy. Late in 2014, a Patagonia store opened in Seoul, South Korea, in partnership with Yong No Jo, a local Korean sports brand agent. In South America, Patagonia has a store in Buenos Aires, Argentina, and a network of thirty dealers. There are also dealers in neighboring Brazil and its spiritual home—Chile.

There are six partner stores in France, five in Italy, and two in Switzerland—clustered in ski centers. In 2014, the company decided to reorganize its European operations to strengthen its position both in terms of countries covered and products sold. The European headquarters was moved from the Alps (Annecy, France) to Amsterdam, the Netherlands, where new distribution, e-commerce, and customer service operations were set up.

In the UK, a new trade and dealer showroom was opened in central London, near Oxford Street. According to Ryan Gellert (Patagonia's European manager) the company already runs a network of 140 dealers in the UK market, including leading sports names such as Farlows of Pall Mall, Ellis Brigham, Cotswold Outdoor, and Snow & Rock (Cave 2015). In 2011, one Patagonia dealer, the Outdoor Group of Hathersage in the Derbyshire Peak District, took the major step of opening a UK flagship Patagonia store in the former Watney Brewery heritage site in Covent Garden, Central London. At the time this received much press attention; however, clearly the venture was not successful and the store closed in January 2014. In 2015, London was again discussed as the site for a new Patagonia store as part of a plan to increase European business. In his words:

The people who know Patagonia in Europe and the UK are often very passionate about the brand but there are not nearly enough people that we have communicated with there and that's something we're going to address. I would like to see our business in Europe come closer to 20pc of the global turnover of the brand .... [Patagonia] will be focusing storytelling around key markets and key stories and working to reintroduce the brand. (quoted in Cave 2015)

However, it was later announced that the city of Manchester, with its proximity to the Peak District, had been selected as the location for a new 307 m² store to be housed in a heritage building at 51 King Street.

Patagonia describes itself as an activist company, which inevitably results in political engagement; in 2017, Patagonia added its signature to the open letter to the international community and parties to the Paris Agreement from US state, local, and business leaders in response to the US president's decision to abandon the 2015 Climate Accord. Patagonia has established itself as an authentic brand and leveraged its compelling business through storytelling. Patagonia's business objectives have never been profit-driven and since 2012, when Patagonia Works was created as a Benefit Corporation, the business has enacted its mission to make a positive impact on society and the environment over shareholder returns.

With its commitment to environmental, social, and financial sustainability the brand faces choices about its future direction. With an anti-consumerist ethos at the core of the business Patagonia has adopted a slow growth business model but its own success and the increasing athleisure segment offers Patagonia potential to expand internationally, and to reconsider whether its focus should be on performance or its fashion offer. In 2009, Chouinard was reported as saying that he could sell US$20 million of merchandise annually if he was willing to supply Nordstrom (the leading US premium department-store group), but he preferred to decline the opportunity. So, if turnover, global presence, and customer numbers are not the measure of success that resonate with Patagonia's management, is there a more innovative direction the business could be taking and what would success look like?

Business Questions

1   Patagonia's view of marketing communication is that it is the glue that binds together all the members of its brand community. It also allows the company to evangelize their environmental message to the wider universe, including key influencers and decision makers. Thus, effective communications are vital to the success of this ambition.Segmentation is a strategic process used to divide a market or group of consumers into subgroups or segments. Targeting is the strategic process of designing products, services, and/or marketing materials for a specific segment. Positioning is how a brand sits in relation to its competitors. These processes are combined within the concept of STP (segmentation, targeting, and positioning). Given that both qualitative and quantitative factors can contribute to a brand's position, analyze Patagonia's approach to segmentation, profiling the brand's target market(s) and analyzing the brand's positioning within the outdoor activity clothing market, and the fashion market.

2   Apply the concept of the marketing mix to analyze the retail-marketing strategy of Patagonia (restricting your analysis to clothing for the purpose of this exercise).

3 Debate the idea(s) behind the "Don't buy this jacket" campaign. Was this a shrewd piece of reverse marketing conspired to take advantage of mass consumerism on Black Friday? Or was this a genuine plea from an authentic, considerate, and sustainable brand? Would this kind of viral campaign work for today's more savvy customers?

4 International business is rather more significant to Patagonia in unit terms than it appears in dollars. Patagonia's cautious international expansion is in keeping with its slow-growth brand ethos, but is this approach putting the company at risk from competitive pressure?

5 Given the brand's slow-growth strategy, to what extent should Patagonia take advantage of its cult status as a fashion brand? Should they undertake a repositioning strategy to do this? What are the opportunities and risks of brand extensions for Patagonia?

6 Digital and social marketing offer the opportunity for increased consumer touchpoints and customized marketing. How are Patagonia's current digital marketing practices performing? Provide a SWOT analysis of Patagonia's digital marketing strategy to help prepare your recommendations for this question.

7 Patagonia uses online and wholesalers to distributes their product in most of their international markets. What are the benefits and risks associated with this retail strategy? You could choose one or several international markets for your answer.

References and Further Reading

Berg, Meredith Derby. 2013. "Why Advertising is 'Dead Last' Priority at Outerwear Marketer Patagonia." *Adage.com*. Accessed July 2018. http://adage.com/article/cmo-strategy/advertising-dead-priority-patagonia/245712/

Bradley, Ryan. 2015. "The Woman Driving Patagonia to Be (Even More) Radical." *Fortune.com*, September 14. Accessed July 2018. http://fortune.com/2015/09/14/rose-marcario-patagonia/

Byars, Tessa. 2017. "Patagonia Wins Circular Economy Multinational Award at World Economic Forum Annual Meeting in Davos." *Patagonia Works*, January 17. Accessed July 2018. https://www.patagoniaworks.com/press/2017/1/17/patagonia-wins-circular-economy-multinational-award-at-world-economic-forum-annual-meeting-in-davos

Cave, Andrew. 2015. "Ethical Outdoor Brand Patagonia Targets 'thoughtful expansion." *The Telegraph*, May 3. Accessed July 2018. https://www.telegraph.co.uk/finance/newsbysector/retailandconsumer/leisure/11580811/Ethical-outdoor-brand-Patagonia-targets-thoughtful-expansion.html

Chhabra, Esha. 2016. "Does Patagonia Have the Answer for Narrowing the Wage Gap?" *The Guardian*, November 17. Accessed July 2018. https://www.theguardian.com/sustainable-business/2016/nov/17/us-companies-gender-wage-gap-patagonia-arjuna-capital-salesforce-expedia

Chouniard, Yves. 2006. *Let My People Go Surfing*. New York: Penguin Press.

Chouniard, Yves and Vincent Stanley. 2012. *The Responsible Company: What We've Learned From Patagonia's First 40 Years*. Ventura: Patagonia Books.

Dun & Bradstreet. 2015. *Patagonia Inc—Comprehensive Report*, published June 15th. New York: D&B.

Hamm, Steve. 2006. "Patagonia—a Passion for the Planet." *Bloomberg*. Accessed July 2018. https://www.bloomberg.com/news/articles/2006-08-20/a-passion-for-the-planet

Hine, Samuel. 2017a. "How Patagonia Became Fashion's Favorite Outdoor Brand." *GQ*. Accessed July 2018. https://www.gq.com/story/patagonia-labels-on-fire

Hine, Samuel. 2017b. "How Dickies, Patagonia and Carhartt are Making Street Style Dope Again." *GQ*. Accessed July 2018. https://www.gq.com/story/new-heritage-dickies-carhartt-patagonia-style.

Ind, Nicholas. 2007. *Living the Brand*, 3rd edn. London: Kogan Page

Little, Jim. 2011. "53 and Growing—Announcing the Opening of Our Latest Patagonia Stores." *The Cleanest Line* (blog) *Patagonia*. Accessed July 2018. https://www.patagonia.com/blog/2011/01/53-and-growing-1/

Lutz, Kristall. 2011. "What Makes Patagonia 'the Coolest Company on the Planet'?" *Opportunity Green*, January 27. Accessed July 2018. https://www.opportunitygreen.com/green-business-blog/2011/01/27/what-makes-patagonia-the-coolest-company-on-the-planet-insights-from-founder-yvon-chouinard/

Miller, Paul. 2006. "Multi-channel Marketing the Patagonia Way." Accessed July 2018. https://www.mytotalretail.com/article/multichannel-marketing-the-patagonia-way-39064/all/

Patagonia. n.d. "Patagonia Works, Annual Benefit Corporation Report May 2012–April 2013." Accessed July 2018. https://www.patagonia.com/pdf/en_US/bcorp_annual_report_2014.pdf

Patagonia. 2018a. "Culture/Life." Accessed July 2018. https://www.patagonia.com/culture.html

Patagonia. 2018b. "Mission Statement." Accessed July 2018. https://www.patagonia.com/company-info.html

Reinhardt, Forest L., Ramon Casadesus-Masanell, and Deborah Freier. 2003. "Patagonia." *Harvard Business School Case* 703-035, March. Revised January 2010.

Reinhardt, Forest L., Ramon Casadesus-Masanell, and Lauren Barley. 2014. "Patagonia (B)." *Harvard Business School Supplement* 714–465, February.

Sherman, Lauren. 2015. "Why Fashion Insiders Are Buzzing About Patagonia." *Wall Street Journal*. Accessed July 2018. https://www.wsj.com/articles/why-fashion-insiders-are-buzzing-about-patagonia-1420825704

Statista. 2018. "Sports & Outdoor Worldwide." Accessed July 2018. https://www.statista.com/outlook/259/100/sports-outdoor/worldwide

The Cleanest Line. n.d. [Blog]. https://www.patagonia.com/blog/

Troy, Mike. 2015. "Patagonia Encourages Consumers to Repair Clothes Instead of Always Buying New." *Chainstoreage.com*. Accessed July 2018. https://www.chainstoreage.com/news/patagonia-encourages-consumers-repair-clothes-instead-always-buying-new/

Wieners, Bradford. 2012. "Environmental Movement has Lost says Patagonia Founder: 10Q." *Bloomberg*, May 2. Accessed July 15, 2015. https://www.bloomberg.com/sustainability/the-grid/77/

Chapter 41

The Industry Versus The Indie:
The case of Zara Versus Tuesday Bassen

Fast Fashion, Unlawful Copying, and Enamel Pins

Roxanne Peters

Fashion is particularly difficult to define in a legal sense and often works are not protected by copyright, a type of intellectual property (IP) that protects original creative works from being "copied" without permission. Reinterpreting popular designs plays a vital role in an evolving fashion industry. Healthy inspiration can drive economic growth and ensures that fashion designers are recognized fairly for their creations. Because of the fast-paced nature of the industry, some designers do not see the value in protecting their IP. They innovate to stay ahead of their competitors. Others would protect their creations but legal fees and a lack of understanding the law prohibit them from doing so. Licensing contracts are often used by those who do wish to collaborate and effectively manage their IP. Therefore, what happens when a global fashion retailer blatantly copies an independent artist's designs with no attribution or prior agreement?This case explores what happens when an independent brand takes on a multinational industry player. In this case, Zara was accused of copying independent designer Tuesday Bassen's enamel pins in 2016. Bassen, a well-respected illustrator uses her original designs for accessories and has collaborated with several high-profile brands including The New Yorker, the United Nations, and Nike. Informed by her online followers that Zara was using her work without crediting her, Bassen challenged the global brand on the basis that her copyright had been infringed. The fashion retailer defended its position by questioning the originality and copyright status of Bassen's accessories.

Learning Objectives

Upon completion of this case, students should be able to:

- Define types of intellectual property that apply to fashion design.
- Explain the challenges that independent designers face working in the global fashion industry.
- Describe and evaluate strategies for protecting and registering intellectual property.
- Describe strategies for how large brands can collaborate with independent designers to realize positive outcomes.
- Discuss and debate the concepts of inspiration versus imitation of other people's works.

Introduction

Fashion is one of the world's most important creative industries. It is a significant contributor to the global economy, estimated to be worth $2.4 trillion in total value in 2016 (Business of Fashion and McKinsey and Company 2016). If ranked alongside individual countries' GDP, it would represent the world's seventh largest economic sector (IMF 2016). The industry is nuanced, the practice wide-ranging, from luxury brands who have traditionally presented collections per season to high street retailers who succeed on a business model of "manufacturing and marketing which thrives on constant change and the frequent availability of new products" (Hanbury 2018). Competing for a place in the market alongside well-established fashion houses and global retailers are independent designers and creatives.

Fast fashion is a contemporary term representing the way high street brands emulate catwalk collections with affordable price tags. The business model underpinning today's fast fashion industry derives from the US in the 1980s. A product-driven concept based on a manufacturing model transitioned to one informed by a market-based model in the 1990s and early 2000s.

Today Zara leads the way as the most successful retailer of fast fashion, ahead of other renowned brands such as H&M, Primark, and Japanese company Uniqlo. Founded in 1975 by Armanico Ortega (one of the richest people in the world in 2018 [Bloomberg Reporting 2018]), it now has an annual revenue of more than 20 billion euros ($25 billion). Zara is part of the Inditex group which includes brands Bershka, Pull & Bear, and Massimo Dutti. The company represents 6,500 shops in 88 different countries and sets itself apart from its competitors with its unique business model of being fast paced and operating in "proximity markets," i.e. Spain, Portugal, Turkey, and Morocco rather than Asia (Ruddick 2014).

Zara's success lies in the unique connection between its stores, in-house designers, and factories. Investment in large commercial and design teams means that the product range evolves quickly and Zara boasts an average two-week turnaround time from production to in-store sales. Its strategy involves stocking limited ranges and updating collections often to deliver the latest emerging trends. This means that customers are encouraged to make quick buying decisions. With a limited supply of merchandise it means that there is little surplus, quick sales, and often no need for markdowns.

Fast-fashion brands, including Zara, make it a priority to stay connected with the latest trends and style formats and in doing so look to independent designers for inspiration. In recent years, many high street brands have been seen to use "copycat" designs and have faced lawsuits from well-known retailers and designers (CBS News. 2017). However, this is only possible if the designer or brand has the resources, finances, and know-how to pursue any unlawful use of their work. Furthermore, intellectual property, the legal right which helps creators manage the way their works are used in enterprise, is complex, differing from country to country and industry to industry. In 2016 Zara was accused of unlawfully using independent designer Tuesday Bassen's enamel pin designs for its popular "it" accessory (*The Fashion Law* 2018).

Business Problem

"You know what? Sometimes it sucks to be an artist because companies like @zara consistently rip you off and deny it," Tuesday Bassen, indie artist, via Twitter (Bassen 2016).

What happened?

LA-based indie illustrator and designer Tuesday Bassen has over 168,000 Instagram followers and is considered a role model for young women with her unique aesthetic take on enamel pins, patches, and clothing. Having collaborated with brands such as Adidas, Nike, and the United Nations which would have involved contractually agreeing the terms and conditions of how Bassen's intellectual property was licenced, she discovered that Zara had copied almost her entire catalogue of work without seeking permission.

In 2016 when enamel pins were the "it" accessory, global brand Zara produced several accessories bearing a very similar resemblance to Tuesday Bassen's creations and other independent designers. When challenged by Bassen, Zara responded by stating that Bassen's designs are "too simple" but also overlooked her talent and reputation within the indie scene by referencing their ninety-eight million monthly online visits. When challenged, Inditex's legal team confirmed that it has "more than 600 designers in house that create more than 50,000 designs a year, it has the highest respect towards each individual's creativity and will investigate this specific case to its end" (*The Fashion Law* 2016).

Zara questioned the designer's credibility, comparing its global trading figures and online traffic to the designer's dedicated fan base. Bassen's experience has led to other designers discovering their works have been copied by Zara and other designers have since legally challenged other brands for unfair exploitation.

What is the legal protection for fashion creatives?

Copyright

Copyright, a type of intellectual property, is the exclusive right a creator has to decide the way his or her work is represented or copied. It arises automatically on creation when a work is fixed (an expression of an idea) and lasts the life of the creator plus seventy years. Copyright protects original creative works such as illustration, music, books, films, photography, and in some cases extends to fashion. For example, jewelry has been considered more valuable in "creative" terms than mass-produced garments.

Historically, in a legal sense, fashion has been regarded as inferior to other creative industries. Until recently the protection of fashion creativity and innovation has varied substantially at a global level (Pouillard 2017). In countries such as the United States and the UK, fashion is often perceived as lacking in originality, seen to reference or borrow from someone else's work. In France and Italy, it is more likely that fashion, particularly couture, would be protected by copyright as an "artistic work."

In a legal sense, cases have focused on the useful, functional role fashion plays rather than considering any aesthetic qualities of a work. What is clear-cut are the two-dimensional creative elements of garments such as a graphic print on a T-shirt, fashion sketches, fashion photographs and illustrations. Creatives may be able to rely on other types of intellectual property such as trademarks, design rights, and patents to help prevent unlawful copying. The way creatives can manage the use of their works is usually via licensing agreements which often involve a fee or a royalty as a source of income. In other cases it may be that other contractual terms are agreed to enable the greatest commercial and creative exchange.

Design rights

Design rights protect the appearance of a product such as the shape and configuration as opposed to its function or the way a product works. Creatives can register a work for a small fee (this varies internationally) on the basis that the work is new and has "individual character." This can last up to twenty-five years from the year a work is manufactured (if renewed every five years). Unregistered design rights automatically protect designs for ten years after they are first sold or fifteen years after creation (whichever is earliest). In terms of fashion, design rights may include the surface decoration of textile fabrics, watch faces, the stitching of jeans, the shape of a jacket.

Registering designs is quick, simple, and relatively cheap, and can work well with trademarks; for example, if a word that is trademarked has a stylistic element, this may be registered as a design right.

Trademarks

A trademark is a symbol used to distinguish the goods and services of one company from those of its competitors and is commonly known as the "brand." Its primary purpose is to identify the origin of a product and examples in the context of fashion brands include the Nike swoosh, the Louis Vuitton print, the Chanel number 5 fragrance, the red Louboutin sole (in certain countries), the stylized wording "Paul Smith." Trademarks need to be registered and are the strongest form of IP protection as they can be renewed every ten years. They vary by territory so it is important that creatives register their trademark per country to ensure that no one else registers the same name. The elements of a strong brand "reflects the corporate image and represents the quality, reputation and character of the company and brand" (Centre for Fashion Enterprise 2012c).

Patents

Patents are registered intellectual property rights which protect certain new inventions and essentially the processes and way that things work. They can take a considerable amount of time to register and are expensive. Fashion design does not generally rely on patents for protection, but by way of example, Levis patented the first denim jeans in the 1800s, protecting the fastening of pockets and later waistbands.

Inspiration vs imitation: Copying and the fashion industry

The fashion industry is constantly evolving. With changes to the speed at which fashion is produced, combined with the rise of social media and its instant access to new trends, being inspired by or replicating what has come before has never been easier. With fast-fashion retailers such as Zara managing the entire production process in ten to fifteen working days, alleged copying can be "last season" before a creator is aware. Copying lies at the heart of fast-fashion where the focus is not on originality but on delivering affordable versions of the latest runway trends. However, there is an important distinction between inspiration and imitation. Imitation "refers to the production of identical copies and/or the substantial copying of other artistic works" (*The Fashion Law* 2017), and "makes a like for like replication of the cut, construction, print, pattern, and/or other features of another garment or accessory" (*The Fashion Law* 2017). Inspiration is different, creating something new from a preexisting work as is common in fashion.

What is the challenge for indie designers?

In short, established global brands have financial resources and legal departments. They also have successful business models which are a significant contributor to the global economy, for example, in 2015, Zara had over 2,000 stores and $14.5 billion of sales (Petro 2015). As fashion design is not recognized or protected in the same way as other types of industry and innovation, creators are unlikely to be able to rely on copyright protection to prevent counterfeiting.

Without financial backing, resources, and legal knowledge, small independent designers like Tuesday Bassen are disadvantaged when it comes to protecting their creative products and building a brand.

Business Questions

Legal

- What intellectual property rights might Tuesday Bassen have for her enamel pins? Do you consider her pins as "artistic works" or something else?
- Did Zara unlawfully copy Tuesday Bassen's designs and if so what did they do wrong?
- For independent designers like Tuesday Bassen, is it beneficial to register their designs?
- What are the risks if an independent designer like Tuesday Bassen does not choose to register their intellectual property?
- What other ways can an independent designer build their brand without registering their IP?
- Should the law be updated to provide stronger copyright protection for fashion?
- Discuss reasons for and against changing the law.

The fashion industry

- Some believe that copying has a positive impact of the fashion industry, encouraging inspiration and commercial opportunities. Others argue that it compromises creativity. Discuss whether copying has a positive and/or negative impact on the fashion industry and explain the rationale for each answer.

- What are the risks to the reputation of a global brand like Zara when exposed to having unfairly copied an independent designer's work?

Collaboration

- Consider how a global brand like Zara might be able to work more collaboratively with independent designers. What opportunities can you identify for Zara? For Tuesday Bassen?

- Tuesday Bassen is one of a number of independent designers whose works have been copied by global brands. How might designers work collaboratively to protect their works?

Ethics

- Is it ethical for global brands like Zara to draw inspiration from independent designer's works?

References and Further Reading

Bassen, Tuesday (@TuesdayBassen). 2016. "You know what? Sometimes it sucks to be an artist because companies like @zara consistently rip you off and deny it." *Twitter*, July 19, 3:29 pm. Accessed July 10, 2018. https://www.twitter.com/tuesdaybassen/status/755530142336688128?lang=en

Bloomberg Reporting. 2018. "Amancio Ortega." Bloomberg. Accessed July 10, 2018. https://www.bloomberg.com/billionaires/profiles/amancio-ortega-gaona/

CBS News. 2017. "Gucci Sues Forever 21 for Trademark Infringement." August 10. Accessed July 10, 2018. https://www.cbsnews.com/news/gucci-sues-forever-21-trademark-infringement-bomber-jacket/

Essemaker, Tina. 2016. "Tuesday Bassen." *The Great Disconentent*, May 23. Accessed March 4, 2018. https://www.thegreatdiscontent.com/interview/tuesday-bassen

Fashion Law, The. 2016. "Zara Comes Under Fire for Copying Indie Artists Designs." July 20. Accessed March 2018. https://www.thefashionlaw.com/home/zara-comes-under-fire-for-copying-indie-artists-designs

Fashion Law, The. 2017. "Why Is 'Copying' So Rampant in Fashion?" November 21. Accessed July 10, 2018. https://www.thefashionlaw.com/home/why-is-copying-so-rampant-in-fashion

Fashion Law, The. 2018. "Pins are Proving a Contentious Issue for Indie Designers and Fashion Copycats." March 8. Accessed March 4, 2018. https://www.thefashionlaw.com/home/pins-are-proving-a-contentious-issue-for-indie-designers-and-fashion-copycats

Gualtieri, Thomas, and Rodrigo Oriheula. 2018. "How Zara Transformed its Hometown into a Spanish Powerhouse." *Business Of Fashion*, March 2. Accessed March 6, 2018. https://www.businessoffashion.com/articles/news-analysis/zara-hipsters-transform-their-hometown-into-a-spanish-powerhouse

Hanbury, Mary. 2018. "Zara and Forever 21 Have a Dirty Little Secret." *Business Insider UK*, March 6. Accessed July 10, 2018. http://uk.businessinsider.com/zara-forever-21-fast-fashion-full-of-copycats-2018-3

International Monetary Fund (IMF). 2016. "List of Countries by Projected GDP." October 21. Accessed July 10, 2018. http://statisticstimes.com/economy/countries-by-projected-gdp.php

Malick, Nicole. 2017. "11 Indie Artists File Suit Against Copycat Retailer Francesca's Collections." *The Fashion Law*, January 19. Accessed March 4, 2018. https://www.thefashionlaw.com/home/11-indie-artists-file-suit-against-copycat-retailer-francescas-collections

Petro, Greg. 2015. "The Future of Fashion Retailing, Revisited, Part 2." *Forbes*, July 23. Accessed July 10, 2018. https://www.forbes.com/sites/gregpetro/2015/07/23/the-future-of-fashion-retailing-revisited-part-2-zara/#11f6c06965e6

Pouillard, Veronique. 2017. "The Milton Case (1955–1962). Defending the Intellectual Property Rights of Haute Couture in the United States." *Journal of Design History* 30, no. 4 (July): 356–70.

Puglise, Nicole. 2016. "Fashion Brand Zara Accused of Copying LA Artist's Designs." *The Guardian*, July 21. Accessed March 4, 2018. https://www.theguardian.com/fashion/2016/jul/21/zara-accused-copying-artist-designs-fashion

Ruddick, Graham. 2014. "How Zara Became the World's Biggest Retailer." *The Telegraph*, October 20. Accessed March 6, 2018. https://www.telegraph.co.uk/finance/newsbysector/retailandconsumer/11172562/How-Inditex-became-the-worlds-biggest-fashion-retailer.html

Chapter 42

Who Owns Genuine Ugg/UGG® Boots in the Global Footwear Marketplace?

Rachel Matthews

There is an ongoing legal dispute surrounding the use of "ugg," "Ugg," and "UGG®," all terms used to describe a form of flat-soled slip-on sheepskin boot. The case raises a number of points of contention concerning intellectual property (IP) in the global fashion marketplace. This case study uses published material to examine differing applications of the term "ugg"/"UGG®" and the issues this raises around IP protection.

Ugg boots have their origins in Australia, produced as a by-product of the wool industry in the early part of the twentieth century, before being adopted by surfers and subsequently becoming fashionable footwear. As such, there is a geographic divide in opinions about whether Ugg boots are a generic product category (like other footwear categories such as ballet flats or desert boots) or whether UGG® boots are a product defined by their branding. Two views on intellectual assets and their protection in relation to Ugg boots are examined in this case study, the first from the perspective of the Australian manufacturers of sheepskin boots and then from the owners of "UGG® Australia." The case study highlights how, despite the Australian heritage of this footwear, using the term "ugg" to market these products has become problematic and legally contestable for Australian footwear manufacturers. The study provides a brief overview of the development of Ugg boots and the "UGG® Australia" footwear line. It discusses concepts of IP through branding, trademarking of terms, and cultural appropriation.

Learning Objectives

Upon completion of this case, students should be able to:

- Review the arguments put forward by the Australian manufacturers of sheepskin Ugg boots and Deckers Outdoor Corp (parent company of UGG® Australia). Using this information, students can examine how each party defines its intellectual property.

- Describe how design protections such as trademarks and intellectual property (IP) function in the fashion industry.
- Describe the impact of internet and online shopping on issues of IP protection.
- Describe how the product's origins and cultural heritage can be leveraged as an intellectual asset.

Introduction

Ugg boots originated in Australia; however, since the late 1990s the popularity of this type of sheepskin boot has increased as many international celebrities have adopted them as their footwear of choice when off-duty. Online shopping has extended the footwear's circulation and allows the promotion and distribution of ugg-style boots in the global marketplace.

In this retail context, there are customers seeking UGG® Australia branded footwear, as worn by models, actors, and celebrities. There are also consumers searching for ugg-style sheepskin boots that are made in Australia due to the product's authentic Australian roots and quality of its sheepskin. Consequently, in the global fashion marketplace buying genuine Australian Ugg/UGG® boots is more problematic than one might expect.

As some sectors of the fashion industry move to develop more robust legal protections for intellectual property (IP), this case study provides an opportunity to examine the complexity of defining IP in a contemporary retail landscape no longer restricted by geographical locations. The study highlights two conflicting yet apparently legitimate positions on IP put forward in relation to this form of sheepskin boot. It calls attention to the contextual factors surrounding IP and challenges some common assumptions regarding legal protections.

To begin, this case study provides background information on the Ugg boot. It then discusses recent developments leading up to the legal dispute between two companies (Australian Leather based in Sydney, Australia versus the owner of UGG® Australia, Deckers Outdoor Corporation based in the United States). The study describes the concept of IP, its scope, and role in protecting ideas as commercial or business assets, before outlining the particular arguments being made by both parties in this legal dispute. Their differing positions highlight how branding, trademarked terms, and the cultural heritage of products operate as intellectual assets.

Background

Ugg boots are a soft double-faced sheepskin boot, with fleece on the inside and tanned skin on the outside. Today they usually have a rubber sole. There are various opinions on the origins of this particular form of footwear. Photographic evidence from the First World War (1914–18) shows pilots wearing fleece-lined boots, then known as "fug boots." These were thigh high and specifically produced for aviators to keep their entire legs warm. However, another view records Australian sheep shearers wearing the original "artisanal" sheepskin boots in the style of Uggs as early as the 1920s. Shearers developed this type of footwear, as it was resistant to wool yolk or lanolin on the fleece that would rot ordinary shearers' boots. In Australia, these soft sheepskin boots also have documented connections to surf culture. Competitive surfers adopted ugg-style sheepskin boots to put on for warmth after surfing during the 1960s. It is through the appeal of the laid-back "Aussie" surfing culture that Ugg boots were first introduced to the United States. Australian surfer, Brian Smith, found a small but enthusiastic customer base in the west coast surfing community and began exporting a limited range of Ugg Australia branded boots to California in 1978.

FIGURE 42.1 Ugg Boot (Credit: MaleWitch/iStock).

In Australia, the ugg-style boot has been a consistent feature of the general footwear market since the 1970s. In 1981 the Macquarie Dictionary (of Australian language) included reference to "Ugg boots" as a generic term for sheepskin boots. In addition to their popularity as a practical accessory for surfers, these boots developed associations with Australian "bogans" (a derogatory slang term for working-class consumers). This connection probably stems from the ubiquity and unrefined structure of the boots. They are adopted more as casual slippers (much like moccasins) rather than as a style statement in Australia and New Zealand.

However, in the international context ugg-style boots have developed other associations. Ugg-style boots gained exposure outside the Californian surfing communities in the United States when the sports stars of US Olympic team wore them to the winter Olympics in Lillehammer in 1994. Subsequently, uggs were spotted on off-duty actors, models, and celebrities, wearing the footwear as part of a carefree and laid-back style statement exemplified by individuals such as Paris Hilton. They received the ultimate media endorsement in the United States when Oprah Winfrey introduced UGG® Australia branded boots to her viewers and bought her entire staff a pair in 2000. Outside Australia, ugg-style boots came to the fashion consuming public's attention via endorsements from sporting heroes and high-profile celebrities. Ugg/UGG® footwear has developed along two parallel paths that have shaped its perceptions differently in different parts of the world.

The evolution of Ugg/UGG®

In developing his export venture selling Australian sheepskin boots to Californian surfers, Brian Smith established a business called Ugg Imports and registered "Ugg Holdings Inc" in 1978 in the United States. Following this, in 1985, he trademarked a ram's head logo with the words "Original UGG Boot UGG Australia"—this trademark protection covered operations in the United States. Smith worked hard to develop the profile of the brand in the United States and heavily promoted the Australian heritage (and production) of his footwear product as part of the branding. The Australian connection resonated well with his target market in the United States.

In 1995, Smith sold UGG Holdings to American firm Deckers Outdoor Corporation. In an attempt to consolidate the Ugg brand identity, Deckers also bought the UGH and UGH Boots trademarks from Australian Shane Steadman and registered trademarks for "UGG" and "UGG Australia" in the United States. Deckers also successfully registered and trademarked the term UGG in a number of countries, including China, Japan, and member states of the European Union. This effectively restricted manufacturers and retailers from offering products described as Ugg boots in any of these countries, unless they are UGG® Australia branded boots.

Establishing trademarks for "UGG" and "UGG Australia" within some countries' borders has been possible; however, trademarking these terms in Australia has been a different story. The term "Ugg" continues to feature as a generic descriptor for this style of footwear in Australia as well as in the branding for companies that manufacture and sell such products. Deckers Outdoor Corporation has initiated a number of lawsuits against Australian companies for breach of trademark in Australia, which have been successfully challenged. The courts have ruled that Deckers Corporation retain the rights to their trademarked UGG logo in Australia, but this trademark is only for the logo as it appears in its entirety. Their logo is protected, but they have no rights over who can use the terms "Ugg" or "Ugg boots" in Australia.

Intellectual property

IP is something that results from original and creative thought. The purpose of IP is to give companies the ability to protect their investments, designs, and creativity. IP forms an intangible nonmaterial asset for a company or business; it is something that allows the business to gain recognition and/or financial benefit. However, the concept of IP is not a universally defined legal framework, certain aspects operate differently in different countries.

Such inventions can be protected by establishing trademarks, copyrights, or patents. Trademarks protect and identify a company's image; a registered trademark can be a word, phrase, symbol, or design. Copyright protection covers material such as textbooks, literature, art, music, and film and patents protect the technical and functional elements of products or processes. In the Ugg/UGG® case, the focus is on trademarks.

In order to register a trademark, it must be:

- Distinctive for the products and services to which it is applied
- Not similar or identical to any earlier marks for the same or similar products and services
- Not deceptive or contrary to law or morality

Business Problem

Two views of intellectual assets

The lawsuit between Deckers Outdoor Corporation and Australian Leather is not about sales of ugg-style boots in Australia, but rather the sales and promotion of this footwear online to a worldwide audience. In an era before internet shopping, the issues at stake in this case study could typically be settled within a country's geographical borders. However, now that consumers have access to a global marketplace, regional protections such as trademarks are harder to determine in a world of selling without borders.

Deckers Outdoor Corporation has taken legal action to prevent the Australian manufacturer promoting and selling its products as Ugg boots online and overseas (in particular the United States). They argue that they have invested in and developed a successful footwear brand—UGG® Australia and that their brand is a registered trademark in the United States which enables its protection as IP. In terms of IP, brand names and logos are recognized as significant business assets and should be protected from use or misrepresentation by others. Deckers are seeking damages from Australian Leather and in addition, want all the company's Ugg boots to be destroyed.

The counter argument put forward by Australian Leather focuses on the status of the term Ugg. They contend that Ugg cannot be protected as an element of IP because it is a common term used to describe this particular type of footwear. Australian Leather argue that the term should not have been trademarked in first place, as it has been in general use since the 1960s. They have provided adverts and articles from surfing magazines from the era to support this claim and will seek to have the trademark overturned in the United States.

Alongside specific issues of trademark, both parties also suggest that the other is misleading the public about the product they are offering. Deckers Outdoor Corporation argues that when consumers are looking to purchase ugg-style boots they want to buy into the branded product chosen by celebrities and models—UGG® Australia, and that where the boots are made is not a significant factor in consumers' motivation to purchase. However,

FIGURE 42.2 Advertisement for Ugg Boots from the February 1970 issue of *Surfing World* magazine (Permission granted from *Surfing World*).

the Australian origins of the product continue to be used by Deckers as a compelling and memorable brand narrative for their product. They appropriate certain cultural associations to connect positive "Aussie" characteristics with the product and the brand, such as the sun kissed, laid-back beach culture that is played out in their advertising material.

The Australian origins of Ugg boots feature differently for the other side in this argument. Nick Xenophon—a former populist Australian senator supporting Australia's sheepskin boot-makers—has stated "Ugg boots are a quintessentially Australian product—the product and the name were invented here," comparing them to Champagne, which is produced only in a particular region of France (Cormack 2017). His comments refer to the idea that geographical indications are also an important element of IP. Geographical indications identify a product that originates from a particular country or region where its quality or reputation is linked to its place of origin; something that can function as both a commercial and a cultural asset for businesses. This is clearly something that Australian Leather would wish to benefit from and pertinent to the notions of Australian-ness that both parties draw upon.

Business Questions

This case study provides contrasting perspectives on the use and value of notions of "country of origin" for products and challenges assumptions around the universality of trademarks. However, many of the issues relating to IP discussed in the study are specific to the current Ugg/UGG® boots situation and cannot be used to generalize about IP protection.

1 What is IP?
2 What is a trademark and what can be covered by a trademark?
3 How do design protections such as trademarks and IP function in the fashion industry? How can a product's origins and cultural heritage be leveraged as an intellectual asset?
4 Review the arguments put forward by the Australian manufacturers of sheepskin Ugg boots and Deckers Outdoor Corp (parent company of UGG® Australia). Using this information, how does each party define its IP?
5 What is the impact of internet and online shopping on issues of IP protection? How has this affected the case of Ugg and UGG®?
6 If you were the judge ruling in this case, would you rule in favor of Deckers Outdoor Corporation or Australian Leather? Which side has the stronger case and why?

References and Further Reading

Al Tamimi, Ahlam. 2016. "Intellectual Property Is an Enormous Asset In the Fashion Industry." The Fashion Law.com. July 27, 2016. http://www.thefashionlaw.com/home/intellectual-property-is-an-enormous-asset-in-the-high-fashion-industry

Anon. 2017. "Ugg: The Battle over an Iconic Australian Boot." BBC News. October 18, 2017. Accessed May 17, 2018. http://www.bbc.com/news/world-australia-41464142

Barker, Anne. 2016. "Ugg Boot-Makers Take Trademark Battle to Court." ABC News. Accessed August 27, 2016. http://www.abc.net.au/news/2016-08-27/sydney-ugg-boot-maker-suing-us-footwear-giant/7786578

Blakley, Johanna. 2010. "Lessons from Fashion's Free Culture." *TED talks*. Accessed April 2010. https://www.ted.com/talks/johanna_blakley_lessons_from_fashion_s_free_culture

Cormack, Lucy. 2017. "Battle to Use the Term 'ugg Boots' Continues in US Courts." *The Sydney Morning Herald*. May 2, 2017. http://www.smh.com.au/business/consumer-affairs/battle-to-use-the-term-ugg-boots-continues-in-us-court-20170502-gvxaju.html

Craik, Jennifer. 2009. "Is Australian Fashion and Dress Distinctively Australian?" *Fashion Theory* 13 (4): 409–442.

Cronin, Emily. 2010. "The Story of Ugg." The Telegraph.co.uk. Accessed January 30, 2011. http://fashion.telegraph.co.uk/news-features/TMG8283572/The-story-of-Ugg.html

Green, Denise Nicole and Susan B. Kaiser. 2017. "Fashion and Appropriation." *Fashion, Style and Popular Culture* 4 (2): 145–150.

"How to Spot Fake Ugg Boots, REAL pictures!" *YouTube*. December 11, 2008. https://www.youtube.com/watch?v=gkItp4k89Os

"Intellectual Property." *Entrepreneur*. https://www.entrepreneur.com/encyclopedia/intellectual-property

"Intellectual Property." *The Free Dictionary*. https://legal-dictionary.thefreedictionary.com/Intellectual+Property

"Intellectual Property and the Fashion Industry." *YouTube*. July 15, 2015. https://www.youtube.com/watch?v=l4KQH47JD_I

"IP Explained." *IP Australia*. https://www.ipaustralia.gov.au/understanding-ip/getting-started-ip/ip-explained

McAllister, Robert. 1996. "Getting Sheepish: It's a Wild and Wooly Battle for Market Share in a Growing Category." *Footwear News*. Accessed February 26, 1996. http://go.galegroup.com/ps/i.do?p=ITOF&sw=w&u=slv&v=2.1&id=GALE%7CA18026064&it=r&asid=dec94e0a7f3cd9367e4e8a221114a665

Meltzer, Marisa. 2016. "Ugg: The Look That Refused to Die." *The Guardian*. March 30, 2016. https://www.theguardian.com/fashion/2016/mar/30/ugg-the-look-that-refused-to-die

Nguyen, Diana. 2016. "Tracking: The Rise and Fall of the Ugg Boot in Recent Fashion History." *E! Online*. February 1, 2016. http://www.eonline.com/au/news/735985/tracking-the-rise-and-fall-of-the-ugg-boot-in-recent-fashion-history

Scheepers, Nicola. 2006. "Ugg Boot-1 Deckers-0." *Mondaq Business Briefing*. November 13, 2006. Accessed August 14, 2017. http://go.galegroup.com/ps/i.do?p=ITOF&sw=w&u=slv&v=2.1&id=GALE%7CA154580728&it=r&asid=25edcdfa329d76c325065ff03878bf85

Stilinovic, Milly. 2016. "Are UGGs Really Australian? Or an American Trademark?." *Forbes* (Asia). Accessed May 25, 2016. https://www.forbes.com/sites/millystilinovic/2016/05/25/should-ugg-really-be-considered-australian/#1e48d2bf768d

This Week In Startups "How to Protect Your Intellectual Property" *YouTube*. November 6, 2014. https://www.youtube.com/watch?v=bfXtUm2A0HQ

Van Caenagem, William and Violet Atkinson. 2016. "Creativity in Fashion: The Complex Effects of Intellectual Property." *Lawadvisor.com*. Accessed November 2016. https://www.lawadvisor.com/articles/creativity-in-fashion-the-complex-effects-of-intellectual-property

"What is Intellectual Property?—Definition & Laws." *Study.com*. https://study.com/academy/lesson/what-is-intellectual-property-definition-laws-quiz.html

Wild, Benjamin. 2016. "Imitation in Fashion: Further Reflections on the Work of Thorstein Veblen and Georg Simmel." *Fashion, Style and Popular Culture* 3 (3): 281–294.

INDEX